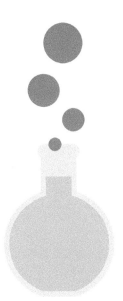

Content Chemistry

The Illustrated Handbook
for Content Marketing

SEVENTH EDITION

BY ANDY CRESTODINA

For my team,
my clients and all
of my teachers.

Contents

✦ Indicates that the section includes AI prompts.

Introduction

Part One: Lecture

Part Two: Lab

INTRODUCTION

01 Welcome to Content Chemistry

THE BOOK YOU ARE HOLDING IS THE RESULT OF MORE THAN A THOUSAND CONVERSATIONS AND COLLABORATIONS SPANNING 24 YEARS.

It started back on January 1, 2000, when I quit my job as an IT recruiter and started a new career in web development and digital marketing. I've immersed myself in digital ever since.

In April 2001, I cofounded a web design company, Orbit Media Studios, with my great friend Barrett Lombardo. Today, Orbit is an award-winning team of 55 specialists with hundreds of happy clients and thousands of successful projects.

Through all of that experience, I've tried all kinds of digital marketing tactics and techniques. Some were amazing successes and others were staggering failures. At times I have been guided by experts. And at other times, I've had to experiment my way through things on my own. Orbit started as a scrappy little company without investors or loans whatsoever. We didn't have any money. So out of necessity, our focus was on organic growth. In digital marketing, that means content.

We've seen huge changes in digital since we first started. We've seen the rise of social networks. We've witnessed the mobile web revolution, the convergence of design trends and the power of influencers. We've seen the birth of digital giants, the dominance of search and now the explosion of generative AI.

But some things do not change. We all still want information, help and advice. We still research our options before making a buying decision, but we do it all online. And we prefer to do it without being interrupted by ads. This alone explains the importance of content marketing.

This book is a compilation of the most important and effective lessons I've learned in content marketing, web design and analytics. The simplest way to summarize all of it goes something like this.

> For thousands of businesses, great content marketing is **the difference between success and failure** on the web.

To be successful, websites must do two things:

1. Attract visitors
2. Trigger action from those visitors, converting them into leads and customers

To do this, web marketers must do two things:

1. Create content
2. Promote that content across digital marketing channels

Simple right? That's where the simplicity ends. Those few big goals and actions break down into hundreds of tactics and thousands of possible actions.

For thousands of businesses, great content marketing is the difference between success and failure on the web.

Once you've finished this book, you'll have a solid understanding of how to grow a business through the creation and promotion of digital content. You'll know which actions lead to which outcomes. You'll know where you're going and how to get there.

Beyond this, my hope is that your new insights into web marketing will motivate you to get started and stay active. Digital marketing is both creative and analytical. It has something for everyone. There's nothing intimidating or mysterious about

it. You may discover that, yes, content marketing is critical to modern business—but it's also a lot of fun.

Andy Crestodina
Chief Marketing Officer, Orbit Media Studios

Who this book is for

This book is for people who want to improve their marketing, increase sales and grow their business. You don't need to be a social media celebrity or a best-selling author to benefit from these lessons. You do need to be yourself. And regardless of who you are, it's almost certain that you're well-suited for content marketing.

If you're a thoughtful, detail-oriented person who enjoys researching and writing well-considered articles, content marketing is for you. If you're a fast, informal writer who can produce quick posts based on today's news, content marketing is for you.

If you're analytical and prefer digging through data over chatting with people, content marketing is for you. If you're a social person who would rather connect with people than analyze numbers, content marketing is for you.

Introverts and extroverts, number-crunching researchers and big-picture thinkers—content marketing has something for everyone. The one nonnegotiable for any content marketer? *You must publish.*

This book is for people who want to improve their marketing, increase sales and **grow their business.**

How to use this book: experiment and measure

This book is called "Content Chemistry" for a reason. As in chemistry, content marketing is about experimentation and measurement. Like a chemist, we'll mix chemicals (content), add energy (promotional activity) and observe and measure the reactions (analytics). Then we'll repeat or try something new.

- **Experimentation:** These practices will continue to evolve. Adapt the techniques to suit your business. It's an ongoing process of trial and error and gradual improvement.

- **Measurement:** Virtually every aspect of web marketing is measurable, much more so than with traditional advertising. This is part of the fun, but it's also a necessary part of the work. *If you're not measuring results, you're not doing content marketing.*

Results will often be unexpected, but the purpose remains constant: We seek awareness, relevance and trust.

How this book is structured

This book is broken into two sections: Lecture and Lab. The Lecture section includes the theory of web marketing, which consists of attracting visitors (traffic) and getting them to take action (conversions). The Lab section covers content marketing in practice, including how to create, promote and measure content.

This book is a training manual and reference guide. It's used by the marketing departments of companies big and small. It's also a textbook in universities. There is no need to read it cover to cover, so feel free to jump around. Each page has insights and ideas for you to try. And in many sections, we've added AI prompts that can help get you started.

The techniques in this book are intended to demonstrate the concepts. I have tried them all and found each to be successful. Once you understand both the theory and the practice, try a little chemistry of your own!

1.1 What Is Content Marketing?

"A strategic marketing approach focused on creating and distributing valuable, relevant and consistent content to attract a clearly defined audience and,

"Smart marketing is about help, not hype . . . Companies have to create content that **transcends the transaction**—content only about your products and services is called a brochure."

JAY BAER, *Convince and Convert*

Fig. 1.1

Content Marketing (inbound)	Advertising (outbound)
Teach, help	Sell
Attract, interact, connect	Distract, interrupt
Brains	Budgets
Slow but durable	Fast but temporary

ultimately, to drive profitable customer action."

That is the definition according to Joe Pulizzi, the founder of Content Marketing Institute and The Tilt. The idea is that your target audience has information, they are looking for answers, products and services right now. If you can connect with them, help them and teach them, some of them will become loyal customers.

Content marketers create and promote useful, relevant information with the goal of attracting and engaging website visitors, and then converting those visitors into leads and customers.

We do this by creating, publishing and promoting content that is relevant to our clients and prospects through three main channels: search engine optimization (SEO), social media and email marketing.

Content marketing is sensitive to the behaviors and psychology of potential buyers. Whether we're looking for jet

engines or consulting services, a wedding DJ or a local florist, we are all more likely than ever to do research online before making a decision. Every day, we search, research, read recommendations and seek advice from experts.

Where traditional advertising aims to interrupt and distract, content marketing aims to attract and assist.

⚠️ CAUTION! Content marketing is a slow process. Although the techniques in this book are things you can start doing today, the effect on sales and revenue may be months or years away. Many of the tactics are cumulative, such as increasing email subscribers, growing social followings and building links. Building up your content and audience takes time. Don't expect to be relevant (or get rich) overnight.

Content marketing vs. advertising

Content marketing (also known as inbound marketing) is actually nothing new. It is simply using content to connect with potential buyers and partners. The content earns the interest and trust of the audience by being informative or entertaining.

Content marketing is not only different from advertising, it's the opposite. Advertisers inject themselves into other relevant media, hoping to be noticed. Content marketers attract their audience by being relevant. It's pull versus push (Fig. 1.1).

The most helpful brand **wins.**

Fig. 1.2

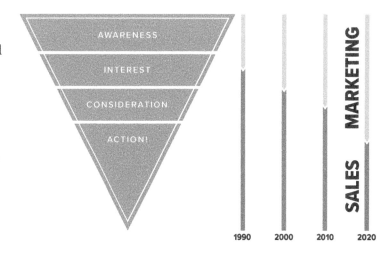

You're probably like us.

You probably don't like to be interrupted by TV or magazine ads. You probably don't click on banner ads. You probably use a spam filter.

You probably like to look for things on your own, research the options and read reviews. You probably listen to input from friends, and you may even share recommendations with them.

That's why content marketing is better aligned with the preferences of the audience. It's a friendlier, more credible and more sensitive way for us to connect with information . . . including the information that drives our purchasing decisions.

In decades past, the sales associate was a key source of product and service information. The prospect had to reach out early in the process just to get information and options. But now that so much information is online, we tend not to reach out until we have a strong sense of what we want. We've read the reviews, qualified (or disqualified) options and we're closer to being ready to buy (Fig. 1.2).

This escalates the importance of marketing and content. It's critical to give lots of information early in the research process, to publish it online, to give away your best advice and answer the top questions your audience is asking. If visitors can't find key information on your website, they'll look for it somewhere else.

1.2 The Evolution of Marketing

To understand the future of marketing, we must first understand the past. Let's take a more detailed look at the history of marketing (Fig. 1.3).

In the beginning . . .

Fig. 1.3

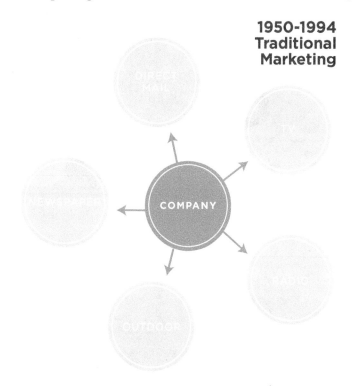

1950-1994 Traditional Marketing

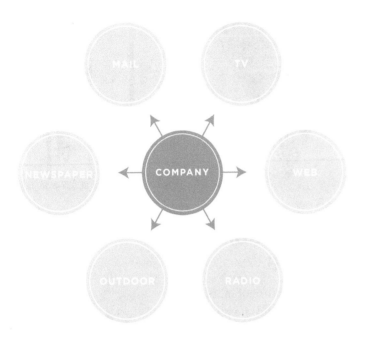

Fig. 1.4

**1995-2004
Traditional Marketing + Web**

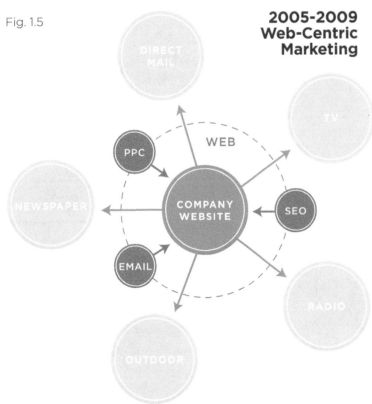

Fig. 1.5

**2005-2009
Web-Centric
Marketing**

Marketing was dominated by advertising, and that meant buying media. It meant buying space in newspapers, hoping consumers would notice before they turned the page. It meant buying time on TV, hoping consumers would keep watching when the show cut to a commercial break.

Businesses sent postcards and letters to our homes and called us during dinner, pushing out their messages with whatever budget they could muster. They hoped that consistent, repeated distractions and interruptions would convince us to buy. Some businesses still do.

But that magazine ad had limited space and the TV commercial had precious little time, giving the business a tiny window to make its case. If the company cut its ad budget, the message disappeared completely.

Even if these methods were successful, it was always so hard to tell which tactic was actually bringing in sales. Maybe you've heard the famous quote, "Half my advertising spend is wasted; the trouble is, I don't know which half." (Fig. 1.4)

Then the web came along and, like magic, advertising messages weren't limited by space and time. Once online, that brochure could be a hundred pages, but printing and postage wouldn't cost you a penny. So, the web became another channel to push out those ads. "Brochureware" websites were born, and businesses simply pasted in the sales copy from other advertisements. They made little, if any, effort to treat the web as a unique channel with new opportunities.

Unlike traditional marketing, web traffic was measurable. People began to talk about how many "hits" their online brochures were getting (Fig. 1.5).

Then, a shift . . .

Slow, steady changes in technology and consumer behavior reached a tipping point. Traditional ad campaigns began directing consumers to the web. Every billboard, TV commercial, radio spot and magazine insert had a web address at the bottom.

Suddenly, the website was the center of all marketing efforts.

As people began to see the value of web marketing, companies moved billions of dollars in marketing budgets toward search engine optimization, pay-per-click advertising and email marketing.

During this time, consumers also gained more ways than ever to dodge the interruptions of advertising. Spam filters blocked unwelcome email. DVRs skipped distracting TV ads. Banner blockers cleaned the blinking boxes off websites. "Do not call" lists helped keep the telemarketers away.

Traditional advertising became less effective (Fig. 1.6).

Welcome to modern marketing! It's new and improved, with more creative ways to connect with the people who matter to you. And the best part is, if you create meaningful content, those people will come to you.

The barriers have been removed, and rather than advertise on television, you

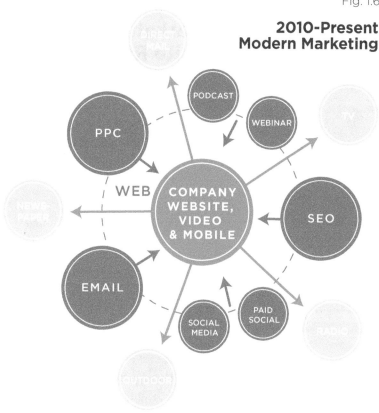

Fig. 1.6

**2010-Present
Modern Marketing**

PODCAST
WEBINAR
PPC
WEB
COMPANY WEBSITE, VIDEO & MOBILE
SEO
EMAIL
SOCIAL MEDIA
PAID SOCIAL

can be your own TV station. Rather than seek publicity through PR, you can start your own online publication and grow your readership. Rather than pay for a celebrity endorsement, you can collaborate with influencers in your niche. You'll spend less money on printing and postage and more time teaching something useful. You are on the web, and the web is in everyone's pocket.

This is a golden era of social, video and influencer marketing, and it's built on content. The simple act of reading this book means you are likely to take advantage of these combined megatrends.

Ready? Let's go.

1.3 Marketing and Website ROI

Whether you're spending your own cash or just investing your time, the return on investment (ROI) in web marketing comes down to three main factors:

- Traffic (number of visitors)

- Conversion rate (percentage of visitors taking action, becoming leads or subscribers, etc.)

- The cost and time invested in marketing

That's it! Traffic multiplied by the conversion rate equals leads. Subtract the time and cost of managing and promoting the site, and you have your ROI. Simple, right?

Everything a content chemist does should increase traffic and conversions, while minimizing the cost and time in any way possible.

Going one level deeper, we can see how the variables are determined. Let's look at a fictional business that wants to generate

> Getting traffic from search engines is great, but **it's not the same as leads.**

leads from visitors who find the site through search engines, and show how that business could calculate its ROI.

Case study: Libby's Laboratory Services

Like a lot of businesses, Libby's business provides a service that people look for online.

Libby offers laboratory staffing and training to research facilities. She's been doing this for a while and she's good at it. But Libby needs more leads if she's going to grow her business, and it's hard to connect with researchers looking for lab services.

So how much money will Libby make from her website and content marketing? How much new business will she get? How many leads would the site need to generate to pay for itself? What is the return on this investment? Let's figure it out.

Traffic . . .

Well, Libby won't have any leads if she doesn't get any traffic. She has a relatively unknown brand. She's in a small niche and wants search engines to help people find her business.

To estimate search engine traffic, she'll need to investigate the popularity of her top keyphrases. She needs to get some sense for how many people are searching for "laboratory staffing" every month. If she can rank high for this phrase, people will find Libby's site in search engines and might visit.

Each time her site appears in search results is an "impression." The more phrases Libby's site ranks for, the more visible she'll become, so she'll want to target a range of phrases.

But how high she ranks for each phrase is also a big factor. A higher rank can mean exponentially more clicks. All other things being equal, the number one ranking page in search results gets a LOT more traffic than number two, and so on down the line. The effect of rank on traffic is exponential.

Two factors determine the total number of impressions: the *number of keyphrases a site ranks for* and the *rank for each keyphrase*. Therefore . . .

$$\text{(Number of Keyphrases)} \\ \text{(Search Volume}^{\text{Rank}}) = \\ \text{Impressions}$$

⚠ **WARNING!** This formula is for illustrative purposes only. Here, a higher rank in search engines would mean a larger "rank" number in the formula. Also, each keyphrase has a unique search volume and rank, so you can't just multiply those factors by the number of keyphrases. Unlike the other formulas in this book, you can't simply plug numbers into this one! It is a heuristic.

When the site ranks, it attracts an audience, and some of them will click.

The percentage of searchers who click on Libby's listing is the "click through rate," or CTR. Each click is a visit.

Impressions x CTR = Visits

So the more phrases Libby ranks for, the more popular those phrases are among searchers, and the higher she ranks for each phrase, the more impressions and, ultimately, the more visits she gets. Sound complicated?

Fortunately for Libby, her cousin Dale is a web strategist. Together they research keyphrases, checking search volume and competition using research tools (see Section 5.5 for details). Then they estimate click through rates and make an educated guess of traffic volume. They estimate that with a well-optimized site, *Libby can eventually expect 1,000 targeted visitors per month from search engines.*

. . . times conversions . . .

Getting traffic from search engines is great, but it's not the same as leads. If a researcher looking for lab services finds Libby's website, he's not a lead yet. He's just a visitor. If (or when) a visitor calls or fills out Libby's contact form, he is officially a "conversion." The more persuasive and informative the site, the higher the "conversion rate."

There are many factors that determine the conversion rate, including design, usability, evidence, specificity and clarity. These factors combine to determine the percentage of visitors who decide to contact Libby for help.

Visits x Conversion Rate = Leads

Libby meets with Dale again to do more research. They study industry benchmarks and look at other laboratory services sites. They assume Libby's new site will be excellent—or at least good—in all of the conversion factors listed above. In the end, *they figure a 2% conversion rate is attainable.* Thanks again, Dale!

. . . equals leads . . .

Now all they have to do is multiply the projected visits by the estimated conversion rate. They calculate that *the site should generate 20 leads per month.*

. . . times closing rate . . .

Now they need to turn these leads into actual customers. Dale can't help here, but Libby has a pretty good sales process in place and she generally closes around 50% of her leads. Each time she does this, she sells $1,000 worth of lab services. It costs her about $500 in time and overhead each time she provides this service. So generally speaking, the value of a lead to Libby is about $250.

Now that we have all the pieces, we can put them together in a (very cumbersome but comprehensive) set of formulas for estimating the return on the investment for a marketing website.*

(Leads x Closing Rate)(Price-Time and Materials) = Profit

$$K \times (SR) = I$$
$$I \times CTR = V$$
$$V \times CR = L$$
$$(L \times CL)(P - Dc) = \$$$

K = number of keyphrases
S = search volume
R = rank
I = impressions
V = visits
L = leads
P = price
$ = profit!

CTR = click through rate (search engines)

CR = conversion rate (website)

CL = closing rate (sales)

Dc = delivery costs or cost of goods and services sold (time and materials)

*There are other variables that could have been incorporated into this formula, including other sources of traffic, but adding them all here would have made the formula more confusing than useful.

. . . equals profit.

Now it's time to do the math. Let's plug in Libby's estimates.

(20 leads x 0.5 closing rate) ($1,000 lab service price - $500 time & materials)=$5,000 profit

If Libby can meet all of the targets above, *her website and marketing efforts will* *bring in up to $5,000 in profitable leads per month. In other words, if she invests $25,000 and ranks well and converts visitors, the website will pay for itself in 5 months. After that, it will be profitable.* Over its lifetime, the new site will likely generate tens of thousands of visitors, thousands of leads and hundreds of thousands of dollars in revenue and profit.

But Libby isn't expecting instant results. She knows something very important . . .

A great site is not enough

Libby knows that launching the site is just the beginning. There's still a lot of work to do, but she's committed to content marketing.

- She's going to create and promote relevant content consistently.

- She's going to network with relevant influencers and build relationships that drive traffic and trust.

- She's going to do the ongoing work to get results in search engines. She knows that SEO takes time.

- She's going to boost traffic with a new email newsletter called *Lab Services Monthly.*

- She's committed to tracking and following up on her leads.

And most of all, Libby is committed to providing the best possible laboratory services. She knows she needs to have a visible presence and a good reputation, both online and off.

"The more informative your advertising, the more persuasive it will be."

DAVID OGILVY, *Founder, Ogilvy & Mather*

1.4 What You'll Need

Now you should have a sense of what content marketing really is and how it differs from advertising. We saw how marketing has evolved and where the big-picture trends are going. And we looked briefly at the end results and how to measure them.

To take advantage of the techniques in this book, you'll need a website. You'll also need some tools to go along with it. Here are the basic tools required for content marketing:

1. A website with sales pages and a contact form: This is the platform for conversions. The pages must be informative, answering questions and addressing objections. Assertions should be supported with evidence. And it needs a simple contact page with a thank you page, allowing you to measure results easily. If yours is an e-commerce business, you need an easy-to-use, mobile-friendly shopping cart and a secure checkout process.

TIP! Buying an expensive marketing automation system isn't step one. Start small. You won't get any value from those tools until you have at least a few strong content assets, a list of subscribers, an active social media presence, etc.

2. Blog: You don't have to call it a blog, but you need a platform for publishing. This is the home of your content marketing program. It should share the same domain as your main website, so the address of the blog is http://blog.website.com or http://www.website.com/blog.

3. Email service provider (ESP) or marketing automation system: ESPs such as MailChimp provide email marketing templates and delivery and reporting tools for sending mass emails. You'll need these tools. They're also built into marketing automation systems such as ActiveCampaign and HubSpot.

4. Customer relationship management system (CRM): This is the database that stores all of your leads and the tool for tracking them through the sales process. It may be part of your marketing automation system.

5. Analytics (GA4): Google Analytics (or similar) is necessary for measuring visitor behavior on the website. Without measurement, there is no data to inform ongoing improvements.

6. Social media presence: For many techniques in this book, you will need a basic presence on social media. This means complete profiles and active streams on X (formerly Twitter), LinkedIn, Facebook or any network where your audience and their influencers are active.

We'll also use generative AI to help us along the way. Probably any of the LLMs will work, but we usually use OpenAI's ChatGPT. For certain methods, we'll upload files, such as screenshots of web pages. For this, you'll need a ChatGPT Plus account.

Once tools are in place and the connections between them are made, you're ready to go.

Notes

PART ONE: LECTURE

How It All Works

THERE ARE MANY FACTORS THAT CONTRIBUTE TO THE SUCCESS OF WEBSITES AND DIGITAL MARKETING.

Let's start by taking a giant step back and looking at all the things required to win attention and generate demand.

Our "How to Generate Leads" infographic on the spread that follows is our all-in-one, super huge, print-this-and-hang-it-up explanation of everything you need to know about how websites and content marketing combine to drive results. There are many elements and tactics that add up to the final outcome. This book includes detailed instructions for each of the tactics mentioned here. It's useful to start with the big picture.

Strategy

It all starts with a clear understanding of why your business exists and how you deliver value to your customers.

1. Mission, Vision and Values
Why are you in business? What is your core offering? What does your company stand for? Know these first, or you're building your business on sand.

2. Research: Audience Needs, Market Size, Competitive Analysis
Know your niche. How do you meet the demands of your audience? What is your place in the market? Are you up against big, consolidated competitors? Or are you in a fragmented market? *Content strategy is the bait, but audience research is the pond you fish in.*

Branding

Branding is the perception of your position in the market, including all your content and imagery. It should be consistent throughout the entire experience of each of your visitors and customers.

Going deep into brand values and voice isn't something you do every day. *This is done at the outset for every business and then revisited every five to ten years.*

3. Position Positioning challenges you to get specific about your target audience and their unmet needs. What is your unique point of difference? What wins the sales conversation? If you haven't created your positioning statement yet, use the template in Section 5.1.

Printable version available at: orbitmedia.com/blog/how-to-generate-leads

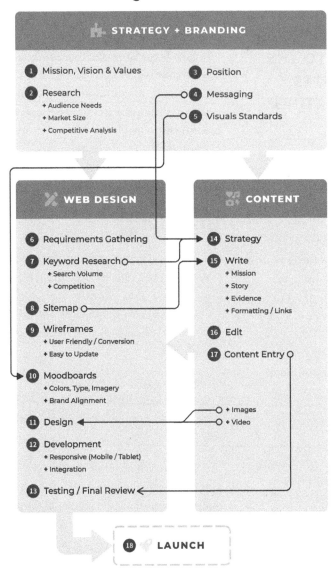

HOW TO GENERATE LEADS

A (mostly) complete guide to everything needed to generate leads
from digital marketing organically through content

Building the Foundation

STRATEGY + BRANDING

1. Mission, Vision & Values
2. Research
   + Audience Needs
   + Market Size
   + Competitive Analysis
3. Position
4. Messaging
5. Visuals Standards

WEB DESIGN

6. Requirements Gathering
7. Keyword Research
   + Search Volume
   + Competition
8. Sitemap
9. Wireframes
   + User Friendly / Conversion
   + Easy to Update
10. Moodboards
    + Colors, Type, Imagery
    + Brand Alignment
11. Design
12. Development
    + Responsive (Mobile / Tablet)
    + Integration
13. Testing / Final Review

CONTENT

14. Strategy
15. Write
    + Mission
    + Story
    + Evidence
    + Formatting / Links
16. Edit
17. Content Entry
    + Images
    + Video

18. LAUNCH

Ongoing Marketing Efforts

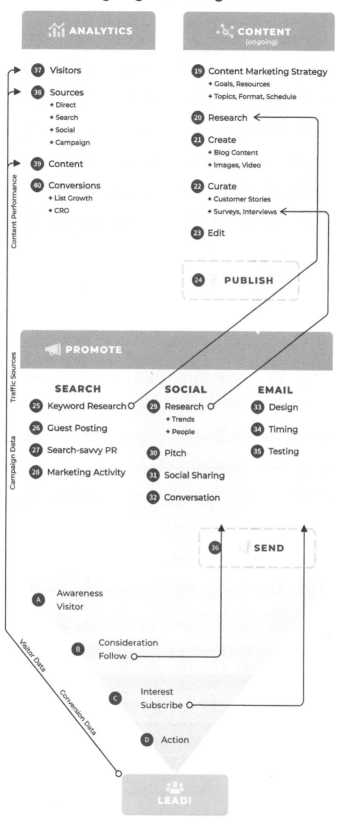

ANALYTICS

37 Visitors

38 Sources
+ Direct
+ Search
+ Social
+ Campaign

39 Content

40 Conversions
+ List Growth
+ CRO

CONTENT (ongoing)

19 Content Marketing Strategy
+ Goals, Resources
+ Topics, Format, Schedule

20 Research

21 Create
+ Blog Content
+ Images, Video

22 Curate
+ Customer Stories
+ Surveys, Interviews

23 Edit

24 PUBLISH

Content Performance

Traffic Sources

Campaign Data

PROMOTE

SEARCH

25 Keyword Research
26 Guest Posting
27 Search-savvy PR
28 Marketing Activity

SOCIAL

29 Research
+ Trends
+ People

30 Pitch
31 Social Sharing
32 Conversation

EMAIL

33 Design
34 Timing
35 Testing

36 SEND

A Awareness
Visitor

B Consideration
Follow

C Interest
Subscribe

D Action

Visitor Data

Conversion Data

LEAD!

4. Messaging How do you best describe the value you provide? What evidence do you have to support your unique point of difference? Align your message with your position and your values. Find a clear and concise voice.

5. Visual Standards Create visual continuity through colors, styles and type. Carry this through your website, your offline materials, your social networks, your email marketing and each piece of your content.

Web design

The website is the platform for publishing and the machine for generating leads. A great site pulls in traffic like a magnet, builds trust and gives valuable information to visitors. It's also easy to update and is integrated with your other systems.

Our research has shown that the top marketing websites redesign every two years and seven months on average. (source: https://www.orbitmedia.com/blog/website-lifespan-and-you/) *For most businesses, the life span of a website is three to five years.*

6. Gathering Requirements Understanding the scope of the website project is the first step. What information and features does the audience need? What will it include? What kinds of changes might you need down the road? How many types of page templates will there be?

7. Keyword Research People are looking for you right now. If you know what they're searching for, you can align pages on the website with phrases that they're searching for. And if you're already ranking for something, you need to protect those rankings by preserving those URLs and content. Do this research before you make the sitemap.

8. Sitemap How will visitors navigate the site? What information do visitors need, and in what order, before they become leads? The sitemap also affects how search-friendly the pages are. What navigation labels best indicate your relevance? Create your sitemap with both visitors and search engines in mind.

9. Wireframe layouts These are the black-and-white layouts for the page templates. Like the sitemap, wireframes have several purposes. They function as a planning tool for the user experience. But these layouts also affect search-friendliness and ease of updates. This is also where you will plan for desktop, mobile and tablet versions of the pages.

10. Moodboards If the wireframes are about structure, the moodboards are about style. Here's where the visual standards are executed online. Moodboards set background colors, button styles, image treatments and type.

11. Design Next, the wireframe layouts and the moodboards are combined into the storyboard designs. Now all the planning comes to life. The visual prominence of each element is balanced in relation to the others as usability and the brand come together.

12. Development First, you'll convert final designs into web pages through front-end programming: HTML and CSS, and browser compatibility testing. Next comes back-end programming: custom features, integration into the content management system and final content entry.

13. Testing and Final Review
Double-check everything to ensure it works properly on all browsers in all devices. Pages must load quickly, and each feature must be bug-free.

Website copy

In the ideal process, the copy for the pages is created during the design, so you can review the content in context. Once the sitemap is final, the full scope of the content requirements is set. Finalize the initial website copy for the main marketing pages before development is complete, or it will delay the launch.

14. Strategy
What questions does your audience have? What concerns? What do they desire, fear, trust and love? The website content topics and tone must align with the people who will be reading it. Create personas if necessary.

15. Write
Write with these readers in mind. What information do they need? What are they hoping for and worried about? What evidence will build their trust? Why wouldn't they buy? How can you handle those objections?

Respect the time of the readers and be concise. Use the target phrases and indicate relevance. Pay close attention to formatting and internal linking. Select images and create videos that build credibility. Put your best foot forward, but be humble.

16. Edit
Make sure the content is accurate and on target, but don't delay the launch while you wordsmith that paragraph for two weeks. Web content is easy to update or change any time.

17. Content Entry
Add all final content to the content management system, including images, videos, metadata and page titles. Check all formatting—including headers, bullets and links—one last time.

18. Launch!
The big day. Hopefully, the design, programming and content are all ready to go. But again, don't let small issues delay the launch. Digital ink is never dry. You can (and should) change the site as time goes by.

Now the platform is in place, and we're ready to start content marketing.

Create content

A website without a steady stream of useful content is just an online brochure. It has no pulse. It is simply an online advertisement. But add useful content regularly, and suddenly there's a compelling reason for people to visit. There's a reason to share, to link and to open the newsletters. Content generates the trust that generates the fans, the leads and the sales.

The strategy, branding and website design were specific projects with a start date and an end date, *but content marketing is done frequently and continually.*

19. Content Marketing Strategy
A sustainable content marketing plan is based on the resources available: people,

Respect the time of the readers and be concise.

money and time, both internally and from vendors and partners. An effective content marketing plan is based on topics, tone and frequency that align with the needs of the audience. Personas and publishing calendars will help.

In the Chapter 5, you'll find a template for creating a simple content marketing mission statement.

20. Research A carefully researched article is more useful to your audience than an opinion piece. Visitors are more likely to search for, share, bookmark and read thorough how-to posts. Do your research and create something valuable. Original research is among the highest-value content on the web.

21. Create Write the posts, record the podcasts or shoot the videos—whichever *format* is best for your audience. Use a ghostwriter, content template, content checklist or restaurant napkin—whichever *method* is best for you and your team.

22. Collaborate Great content programs aren't islands. They're connected to communities. Work with experts and influencers to cocreate content. It's good for quality, social reach and even search rankings.

23. Edit Your process should include an editorial review to make sure you don't publish typos and mistakes. Take the time to have an editor review the work.

24. Publish! Make it live. For posts, publish using a URL that includes the target keyphrase. For videos, embed them into your site using a professional hosting service.

Content promotion

Now you're ready to promote your content. Our focus here is content marketing, not advertising. That means making your content visible through search engine optimization, social media and email marketing. It's time to market your marketing.

Search engine optimization

Ranking in search engines can provide a durable, consistent source of traffic. It requires research, careful writing, and a credible website and domain. This means enough link popularity (also known as "Domain Authority") to compete for the phrases you're targeting.

25. Keyword Research As with web page content, blog posts and other content marketing should be aligned with keyphrases. Select phrases based on search volume, competition and relevance.

26. Guest Blogging Your content shouldn't be limited to your own site. Writing high-quality content and pitching it to relevant blogs is good for branding and SEO. It's a way to put your message in front of a new audience and make new friends.

27. Search-Savvy PR Public relations activity can also create great linking opportunities. PR professionals who know the value of links take advantage of any media attention to seek authoritative links to specific web pages and blog posts.

28. Other Marketing Activity Of course, this goes beyond search optimization, but all kinds of offline marketing have potential search benefits. Events, partnerships, advertising, association memberships and sponsorships can all create link opportunities.

Social Media

Social media marketing is a powerful channel for promoting content and an indispensable tool for online networking. Both of these outcomes are important for lead generation. Great social media marketing includes content promotion, content curation and one-to-one conversation.

29. Research Find specific people to connect with, such as prospects, bloggers, journalists, editors and influencers. Build lists of people to watch. Carefully research publications and blogs before pitching content.

30. Pitch For both PR and guest blogging, pitching content goes hand in hand with social media. Use social channels to build stronger connections gradually. Submit content with humility and sensitivity to the audience of the blog or publication. Always be thoughtful of editors' time.

31. Social Sharing Post your content on the social networks where your audience spends time. Don't be shy. Believe in your content, and share each post multiple times over days, weeks and months. Deliberately share the post on social media with people who will love what you wrote. You can even share your content via personal emails.

> A website without a steady stream of useful content is just an online brochure.
> **It has no pulse.**

32. Conversation Don't let your social stream fill up with promotional posts. Talk to people! Use social media as a tool for networking. When possible, move the conversation from casual mentions on social media to email, phone and face-to-face meetings.

Email marketing

Search engines and social networks are all owned by companies—but your email list belongs to you and your business. An engaged list of subscribers who look forward to your content is one of the most powerful tools for generating long term awareness and demand.

33. Design and Production
Your email template should be lightweight, mobile-friendly and easy to manage. Your subject line should be descriptive but leave room for curiosity. You should craft your teaser text and call to action to maximize click throughs.

34. Timing and Frequency When
is your audience most likely to open? Friday at lunch or Saturday morning? How often should you send email? If your sales cycle is long, you may only need to send something monthly. Focus on quality, not quantity. Grow your audience by politely inviting your current prospects to join your list.

35. Testing Email marketing is easy to track, so each email is an opportunity for measurement and improvement. A/B test subject lines and experiment with timing. Add tracking codes using the Google URL Builder to compare campaigns. Keep experimenting and improving. We'll talk more about adding tracking codes in Section 3.4.

36. Send! Send emails using a professional service with good deliverability (99%) and easy-to-read reports. Keep your list clean by checking bounces and removing old addresses.

Analytics

Google Analytics (GA4) is a decision support tool. Use it to do real analysis, not just reporting, and check the results of experiments. The two most important numbers for lead generation are total traffic and conversion rate. Focus all your efforts on these two numbers.

37. Visitors and Overall Traffic
Levels Adjusting for seasonality, is traffic up or down? Is your content attracting more visitors over time? Are the visitors bouncing after one page or going deeper into your website?

38. Traffic Sources Where are visitors coming from? Which of your promotion channels are effective? Which keyphrases, email campaigns and social channels are pulling in the most engaged visitors?

39. Content Performance
Which pages are connecting with visitors? Which topics and formats are getting traction? Which are most successful at generating traffic and conversions?

40. Conversions The bottom line is the total number of leads or ecommerce sales. The *total traffic* times your *conversion rate* equals success. Other conversions include newsletter subscribers, job applicants and event registrants. Social follows are also conversions, but they don't appear in Google Analytics.

Let's start from the beginning and take a look at the different sources of website traffic.

The Myth of Content Marketing

Keep on blogging, and eventually, you'll create a river of leads. They'll flow in all day every day. You'll rank, convert and create demand, just as long as you keep blogging.

That's what they say. Blog enough and you'll eventually win.

That idea—blog and grow rich—fails because it misses the key connection between content and traffic. Here's the myth: visitors click from blog posts to service pages and then become leads (Fig. 2.1).

But this is actually very rare for B2B service companies. If you consider a "lead" to be anyone who enters an email address to download your e-book or guide, then yes, your blog readers will become leads. But let's be honest. These are email addresses, not marketing-qualified leads. They want your e-book, not your help.

These visitors have information intent, not commercial intent. It would be nice if a blog reader suddenly realized they need your business services, but it doesn't happen a whole lot. It's not why they're visiting.

When you look at the conversion rates *for marketing-qualified leads* when that visitor starts their visit on a blog post, it's abysmal. Usually just a fraction of one percent. *But the blog is critical anyway.* Even if our conversion rate from blog readers is zero.

Why? The indirect benefits from blogging and content marketing are critical to attracting qualified visitors from search.

- With no content, there is nothing on your website worth linking to.

- With no links, your website will never have authority in search engines.

- With no authority, you will never rank for those competitive commercial-intent keyphrases.

- With no rankings for those more valuable phrases, you'll never attract the targeted visitors.

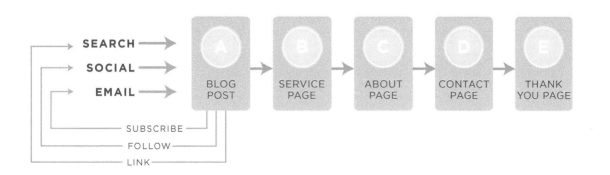

Fig. 2.1

- With no targeted visitors, you'll never convert visitors into qualified leads.

The high-quality blog post, combined with a strong network of content creators and a collaborative approach to content marketing, is what drives the SEO.

One of the primary goals of the B2B content strategy is this: get the service pages to rank for commercial-intent phrases, and attract visitors who really need your products, your services and your help.

Very few blog readers ever become leads . . . and that's ok.

I've seen this in action on dozens of websites, digital marketing programs and GA4 accounts. But here's an example from our own marketing and lead generation program.

The screenshot below (Fig. 2.2) shows an account with around half a million blog readers per year. But do these people ever really turn into leads? Nope! With a few quick comparisons in GA4 (landing page contains "blog" vs landing page does not contain "blog"), you can see the conversion rates for the two types of visitors for this website.

It's just rare for someone who drops by for a bit of advice to convert into an actual qualified lead. In this GA4 account, it happens in just .03% of visits. But the visitors who start their visit on a service page are much more likely to convert into a lead. (Note: In GA4, conversions are now "key events", and conversion rates are "session key event rates".)

Obviously, if we had no blog, we'd have no subscribers, no followers and half a million fewer visitors per year. That's a lot less brand awareness. More importantly, no one would ever link to us.

Fig. 2.2

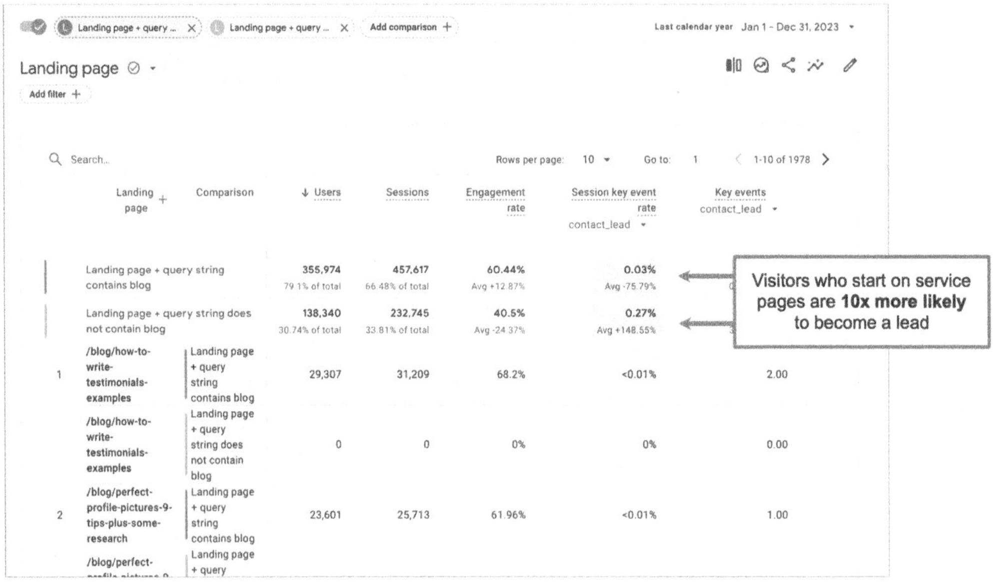

According to Ahrefs, 9,000 websites link to orbitmedia.com. 87% of those links are to blog posts. Except for the home page, the top 217 linked-to pages are all blog posts!

So without these pages, we'd have no authority . . . and no ranking for the "money phrases." Here are the search results for "Chicago web design" with MozBar turned on. You can see the Authority for all the top-ranking pages (Fig. 2.3).

So if you want to attract visitors who have strong intent, who actually may need your services, who actually may

Almost no one links to sales pages or brochure websites. But people link to **useful articles every day.**

become a lead, you have to have a lot of links and, therefore, link-worthy content. And service pages are not link-worthy. Have you ever linked to someone's service page? Probably not. A website without a blog is an online brochure, one with very low domain authority and rankings.

Fig. 2.3

Orbit Media: Web Design and Development Chicago
https://www.orbitmedia.com/ ▾
Orbit Media is a **web design** and development firm in **Chicago**, creating custom, clean and results driven websites since 2001.
Web Design & UX · Web Services · Web Development · Marketing Website Design

1) PA: 77   102,359 links / 558 RDs   DA: 72   123,736 links / 1,564 RDs   ⊘ Link Analysis

Top 15 Web Designers in Chicago - January 2018 Reviews - UpCity
https://upcity.com/local-marketing-agencies/lists/top-2...
As one of the largest cities in the America, **Chicago** is known...
skyline, the **Chicago** Bulls, and, of course, the deep dish pizza...
and business hub of the midwest. Come along as we discove...
selected these ...

2) PA: 47   889 links / 3 RDs   DA: 50   245,690 970 RDs

That explains why we have more authority and higher rankings for "chicago web design" and all of our other commercial-intent keyphrases.

Top Web Designers in Chicago - 2018 Revie...
https://clutch.co/web-designers/chicago ▾
5 days ago - Detailed client reviews of leading **web design** companies in the greater Chicago, Illinois area. Find the best **web design** agency for your needs.

3) PA: 42   221 links / 6 RDs   DA: 67   170,788 links / 2,368 RDs   ⊘ Link Analysis

Chicago Web Design Firms (Top Chicago Developers - Jan)
https://www.10bestdesign.com/firms/chicago/ ▾
Jan 1, 2018 - Give your Illinois business an edge by working with the best **Chicago web design** firms. Our research helps you identify the most reputable companies quickly.

4) PA: 32   1,591 links / 5 RDs   DA: 41   149,399 links / 341 RDs   ⊘ Link Analysis

25 Best Chicago Web Designers | Expertise

So let's tweak that first chart. Here you see how the blog posts attract the authority that drives the rankings, and how those rankings attract the more qualified visitors (Fig. 2.4).

Now, we've properly set our expectations. We recognize how many factors contribute to success. We appreciate the powerful but indirect benefits of content marketing. We are ready to explore the strategies that drive awareness, demand and growth through content.

This is what many B2B companies don't understand about content marketing. It's part of a broader lead generation strategy that takes into account Domain Authority. If you understand search, the benefits of blogging are very powerful. Indirect, but powerful.

Fig. 2.4

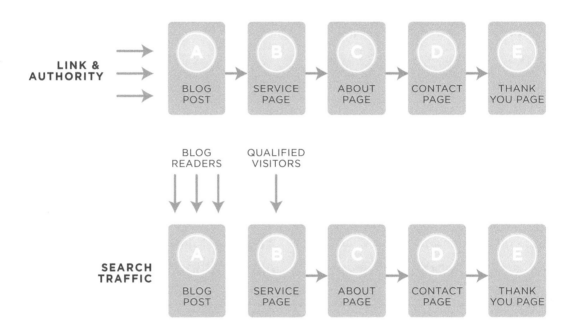

③ Traffic Sources

WHERE THERE'S TRAFFIC, THERE'S HOPE.

Because every visit is a chance for something good to happen.

That's why increasing website traffic is the first goal of most digital marketing strategies. It's the equivalent of traditional marketing's goal of *brand awareness.*

If we're going to spend all this time, energy (and maybe money) to generate traffic, let's first spend a few minutes to understand the sources of website traffic, how they're defined and how they're measured.

- *How is website traffic measured? Categorized?*

- *How can I increase traffic from each traffic source?*

- *How accurate are traffic sources in Google Analytics?*

This guide breaks down the sources of website traffic and includes tips for increasing traffic from each.

A quick breakdown of website traffic sources

Traffic flows in from all over: websites and apps, search engines and social networks, links and buttons, ad campaigns and word of mouth. Google Analytics puts these visitors into six big groups, called "Default Channel Groups" (Fig. 3.1):

Fig. 3.1

Traffic Source	Visitor Action[1]	Context/Intent
Organic Search	... clicked a link in a search engine	... knows what they want
Social	... clicked a link in social media	... just browsing the web
Paid	... clicked an ad	... impatient, wants something specific
Email	... clicked a link in an email	... been here before
Referral	... came from another website	... interested in learning more
Direct	... typed the address into a browser	... remembers us, or heard about us

---

1. Not always the case. This guide shows why these aren't quite what they seem.

Here's how the traffic sources look in GA4.

Assuming that email campaigns are tracked using UTM tracking codes, the Acquisition > Traffic acquisition report will look something like this. Look at the "Session key event rate" column to see the likelihood that visitors take action for each source of traffic (Fig. 3.2).

This is useful for tracking the effectiveness of various marketing efforts (Fig. 3.3).

Let's look more closely at each specific source of website traffic, including their technical definitions in Google Analytics. But first, here's a helpful way to think about the sources and the efforts that make them go.

Fig. 3.2

Session primary...Channel Group) ▾ +	Users	↓ Sessions	Engagement rate	Average engagement time	Session key event rate All events ▾
	26,277 100% of total	37,004 100% of total	60.35% Avg 0%	1m 29s Avg 0%	0.72% Avg 0%
1 Organic Search	17,512	23,359	65.51%	1m 24s	0.45%
2 Direct	5,350	7,588	46.05%	1m 02s	0.99%
3 Email	1,467	2,614	47.97%	2m 12s	0.38%
4 Referral	1,128	1,808	63.38%	2m 32s	1.33%
5 Organic Social	910	1,751	53.23%	2m 06s	2.57%
6 Unassigned	219	328	23.48%	2m 35s	1.22%
7 Organic Video	39	77	61.04%	1m 48s	2.6%

Where visitors are coming

The likelihood that they take action

Fig. 3.3

Q Search...   Rows per page: 10 ▾   Go to: 1   ‹ 1-10 of 191 ›

Session campaign ▾ +	↓ Users	Sessions	Engagement rate	Average engagement time	Session conversion rate All events ▾	Conversions All events ▾
	7,310 100% of total	17,151 100% of total	47.33% Avg 0%	2m 44s Avg 0%	0.55% Avg 0%	99.00 100% of total
1 laster_safety	1,590	3,063	54.75%	3m 44s	0.49%	15.00
2 diode_installation	724	1,711	45.41%	2m 17s	0.88%	16.00
3 energy_particles	576	993				6.00
4 photon_tips	491	888				5.00
5 spectral_analysis	463	766	45.43%	1m 50s	0.13%	1.00
6 zapper_mistakes	453	852	47.3%	1m 26s	0.35%	3.00

Traffic, engagement and conversions from each email campaign

Oars, sails and the motor

Here's a fun little metaphor we'll use to help you understand the sources of traffic to websites (Fig. 3.4).

Imagine weighing anchor and heading out to sea for a fishing trip. The farther you go, the more fish you'll catch. You want to go far and go fast, and you don't want to break your bank account (or your back) in the process.

You've got a few options: row, sail or fire up the motor.

Social media (Oars)

Stroke! Stroke! Stroke!

Social media traffic requires social media activity. Every time you pull those oars, you can move ahead a little bit. But if you stop, you won't coast for long. You'll soon be dead in the water.

Here are the defining traits of social media traffic:

* **Social media is unpredictable**
  Even with consistent activity, you're going to see big spikes and valleys in traffic patterns. Anyone know what's going to trend tomorrow?

Fig. 3.4

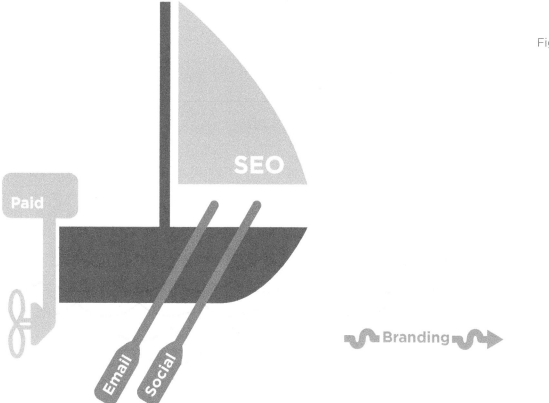

Is anybody really good at "viral marketing"?

- **Social media isn't just about traffic**
It's about networking, PR, customer service, influencer marketing and listening. None of these are measured in Analytics. If your only reason for being active on social media is to attract visitors, you're probably going to be disappointed.

- **(Some) social media can be delegated and/or automated**
You can't replace yourself with a robot. But the types of social posts that drive traffic can certainly be scheduled, or even automated, as we'll see in a bit.

Here's what social media traffic often looks like in GA4 (Fig. 3.5). Spikey, isn't it?

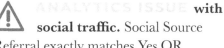 ANALYTICS ISSUE **with social traffic.** Social Source Referral exactly matches Yes OR Medium matches regex ^(social|social-network|social-media|sm|social network|social media)$

That's how GA4 knows what traffic to categorize as social media in the Channels report.

So "social media traffic" drastically undercounts traffic from social shares. Here's why:

Something like 80% of all sharing is not trackable as social shares.[1] This traffic is called "dark social" because it's not attributable to any source. Dark social includes:

- Clicks on links shared in text messages

---

1. https://blog.smarp.com/finding-your-dark-social-traffic-and-why-it-matters

Fig. 3.5

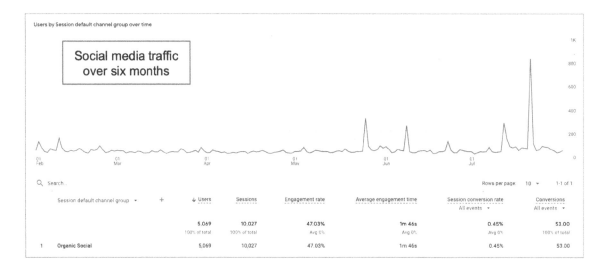

Users by Session default channel group over time

Social media traffic over six months

- Clicks on links shared in personal email messages

- Clicks on links shared in messaging and chat apps (WhatsApp, Slack, etc.)

There is simply no way to accurately track these kinds of social activity, because no referral data is passed in the link when it's clicked. They're just links floating around, inside of software apps and outside of browsers.

Email marketing (Oars)

Sometimes there is no giant tech company, such as Google or Facebook, between you and your potential visitor. That's email. It's the one digital channel you own and you control. You don't own your social followers or search rankings, but you do own your email list.

Email is very spiky like social but more consistent over time (Fig. 3.6).

A rowing team gets results through repetition and coordination. The Olympic-level email marketers are just as consistent and organized. Here are the defining traits of an email marketing program:

- **Email marketing is about consistency**
  Email drives the cadence of a content strategy. It's in sync with publishing calendars, event schedules and product launches.

- **Email marketing is about trust**
  The subscriber has control. You have a sender name and subject line. To win an email visitor, you need to first build enough trust through your content to get their email address. Gradually, you will build your reputation with them and get opened and clicked.

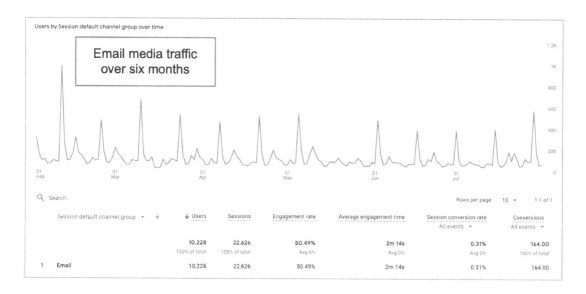

Fig. 3.6

- **Email gets a little easier**
  Results gradually improve as you build your email list and try new things. What's working? Ever tried sending on a weekend? Changing the sender name? Doubling frequency?

⚠ ANALYTICS ISSUES: **Email Traffic.** Medium exactly matches email

That's how GA4 knows what traffic to categorize as email in the Channels report.

Simple, right? Yes, but only if you add campaign tracking code to every inbound link in every email you send using a URL builder. We'll show you how later in this section.

Search engine optimization (Sails)

Just like sailors rely on the weather, SEOs are subject to the winds of Google. But sailors who know search optimization often go very far, very efficiently.

Here's why: **every page can catch traffic, like a sail catches wind.**

- **Search traffic is durable**
  A page that ranks for a given phrase is likely to keep ranking over time. Many of the listings you see in search results have been there for months or years.

- **Keyword opportunities are virtually limitless**
  Unlike a boat, which can only hold so many sails, there is no limit to the number of pages you can publish and phrases you can target. Some sites rank for millions of phrases.

- **Search is hypercompetitive**
  You need super-high-quality content, because you're competing with the 10 million other pages that are also relevant for your target phrase.

Beyond that, every brand now has to compete with Google itself. Each year, there are more "SERP features" which pull attention away from organic listings and reduce click through rates to websites. More about that in a minute.

When it works, organic search is a durable, almost passive source of "free traffic." You get more traffic with less continued effort. You could stop marketing completely and keep pulling in visitors for years (Fig. 3.7).

But it's hard to predict and it's often slow, uncertain work. If this is your maiden voyage (new website, young domain) be patient. It'll take a while.

That's how GA4 categorizes organic visitors in the Channels report.

⚠ ANALYTICS ISSUES **with organic traffic.** Medium exactly matches organic

But here's the problem: Many of these visitors didn't "discover" you in search at all. A lot of them were already brand-

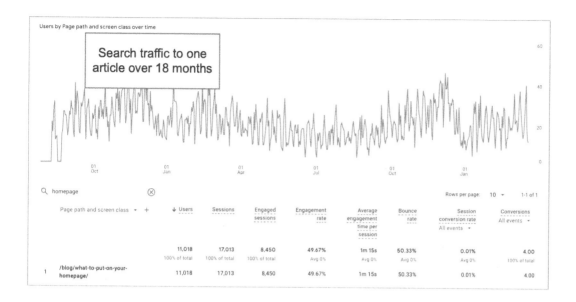

Fig. 3.7

aware but forgot your web address. So they searched for your company name, saw you there in the top spot and clicked. This is organic traffic, but not discovery. **So a lot of organic traffic is basically direct traffic.**

You can check Google Search Console to see what percentage of your organic traffic was for branded (navigational) queries, as in your company name.

Paid advertising (The motor)

Anyone can buy traffic. Social ads, pay per click (PPC), retargeting and banner ads (usually called display ads) are all ways to get the boat moving.

Here are the defining traits of paid traffic.

- **Advertising is fast**
  Pick your platform, set a budget, create your ads. Day after tomorrow, you'll have paid traffic.

- **Advertising is temporary**
  You've got to keep buying gas or the motor doesn't run. Turn the motor off and it stops as quickly as it started. The other sources of traffic are more durable.

- **Advertising is expensive**
  We all know tales of captains running huge, expensive motors at full speed and not catching a single fish.

- **Advertising is targeted**
  The quality of the visitor is high because you often know more about them based on the click. They must be interested or they wouldn't have tapped on your ad. But there are really two kinds of ads and, therefore, two kinds of targeting (Fig. 3.8).

Fig. 3.8

The two (opposite) types of digital advertising

Search Ads (PPC)	Social Media Ads (paid social)
You know what they're thinking (but not who they are) Great for products/services/topics: • That require research • That are needed urgently • For which the category is well-defined (there's a keyword for it)	**You know who they are** (but not what they're thinking) Great for products/services/topics: • That are visually interesting • That are useful to a very specific audience • That don't fit into a well-defined category (no one is searching for it)

Fig. 3.9

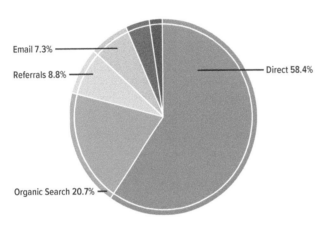

Email 7.3%

Referrals 8.8%

Direct 58.4%

Organic Search 20.7%

share the traffic source estimates from the top online marketing companies. Direct traffic is the top traffic source by a lot, more than all other sources of traffic combined.

Probably most internet traffic is direct traffic, but people don't talk about it much. There's also a lot of confusion about it (Fig. 3.9).

ANALYTICS ISSUES WITH DIRECT TRAFFIC

Source exactly matches direct and Medium exactly matches (not set) OR Medium exactly matches (none)

That's how GA4 knows what traffic to categorize as direct traffic in the Channels report. Look at that last part. If there is no medium for the visit, it gets counted as direct!

So here's the misunderstanding:

Direct traffic is supposedly from visitors who typed your address into their browser, but it's actually **all unknown sources of traffic**. It's direct traffic if the visitor . . .

A skilled digital strategist can look at a product, service or headline and know where it will perform best: paid search or paid social.

Direct traffic (Current)

Just like the current under a boat, brand awareness drives traffic. They know the brand, they type the address into a browser, and a direct traffic visitor arrives.

It's probably the least discussed source of traffic, but it's the most important. We asked our friends at SimilarWeb to

- Typed the URL into the address bar

- Clicked a bookmarked page or a page in browsing history

- Clicked a link that wasn't in a browser (PPT, PDF, QR code, app, etc.)

- Shared something in dark social (links in email apps, chat, Slack, SMS text messages)

- Clicked a link in incognito/private browsing mode

- Clicked a link with bad campaign tracking code

- Clicked from an HTTPS to an HTTP page

Any visit that isn't from a search engine, social network or referring website and has no tracking code is lumped in with direct traffic. A better name for it would be "All other traffic."

There are ways to minimize these issues, but Google Analytics will never be 100% accurate, and that's fine. You only need it to be accurate enough to help you make good marketing decisions.

Referral traffic (Current)

Here's another source that people don't talk about much, probably because it doesn't align with a marketing activity, unlike search, social and email. But like direct, it can be a consistent current under your boat.

Spikes usually come from news mentions and links on blog posts. Steady referral traffic often comes from directories (Fig 3.10).

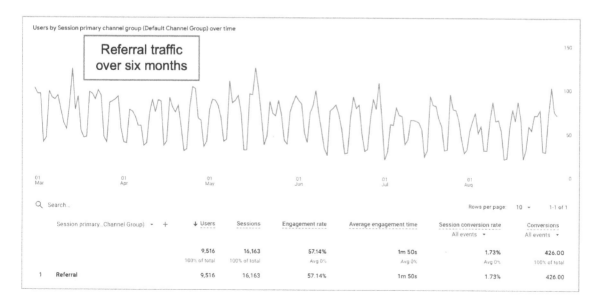

Fig. 3.10

⚠ ANALYTICS ISSUES WITH REFERRAL TRAFFIC Medium exactly matches referral

That's how GA4 knows what traffic to categorize as referral traffic in the Channels report.

That's pretty straightforward. It is all traffic from websites that are not search engines or social networks. But in reality, a lot gets caught in here, including a bit of search and a bit of social.

Check your Acquisition > All Traffic > Referrals report to see which sites are sending you visitors. You're likely to see sources that are obviously email (mail. google.com) or search (uk.search.yahoo. com).

You can increase traffic from referral sources by submitting your site to relevant directories and writing guest posts for other websites. And of course, doing anything newsworthy that leads to press coverage will lead to a spike in referral traffic.

Diversity is good, matey!

The best fishermen don't always fish in the same lake.

The best marketers don't rely on one source of traffic.

Smart marketers diversify their traffic sources. It's risky to rely too heavily on one traffic source, especially search and social. We can't control what big tech companies do with their algorithms.

A friend of ours shared the breakdown of his default channel groupings. It's impressive. None of his traffic sources make up more than 23% of his traffic (Fig. 3.11).

Clearly he has a budget. In fact, he has a team dedicated to each channel. Must be nice to have that kind of fishing fleet!

OK, enough with the boat metaphor. Let's go deeper and get a better understanding of the three main promotion channels for content marketing: search, social and email.

Fig. 3.11

Default Channel Grouping	Users	Users
	651,310 *% of Total: 100.00% (651,310)*	651,310 *% of Total: 100.00% (651,310)*
1. ■ Paid Social	164,917	22.55%
2. ■ Organic Search	119,084	16.29%
3. ■ Paid Search (Nonbrand)	100,002	13.68%
4. Direct	66,533	9.10%
5. ■ Shopping Ads (Smart)	58,615	8.02%
6. ■ Email	57,314	7.84%
7. ■ Social	50,528	6.91%
8. Shopping Ads (Standard)	36,805	5.03%
9. Paid Search (Brand)	30,658	4.19%
10. Referral	25,878	3.54%

Contribution to total: Users

3.1 Search Engine Optimization (SEO)

Just watch your own behavior online for an hour, and you'll probably find yourself using a search engine. If you searched Google, it was one of trillions of searches done today, literally. Nearly 90% of all searches happen within Google, so we'll focus there. But the principles of ranking in Google are fundamentally very similar across all search engines.

The outcomes of successful SEO efforts can be impressive (Fig. 3.12):

As the page gradually ranks higher, traffic climbs. As the page gradually ranks for a wider range of phrases, traffic climbs. As the site gradually has more high ranking pages, traffic climbs.

The power curve of rankings and clicks

Pages that rank high don't just get more traffic, they get a lot more traffic. Ranking high in search results is exponentially better than ranking low. According to Advanced Web Rankings' ongoing tracking of click through rates by search position, the first three spots in Google get almost 54% of all clicks on average. The top spot gets 26%, second place gets 17% and so on down the line, er, page. The numbers are even higher when the search term includes a brand name, the so-called "navigational queries."

Everyone knows that page two is no-man's-land, but not everyone realizes that *ranking first might drive six times as*

Outcomes of Successful SEO Efforts   Fig. 3.12

Click Through Rates by Search Position   Fig. 3.13

Source: https://www.advancedwebranking.com/ctrstudy/

much traffic as ranking fifth. Here's the data (Fig. 3.13):

So, a top search engine position is worth a lot. The marketers who dedicate the time and energy in this channel can drive huge visibility. And it aligns well with the helpful nature of the content marketer. The goal is simply to help Google help people find you. Make the best page on the internet for the topic and indicate its relevance. And whenever possible, build up the credibility of your website by attracting links and collaborating with others.

Three types of phrases, three types of visitors

Before getting into the details, let's first break down the types of phrases, visitors and intent.

Every keyword indicates intent

People actually search for three distinct kinds of phrases. Each type of phrase has a specific type of intent and each attracts a different type of visitor (Fig. 3.14).

1. **Know** (informational queries)
   These people are just looking for information or answers. They have an idea or question but no plans to take action. Or maybe they want to solve their problem themselves. *They are problem aware.*

2. **Do** (transactional queries)
   These people are researching a product or service. They know they need something and they may be ready to act. *They are both problem and solution aware.*

3. **Go** (navigational queries)
   This third group is usually just trying to get to a website. Or they may have a question about a company or a specific product. The company name is all or part of their query. *They are brand aware.*

The Three Types of Keyphrases

Fig. 3.14

Type of keyphrase	Searcher's intent	Page types and keyword examples
Informational/Content	**KNOW (problem aware)**	**Blog Articles**
	Looking for answers, researching	"Can a microscope see cells?"
	May want to do it themselves	"How to replace a microscope lightbulb"
Transactional/Commercial	**DO (solution aware)**	**Service/Product Page**
	Has product/service in mind	"USB microscope"
	Choosing between options	"Microscope replacement bulb"
Navigational (branded)	**GO (brand aware)**	**Homepage**
	Knows where they want to go	"SciencePlus"
	Wants to get there fast	"SciencePlus near me"

Fig. 3.15

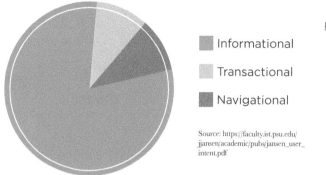

Informational

Transactional

Navigational

Source: https://faculty.ist.psu.edu/jjansen/academic/pubs/jansen_user_intent.pdf

Navigational queries are often ignored by SEOs. In fact, some will tell you that the point of SEO is to attract visitors for non-branded keyphrases. But researching your own branded queries is often a gold mine of insights.[2] And the Google search results page for your brand is really your "other homepage."

Eventually, as a content marketer, you'll be able to categorize keyphrases at a glance. You'll develop the skill of knowing the general intent behind any keyphrase, what type of page or content would best align with that visitor's intent and if creating that content would support your business goals.

Most searches are done by people who are just looking for content. The research shows that 80% of all searches are informational, 10% are transactional and 10% are navigational (Fig. 3.15).[3]

Here again, you see the power of content marketing. There are eight times as many people looking for information as there are people who are ready to spend money or become a lead. If you're not publishing information and answers, you'll never catch their attention early. You're letting your competition be relevant for your topics. You're missing out on a river of potential traffic, brand awareness and future demand.

Yes, the ideal visitor is one that is likely to buy. But even "low-quality" visitors are valuable. They may share your content, subscribe to your newsletter, follow you on social media or link to you from their blog.

Every visit is a chance for something good to happen. If you want a lot of leads, you have to help a lot of information seekers.

The "zero moment of truth" is when the visitor is about to start their search. Their fingers are on the keyboard and they're about to type in a keyphrase. Understanding what your potential visitor is thinking in this moment is the first key to SEO.

The two types of visitors from search

Let's set aside the navigational queries. Those people already have a company or website in mind. That leaves us with the informational and transactional keyphrases. Think of them as **question marks** and **dollar signs**. These are two very different types of phrases, attracting

2. https://www.orbitmedia.com/blog/branded-keywords-seo/
3. https://faculty.ist.psu.edu/jjansen/academic/pubs/jansen_user_intent.pdf

Fig. 3.16

TYPES OF VISITORS

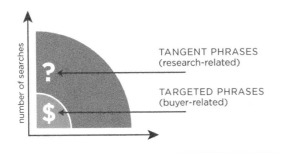

Wants a product / service. Ready to make a buying decision or become a lead.

Wants answers. Doing research. May want to solve their own problems.

TYPES OF SEARCH PHRASES

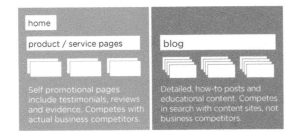

number of searches

?

$

TANGENT PHRASES (research-related)

TARGETED PHRASES (buyer-related)

TYPES OF PAGES

home

product / service pages

blog

Self promotional pages include testimonials, reviews and evidence. Competes with actual business competitors.

Detailed, how-to posts and educational content. Competes in search with content sites, not business competitors.

TYPES OF VISITS ACCORDING TO ANALYTICS

Fewer visits are this type. They have lower bounce rates, less time on page and more pages per visit.

Most visits are this type. They have high bounce rates, more time on page but few pages per visit.

FUNNEL IMPACT, DESIRED OUTCOMES

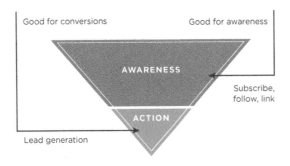

Good for conversions

Good for awareness

AWARENESS

Subscribe, follow, link

ACTION

Lead generation

two distinct types of visitors to two different areas of our websites. They even look very different within Google Analytics.

- Articles and blog posts target information queries (question marks)

- Products and services pages target transactional queries (dollar signs)

We'll look more closely at how pages align with phrases in the Keyphrase Research section in Section 5.5. For now, here's a quick breakdown of the difference (Fig. 3.16):

Sites without content marketing are truly just online ads. They're known as brochureware websites. They don't have pages that teach, help, inspire or entertain. They don't target the broader set of phrases. They don't attract a larger audience.

Sites that do publish search-optimized educational content often attract huge audiences. The goal of the content marketer is to unlock the expert knowledge within their organization and offer it to the world, growing attention and, ultimately, demand.

SERP features and SEO real estate

There is another important reason to targeting the question mark phrases, and its related to a megatrend in search engine optimization. Besides organic listings, there are a lot of features that appear in search engine results pages (or SERPs as they are called). Many search engine results pages feature ads, images, maps, answer boxes and other "SERP features." These all push the top-ranking organic search results down.

Gone are the days of ten blue links. High-ranking pages aren't as visible as they used to be. This is more often the case for transactional, dollar sign phrases.

Here are two search engine results pages, side by side. The left is for a very valuable, competitive transactional phrase—"wedding dresses." This phrase indicates a strong commercial intent. If you searched for this, you probably are getting ready to spend some money.

Build a mini-version of
Wikipedia for your industry.

The right is for a more informational, research-related query of the phrase—"modern wedding dresses."

We've shaded various SERP features in different colors: pink for ads, purple for images, gray for local listings and blue for pages that rank organically (Fig. 3.17).

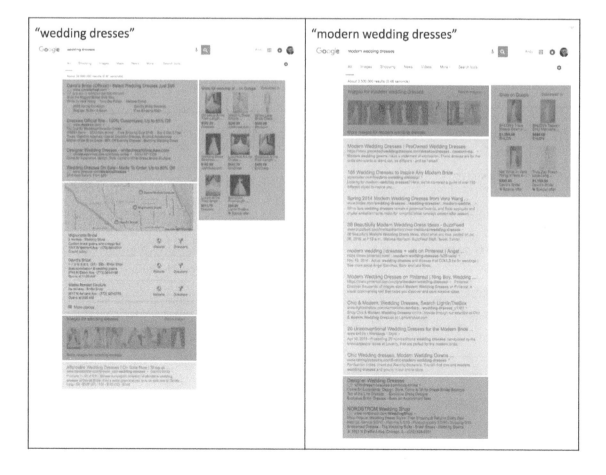

Fig. 3.17

Notice how much less visible the top-ranking page is for the transactional phrase. It's pushed way down. So you always need to actually search for any keyphrase you're considering to see how high you would appear on the page if you're successful and you do rank. Is it below ads, images, local listings and other features? That's the size of the prize.

Dollar sign phrases are dollar signs for Google too, so Google is likely to push organic search results down, below ads and other SERP features. This, in turn, reduces the click through rates on websites in organic listings and increases the click through rates on ads and Google products.

Why do sites rank?

Answering this question is the first step in winning a steady flow of high-quality visitors. Google famously includes 200+ search ranking factors in its algorithm. That sounds complicated. But really, there are fundamentally two reasons why a page does or does not rank. The two main search ranking factors are *authority* and *relevance* (Fig. 3.18).

- **Relevance**
  A page doesn't rank unless it is sufficiently detailed on the topic, relative to the other pages that rank for the phrase. It needs to use the target keyphrase and the related phrases. Relevance is about content quality, depth and keyword usage.

- **Authority**
  A page doesn't rank unless the page is viewed as sufficiently credible by the search engine, relative to the other pages that rank for the phrase. Credibility is passed to the website from other websites through links. The quality and quantity of links to a page and its website determine it's authority.

NOTE! Even if you're not a marketer, you should have a basic understanding of how these giant digital companies are guiding your attention around the internet, and how marketers are trying to capture your clicks. This is basic, modern consumer education.

Authority

Google is the most popular search engine because of one truly original innovation and an amazing insight from its cofounder Larry Page. Remember, the mid-to late-1990s were dark days for search engines. Spam was easy and search results were terrible. Researchers were experimenting with all kinds of algorithms, trying to figure out how to improve the quality of search results.

What were the most important factors to consider? Was it the title of the page?

Fig. 3.18

RANK

Authority
What's on **other** websites
Links and mentions
"Off-site SEO"

Relevance
What's on **your** website
Keyphrases and content
"On-site SEO"

Was it the number of times the phrase appeared in the body? The relationship between words? The amount of traffic the website seemed to be getting?

Larry's brilliant insight was to consider a completely separate factor, one that wasn't on the website at all. His idea was to consider links to the website and to the specific page when deciding if the page was relevant for the phrase. And link popularity was born as a search ranking factor.

Suddenly, Google's search results were so much better than those of Excite, Lycos and AOL that within a few years, it established a position of dominance. To this day, links and authority remain a critically important ranking factor.

It makes sense. A link from one website to another is like a vote of confidence. If many websites link to a page, that page is probably good. Otherwise, why would those editors, bloggers and journalists have linked to it? Links are an excellent ranking factor because they're hard to fake. Google made the editors of all the websites into the arbiters of quality.

For example, if there are one million pages on the web about "jetpacks for kids," but one of those pages has been linked to from 100 other websites, that page is probably a credible source of information on the topic.

And if the links to the kids jetpacks page are from sites that are themselves very credible—sites with many hundreds of inbound links of their own—then it's even more likely that the jetpacks page is a good one . . . and it's even more

likely to rank. It's getting votes from authoritative sites.

And if the links are from kids sites or sites about space travel, then it's also more likely that the jetpacks page is a quality source of information, and it's even more likely to rank. It's getting votes from relevant sites (Fig. 3.19).

Fig. 3.19

When another website links to one of your pages, it's a vote of confidence and Google notices.

When many sites link to one of your web pages, even better. Link popularity works like any popularity contest. It's good to have a lot of votes.

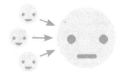

The best links are from sites that have a high link popularity themselves. These links are worth more. Just like a popularity contest, one vote from someone popular is worth more than a dozen votes from the unknown.

If a page is linking to several sites, the value of those links is divided. So a link to you from a page that's also linking to all kinds of other pages isn't as valuable.

Again, in a popularity contest, if the person who votes for you is voting for three people at once, it's not as good. You're really only getting a third of their vote.

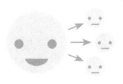

Links from related sites are generally better. A link from a completely irrelevant site is not as valuable, since that site doesn't have as much credibility on that topic.

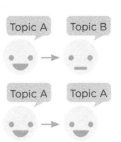

"**Google is a lot like that really mean girl from high school.** Your best shot at getting her to like you is to ignore her while you go about getting social sharing, links and publicity because you're trying to reach people. The less you care about what she thinks, the better light she tends to see you in—because real people already like you."

SONIA SIMONE, *Chief Content Officer, Copyblogger and Rainmaker Digital*

WARNING! Some links may actually hurt your rankings. Anything that looks spammy or unnatural could be bad. For example, if suddenly there are 500 new links to your site from low-quality pages with irrelevant content, Google may see this as artificial manipulation and penalize you.

Competition and keywords

Next, it's important to understand what is actually ranking here. Google doesn't rank websites. **Websites never rank.** Only web pages rank.

For a lot of people, this realization is a light-bulb moment. The URL is the unit of currency on the web. Google is trying to bring the visitor to the best page on the web for the topic. This is why "sprinkling" phrases around a website is a waste of time. But building rich, deep, super-useful pages works really well.

TIP! If you've ever wondered why you don't rank for a phrase, ask yourself this question: which page on my site is the most relevant page for that phrase? Then, look carefully at that page and ask yourself this second question: why would Google believe this page to be the best page on the internet for that topic?

So the likelihood of ranking for any phrase depends on the competition for that specific phrase. If the other high-ranking pages for a phrase are very authoritative, with high link popularity, then it's unlikely you'll rank unless you are in that same range of authority. This is why famous brands typically dominate search results for the most popular and valuable keyphrases.

Keyphrases generally fall on a spectrum of competition, popularity and length. Later we'll look at the relationship between keyword length, search volume and competition. For now, we'll keep it simple (Fig. 3.20).

Authority is a quantifiable metric. Back in the day, everyone knew the general level of authority of websites on a scale of one to ten, as designated by Google. This metric was called PageRank (named after Larry Page) and using a Google toolbar, you could look it up for any website.

Around 2012, Google stopped updating the PageRank data behind this toolbar. Then in 2016, it disappeared entirely. So today, SEOs use proxy metrics, created by SEO software companies, that emulate PageRank.

Their bots crawl the internet and track all the links to all the websites. Then they estimate the authority of every website on a 1-100 scale. Here are some of the more popular SEO tools and the names for their respective metrics for authority:

- Moz: Domain Authority

- Semrush: Domain Score

- Ahrefs: Domain Rating

- Searchmetrics: Page Strength

They are all essentially the same thing: an estimate of link popularity and the likelihood of ranking. We'll use the Moz proxy metric, Domain Authority (DA), when researching keyphrases in Section 5.5.

Knowing and measuring authority is important to you, the content marketer, in two ways. Your authority indicates the ranking potential of the pages on your website. The authority of other websites indicates the value of a link if they link to you.

Do the high-ranking sites for the keyword have higher link popularity than you? Then choose another keyword.

If your link popularity is low, start with a narrow niche and target longer, more specific keywords. It's better to rank first for a less popular phrase than rank on page 50 for a big-money keyword.

Let's look more closely at what determines the value of a link.

Anchor text: the words within those links

Anchor text (also known as link text) is another aspect of authority. Link text is the word or words that make up the link itself. For example, the link text for <u>this link</u> is "this link."

Most link text is not keyword-focused. A lot of links simply say "click here," "learn more" or "www.website.com." But when link text to a page includes a keyword, it is another indication of the relevance

Every phrase is a competition.
Every page is a competitor.

of that page. It's another way to help Google know what the page is about.

If you're hoping to rank for "kids jetpacks," then it's helpful if at least a few of the links to your page include the words "kids" or "jetpacks" within the link text (Fig. 3.21).

Fig. 3.21

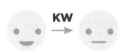

It's good to have links that include the target keyword.

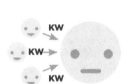

When too many links to a page include the target keyword, it may look spammy. Google may penalize you for "over-optimization."

Don't try too hard to get links with your exact keyword as link text. It looks unnatural. Balance is good.

⚠️ WARNING! Some search optimizers used spam tactics to get keyword-focused link text in tons of links to their websites. Google identified this as a problem and penalized these sites. It's good to have a few, but don't overdo it. If your business is called "Space Express" but every link to your site says "discount jetpacks," you're probably a spammer and you could get penalized.

Follow vs. nofollow

Some links are given a special tag that literally tells the search engine not to "click" on them, not to follow them and not to attribute value to them. When this tag appears on a link, the SEO value of that link is zero.

The "nofollow" parameter can be used in a meta tag for the page or the robots.txt file for the entire website, but usually it's added to a specific link.

<a href="www.website.com/page" rel="nofollow">click here</a>

Why would a website do this? To reduce spam.

Commenting on blogs often creates a link back to the website of the commenter. Years ago, when search engine optimizers realized they could generate links to themselves just by leaving blog comments, they flooded blogs with low-value, spammy comments. This quickly became a problem for both the blogs and the search engines. Website owners dealt with this problem by adding the "nofollow" tag to the code within links in blog comments.

When nofollow appears in the code of a link, the search engines know not to pass authority from that link to the subsequent page. This ended blog comment spam, at least from SEOs. The spammers moved on.

Today, this tag is for more than just blog comments. Some blogs and media sites add "nofollow" tags to all links in their content. Wikipedia, Forbes, Inc and Entrepreneur add "nofollow" tags to all external links as a way to reduce SEO spam. They don't want people buying and selling links on their websites.

This doesn't mean that "nofollow" links are worthless. They may still get clicked and send visitors your way. There's more to life than SEO.

💡 TIP! When you're considering a website as possible linking opportunities, check to see if links from that website are tagged as nofollow. It would be frustrating to spend hours writing and editing a high-quality guest blog post, pitch it to a relevant site, see it go live . . . and then realize that the link back to you passes no authority. More on guest blogging in Section 6.7.

Links to deeper pages

Is the link to a specific service page? Or is it just another link to your homepage? Links to deeper pages are likely more valuable for your search rankings. Homepages are almost always the most linked-to, most authoritative page on a website. It's already got plenty of links. So never miss the chance to get a link to a deeper interior page.

Diversity of the sources of links

Is the link from a site that has linked to you many times already? If so, it is likely less valuable than a link from a website that has never linked to you before. When the same site links to you again and again, there is probably a point of diminishing returns and a diminishing value of those later links. As if Google says, "I got it. Ok. This site likes you."

Here's a very unscientific chart that describes those diminishing returns and the importance of a diverse source of links. Many SEOs suspect that this is the case (Fig. 3.22)

Fig. 3.22

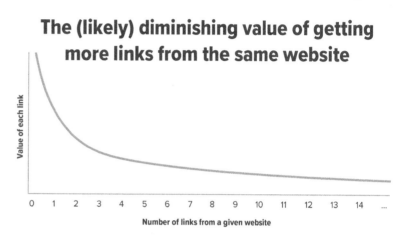

This is something to consider before becoming a regular columnist for a digital publication. Getting links shouldn't be the only reason you write a weekly column for a media publication. That's a lot of effort for links from a single domain. If the goal is to build your Domain Authority, you're probably better off building relationships with lots of columnists and spending the time working to appear in many publications.

But remember, this is just one factor in the value of a link. If it checks other boxes (it's a keyphrase-focused link to an important service page, deep in your website) then it may be a great link, even though it's from a site that links to you a dozen times already (Fig. 3.23).

Links that do not affect you website's Domain Authority

These links have no impact on the credibility of your overall website.

1. **Links between pages on your website**
   Internal links may pass authority from one page to another, affecting the authority of specific pages (Page Authority, or PA), but they don't increase the authority of your overall website (Domain Authority, or DA). We'll talk more about the difference between PA and DA later on.

2. **Links in social media posts**
   Sure, a link from Facebook is a link from a site with a DA of 100, but the link is on a social post, which is one of billions of URLs on Facebook, each of which enjoys only a tiny share of Facebook's overall authority. So the URL where the link appears has no real authority. It passes no value along to your domain. This is also true of links from YouTube channels and Reddit forums.

3. **Links in press releases**
   Google knows that press releases are a special type of content. They

---

Fig. 3.23

Authority flows through links, internal and external.

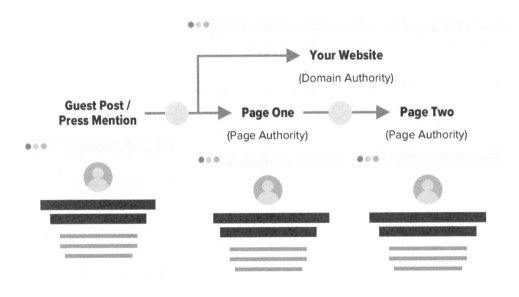

External Link
(backlinks, inbound links)

Passes authority to your page, plus a little bit to your overall domain

Internal Link
(links between pages on your site)

Passes authority between pages on your site, but doesn't improve your domain's authority

appear everywhere as duplicates very suddenly. Few SEOs believe that press release links offer any SEO value.

Let's recap. The following types of links have the biggest impact on your ranking potential:

- A link from a high Domain Authority website

- A link that is not tagged with "nofollow"

- A link to a specific service page, not just your homepage

- A link with a relevant keyphrase in the text of the link

- A link from a website that hasn't linked to you before

Off-site SEO

So how do you get other websites to link to you? This is one of the best questions in all of marketing.

There are dozens of ways to win links and mentions from other websites. Some SEO companies are totally focused on "link building" and increasing the authority of their clients' websites. The best are both very creative and very good at reaching out. Others are simply traditional PR firms who have learned SEO and the value of links.

So what does increase your Domain Authority? Good marketing. Here are

some of the actions that lead directly to links:

- Digital PR

- Guest blogging

- Blogger relations/influencer marketing

- Submitting to directories

To win links, publish **high-quality, original content** and make it visible to people who also create content. Or just do something really interesting and newsworthy.

Beyond these, there are many powerful tactics that may not lead directly to links and authority, but they often pave the way for the relationships and content that lead to links. Here are 22 marketing activities that often attract links organically.

Hosting webinars, hosting live events, chats on X (formerly Twitter), public speaking, sponsoring events, podcasting, publishing original research, eBooks, whitepapers, embeddable infographics, being a guest on the radio, appearing on television, writing books, advertising on websites, social media ambassador programs, running contests, running online promotions, guerilla marketing, winning awards, joining networking groups, forming mastermind groups with other marketers, and email outreach.

Link building (and link attraction) campaigns that increase Domain Authority are often very clever combinations of several types of marketing.

⚠ WARNING! Paying someone to link to you for the sake of search engine rankings is a violation of Google's Webmaster Guidelines. This is a kind of "link spam," and it's both unethical and risky. Influencer marketing is about relationships with people, not links.

Later we'll look at what content is best for attracting links and how to build relationships with content creators. But any piece of quality content might win the attention, the love and a link from a blogger or editor. Content marketing itself has the great benefit of organically building the authority of a website. But that authority is only helpful if you focus on the second aspect of SEO as well: relevance.

Relevance

Websites are like people. Some you don't listen to because they aren't credible. No one believes them. That's authority. But other people you don't hear because they don't really say much. They're quiet. That's relevance. So next we'll look at the ways in which a page can speak up.

This is called "on-page SEO" because it's focused on the pages themselves.

Everyone knows that you need to use the phrase on the page. But a lot of people seem to think that there is some magic to it, as if the key to ranking is to use the phrase in just the right place or the right number of times. Meanwhile, they publish content that no search engine (or human) would ever consider useful or good.

Before you start counting keywords, think about the big picture. Let's consider what kinds of pages we tend to see at the top of search results.

Bad on-page SEO	Good on-page SEO
Short pages with few details and low word-count	Long, detailed pages that cover the topic from many angles
General pages that say a little bit about a lot of different things	Focused pages that go deep into one specific subject
Spammy pages that repeat the same phrase over and over	High-quality content that incorporates many of the related words and phrases

Ultimately, the goal is to make a high-quality piece of content, but also **to indicate that the page is relevant**. Every time you see or hear the phrase "search engine optimization," substitute the words "create quality and indicate relevance" and you'll have the right mindset for good SEO work.

 WARNING! **The "Services Page"**
Although you may have a page that lists all of your services, this page is unlikely to rank because it's not focused on any one specific topic. Create a separate page for each service and on those pages, indicate the relevance for each specific service. Fill it with answers, details and testimonials.

Pick your battles: keyphrase research

The first step in search marketing is always the same: choosing your target keyphrases. If you do everything else right but get this wrong, you won't see yourself in search results. As a content marketer, you must carefully choose phrases that meet three criteria:

- **Search volume:** How many people are searching for this phrase?

- **Competition:** How many websites are relevant for this phrase? Are they powerful sites?

- **Relevance:** If someone found your site while searching for this phrase, would they be happy? Would you be happy they found you?

The goal is to align the page with a relevant phrase. The ideal keyphrase has high volume and low competition and is highly relevant to your business (Fig. 3.24). We'll go deep into the specific techniques in Section 5.5.

A well-planned marketing website has a dozen or more sales pages optimized for many phrases. A thoughtful content marketing program regularly publishes keyphrase-focused content. Eventually, there may be hundreds of high-ranking articles. Together, these efforts drive a steady stream of both brand awareness and demand.

Using keyphrases

In the Lab section, you'll find detailed instructions and checklists for indicating relevance and search optimizing your content. There are probably dozens of places you can use a target keyphrase, but the most visible places are more important. They are more likely to indicate the relevance of the page.

Fig. 3.24

Choose a keyword for which people are really searching and that is relevant to your topic.

You're unlikely to rank if you don't deliberately target a phrase. SEO doesn't happen by accident!

You could also hurt your rankings if you overuse the keyword on the page. Keyword stuffing is spam. Indicate relevance, but don't try too hard.

These are the three most important places to indicate relevance:

- Title tag
- Headers and subheads
- Body text

Writers never used to worry about keyphrases. It's a concern that we never had prior to the digital era. It's still a foreign concept to a lot of marketers. But if done well, using keyphrases requires only minor compromises to the writing. And there are times when it might push you deeper into the content, adding more research and details. Yes, SEO might even make you a better writer!

And once the page is live, the work continues. As the name "optimization" suggests, it's an ongoing job. If you think it's a one-time effort, you've misunderstood the nature of the work. The greatest opportunities come after the page is live when you can see how the page performs.

The best SEOs use data to see what's working and what isn't. They make small, ongoing changes, tweaking the text, adding details, linking between pages. These are the pros who gradually improve their rankings and visibility over time. They trim the sails to better catch the wind.

Chapter 8 includes a detailed process for auditing your content, updating your articles and improving your search performance with ongoing search optimization.

User signals

Authority and relevance might determine if you rank. But there's a third factor that determines if you're going to keep ranking. It's how your visitors are interacting with the page.

Is your page getting clicked in search results? Do visitors who land on your page stay for a few long minutes or just a few short seconds? Do visitors quickly hit the back button and go back to search results to try another page?

Google knows the answers to all of these questions. Each answer is a different "user interaction signal," and together they help Google determine if the page is good and if the page is worthy of continued ranking.

So we add user signals as a third major search ranking factor. (Fig. 3.25)

Fig. 3.25

USER SIGNALS

RANK

AUTHORITY   RELEVANCE

There are three user signals that Google is most likely to use as search ranking factors, along with contributing factors for each:

1. **Click through rate from search results.** Was the search listing compelling? Does the title tag and description indicate a specific benefit or use unexpected words?

2. **Bounce rate for visitors from search results.** Was the page immediately useful? Do internal links and calls to action guide the visitor deeper into the site?

3. **Time on page for visitors from search results ("dwell time").** Was the page formatted for easy scanning? Are there visuals? Are they compelling? Is it a long, detailed, useful page?

Visitors who come to your page from a search engine sometimes leave without visiting another page. This kind of one-page visit is called a "bounce." There are two types of bounces:

*   The visitor hated the page and hit the back button after 10 seconds. (the short click)

*   The visitor loved the page, read every word, stayed for 10 minutes and then finally left (the long click)

So a "bounce" doesn't necessarily correlate with high or low quality. But "dwell time" does.

In our experience, it's very important. We've seen many high ranking pages with high bounce rates. But if a visitor comes to your page from search and hits the back button after just a few seconds, that's a big problem for your rankings (Fig. 3.26).

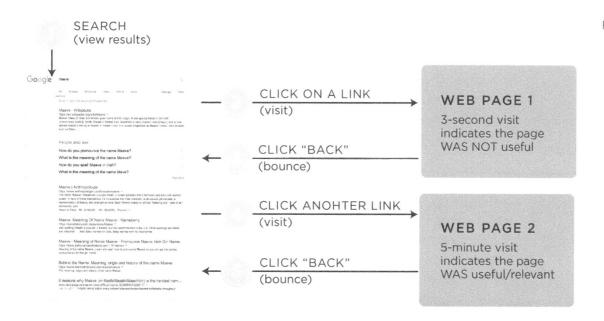

Fig. 3.26

The first example is a "short click" and the second is a "long click." The difference is the dwell time. Dwell time is the average time on page for visitors from search engines, and it's a powerful indicator of quality and relevance.

The key to long clicks with high dwell time is to create content that makes the visitor want to stay. That means using visuals that capture attention, formatting that keeps them scanning and depth that offers them enough details and utility to draw them deep into the content.

When you understand user interaction signals, you understand the correlation between search rankings and video, image, details and great writing. You understand the mechanism that connects high-quality, engaging content and high rankings.

Black hat SEO and spam

Some search optimizers try to trick Google by using aggressive techniques that go beyond normal SEO. They stuff pages full of keyphrases and try to hide text behind images. They buy links from private blog networks (PBNs). Some even program their websites to show different content depending on whether the visitor is Google or human.

These are all considered "black hat" techniques and web spam. If you violate Google's guidelines you risk having your domain blacklisted from Google's index. Once blacklisted, pages on your domain won't rank even when people search for the business name. This is a devastating outcome for a content marketer.

Anything that you do purely for the sake of Google, with no consideration for human visitors, is likely spam. Stick to the ethical, sustainable "white hat" techniques found throughout this book and in Google's Webmaster Blog (https://webmasters.googleblog.com/). Create great content (quality), indicate your relevance (keyphrases) to your audience and build genuine connections (links) with related websites.

Google famously has 2,000+ Mathematics PhDs on staff. We assume they are smarter than us, so we want them on our team. We don't want a small army of geniuses working against us. So here's how we think about SEO:

- If you made the best page on the internet for your topic, *there are 2,000 Math PhDs trying to help you.*

- If you didn't make the best page on the internet for your topic, *there are 2,000 Math PhDs trying to stop you.*

SEO summary

In the end, ranking in search engines is all about quality writing that goes deep and indicates its relevance. It's posted on an authoritative website, supported with links from other websites. And visitors who find it love it. They stay on the page and engage with the content.

In other words, if you want to rank high, be good. Build and maintain a great online presence. If you are the best site on the internet for that topic, the engineers at Google will try very hard to help people find you.

3.2 Social Media Marketing

If search is a slow climb up, social is the opposite. It's fast, spikey and unpredictable. It doesn't become a passive source of traffic. It requires ongoing activities. When activity drops, results drop. That's because social streams move fast. Most of the clicks, shares and interactions happen within the first minutes or hours of creating a social post.

⚠️ **WARNING!** Social media experience does not necessarily translate into social media marketing skills. Billions of us have experience using social media, but this doesn't qualify us as marketers.

It's very hard to predict what people will share or click. Who knows what's going to go viral tomorrow? Your audience may love something on one social network but ignore it on another. Last month everyone liked that topic, but today it's been mostly ignored. Social traffic is notorious for spikes and troughs, peaks and valleys.

It's unpredictable but, of course, there are ways to dramatically increase the likelihood of social media success. Careful use of headlines and visuals and collaboration with influencers can

> Content optimized for search includes **keywords**. Content optimized for social includes **people**.

all give your content huge advantages. Content can be designed specifically for success in social media.

Networking with influencers on social media

Traffic from social sources is good, but it's not the only reason to be active on social media. Social is also a powerful networking tool. You can use social media to find, connect with and collaborate with people who are influential in your industry. Social media is a powerful, efficient way to connect with the people who have already built the audience you're targeting.

Our goal is to connect with people who have already built the audience you need to reach . . . Then borrow that audience in a sensitive and considerate way.

There are names for this kind of work: online networking, influencer marketing, blogger relations or just digital PR.

The benefits are huge. First, if an influencer shares something, you're likely to see a spike in traffic. Second, if a member of the media covers you, you may see that spike in traffic, but you may also be able to add an "as seen in" logo to your homepage. This increases trust, which can increase the conversion rate, which we'll talk about shortly.

TIP! Social media is a powerful source of social proof in two ways. First, people and brands with large social followings look credible. Second, testimonials and positive reviews that appear in social streams can be captured and added to web pages.

Social media vs. search optimization

The audiences, the actions and the outcomes are very different. Understand the differences and you'll make better decisions about which content to promote

in which channel, how to spend your time and where to set your expectations.

Let's compare social and search. The differences are so interesting (Fig 3.27).

In many ways, social and search are opposites. But they are also complementary and interdependent. Smart use of social media and online networking can do wonders for your search engine rankings.

How social media affects search rankings

There is a lot of confusion on this topic among marketers. Some believe that social activity directly causes pages to rank higher as if Google uses Facebook likes as a search ranking factor. Not so.

Some believe that links from social networks are valuable and that those links pass along some amount of authority. Not really. Others believe that just being generally active in social media has some general benefit on search rankings. This is also not true.

Social media has a very specific but indirect benefit on search rankings. Social media is a way to connect with people who create content. People who create content create links. Links pass authority from those websites to your site and authority increases the likelihood of your pages ranking (Fig. 3.28).

So, to get an SEO benefit from social media, the key isn't to connect with just anyone. You're looking for relationships with content creators. People like us.

Fig. 3.28

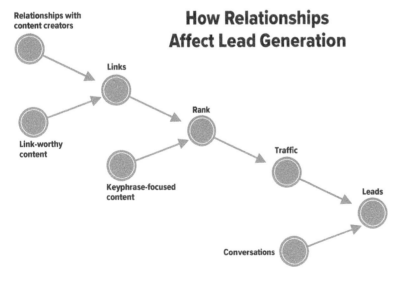

How Relationships Affect Lead Generation

Relationships with content creators

Links

Link-worthy content

Rank

Keyphrase-focused content

Traffic

Leads

Conversations

Fig. 3.27

Social	Search

Targeting

You know a lot about who they are but nothing about what they're thinking.

Visitors are likely bored.

You know nothing about who they are but a lot about what they're thinking.

Visitors are likely busy.

Topics

Content that stirs an emotional response often does best, especially emotions such as anxiety, anger and awe.

Research-based content often performs best, such as detailed, how-to topics and articles that answer common questions.

Formats

Visuals perform best in social media. Posts with images get more shares, clicks.

Long-form text performs best. The average high-ranking page is 1,500+ words long.

Conversion

Visitors from social are less likely to buy, but more likely to share and spread awareness. Fans may influence potential buyers.

Visitors from search are more likely to be ready to purchase, but less likely to share and interact. They have a specific purpose, need or question.

Speed

Social posts appear instantly and results can happen within minutes. But growing a loyal following takes time.

SEO is slow and uncertain. Even relevant pages take days to get indexed and rank. It often takes years to build enough authority to compete for valuable phrases.

Durability

Social involves many short-lived actions. Outcomes may only last for minutes. Requires a continuous, ongoing effort.

Once it's working, search traffic can be an ongoing, passive source of visitors. High rankings often endure for weeks or months.

Upper Limits

Virtually no limit to the number of people who share. Mini viral events can drive huge amounts of attention.

Traffic from search will never exceed the number of people who search for that phrase each day.

Measurement

Engagement metrics (shares, likes and comments) are all highly visible, but ROI is difficult to report.

Visibility and traffic from search is easy to report, but engagement is harder to measure. Keyword data at the page level is no longer provided.

Fig. 3.29

There Are Two Types of People on the Internet

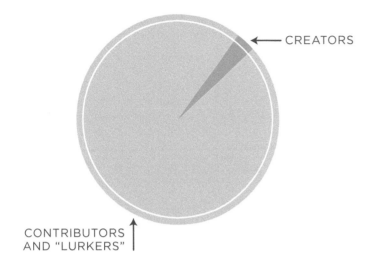

CREATORS

CONTRIBUTORS AND "LURKERS"

According to the "1% Rule," this is a small minority of people online (Fig. 3.29).

So who creates content? Who can you connect with that might mention, link and share their authority?

- Bloggers and editors
- Journalists and columnists
- Authors
- Podcasters
- Event and webinar producers
- Academic researchers

Content marketers who have a focus on PR, SEO or influencer marketing look at the social streams in a very different way. They pay careful attention to who is interacting with their content, who is sharing, who is engaging. When

they notice that they've captured the attention of a content creator, they slow down and start a conversation. They begin networking.

In Section 6.6, you'll learn specific ways to find and connect with these people, along with tips for guest blogging and collaboration.

To summarize, there are two main approaches to social media, each with separate benefits:

- **Traffic:** Promoting content to a large audience through a social network
- **Networking:** Connecting to a few influencers through many networks

It's about making friends! Building an active social media network of bloggers and content creators will do wonders for your future search rankings and your long term visibility. This cannot be overstated (Fig. 3.30).

Smart marketers also use social media as a listening tool to discover trends, as a testing tool to try out headlines and as a customer service channel to connect with clients. We're focusing on social media for content marketing, but there are lots of reasons to be social.

The rule of thirds

Promoting your own content is only one type of social media post. If that's the only thing you share, you're missing out on those networking benefits, and your account won't be a lot of fun to follow. You're really just using social media as a dumping ground for links.

CONTENT PROMOTION
TRAFFIC & BRANDING

ONLINE NETWORKING
RELATIONSHIPS WITH INFLUENCERS

Fig. 3.30

There are three types of social media posts (Fig. 3.31).

- **Creation**
  These of your posts are self-promotional, sharing content created by your brand, driving traffic to your website.

- **Curation**
  These of your posts are news, ideas and advice from other people in your industry, shared partly to help your audience and partly to build relationships with those influencers.

- **Conversation**
  These of your posts are personal interactions, saying thank you, asking questions, answering questions and talking to people directly. That includes influencers, customers, strangers, friends and anyone else!

They are never equal thirds. Most social posts from most brands are self-

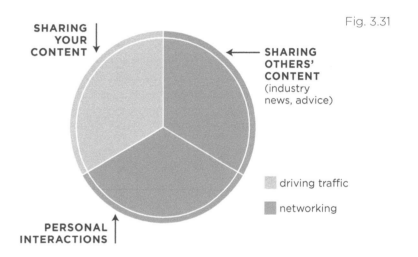

Fig. 3.31

SHARING YOUR CONTENT

SHARING OTHERS' CONTENT
(industry news, advice)

PERSONAL INTERACTIONS

driving traffic

networking

promotional. But every great social media account includes a mix of all three, and there is plenty of sharing, generosity and interaction. Together, they combine to drive traffic, build a brand, grow relationships and, eventually, drive rank and revenue.

Social media network comparison

Each network has its own pros and cons. Depending on your audience, some networks are more useful than others. Facebook and Instagram are typically more relevant for *business-to-consumer* companies, whereas LinkedIn is better for *business-to-business*. X (formerly Twitter) is so versatile that it is relevant to both B2B and B2C companies. (Fig. 3.32)

Social media and analytics

Traffic from social sources is notoriously difficult to measure. Social media is platform-independent, and you can access it from a huge range of mobile apps and websites. This means that in GA4, social media traffic numbers are often inaccurate. Social traffic may be recorded as coming from a *referring site* if the click was on facebook.com, but may look like *direct traffic* if the click was on the Facebook app. Analytics is getting better at this, but it isn't perfect.

Fig. 3.32

	Facebook	Instagram	X (formerly Twitter)	LinkedIn
Relevance	B2C	B2C	B2C/B2B	B2B
Follow, add, or invite	Two-way connecting, one-way following	One-way following	One-way following	Two-way connecting, one-way following
Categorizing connections	Friends list		Lists	
Share a . . .	Post	Post	Post	Update
Character limit	63,206 character max	2,200 character max	280 character max	700 character max
Media	Video, images, text, gifs, hashtags	Video, images, text, stories, hashtags	Video, images, text, gifs, hashtags	Video, images, text, hashtags
Live streaming	Facebook Live	Instagram Live Video	Live Events	LinkedIn Live Video
Visibility	Facebook's "EdgeRank" determines which fans/followers see posts	Instagram determines who sees posts; engagement increases visibility	Posts visible to any follower and the public	Post visible to your connections
Engagement	Likes, reactions, shares, comments	Likes, reposts, comments	Likes, reposts, comments	Likes, shares, comments
Segmented messaging	Groups	Direct sharing		Groups
Private messaging	Messages	Direct messaging	Direct messages	Direct messages
Live chat	Facebook Messenger	Direct sharing	X spaces	Messages

Serious social media marketers often add campaign tracking code, which you'll learn about in Section 3.4, to links that they share on social media. This allows them to track social traffic from their own efforts separately in the campaign reports. But traffic generated from other people sharing content could still appear in several places.

We encourage marketers to consider the indirect benefits of social media, the benefits beyond the traffic itself. Networking, research, listening and conversation are all critical, but they don't show up in your GA4 reports.

3.3 Email Marketing

Virtually all content marketing programs share one common goal: capture the email addresses of visitors. Visit any major blog or media website and you'll see email sign-up forms pop up, slide in and dropdown. You'll see them right when you land and right as you're leaving.

Why are brands so eager to collect email address? It's because email is the only direct connection they have to their audience. With the search and social channels, there is a company between the brand and their audience. Google, Facebook and the other digital giants are intermediaries. They stand between you and your potential visitor.

But with email, you can connect with your audience directly. **Email marketing is disintermediation.** It's the traffic source you can best control. You do not own your social connections

Every serious content marketing strategy is focused on **email list growth.**

or your search rankings, but you do own your email list.

Although it's spikey, it's regular. Email appears as a pulse in your analytics, as steady as a heartbeat on an EKG.

- B2B service companies with long decision cycles love email marketing because consistent emails help them keep in touch over weeks and months.

- B2C product companies with short decision cycles love email marketing because a well-timed email can drive sales almost instantly.

Email is a permission-based channel. You are asking for a reader's permission to send them emails. Your job is to deliver quality content and build trust with your subscribers. These are the email marketing success factors:

- List growth/quality

- Deliverability

- Email timing

- Sender names

- Subject lines and preheader text

- Content and calls to action

- Testing and reporting

⚠️ **WARNING!** Never buy or rent an email list. The key to email success is to only send mail to people who have asked for it! According to the U.S. CAN-SPAM Act, it is legal to send unsolicited commercial email, but only if you make it possible for recipients to unsubscribe. European and Canadian laws are more strict. These laws apply to you if any of your recipients are in Europe or Canada.

Email service providers

Although there isn't a company that controls access to your audience, you still need a service to deliver the mail. Your email service provider (ESP) is the tool you use to create emails, send them to your list and measure opens and clicks. There are dozens of ESPs to choose from. Some cost nothing until you have several thousand subscribers. Others provide a more personalized service, even offering creative design.

Here are some general criteria for selecting an ESP:

- **Deliverability**
  One of their main jobs is to make sure your subscribers get your emails. Unless there's something wrong with your list, you should expect at least 96% of emails to be delivered. These companies have full-time staff dedicated to keeping their email servers from getting "blacklisted" by Gmail, Outlook and other inbox providers. These people have titles like "ISP Relations" and "Director of Deliverability."

- **Easy-to-Use Interface**
  The tools you use to create and send emails should be simple and require no more time or effort than necessary. It should be easy to manage your list. None of the ESPs are perfect. They all take a bit of getting used to.

- **Reporting**
  Percentage delivered, percentage opened, percentage clicked. Without this data, you can't get smarter. Reports should be easy to access and to analyze. The faster you can find insights, the sooner your email program will improve.

⚠️ **WARNING!** Marketing automation systems all include email marketing features, but don't buy them unless you have a serious, short-term plan to use their many other features as well. There are many small businesses who spend $1,000 per month for HubSpot but really should just be spending $100 per month on MailChimp.

Other ESP features to consider: the ability to segment lists, create an email welcome series for new subscribers, easy A/B testing and the ability to integrate with your CRM (customer relationship management) database. Of course, price is also relevant. Don't pay for features you don't use. Marketers are notorious for overbuying technology.

3.4 Tracking Traffic from Campaigns

Email reports appear in two places. First in your ESP, and then in Analytics. The ESP reports on open and click through rates. GA4 reports on what the visitor did after they clicked on the email and landed on your website. You'll need both to get the complete picture (Fig. 3.33).

As with all reporting in digital marketing, the reports from your ESP are never 100% accurate. The way ESPs track emails is a little bit strange. To track open rates, ESPs add a tiny invisible pixel to every email. If this pixel loads, they know the email was opened. But some subscribers may have images turned off, so their open is never recorded. Other subscribers may open the email from several devices, so their opens are recorded twice.

To track the visitors from your email campaigns separately in GA4, you have to add a little tracking code to each link in each email, so GA4 can report this traffic separately in your campaign reports.

"Treat your email subscrubers like friends. Write human copy. No jargon. No corporate speak. Personalize and segment your messages. Stay in touch regularly but don't harass subscribers with unwanted sales messages. **It's a frienship. If you wouldn't treat a friend like that, don't treat a subscriber that way either.**"

LIZ WILLITS, *Founder of LizWillits.com*

TIP! One useful email marketing metric is the "click-to-open rate" (sometimes shown as CTOR or CTO). This is the number of unique clicks divided by the number of unique opens. It's useful because it shows how likely people are to engage with your emails after they open them. This removes factors like email timing and subject lines, allowing you to analyze the performance of the email's creative content and call to action. A CTOR of 25% is considered excellent.

Fig. 3.33

	Email engagement			Website engagement		
ESP Reports	Delivery Rate	Open Rate	Click through Rate			
Analytics Reports			Visits from email	Bounce Rate	Time on page/ Pages per visit	Conversion Rate

Perfect data is not the goal. **Useful insights are the goal.** You only need information accurate enough to guide your next decision.

Your ESP may have a feature that helps you add tracking codes or you can create them using a URL Builder.

Google has one but it's not the easiest. We built one on our site that makes basic tracking easy. It's simple. It makes sure all codes are lowercase and it previews the campaign report for you. You'll see a screenshot of it shortly.

Whichever tool you use, they all do the same thing: append tracking code that allows traffic from specific sources to be reported on separately.

They are very simple to use. Just paste in the destination URL of the link, then add the three main parameters into the form: Campaign Source, Campaign Medium and Campaign Name. There are other parameters that email marketers sometimes use (Campaign Term, Campaign Content) but these three are the basics. They tell Analytics which email the visitor came from (Fig. 3.34).

TIP! As a rule, never use capitalized letters in campaign tracking. "Newsletter" and "newsletter" would show up as separate sources. Consistency matters and it's simpler to just always use a lowercase naming convention.

The tool will add these parameters to the end of the link. You then you use that new link in your email.

If you don't add this tracking code, the traffic from your email campaigns will be mixed together with all your other traffic in Google Analytics. Visitors who clicked from an email app on their phone get

Fig. 3.34

Parameter	Definition	Examples
Campaign Medium	The broadest origin of traffic	email
Campaign Source	The specific origin of traffic	newsletter or mailchimp
Campaign Name	The specific email send	july_sale or campaign_tracking_article

mixed in with direct traffic. Visitors who clicked from browser-based web mail get mixed in with referral traffic. This makes it impossible to measure the performance of your email efforts.

You can also use the URL Builder to add tracking codes to links in other places besides email, such as traffic from display ads and social media. You could even track traffic from links in PDF files, presentations, email signatures or any other marketing effort.

⚠️ WARNING Never use campaign tracking to track internal links from one page on your website to another. A click on any of these links would overwrite the original source of traffic for that visit, making your GA4 less accurate. Campaign tracking is used to measure the performance of specific marketing efforts, not links on websites.

Example: Laser safety email newsletter

Ted publishes an article about laser safety on his blog and he's getting ready to send it to his subscribers. The article is live on his website at www.megalasers.com/blog/laser_safety and the email is written and ready to go.

There are two links in Ted's email that guide visitors to the article, a big link in the top of the email and a call to action at the bottom. He'll need to add tracking code to both. But they go to the same page, so he just needs to use the URL Builder once.

He copies the link into the URL Builder, then enters "july-newsletter" as the campaign source, selects "email" as the campaign medium and adds "laser_safety" as the campaign name (Fig. 3.35).

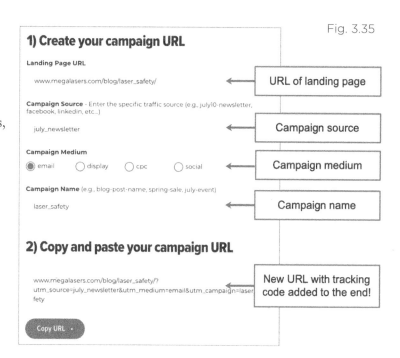

Fig. 3.35

1) Create your campaign URL

Landing Page URL

www.megalasers.com/blog/laser_safety/ ← URL of landing page

Campaign Source - Enter the specific traffic source (e.g., july10-newsletter, facebook, linkedin, etc...)

july_newsletter ← Campaign source

Campaign Medium

◉ email ○ display ○ cpc ○ social ← Campaign medium

Campaign Name (e.g., blog-post-name, spring-sale, july-event)

laser_safety ← Campaign name

2) Copy and paste your campaign URL

www.megalasers.com/blog/laser_safety/?utm_source=july_newsletter&utm_medium=email&utm_campaign=laser_fety ← New URL with tracking code added to the end!

Copy URL

The new link is auto generated with the tracking code appended to the end. It's now www.megalasers.com/blog/laser_safety?**utm_source=newsletter&utm_medium=email&utm_campaign=laser_safety**

Now, Ted uses the new URL in all of the calls to action within the email and blasts it out to his loyal laser subscribers. A week later when he checks the Acquisition > Traffic acquisition report in GA4 (setting the dimension in the dropdown above the first column to "Session campaign") he sees the performance of that specific email. (Fig. 3.36).

It looks like the visitors from this email spent more time on the article than visitors from his other recent newsletters. People must have liked it! Maybe safety is a good topic for Ted. He's thinking about writing about plasma safety next . . .

Fig. 3.36

Session campaign ▾ +	↓ Users	Sessions	Engagement rate	Average engagement time	Session conversion rate All events ▾	Conversions All events ▾
	7,310 100% of total	17,151 100% of total	47.33% Avg 0%	2m 44s Avg 0%	0.55% Avg 0%	99.00 100% of total
1 laster_safety	1,590	3,063	54.75%	3m 44s	0.49%	15.00
2 diode_installation	724	1,711	45.41%	2m 17s	0.88%	16.00
3 energy_particles	576	993				6.00
4 photon_tips	491	888				5.00
5 spectral_analysis	463	766	45.43%	1m 50s	0.13%	1.00
6 zapper_mistakes	453	852	47.3%	1m 26s	0.35%	3.00

Traffic, engagement and conversions from each email campaign

Search...
Rows per page: 10 ▾ Go to: 1 ‹ 1-10 of 191 ›

Notes

04 Conversions

CLICK! THE PAGE LOADS. A VISITOR HAS LANDED ON YOUR WEBSITE. WHAT HAPPENS NEXT?

The visitor takes action or they don't. During their visit they may become a lead, a subscriber, a registrant, an e-commerce customer . . . or they may do nothing at all.

When they do fill out the contact form and click "submit," a lead is born. We call this a conversion. The percentage of visitors who takes one of those desired actions is called the conversion rate.

It happens a million times a day, all over the web. They searched; they found a website; it was clear and persuasive; they filled out the contact form. This is the job of the content marketing program and the lead generation website it feeds: **to build a bridge from a traffic source to a thank you page** (Fig. 4.1).

This chapter is about understanding conversions—why visitors act and why they don't. It's about how conversion rates are measured and how to improve them.

4.1 Types of Conversions

Generating leads and sales is the ultimate goal of most websites, but there are many indirect routes to getting there. There are at least twelve types of conversions, and all of them are good. These smaller conversion successes are important steps toward turning visitors into a loyal audience and eventually into customers and clients down the road (Fig 4.2).

Lead, customers and donors are the most important because they affect the bottom line directly.

Subscribers, followers and fans are are also important because *they allow you to connect with people later, after they've left your website*. They've asked for more. When you increase these types of conversions, your content will reach farther, drive greater traffic, and lead to higher conversions in the future. We've included a section here about

Fig. 4.1

Traffic Source　　　　　**Thank You Page**

Fig. 4.2

12 Types of Conversions	Revenue	Content	Brand
Lead	💀		
Customer (ecommerce)	💀		
Donor	💀		
Event Registrant	💀	🏆	
Subscriber		🏆	
Downloader (guide, ebook, whitepaper)		🏆	
Webinar Registrant		🏆	
Follower/Fan (social media)		🏆	★
Entrant (sweepstakes, promotion)		🏆	★
Member (community, directory)			★
Reviewer (products, businesses)			★
Job Applicant			★

maximizing the percentage of visitors who subscribe.

How can you increase the conversion rate on your website?

First, we need to understand why visitors convert. All visitors—all of us—want answers to our questions and solutions to our problems. Usually, we visit a website with a question or problem in mind. We want a product, a service or just a little advice.

Regardless of the goal, *visitors take action when the hope for a solution is stronger than the fear that they'll be disappointed.* So there are two factors at work: One is the motivation that is pulling them toward the conversion, and the other is friction that is keeping them away (Fig 4.3).

Fig. 4.3

MOTIVATION
compelling content,
easy to use site,
strong design, trust,
urgency

FRICTION
weak or unclear content,
unanswered questions,
hard to use site,
lack of trust, confusion

VISITOR

GOAL

Which force is stronger?

If the **perceived value** is greater than the **effort required** and fear of disappointment, they convert. That means the motivation is stronger than the friction, and they move forward, reaching their goals and yours.

Each of your visitors is doing a quick cost-benefit calculation in their mind. Do the rewards outweigh the effort? *What's in it for me?*

There are two ways to increase your conversion rate: **increase their motivation/reduce their uncertainty** and **make it easier to take the action**. The key in both cases is to understand the visitor. If we know what they're thinking, we can assure them that we are the best solution, increase their confidence and reduce their uncertainty.

This section is in two parts. First, we'll learn how to improve the conversion rate of the parts of the website that sell things (the products and service pages). Then we'll see how to increase the percentage of visitors who subscribe for more content.

4.2 Questions → Answers → Evidence → Action! Calls to Action

To guide our thinking while we optimize our conversion rates, we'll draw a map. This **conversion map** will describe how we connect with the mindset of our visitors, guide them toward actions, and move them from suspect to prospect (Fig 4.4).

Our map begins in the hearts and minds of our visitors and ends with the triggers that inspire action.

1. Understand our visitors top **questions**
2. **Answer** those questions and address concerns
3. Support our answers with **evidence**
4. Provide clear, specific ways for them to **act**

Simple, right? Not really. Most websites fail at this completely. They leave questions unanswered and claims unsupported and provide no specific calls to action. Every marketing website succeeds or fails based on these criteria.

This map to conversions is relevant to any visitor, looking for anything at all—from a quick decision about plumbing to a long, multi-stakeholder, million-dollar-decision about buying technology (Fig 4.5).

Fig. 4.4

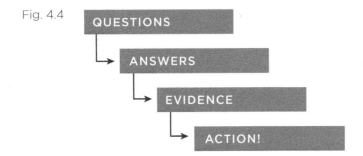

QUESTIONS

ANSWERS

EVIDENCE

ACTION!

Fig. 4.5

Question/Concern →	Answers/Information →	Evidence →	Call to action
Visitor has a leaky faucet			
How soon can you come?	Same day, on-time service	Testimonial: "I was so glad they came right away!" 20 years of fast service	Speak to an operator to schedule a quick visit >
Visitor is evaluating marketing technology			
Does this system connect with my database?	Integrates with the most popular systems	Testimonial: "Thank you for all the help connecting my existing tools" Logos of systems	Chat with an expert about integration > Download the complete guide to database integration >

Questions: Understanding your audience

Empathy is everything in marketing. Understanding the perspective of your visitor is the key to conversions.

What is the true story in the life of the visitor to this page? What are they looking for? What problem are they trying to solve? What are they hoping for and worried about? What do they need?

They came to your site for a reason. They have questions and desires, hopes and fears. They won't take action until their questions are answered and their objections are addressed. Immediately after the page loads, the visitor begins scrolling and scanning, looking for answers.

Below are two studies that give powerful insights into why visitors really go to websites. They both arrived at the same conclusion for why websites succeed or fail (Fig. 4.6).

In both studies, the majority of respondents reported that getting to information easily is the most important aspect of a website. They came for answers, not pretty pictures or fancy features. So the job of the site is to provide that information in a way that's easy to find. If your website doesn't accomplish this, your visitors are likely to leave and look somewhere else.

Fig. 4.6

What is the most important factor in the design of a website?

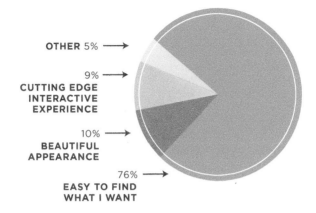

OTHER 5% ⟶

9% ⟶
CUTTING EDGE
INTERACTIVE
EXPERIENCE

10% ⟶
BEAUTIFUL
APPEARANCE

76% ⟶
EASY TO FIND
WHAT I WANT

Source: Hubspot, https://blog.hubspot.com/blog/tabid/6307/bid/14953/What-Do-76-of-Consumers-Want-From-Your-Website-New-Data.aspx

Causes of user failure

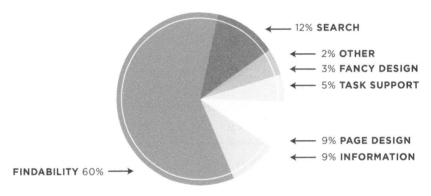

⟵ 12% SEARCH

⟵ 2% OTHER
⟵ 3% FANCY DESIGN
⟵ 5% TASK SUPPORT

⟵ 9% PAGE DESIGN
⟵ 9% INFORMATION

FINDABILITY 60% ⟶

Source: NN Group, https://www.nngroup.com/articles/top-10-enduring/

What questions do people always ask before buying from or hiring us?

If you aren't sure what visitors are looking for, ask the sales team, customer service or anyone who works on the front line with clients and prospects. Better yet, talk to customers yourself. Create simple personas, send a survey or put together a small focus group. Here is a set of questions you can ask your clients and customers during the research process, prior to writing conversion-focused copy:

- Take me back to that moment when you first realized you needed help. What was going on in your business that sent you looking for a solution?

- What was the biggest problem you were trying to solve?

- What else did you try and what didn't you love about it?

- What almost kept you from buying from us?

- What made you confident enough to give us a try?

- What made this the best solution for you?

- When evaluating your options, what was most important to you?

- What can you do now (or do better) that you couldn't do before?

- Give me an example of when this product or service made a difference for you.

- If you never worked with us again, what would you miss the most?

- What would you tell a friend if you wanted to convince them to hire us?

You can also get insights by talking to the frontline sales reps:

- What questions are you just sick and tired of answering?

- What is the aha moment prospects have during sales calls?

- What analogies do you use to explain what we do?

- What should prospects ask you, but they usually don't?

- Fill in this blank: people can work with us, even if they _____.

You can imagine how valuable the answers to these questions will be in your

marketing. In fact, it's next to impossible to write a high-converting page without asking these questions first. We do it on every website redesign project.

If you are looking for quick insights and don't have time to do detailed stakeholder interviews, you can use AI to quickly generate personas. In Section 4.8, you'll find prompts that can help.

As you gather the data from these interviews, look for opportunities to use their actual words and phrases as the copy for the website. It's often more direct and disarming than anything you could ever write yourself.

The best marketing copy is written by the audience, not the marketer

After researching your audience and asking the right questions, you should have a strong sense of their biggest questions, challenges, concerns and motivations.

Answers: Satisfying your visitors' needs

Now your job is to structure the pages of the website to answer each of the top questions according to the needs of the typical visitor. In the end, the website

should emulate a conversation between a sales associate and a prospect.

Like a conversation, the content on the site should flow in a smooth, frictionless way.

Here are the types of answers found on various types of pages.

Homepage
Where am I? Am I in the right place?
Shows and tells visitors what the company does and what makes the company different

Service Pages
How can this company help? Would this actually work for me?
Answers top questions about the specific service and the benefits

Product Pages
Is this the right thing for me? How much is it? When can I get it?
Answers the top questions about the product, options, specifications and fulfillment

About and Team Pages
Who are these people? What do they believe? How did they get started?
Answers questions about qualifications, personalities, origin and values

WARNING! Avoid putting answers to important questions on an FAQ page. If the question is frequently asked, add the answer to a page that is relevant to that topic. FAQ pages tend not to get a lot of visits, probably because the navigation label "FAQ" is so vague. Put answers to top questions on the pages that get the most visitors and are the most relevant. Don't make visitors hunt for answers.

Can visitors tell what you do at a glance?

Every visitor starts with the same question: Am I in the right place? So a great page answers that question in the first split second of the visit, especially on the homepage. Clarity is key. Is the homepage headline descriptive? Or is it general and vague, such as "world class service?"

What is the best order for the information on this page?

Not all answers are equally important. Some things are deal-breakers. Some things are just nice-to-haves. Some things matter to everybody. Some things are relevant to only a few visitors. Prioritize the messages and visuals with this in mind.

Are the sections for headers meaningful? Are they helpful?

All web pages are divided into sections with headers. These headers tell the

To confirm that the site communicates quickly and clearly, show it to someone who isn't familiar with the brand. Don't prepare them. Just say "I want to show you something" and pull up your site. After five seconds, turn off the screen. Now ask them "What does this company do?" If they can't tell you, your site just failed the test. If the site can't pass the 5-Second Test, expect a low conversion rate.

Use Lyssna (lyssna.com/features/five-second-testing) to do a 5-second test with a larger group and get answers to more specific questions about your design. Or test two designs with two different H1 headers.

visitors what that section is about. But often, they are too big, lack value and are basically unhelpful (such as "what we do"). Meaningless headers distract from the more important messages in the section (Fig. 4.7).

Is everything visible? Or is anything hidden behind a click?

Are important things tucked away behind tabs, a carousel or a slideshow? If so, those messages are invisible until the visitor clicks, taps or waits. That content is hidden by default.

If you're using a slideshow and the second and third slides include important messages (or calls to action), keep in mind that most visitors won't see them. But by simply stacking those messages as rows of content on a taller page, they'll be seen by a greater percentage of

Fig. 4.7

Fig. 4.8

Other sources of data-driven empathy:

1. Enter your business category into Answer the Public (www.answerthepublic.com) to see what potential customers are asking about online

2. Visit Quora (www.quora.com) to read questions and answers from your industry

3. Search for "day in the life of [job title]" to see examples of challenges your potential buyers face day-to-day

4. Read negative reviews of competitors to get ideas for the frustrations your audience is having elsewhere

5. If your site has a chat feature, scan the chat logs for questions

6. If your site has a site search tool, check the Site Search report in Google Analytics to see what your current visitors are searching for

visitors. Your visitors are more likely to scroll than to click.

Do 100% of visitors know the meaning of these words?

You're an insider in your industry, and your industry has words and phrases that only insiders will know. But a percentage of your visitors are new in this industry, and they don't know the jargon.

Short, simple words are better for clarity and conversions. So ask this question of each word on your page. Does every visitor know what this means? If not, what percentage of visitors may be confused by it?

You want to avoid jargon, with one exception. If you're positive that your audience knows the lingo and you are confident that using that specific language will build their trust, then go

ahead and use jargon. But keep in mind that some visitors won't understand that part of the page (Fig. 4.8).

If your goal is to rank for a bit of jargon, then of course make a page on the topic and use that phrase throughout the page. This may attract people searching for that specific term without alienating people who land on the homepage or other primary pages. People search for niche, industry-specific phrases all the time.

Is the content formatted for people who scan?

Your visitors are scanning more than reading. With this in mind, you can make a page that works for scanners by adding formatting that makes the page easy to browse through.

If you don't adapt for scanners, visitors will be less likely to see something of interest, and less likely to slow down, less likely to read something in depth. That means short paragraphs, multiple images, bullets, bolding and internal links. In Section 5.11, you'll find a complete checklist of formatting that will make your pages easier to scan.

Evidence: Supporting our claims

Now that you've given them what *they* want, it's time to give them what you want them to have. This is where you'll add evidence to support your answers and show that you're legitimate. This evidence will build trust and differentiate you from the competition.

Most websites are filled with unsupported marketing claims. But great marketing websites *support their claims with evidence* (Fig 4.9).

Answering the price question If you don't want to (or can't) answer a question about price, you can still address the question without answering it directly. You can write a call to action in the form of a question. This both aligns with their needs and becomes the start of a conversation.

QUESTIONS ABOUT COST?
Talk to Sarah about financing options >

Pile of unsupported marketing claims

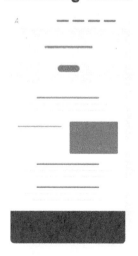

Page filled with evidence

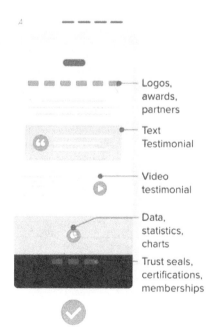

- Logos, awards, partners
- Text Testimonial
- Video testimonial
- Data, statistics, charts
- Trust seals, certifications, memberships

Fig. 4.9

Fig. 4.10

Two kinds of evidence		
Stories	Qualitative and personal, *appeals to the heart with emotion*	"Thanks so much for super-fast delivery!" • Testimonials • Case studies • Reviews
Data	Quantitative numbers, *appeals to the mind with reason*	99% on-time delivery record • ROI, hours and dollars saved • Percent increases • Years in business • Number of happy customers • Best seller

Did you add evidence to support your marketing claims?

Did you augment every one of your marketing claims with data and/or stories? Or did you leave many of your claims unsupported? Do all of your top pages include some form of evidence?

Visit any page on your website and count the marketing claims. How many times is your business described as *trusted, easy, smart, effective, or reliable?* Now look at the same page and count the number of claims that are supported with evidence. How many *data points, statistics, case studies* and *testimonials* are there?

There are two kinds of evidence you can use to support your marketing claims (Fig. 4.10).

Some visitors are influenced by data and statistics. Others are affected more by the stories and firsthand accounts. You have plenty of room on your pages to include both.

Conversion optimization experts will tell you that stories and testimonials are a more powerful factor than data and statistics, so we've included a section about testimonials later in this chapter.

"Facts are called 'cold and hard' for a reason. They don't have the ability to warm hearts, which is the key to changing minds."

ROB BIESENBACH

Calls to action: Simple and specific

The final step on our conversion map is the call to action. High-converting websites don't just have a contact link in the top right. They trigger action through prominent, specific calls to action placed strategically throughout the website.

Does the site offer easy-to-find calls to action?

A call to action (CTA) can appear almost anywhere: in headers, popup windows, within the content, in the right rails and at the bottom of pages. The location of the CTA is a big factor in its visual prominence. They should appear at least once on any page that makes an offer, usually at the bottom.

Do the colors guide the visitors' attention to the desired actions?

Color is another factor in visual prominence (Fig. 4.11). Our eyes are constantly scanning for pattern interrupters. Anything that contrasts with its surroundings automatically gets our attention and is more memorable. This contrast is fundamental to the biology of the human eye and occipital lobe in the brain. The effect of remembering the contrast is called the Von Restorff Effect.

Color & Visual Prominence

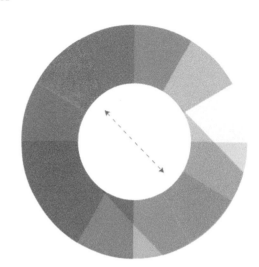

WARM COLORS
Red
Orange
Yellow

COOL COLORS
Blue
Green
Purple

COMPLEMENTARY COLORS
Red / Green
Orange / Blue
Yellow / Purple

Fig. 4.11

WARNING! **Candy colored exit signs!** Using color as a pattern interrupter can backfire and cause you to lose visitors. Colorful social media icons are super prominent when used on a cool, light web page, especially if they appear in the header. But these icons take people away from the site. Do you want the most visually prominent thing on your page to be an exit sign? (Fig. 4.12)

Fig. 4.12

Designers can take advantage of the Von Restorf Effect by using contrasting colors to draw attention to desired actions. On a page with mostly cool colors (blue, green and purple), a call to action in a warm color (orange, red or yellow) will be visually prominent.

Colors on opposite sides of the color wheel have the strongest contrast: blue/orange, purple/yellow, green/red. These are called complementary colors. Notice how prominent a warm-colored button can be in the context of a cool-colored design. Here we see how a complementary color guides the eyes toward action (Fig 4.13).

Fig. 4.13

TIP! Choose one contrasting color to be the "action color" and use it throughout the site on all the most important links and buttons.

It's usually not great if your visitors leave your site and go to a social network. Those sites are filled with distractions, ads and competitors. Visitors who click on one of those social icons are unlikely to return and, therefore, are less likely to convert.

Do the CTAs use compelling action words?

Every click of every button is a metaphor for an action. So buttons need action words. Begin with a verb. That little word explicitly tells the visitor what action they're taking when they click. *Read*, *learn* and *click* aren't usually the most compelling verbs.

Do the button labels indicate specific benefits?

Beyond just using verbs, CTAs can let the visitors know what they'll get if they click. What's on the next page? Why is this worth 10 seconds of their day? What problem is going to be eventually solved?

Naming the benefit in the button text reminds them why they would take the action. It reminds them why they're on the website. There is a strong correlation between specificity and conversion. Take a look at these tests run by conversion expert, Michael Aagaard:

Fig. 4.14

When a bit of text is added telling the visitor more about what they get and what's about to happen, the click through rate jumps.

Every visitor who sees your CTA is doing a split-second cost-benefit calculation. What's in it for me? This goes far beyond buttons and into every aspect of digital marketing. Anytime anyone sees something clickable, they ask themselves if it's worth their time. That includes every email subject line in our inboxes, every post in our social streams and every search listing on every search results page. This is why headline writing is such a critical skill.

Click through rate is the one metric that unites all digital marketers.

Do your CTAs use first- or second-person language?

Pick your pronouns carefully. They may affect conversion rates. Website copy is generally written in second-person language ("*Your* trusted partner in roof repairs"), which makes sense because the website is speaking to the visitor.

But some studies have shown that CTAs are more effective if they are written in first-person language ("Get an estimate for *my* roof repairs"). Tim Paige of Leadpages tested first-person and second-person language in button text. Here's what he found.

Account). Point of view and pronouns can sometimes impact conversion rates. Tim's study suggests that the first-person labels on buttons perform better because they speak from the perspective of the action taker, the person holding the mouse or touching the screen. Use second-person language (you, yours) in headlines and text, but first-person pronouns (I, me, my) in buttons.

Are there distractions near your calls to action?

The area around your call to action should be free from distractions. Any links or buttons that guide visitors away from the desired action may reduce your conversion rate. Take a look at this email sign-up box. The goal of this feature is to get visitors to subscribe, but it offers six other links at the same time. The call to action is just one of seven things the visitor can do within this box (Fig. 4.16).

Fig. 4.15

The button with first-person perspective (Create My Account) was clicked by 24% more visitors than the buttons with the second-person perspective (Create Your

Fig. 4.16

The "attention ratio" of any page (or area of a page) is the number of things the visitor can do divided by the number of things you'd like them to do. The closer the attention ratio is to 1:1, the higher the conversion rate will be.

Does the website miss an opportunity to create urgency?

We all hate to miss out on opportunities. We all have a built-in cognitive bias that overvalues losses and undervalues gains. In psychology, this is called "loss aversion." So whenever we are reminded that we might lose a chance at something, this information is given extra weight as we make decisions. We humans are not very good cost-benefit calculators.

The marketer can use this aversion to increase conversions. **Use language that reminds visitors what they'll risk, miss or lose by not acting now.** In other words, if there is any scarcity in the offer, make sure to mention it in or near the call to action

Is there a limited supply of the product? Is it only available for a certain amount of time? Are a limited number of people accepted? Is there a deadline? Never miss the change to trigger FOMO (fear of missing out).

Of course, you can find examples everywhere of marketers creating artificial scarcity (Sale Ends Saturday!) but lots of offers are legitimately limited. For example, school starts in the fall. There's a deadline to apply and a limited number of classrooms. So instead of "Apply Now," try a call to action such as "Save My Spot." It reminds visitors that there is a chance of losing this opportunity.

Are the forms short and easy for visitors to complete?

There is an inverse correlation between the length of a form and the percentage of visitors who fill it out and submit. Most studies show that shorter forms convert at a higher rate. Lead generation forms should include a minimum number of required fields: name, phone number, email. You can also include company name and message, depending on the goals of the form (Fig. 4.17).

Fig. 4.17

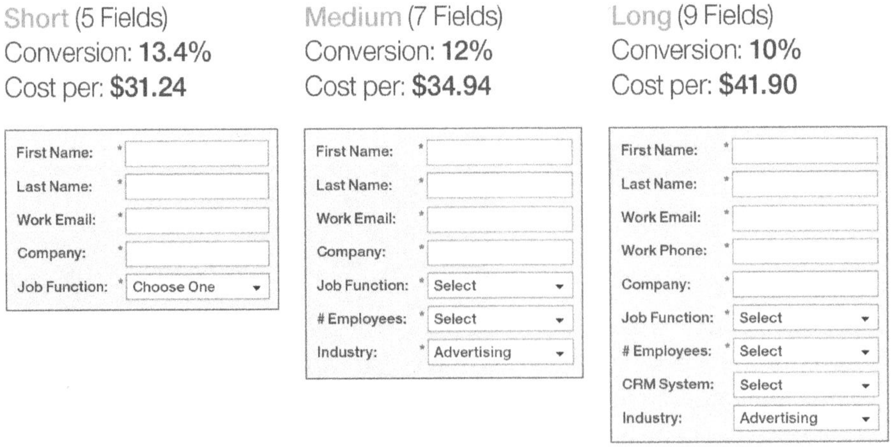

Short (5 Fields)
Conversion: **13.4%**
Cost per: **$31.24**

First Name:
Last Name:
Work Email:
Company:
Job Function: Choose One

Medium (7 Fields)
Conversion: **12%**
Cost per: **$34.94**

First Name:
Last Name:
Work Email:
Company:
Job Function: Select
Employees: Select
Industry: Advertising

Long (9 Fields)
Conversion: **10%**
Cost per: **$41.90**

First Name:
Last Name:
Work Email:
Work Phone:
Company:
Job Function: Select
Employees: Select
CRM System: Select
Industry: Advertising

Source: Marketo: The Definitive Guide to Lead Generation

⚠ WARNING! Resist the temptation to create a "warmer lead" by asking for too much information. Long forms are considered "greedy" if they ask more questions than the visitor feels are necessary. Often, you can gather the information you're looking for when you follow up with the prospect offline.

4.3 Messages, Messengers and Format

We've talked about the messages (answers for our specific audience) and the messengers (testimonials from third parties) but there's one other key factor in the conversion power of our content: the format.

Words aren't always the strongest way to deliver a message. Visuals are often a far more powerful, compelling way to deliver both answers and evidence. Just as third parties and customers are stronger messengers, images and videos are stronger formats.

Is the content all text? Or can it be upgraded to more visual formats?

Imagine an audience that needs to know how soon things will be delivered before they commit. In this case, "fast service" is an important message. That message can be delivered in different ways, some strong, some weak.

Here are examples of how messengers and formats combine for the "fast service" message.

Fig. 4.18

#1 in on-time deliveries. Fast service every time!

John Customer
Unsupported marketing claim

The brand makes a claim about themselves in text. It's common, expected and weak. Don't expect this approach to improve your conversion rates.

Fig. 4.19

"That was quick! Thanks so much for being prompt!"

Written testimonial from a customer

The voice of the customer adds evidence. Now the claim is supported in a qualitative way using social proof. But text has limited ability to maximize conversions.

Fig. 4.20

Certification or seal from third party.

The certification or award comes from a third party. It's not a customer, but it's still coming from a source other than the brand. And the visual adds interest and credibility.

Fig. 4.21

"Everything was right on time. What great service!"

Video testimonial from a customer.

Images might catch the visitor's attention, but video is more likely to hold it. This is the law of visual hierarchy of web pages: *Images are more powerful than text. Movement is more powerful than images.*

So video, or any movement, is always among the most visually prominent elements on any page (or at any scroll depth of any page). Movement is just one of several ways to build a hierarchy that guides the visitor's attention around a page (Fig. 4.22).

This is how web designers create the user experience. They use design and content, formats and messages to create a visual hierarchy that guides the eyes through the page. The hierarchy aligns with the messaging priorities, putting the strongest assets in the best positions.

So the video testimonial is the strongest combination of messenger and format. It's likely the single most powerful piece of conversion-focused content you can add to a website. Aside from an in-person referral from a trusted friend, nothing is more effective.

These videos are worth investing in. Unlike social media videos and content marketing videos, these conversion-focused videos should be high production quality. Use a professional looking player. That means a pro hosting and streaming service, like Wistia or Vimeo, not YouTube.

Fig. 4.22

The Laws of Visual Hierarchy

	low visual prominence		high visual prominence
Size	small		large
Position	bottom of the page		top of the page
Color	low contrast		strong contrast, unique color
Format	text	images, icons	movement, video
Position relative to other elements	crowded on the page		surrounded by whitespace

Here is a breakdown of the three main types of marketing videos, showing their location and purpose (Fig. 4.23).

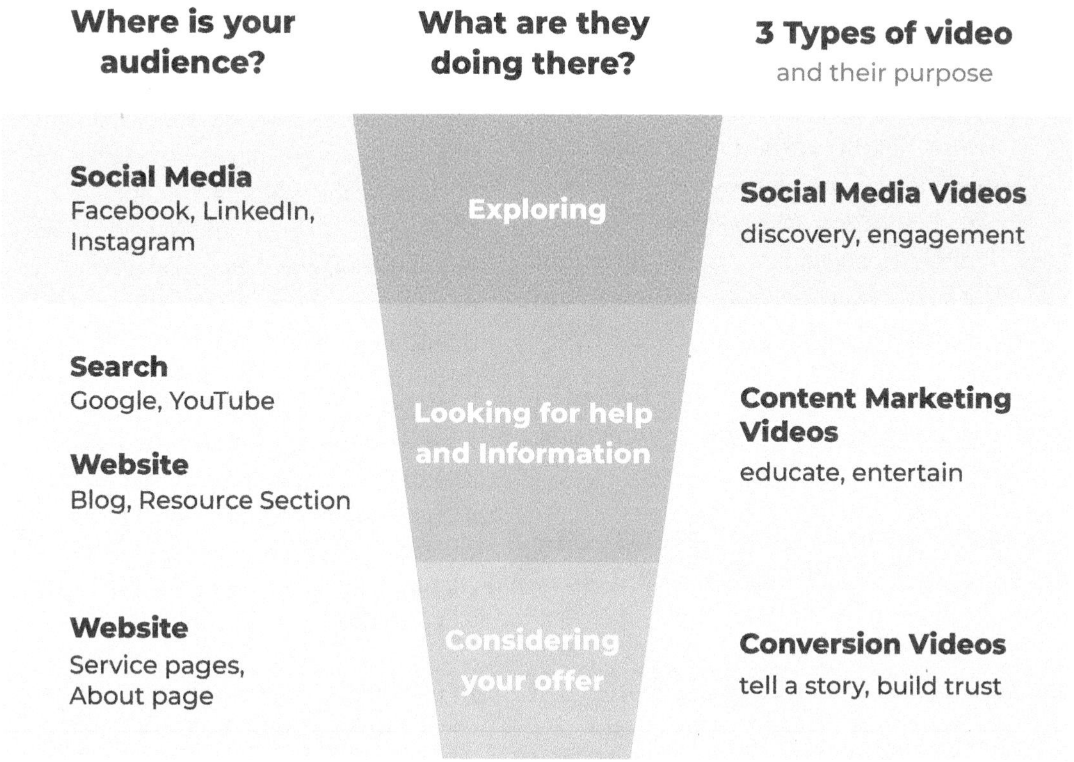

Fig. 4.23

Where is your audience?	What are they doing there?	3 Types of video and their purpose
Social Media Facebook, LinkedIn, Instagram	Exploring	**Social Media Videos** discovery, engagement
Search Google, YouTube **Website** Blog, Resource Section	Looking for help and Information	**Content Marketing Videos** educate, entertain
Website Service pages, About page	Considering your offer	**Conversion Videos** tell a story, build trust

We'll look at social media and content marketing videos in the next two chapters. Those videos drive traffic and engagement. But when the goal is lead generation, the videos are all about building trust. Here are the four most common conversion-focused videos and the goals for each: (Fig. 4.24)

Fig. 4.24

Type of Conversion Video	Goals
About Us Video	Tell the story about the origin and purgose of the company. Personalize the brand.
Explainer Video	Break down complex offerings using movement and visuals. Show processes.
Product/Service Video	Sell by showing/explaining benefits. Differentiate.
Testimonial Video	Build trust and credibility through social proof.

Keep visitors moving

Are there dead ends on your website?

Do your sales pages end without suggesting an action? Does the page just stop? No call to action, no button, no link, no guidance for the visitor on what to do next? If so, the page is a dead end, providing no guidance to the visitor, and erasing any action to which the page may have been leading.

Add a suggested action to the bottom of every page to keep the visitor flowing (Fig. 4.25).

Fig. 4.25

Page Type	Suggested Action
Service pages	Call to Action
Blog post	Subscribe, Comment, Related Posts
"No results" search results page	Were you looking for any of these pages?
"Page not found" 404 error page	You may find these pages helpful . . .
Thank you pages	Subscribe, follow, create an account

Fix the dead ends by adding links that help guide the visitor deeper, toward your best content and toward even more calls to action.

Adding more conversion opportunities to thank you pages

In our experience designing and building websites at Orbit Media, we have found that the thank you page is an excellent place to let the visitor take action again. If visitors had enough interest and trust to take action once, they may take action twice if offered the opportunity on the thank you page.

The trick is to first give visitors what they want. For example, many ecommerce shopping carts ask visitors to create an account before checking out. This isn't what the visitors were hoping for. They clicked "buy now," not "buy after I give you my email address and password."

In the Google Analytics accounts of our clients, we've seen the lack of a "guest checkout" option *reduces sales by 30-50%*. Requiring visitors to create accounts before buying is simply a self-centered website owner being greedy. This is counter to the principles of content marketing. First, we give visitors what they want. Then, they may give us what we want.

On one website, we added the option to create an account after the checkout process. We included two simple sentences of benefit copy: "We'll remember your address for a faster checkout next time. We'll also store your order history and let you create a wish list." The percentage of shoppers who created accounts increased by 40%.

Thank you pages are often missed opportunities to let the visitor become more engaged:

- A lead generation thank you page may offer a newsletter sign-up: "If you'd like to receive our best advice as a monthly email, sign up below."

- A job applicant thank you page may offer social media buttons: "To be the first to know about open positions, follow us on Facebook."

- An event registration or donation thank you page may offer to let the visitor share the news: "Share this on social media and let your friends know you're going/you donated."

The Orbit Media site has a thank you page with an offer to subscribe to our email list. Each year, hundreds of people subscribe to our newsletter from that thank you page (Fig. 4.26).

Even if it doesn't offer a subsequent conversion, the thank you page doesn't have to be a dead end. Add links to guide the visitor toward more content.

4.4 Testimonials

There is a reason that testimonials are the most powerful content for conversions. They show that someone

"**For you to achieve your goals,** visitors must first achieve theirs."

Bryan Eisenberg, *Founder & CMO, IdealSpot*

got value from your service, that someone believes in your brand. The voice of that customer is more credible than the voice of the company. It's a form of social proof.

As empathetic humans, we have a tendency to do what other people do. It's called conformity bias, also known as the bandwagon effect. A testimonial reinforces this bias, transforming an abstract product or service a visitor might exchange money for into something real that has benefited real people.

When you say it, it's **marketing**. When they say it, it's **social proof**.

Fig. 4.26

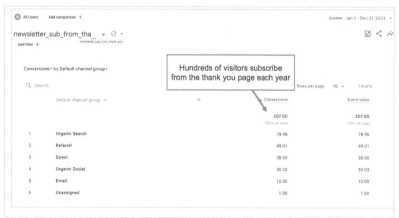

Endorsements vs. Customer testimonials

An endorsement is typically a well-known influencer giving their public support for a brand. But a testimonial is from a customer or client. They may be an unknown person to the reader, but they have personal experience with the product or service. Since they're a paying customer, the testimonial is authentic, like a review.

Everything you say and write as a marketer is marketing. You can't help it. But when your audience says it, it's often unexpectedly candid. Even blunt. It's virtually impossible for a marketer to write copy as authentic as a customer. Check out this example:

"Wow. I just updated my site and it was SO SIMPLE. I am blown away. You guys truly kick ass. Thanks for being so awesome. High fives!"

The tone is so authentic, it's disarming. Don't try to write this way. Let your customers do it for you.

But how you construct the testimonial and where you put it is up to you. Let's take a look at what effective testimonials include and where you can put them for the greatest impact.

7 things to add to your testimonials

The more information in a testimonial, the more credible it is. Yet many websites have weak, almost naked, testimonials with very little supportive information. Here is a miniguide with all the little things you can add to increase the power and credibility of the testimonials on your site (Fig 4.27).

1. Logo (for B2B websites)
If you're a business-to-business company, adding logos to your testimonials will make them more credible and more visually prominent. This is especially effective if the company is well known.

Fig. 4.27

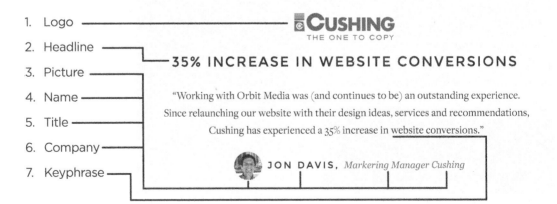

2. Headline

Rather than jump right into the text, take the five to seven words that have the greatest impact and use them as a little headline above the testimonial itself. This will make it more scannable and more likely that visitors will slow down and read the text.

There's a good reason why Amazon makes you write headlines for reviews of products. They know visitors are quickly scanning through the page and that headlines can draw visitors into the reviews.

3. Testimonial text

The testimonial itself should be short and direct. Long testimonials (or long paragraphs of any kind) are less likely to be read by visitors. A long, rambling testimonial might get scanned, but it's unlikely to be read. So keep it short.

If the testimonial is very long, but so compelling that you don't want to edit it down, put the most impactful words at the beginning, especially if those words align with the hope and concerns of the visitor. Frontload the testimonial with these words.

"You made it so simple. My new site is so much faster and easier to work with than my old site. I just choose the page, make the change and click save. Thanks, guys!"

If you don't have an opportunity to edit the testimonial (more about how and when to write testimonials in a minute), you can also try bolding the most impactful words or breaking a long testimonial up into shorter paragraphs. And make sure everything is in quotes.

"By adding a sub-headline, you'll not only draw more **attention to your testimonial** but entice your visitor to actually read what should be your most powerful form of social proof on your site."

JEN HAVICE, *Conversion Copywriter, Make Mention Media*

4. Picture of their face

The human face is a very powerful type of imagery, as we mentioned above and will discuss again later. It makes the testimonial both more visually prominent and more credible. Research suggests pictures of people are especially effective in testimonials. Basecamp, the project management software company, once A/B tested two landing page designs. The design that featured a face of a happy customer increased conversion rates by 102.5%.[1]

"Quotation marks are **the most powerful punctuation** on your keyboard."

1. Source: https://signalvnoise.com/posts/2991-behind-the-scenes-ab-testing-part-3-final

5. Name

Whenever possible, add the full name. Second best is the first name and last initial. If that's not possible, add the initial and a few words describing their industry, role or location. The more anonymous the testimonial, the less credible it will feel to visitors.

6. Title and company (for B2B websites)

If your company sells to other businesses, adding the job title and company will also add credibility, especially if the company is well known to your visitors and the job title is similar to the job title of your typical buyer.

Should you link the company name in the testimonial to the website of that company?

Sure! Why not. It's a nice little way to say thank you, and it's not likely to cost you many visitors. We track exit clicks on our site and found that links in testimonials rarely get clicked. But they do pass a bit of SEO value. That's a nice way to show your gratitude.

Fig. 4.28

Highly Credible, Compelling Testimonial (image, name, title, company)

"You guys rocked on the sculpture project. Thanks so much for doing a great job!"

George Washington
First President, United States of America

Anonymous Testimonial

"You guys rocked on the sculpture project. Thanks so much for doing a great job!"

-G.W., Federal Government Executive

But my clients won't let me use their names or company names. What can I do?

This is a common problem. There is no easy way around it. If you cannot find any happy clients willing to let you use their name, anonymize the testimonial by using initials and the industry. And look for other types of evidence to add. Don't let this stop you from supporting your marketing claims in some way.

Compare these examples in Fig. 4.28. The testimonial text is the same. But which of these is more credible, trustworthy and compelling?

7. Keyphrase

The seventh thing to add to your testimonials isn't about evidence or conversions. It's about search rankings and traffic. A text-based testimonial can help your rankings *if the testimonial includes a target keyphrase or related phrases.*

Here's an excerpt of a page about "raccoon removal service" and optimized for that phrase. We've marked in red the instance of the target phrase and the related words (Fig. 4.29).

The phrase is in the header and the first paragraph. A keyword-focused testimonial can increase both rankings and conversion rates. It is both cheese and mousetrap.

Fig. 4.29

Humane Raccoon Removal Services

We offer 24-hour raccoon removal of all sizes from attics, garages and crawl spaces.

"I so glad you came over quickly. It was the middle of night and that sucker was huge! It's amazing you removed that raccoon without hurting him. That was great service. Thanks guys!"

How to gather testimonials

There are two ways:

- Ask for them

- Catch them as they flow past

The first approach is faster. The second approach is easier.

Asking for testimonials

Start with your happiest clients and customers. These are your superfans. They may have already offered to be a reference so they won't mind the request. They might really want to help you! So send them an email. Here's an example of an email that asks for a testimonial:

> *Hi there, Bob.*
>
> *I'm writing to ask if you wouldn't mind giving us a short testimonial for our website. We're updating a few pages, and I'm hoping to add a quick quote from you. It would link back to your site, so it actually might be a good thing for you and your website.*

> *Would this be ok with you? If this makes you even a little bit uncomfortable, no worries at all. But if you are ok with it, I can send you a very short blurb for you to review, or you can write a sentence or two and send it over. Whatever is easiest for you.*
>
> *Thank you, Bob!*

⚠️ WARNING! If you write and post without the review and approval of the person you are attributing it to, it's fake. It may even be illegal. But if you write a draft and then allow the customer to make edits and give approval it's real and legitimate.

Now let's break it down. This email needs to be *short, considerate* and *easy to respond to*, whether that response is a yes or a no.

Did they say yes? Great. Now say thank you. And make that thank you more than just a short email message. Go overboard on gratitude with a handwritten note, a small gift or a LinkedIn recommendation.

Catch them as they flow past

Testimonials happen every day, or at least the seeds of them do. A smart marketer knows how to spot these seeds. Here's what they look like in the wild:

- **Grateful email messages . . .**
  "Thank you so much for a job well done."

- **Social media love . . .**
  "You guys are the best! Keep up the great work!"

- **Happy, handwritten thank you notes . . .**
  "I just wanted to let you know that it's been great working with you."

- **Gushing in-person gratitude . . .**
  "You've been so helpful. Is there anything I can do for you?"

If you're good at your job, you'll see these flow past from time to time (if you don't ever get positive feedback from customers, you have bigger problems you should fix before worrying about getting testimonials). The key is to keep an eye out for testimonials and when you see one, stop and make the most of them.

1. Save them in a "Good File." Keep a folder of emails or screenshots from these appreciative moments.

2. Reach out with an immediate reply, thanking them for taking the time. Never, never ignore these messages. That would be rude.

3. If appropriate, ask the sender if they wouldn't mind letting you use some of those words on your website.

TIP: If you have a process for gathering feedback from clients (important if you ever hope to calculate your Net Promoter Score) then this is also a moment to capture testimonials and reviews. When you get strong, positive feedback, make that the moment you ask for permission to use it on your website.

Once you know how to spot testimonials and how to ask for them when necessary, you're on a path to fill your site with glowing evidence and social proof. The next question is where to put them.

Where to use testimonials?

Now that you've got 'em, where should you put your sparkling new gems of social proof? Our first tip is a bit counterintuitive:

Never make a testimonials page. **Make every page a testimonials page.**

The reason is simple: visitors rarely go to testimonials pages. They can smell the marketing a mile away. The navigation label "Testimonials" doesn't suggest that they'll find answers to questions there.

Fig. 4.30

28		46	38	1.21	26s	104
29		42	29	1.45	49s	121
30		41	5	8.20	4m 30s	92
31			29	1.34	29s	117
32		30	24	1.50	1m 16s	97
33	/testimonials/	35	24	1.46	17s	77
34		35	23	1.52	48s	109
35		34	27	1.26	36s	96
36		34	27	1.26	30s	107
37		34	33	1.03	53s	135
38		33	29	1.14	1m 13s	84

Pages and screens: Page path and screen class · Custom Jul 1, 2023 - Jan 11, 2024

The testimonials page is the 33rd most popular page

It sounds more like a sales pitch. That's why testimonial pages get less traffic than other pages. Ironically, putting your social proof here actually makes it less visible to your visitors.

Here is the GA4 Pages and screens report for a website that has a testimonials page. You can see there are 32 pages on this website that are visited more often than this page. It's never popular (Fig. 4.30).

Here's the problem: putting them all together on one page also takes them out of context. They aren't near the messages and answers they need to support.

Put the testimonial next to the product or service it mentions. Does the testimonial mention a service? Put it on that service page. Is it about a product? Use it as a review on the product page. Does it mention your speedy delivery times? Put it on the shipping page.

It should be mere pixels away, literally, from the claim it supports.

Put your best testimonials on your most popular pages. Just look at GA4 to see how visitors tend to flow through your website, or just look for the most visited pages. Put your best foot forward by putting your best evidence in your top path and on your top pages.

- Unsurprisingly, this typically means putting your best testimonials on your *homepage*.

- Surprisingly, this typically means adding testimonials to your *about page*. Why not, right? Put the best stuff anywhere people will see it. Put billboards on highways, not backstreets.

✦ Use AI to check your pages for evidence

If you give ChatGPT a full-page screenshot of any of your service pages, you can ask it to evaluate the extent to which you added support for your marketing claims. You'll need a Chrome extension such as GoFullPage to capture a screenshot of an entire webpage. Upload the screenshot along with this prompt.

 Prompt:

You are a conversion optimization expert, skilled at using evidence to support marketing messages. The following are types of evidence that can be added to webpages: testimonials, reviews, case studies, success stories, data and statistics, years in business, number of happy clients, client logos, awards, association memberships, etc.

The attached image is a screenshot of a webpage. Rate the extent to which the page does and does not use supportive evidence. Which marketing claims are unsupported? Show your thinking.

[attach the full page screenshot of a page]

You may find that your page is filled with many unsupported marketing claims. For best results, first give AI your personas so it knows your target audience. You can also use AI to generate personas using the prompts in Section 4.8.

4.5 Sign-up Forms: The 3 Conversion Factors in Email List Growth

To be successful at email marketing, you need to grow your list of email subscribers. To grow your list of subscribers, you need a great email sign-up form. The growth of your email list depends on how you design that little box. In this section, you'll learn how to grow your email list by conversion optimizing your email subscriber form.

It's actually very simple. There are three main factors that all of the best newsletter sign-up forms have in common. Coincidentally, they all start with the letter "p," so we'll call these the *3 P's of Email Sign-up Forms* (Fig 4.31).

1. Prominence

The sign-up form is visually prominent on the page. You can't miss it. That probably means it's big, but it's more than that. Here are a few ways to make your email sign-up box more visible (Fig 4.32).

Fig. 4.31

- **Color contrast**
  The color contrasts with the colors around it, especially the subscribe button. See a few examples below.

- **"Sticky" elements**
  It's a "sticky" element, so it's always visible no matter how far down the visitor scrolls.

- **Multiple locations**
  It's all over the place. At the top of the blog main page. At the bottom of every post. On the about page, in the footer, etc. We get a lot of subscribers from the sign-up box on our contact form thank you page.

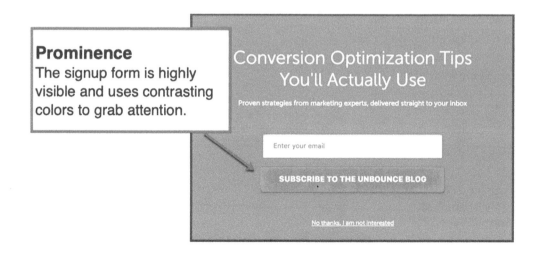

Fig. 4.32

- **The pop-up**
  The email sign-up popup window (aka lightbox, aka modal window) is everywhere. Of course, 0% of visitors like them. But 100% of marketers report that they are effective at list growth. It's a judgment call. We've resisted them for years, but we're starting to experiment.

Now that everyone is seeing your sign-up box, let's look at what we have inside . . .

2. Promise

Make a promise to the visitor. Tell them what they'll get if they subscribe. Sadly, most sign-up forms don't do this. The best newsletter sign-up forms tell the visitor two things:

- The topic of the email newsletter
- How frequently they'll get your emails

If you don't tell them these things, why would they subscribe? You need to answer the question "what's in it for me?" and tell them the benefits of being on the list. Keep reading to see good and bad examples of this.

If our sign-up form has just three lonely words, "subscribe for updates," we're not promising anything. It would be weird if anyone subscribed.

PRO TIP! Publish your content marketing mission statement at the top of your blog and every visitor can see what you publish and why they should sign up. The promise is basically an edited version of the content marketing mission statement, which we'll cover in Section 5.1.

3. Proof

The third P is proof, as in social proof. To get visitors to act, you need to add evidence that the blog is worth reading and the newsletter is worth subscribing to. Here again, we can use either of the two kinds of evidence:

- **Number of subscribers** (quantitative)
  You should have at least 1,000 subscribers before this works well, so this is best for established blogs.

- **A testimonial from a fan** (qualitative)
  A quote from a fan who loves you is effective because it's personal. If it comes from someone well known to your readers, it's more than a testimonial—it's an endorsement.

You'll see subscriber counts and qualitative proof in the examples below, but here's a nice example of an endorsement. Rather than show numbers, Brian Dean of Backlinko adds a short quote (Fig. 4.33).

Fig. 4.33

Bonus P's: More ways to improve your email conversion rates

Beyond those three, most important basics, there are other ways to make your sign-up boxes even more effective. And yes, they all start with P.

- **Presents**
  Offer a present or a gift to the visitor. This is often called a "content upgrade" or "lead magnet" and it's one of the most popular tactics for companies that use marketing automation. The visitor trades their email address for a piece of high-value content. Technically, they're not subscribing to the newsletter, but visitors know that you'll be sending them email.

- **Personality**
  We've already looked at the power of faces as imagery. Using a face also gives you a chance to get the visitor to look in a certain direction with the "you look where they look" phenomenon. Erikson does this beautifully, directing your eyes to the headline (Fig. 4.34).

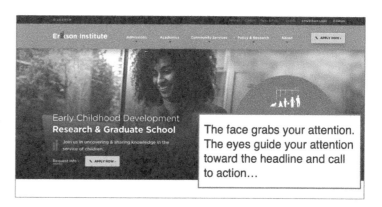

The face grabs your attention. The eyes guide your attention toward the headline and call to action…

Fig. 4.34

- **Privacy**
  The final P is for privacy. If trust levels are low with your audience, you can add a note that reassures them that you won't share or sell their information with anyone else (Fig. 4.35).

TIP: Our friend and conversion expert Justin Rondeau has tested everything and found that some content upgrades work better than others. He suggests offering tool kits, case studies, assessments, quizzes and cheat sheets.

Fig. 4.35

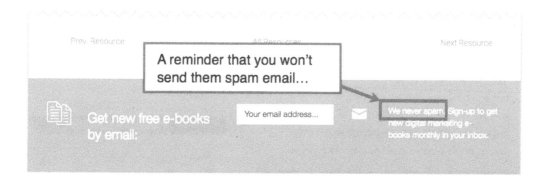

A reminder that you won't send them spam email…

Fig. 4.36

 WARNING! **Privacy reminders can backfire!**
A negative word like "spam" can reduce sign ups because it triggers anxiety. Michael Aagaard of Unbounce ran a test that showed the text "100% spam free" reduced conversion rates by 18%.[2] He recommends avoiding using the word "spam" anywhere near newsletter sign-up forms (Fig. 4.36).

2. https://unbounce.com/lead-generation/32-lead-generation-tactics/

Example: Orbit Media: 4,863% increase in subscribers

For years, we had a sign-up CTA at the top of our blog. It was a vague, wordy paragraph with a link at the end. The actual sign-up form was on a separate page (Fig. 4.37).

Fig. 4.37

One day, we made a change. We let people subscribe without leaving the page. We also trimmed the text and added the three P's (Fig. 4.38).

Fig. 4.38

There was an immediate, dramatic impact on our conversion rates. Look at the report for sign-ups and conversion rates during this period, compared to the previous year (Fig. 4.39).

Yes, you are reading that correctly. That's a 4,863% increase in newsletter subscriptions and an 806% increase in the conversion rate. Aside from the change to the form, the only other change we made in our content marketing was an increase in publishing frequency during that time frame.

Also, notice how the abandonment rate dropped to zero. That's because the form wasn't on a separate page. There's nothing to abandon because it's all on one page.

Since then, we've experimented with other designs. Our latest blog landing page increases the prominence by making the header a large CTA area, with a big red button. The promise is there in huge bold letters. The supportive proof is the number of subscribers (Fig. 4.40).

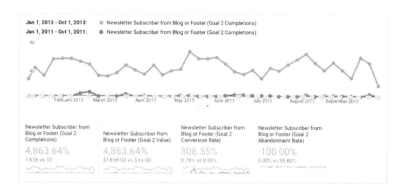

Fig. 4.39

We also removed the name of the blog, "The Orbiter." No one seemed to notice. The subscriber rates didn't change. This suggests that the visitor doesn't care what you name your blog. They are interested in the content, not the branding.

Footer email sign-up forms

It's common to add an email sign-up form to the footer of a website. We've built them into dozens of websites. These footer forms can still include the three P's.

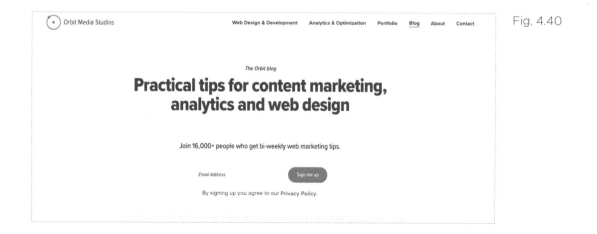

Fig. 4.40

If the subscribe form is nothing more than a lonely box with the words "email sign-up" and a submit button (Fig. 4.41), then it's not likely to grow your list. In fact, it would be strange if anyone entered their email address here:

Fig. 4.41

Here is a more compelling example on the Acquirent website (Fig. 4.42). It has visual prominence (the green color), promise (sales and marketing tips) and proof (13,000 subscribers).

Fig. 4.42

Footer sign-up forms shouldn't be the only place for visitors to subscribe. This should be one of several places. This is just the final call to action, visible on every page, similar to social media icons.

4.6 Thank You Pages and Conversion Tracking

Success! The visitor takes an action and becomes a lead, buys a product, subscribes to the newsletter, applies for a job or makes a donation. But there are a lot of ways that visitors can take these actions. How they take action and what happens after that final click determines how easy success is to measure.

If you can't measure conversions and conversion rates, you'll never have the data to inform the decisions on making improvements. You can never successfully perform conversion rate optimization.

Fig 4.43 shows the main ways in which visitors take action and convert on websites. This also shows the advantages or disadvantages for measurement.

The problem with email links

If you have a contact page with an email address rather than a contact form, you will not be able to track conversions accurately. Actually, there are lots of disadvantages to using an email link, beyond the tracking problems. Compare the differences between email link and contact forms in Fig. 4.44.

Fig. 4.43

Type of Action	Measurement Implication
Phone call	Untrackable in GA4. But can be tracked using a service such as DialogTech.
Email link click	Untrackable in GA4 without "event tracking." Even then, only the email link click is measured. GA doesn't know if an email was actually sent.
Contact form with thank you message	Trackable in GA4 only through event tracking.
Contact form with thank you page	*Preferred.* Easily trackable using simple destination goals.
Contact form or shopping cart on third-party website (such as Unbounce, PayPal or EventBrite)	Trackable in GA4 only through cross domain tracking and only if the third-party site allows (Amazon, for example, does not)
Shopping Cart with "thank you" pages	*Preferred.* Easily trackable using simple destination goals.

Fig. 4.44

	Email Link	Contact Form
Easily trackable In Analytics	No	Yes
Can store a backup in a database	No	Yes
Leads to a thank you page with additional content	No	Yes
Sends an auto-response email with additional content	Mostly No	Yes
Can ask specific questions	No	Yes
Can route message depending on answers	No	Yes
Can route message to multiple people	No	Yes
Works on any computer, no email software necessary	No	Yes
Increases spam	Yes	No

The winner here is obvious. Email links fail on every criterion for good marketing, from messaging to lead management, from usability to tracking. Beyond that, email links are magnets for spam. Spammers use robots that scrape the web for email addresses. So that little email link on your website might lead to a lot of junk in your spam folder.

4.7 Lead Generation Website Best Practices

Clearly, there are a lot of little factors involved in the success or failure of a lead generation website. They all work together to create visibility, then clarity, then trust.

There is one feature that every lead gen website has in common: *the back button*. One mistake and the visitor will simply leave and find an alternative. We need to avoid that click and keep visitors in the flow.

A lead generation website has a specific set of pages, each with a specific job and specific elements. Each element aligns with the psychology of the visitor and the marketing goals of the business.

The website is gently guiding the potential customer through a series of steps: awareness, interest, trust, then action. That's a classic "conversion funnel." Notice how the pages align with steps in the funnel in Fig. 4.45.

But this only works if each page in the process is built specifically for the purpose.

Each page needs a set of elements that keep the process moving and the visitor flowing. So to avoid mistakes and missed opportunities, here is a set of best practices for lead generation websites, including a breakdown of all the elements on all the pages involved.

Fig. 4.45

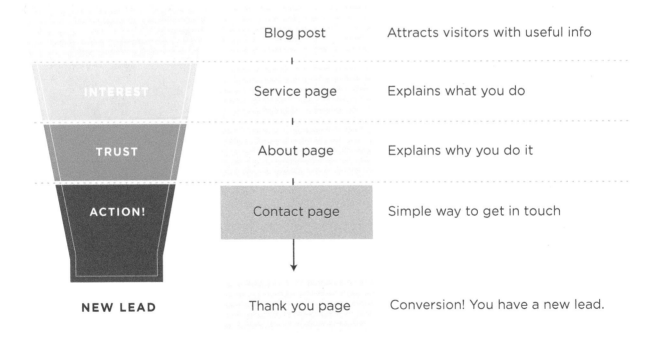

	Blog post	Attracts visitors with useful info
INTEREST	Service page	Explains what you do
TRUST	About page	Explains why you do it
ACTION!	Contact page	Simple way to get in touch
NEW LEAD	Thank you page	Conversion! You have a new lead.

Blog post: Helpful advice

The process starts even before the visitor lands on the website.

Your audience is looking for information and answers. To pull them toward you, you need to give them a reason to visit. The better you are at getting your expertise out of your brains and into your content marketing, the more visitors you'll attract.

The article should be so useful that the reader will be thrilled to have found you. And during their visit, they'll find easy ways to engage:

- Get more of your advice via your email program (a prominent sign-up form)

- Get more or share via social media (social icons, share buttons)

- Get more content during this visit (internal links to related content)

The likelihood that they do any of those things is partly a result of the blog template itself. So a great blog post template is key to the lead generation process (Fig. 4.46). It should include all of the following elements:

1. Keyword-focused header
If the topic is something your audience is searching for AND your website has sufficient authority to compete for the phrase, you have an SEO opportunity. You'll learn all about keyword research in Section 5.5.

To capture a keyword opportunity, you'll need a super-high-quality article that indicates its relevance for the phrase. That starts at the top. Use the target keyphrase once in the <h1> header. Along with the <title> tag, this is the most important place to use the primary keyphrase.

2. Featured image
Every great post has a great image. This makes the post more attractive, both on your site and in the social streams when it gets shared. Bright, unexpected or provocative images may increase engagement when the post appears in social streams.

3. Email sign-up box
We'll use those three P's of email sign-up forms we already covered: prominence, promise and proof. Of course, even the best blogs have extremely high bounce rates. One of the best outcomes from a blog visit is a new subscriber. Or maybe they'll help with a bit of social promotion . . .

4. Social sharing buttons
Make it easy to share by putting your share buttons in several places. Here's where top blogs put their share buttons.[2]

- Above the article: 36% of blogs

- Next to the article: 33% of blogs

- Below the article: 35% of blogs

Many blogs put share buttons in several places. Also, there are different styles of share buttons. Some show the number

---

2. How to Design a Blog, Orbit Media https://www.orbitmedia.com/blog/how-to-design-a-blog/

Fig. 4.46

Elements of a High-Performing Blog Template

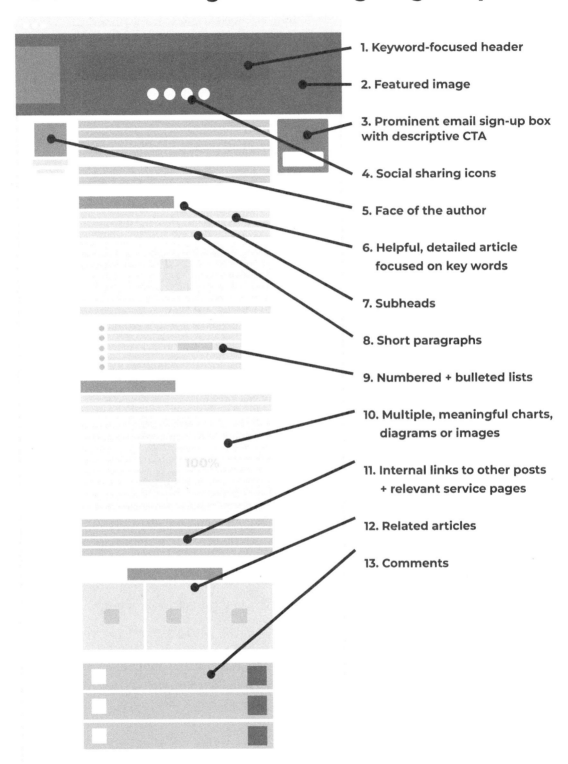

1. Keyword-focused header

2. Featured image

3. Prominent email sign-up box with descriptive CTA

4. Social sharing icons

5. Face of the author

6. Helpful, detailed article focused on key words

7. Subheads

8. Short paragraphs

9. Numbered + bulleted lists

10. Multiple, meaningful charts, diagrams or images

11. Internal links to other posts + relevant service pages

12. Related articles

13. Comments

of shares in a little counter; others do not. Which to use should be a deliberate decision.

- If sharing is high, use share widgets with counters to show the number of shares.

- If sharing is low, don't show a counter . . . those zeros are negative social proof.

5. Face of the author

Never miss the chance to make your marketing more human.

The byline is one of the defining features of blog templates. Adding a face to the byline makes it all the more personal. It supports thought leadership (leaders are people, after all) and gives a little networking boost to the author (Fig. 4.47).

What about the date?

If your content strategy is to publish evergreen, how-to articles, rather than news, then we recommend against using a blog post template that shows the publishing date. Dating your content makes it look older faster, increasing the bounce rate and reducing social sharing—even if it's the best page on the web for the topic.

If the design of your blog doesn't include a date, you still always have the option, as a writer, to include it or not in the title and the body text.

6. Depth, detail and related phrases

It's the deep, how-to articles that position your site as the go-to resource. If they trust your content and visit regularly, they'll think of you the moment they need help, the "zero moment of truth" in lead generation.

And the extremely detailed articles are more likely to rank in search engines, partly because they have more opportunities to use both the target keyphrase and the semantically related phrases. They answer more of the related questions. They touch on more of the subtopics.

Fig. 4.47

BY LAUREL MILTNER

We've all been there. You know you have a ton of content, but you don't know 1) what everything is, 2) where it is, or 3) if it's even still any good. When your content management hinges on going to that one person you know did that one thing that one time to find it, it's time for a content audit.

Let's be real. Conducting a website content audit can be a little intense. A lot intense, actually, if you have a lot of content or it's been a really long time since someone did one. But they're important—critical even—to your ongoing content marketing success. And I promise: they aren't really that hard. Just time-consuming.

Why should you do a website content audit?

Fig. 4.48

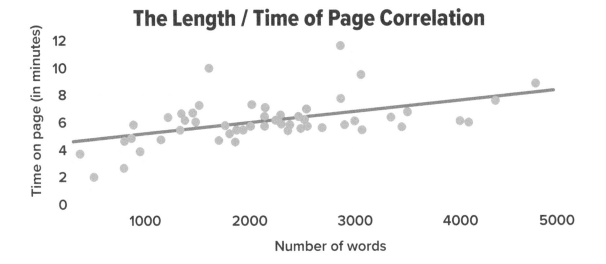

The Length / Time of Page Correlation

Detailed articles are also more likely to engage visitors. There is a clear correlation between length and time on page. You can do the analysis for your own content using your own data. That's just what we did for our top 50 articles, in this scatter plot chart (Fig. 4.48).

7. Subheads
Long articles don't have to be dense and blocky. Break up the article with plenty of subheads. Remember, most readers are actually scanners. The structure provided by subheads will help your scan reader quickly find answers to their specific questions.

8. Short paragraphs
The longer the paragraph, the more likely it will be skipped.

As a general rule, don't write paragraphs longer than three or four lines. And look for opportunities to write the occasional very short paragraph of just a few words. *Designers know that visitors love white space. But somehow, writers didn't get the memo.*

9. Numbered and bullet lists
Lists are another type of formatting that keep the scan reader flowing.

Beyond being easy on the eyes, numbered lists have another advantage: they give you an opportunity to use a number in the headline. And since numerals are more visually prominent than letters, this can help the article stand out when it appears in social streams and inboxes.

10. Multiple meaningful charts, diagrams and other images
We started with a great featured image, but don't stop there. It's impossible to overstate the importance of visuals. Here's how our recommendations have changed:

2010: "Make sure to include a great image on every post."
2020: "Make sure there is something of visual interest *at every scroll depth on every post.*"

This will keep the reader from reaching a wall of text. If they get to a desert of words, without an image in sight, they're more likely to bounce.

The best images are supportive, not generic. Later we'll go into detail about best practices for blog images. For now, we'll recommend skipping the stock photos and instead adding images that improve clarity (diagrams) or support the message (charts and graphs), such as the one in Fig. 4.49.

11. Internal links to other blog posts and service pages

Guide the visitor down the funnel through internal links. Each blog post should have at least two links within the body text:

- Link to a relevant service page

- Link to another blog post

12. Related articles

This is the most common feature on blog templates. 80% of the top blogs show related articles.[3] It's a way to encourage readers to dig deeper (reducing bounce rates) and build interconnected hubs of content.

The recommended articles can be automatically selected based on category and relevance or can be manually curated. Ask your developer to show you options.

13. Comments

Still a popular feature and possibly the most social element on the page, blog comments are a golden opportunity to get feedback from your readers. They're also an opportunity to grow your network. And finally, they can be a magnet for social proof.

---

3. How to Design a Blog, Orbit Media https://www.orbitmedia.com/blog/how-to-design-a-blog/

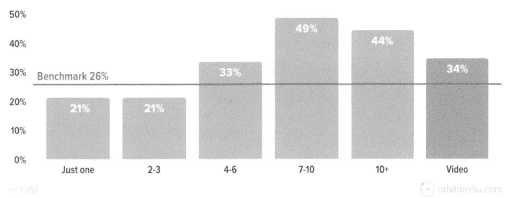

Bloggers who add more visuals get better results

Fig. 4.49

Percentage of bloggers who report "strong results" based on use of visuals

	Just one	2-3	4-6	7-10	10+	Video
%	21%	21%	33%	49%	44%	34%

Benchmark 26%

orbitmedia.com

Source: Blogging Statistics, 2023, Orbit Media https://www.orbitmedia.com/blog/blogging-statistics

Yes, it's hard to get readers to comment. To help trigger more comments, end the post with a question or suggestion that the reader shares their thoughts.

Service page: Simply what you do

This is the workhorse of the lead generation website. The blog post teaches; the service page sells. But it's still educational. The content needs to answer the prospects' top questions and address the top objections. It describes how you do the work.

Fig. 4.50 gives a quick breakdown of the differences between the services pages and blog posts.

Here are the three key ingredients of service pages with high conversion rates.

- **Answers** to visitors' questions, adding clarity and addressing objections

- **Evidence** to support those answers, without which the page is a big pile of unsupported claims

- **Calls to Action** that are specific and clear

The next level of detail is much more interesting.

The little diagram in Fig. 4.51 shows a one-column layout. For most B2B lead gen websites, it's more likely a two-column layout with a series of page blocks. Each page block shows text and visuals in various layouts, guiding the visitors' eyes down the page.

Fig. 4.50

	Service Pages	Blog Posts
Goal	Sell (generate qualified leads)	Teach (grow awareness, subscribers, links, etc.)
SEO	Commercial intent pharese ($)	Information intent phrase (?)
Writing	"Copy"	"Content"
CTAs	Get in touch, Schedule a demo	Subscribe
Also links to	Case studies, other services	Third-party research, other blog posts
Doesn't have	Links to blog post or other websites	Self-promotional sales messages
Typical Analytics	Lower bounce rate Lower time on page	High bounce rate High time on page

Elements of a High-Performing Service Page

Fig. 4.51

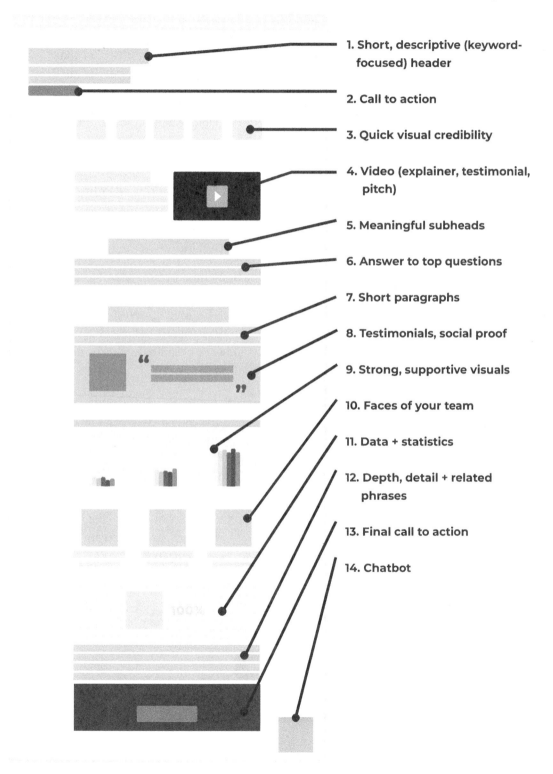

1. Short, descriptive (keyword-focused) header

2. Call to action

3. Quick visual credibility

4. Video (explainer, testimonial, pitch)

5. Meaningful subheads

6. Answer to top questions

7. Short paragraphs

8. Testimonials, social proof

9. Strong, supportive visuals

10. Faces of your team

11. Data + statistics

12. Depth, detail + related phrases

13. Final call to action

14. Chatbot

Either way, it has a clean, simple flow. The visual hierarchy is in line with the messaging priorities, which are in line with the information needs (top questions) of the target audience.

1. Short descriptive (keyword-focused) header

It's the first question of every visitor to every web page: "*Am I in the right place?*" So the header should simply say what you do.

Do it in plain English. Call your services what your visitors would call them. Avoid vague benefits statements such as "Experience Excellence" or "Humanizing Technology." A descriptive header is good for visitors and good for search rankings.

2. Call to action

It may seem early to ask for the lead, but this may not be their first visit. For the visitor who is ready to go, a CTA high on the page helps trigger that action. But first we need to understand the psychology behind the click.

No one clicks anything until they've done a split-second cost-benefit analysis. Do the benefits exceed the costs? They click. If not, they'll dismiss the CTA and keep reading and scrolling or they'll simply leave. So to increase the click through rate of your CTAs, make the cost appear smaller (it's easy/fast/free) or make the benefit appear bigger (it's valuable). (Fig. 4.52)

Pay close attention to the verbs in your buttons. "Click," "Read," and "Learn" are probably not your strongest options.

3. Quick visual credibility

A split second after they see what you do, they'll start scanning for evidence that you are legitimate.

Remember, your visitor has been on hundreds of spammy, sketchy, and even fraudulent websites. They're understandably skeptical. So we need to show our credibility fast by adding one of the following:

- Logos of clients or press mentions (triggers a cognitive bias known as the "halo effect")

- Certifications, awards, memberships (known as trust seals)

- Number of happy clients, years in business, projects, team members, etc. (data points)

Fig. 4.52

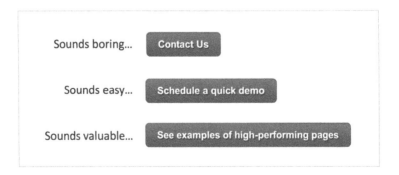

Fig. 4.53

Put these little nuggets of differentiation high on the page. Ideally, above the fold. Here are three examples from recent web development projects (Fig. 4.53).

4. Video explainer, testimonial or pitch

Sometimes, text is insufficient. Video is generally more effective at building trust and explaining complex concepts. Sometimes you'll need to upgrade to more visual formats, like video.

When is it best to show, rather than tell? Here are times when it may be best to use video:

- **The service is complicated**
  Are there many interrelated or abstract concepts involved?
  If so, add an explainer video.

- **Trust is especially important**
  Is the visitor especially fearful?
  Have they been burned before?
  If so, add video testimonials.

- **The service is very high-touch**
  Is personalized service important to the visitor?
  If so, add videos showing your people.

These are all conversion-focused videos. Their job is to support the lead generation process and increase conversion rates. These videos should be higher production quality than the content marketing videos on the blog. These are worth spending money on.

5. Meaningful subheads

Subheads are the little section headers on web pages, usually formatted using <h2> tags. Their job is to tell the visitor what follows, so it makes sense that web designers want them to stand out.

The problem isn't the design; it's the content.

They often add zero value because they are so vague that they're meaningless. Not only is a meaningless subhead

adding visual noise without adding value, it's a missed keyword opportunity. We showed an example earlier in this chapter. Here are a few more:

Meaningless (+ Boring) Subhead	Descriptive (+ Search-Friendly) Subhead
What We Do	**Lead Generation Services**
Our Work	**Recent Landing Page Design Projects**
What Our Clients Say	**"I was thrilled with the marketing results!"**
Recent Articles	**Our Latest Lead Generation Tips**

Fig. 4.54

Look at any of the subheads on your service pages. *Would the page be just as strong without it? Is it adding clarity, value or keyphrase relevance?* If not, change it or remove it.

6. Answers to top questions

There is a true story in the life of every visitor to every web page.

They have questions and concerns. The better you answer those questions and address those concerns, the more likely they will get in touch and become a quality lead. This is, after all, the reason they're here.

Every unanswered question increases the odds that they'll leave and visit a competitor's website. So the job of the conversion copywriter is to write a page that builds clarity and trust by answering visitors' questions.

7. Short paragraphs

As above.

Visitors to service pages have stronger intent, so they are more likely to read deeply. But it's still important to avoid long blocky paragraphs, whenever possible.

8. Testimonials, social proof

Anyone can claim to do something, but not everyone can prove it.

Add evidence of your legitimacy and the value of your services. This may include examples, statistics and research. Better yet, add social proof in the form of testimonials, using the voice of your happy customers. Fig. 4.55 shows a testimonial that includes the best elements.

Fig. 4.55

9. Strong, supportive visuals (avoid stock photos)

Humans are visual creatures and the internet is a visual place. Obviously, all lead generating websites have images. But the best lead gen sites have relevant visuals that support the message. They add information.

- Charts and diagrams, visualizing supportive data

- The product in use or the service being performed

- Before and after real-world examples

- Brand-aligned visuals, including textures and patterns

- Building exterior or place pictures

Stock photos are not strong. They're expected and boring. Avoid them if possible.

10. Faces of your people

Pictures of faces are uniquely powerful. Even from infancy, we tend to look at faces more than other types of images.[4] This also works in web design. Add a face and it's almost automatically at the top of the visual hierarchy for that scroll depth.

And faces of people on your team are automatic differentiation, since they are unique to your business. You are the only business with your people. Showing their faces helps position them as thought

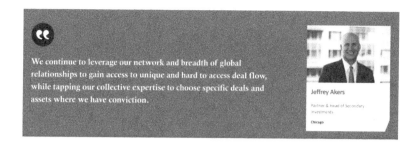

Fig. 4.56

leaders while making the company more approachable.

One way to showcase your team is to treat them like testimonials. Add a quote, along with the face, title, location, etc. (Fig. 4.56).

11. Data and statistics

Support your value proposition with numbers.

When the visitor begins leaning toward action, data helps them justify the decision. Humans aren't very rational decision-makers. But once we begin to decide, our brains seek to rationalize the decision with hard evidence.

Data does that job (Fig. 4.57).

Fig. 4.57

4. Early cortical specialization for face-to-face communication in human infants
https://www.ncbi.nlm.nih.gov/pmc/articles/PMC2572680/

Fig. 4.58

Here are examples of data points that support lead generation messages.

- Years in business

- Number of happy clients

- Number of team members

- Projects completed

- Return on investment

- Dollars sold/saved/earned

12. Depth, detail and related keyphrases

As described above, the page should be detailed and complete. With very few exceptions, longer pages tend to convert visitors into leads at higher rates than short pages.

TIP! If you're thinking "but my visitors have short attention spans," that may be true. But that is no reason to build less informative pages. Visitors who don't want a lot of info won't read everything. That's fine. But some visitors will go deep and read everything. A short page is the equivalent of a salesperson who hangs up during a sales call.

13. Compelling call to action (CTA)

As described above, here at the bottom of the page, the call to action is another opportunity to use faces within a visual hierarchy. The face can pull the visitor's attention toward the desired action (Fig. 4.58).

14. Chatbot

These are now super popular with B2B marketing programs. Conversational marketing is almost a new standard on lead generation websites. You see chatbots on all kinds of sites, trying to catch your eye from the bottom right corner of pages everywhere.

They're very clever. They ask qualifying questions to quickly engage with visitors (improved lead flow) and help visitors who aren't a fit disqualify themselves (improved lead quality).

You can write different "playbooks" (a series of multiple-choice questions) for different pages and different types of visitors (Fig. 4.59).

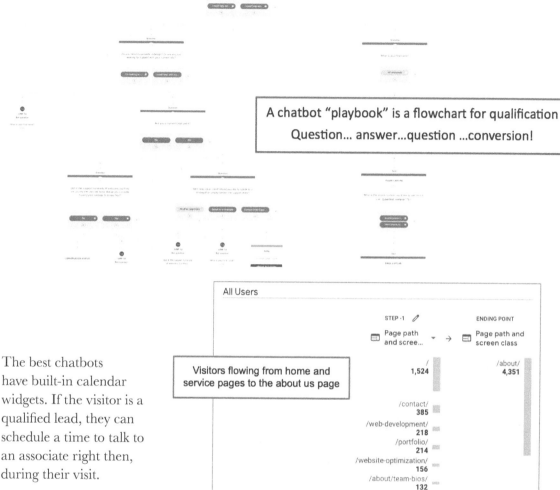

Fig. 4.59

A chatbot "playbook" is a flowchart for qualification
Question... answer...question ...conversion!

Fig. 4.60

All Users

STEP ·1

Page path and scree... → Page path and screen class

STEP ·1 / ENDING POINT

Visitors flowing from home and service pages to the about us page

/ **1,524**

/about/ **4,351**

/contact/ **385**

/web-development/ **218**

/portfolio/ **214**

/website-optimization/ **156**

/about/team-bios/ **132**

+14 More **1,108**

The best chatbots have built-in calendar widgets. If the visitor is a qualified lead, they can schedule a time to talk to an associate right then, during their visit.

About page: Building trust

You've shown the visitor **what** you do and **how well** you do it. Next they'll start to wonder **who** you are, **how big** you are and **what** your company believes.

If you doubt the importance of your about page, just look at your GA4. A path exploration with the about page as the ending point will show you which pages are sending visitors to that URL. It's often the high-intent visitors who are

considering your services. These visitors want to know who you are (Fig. 4.60).

The about page is one of the most popular pages on virtually every lead generation website we've analyzed. It's rare to see an Analytics account where the about page wasn't one of the top five pages, excluding blog posts.

On this page you'll put a face to the name, explain your mission and tell your story. You can build an entire about section with many pages, but it's not necessary. Usually, all of the most important elements fit on one page (Fig. 4.61).

1. Mission, vision and values
These are short, big-picture statements.

Often, they're just a statement of the business category: *"Our mission is to be the best web design company . . ."* That's fine, but expected. If it's boring, keep it short.

A mission or vision statement can also be a call to arms. It's your chance to plant your flag and take a stand. The best statements are strong, direct and a little unexpected. Consider these:

Fig. 4.61

Elements of a High-Performing About Us Page

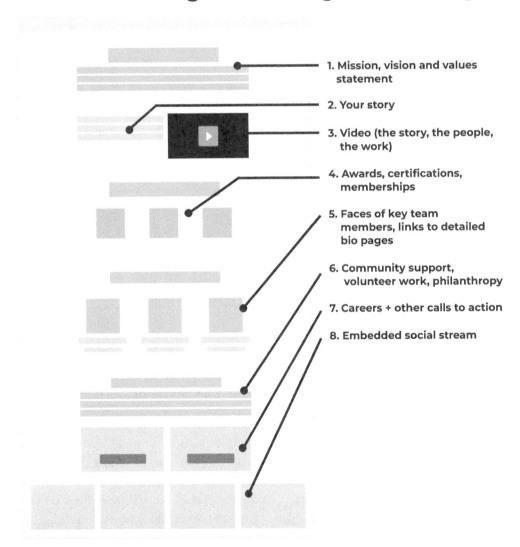

1. Mission, vision and values statement
2. Your story
3. Video (the story, the people, the work)
4. Awards, certifications, memberships
5. Faces of key team members, links to detailed bio pages
6. Community support, volunteer work, philanthropy
7. Careers + other calls to action
8. Embedded social stream

- We believe in being relentlessly helpful.

- We believe in a healthy obsession with the experience of website visitors.

- We believe in accessibility. Because access to information is a human right.

- We believe in sweating the small stuff. Because little details make all the difference.

- We believe in generosity. We share everything we know with anyone who is interested.

- We believe in inclusion. Because the best answers are discovered when many voices are heard.

"Origin stories are as old as the universe itself. People crave knowing it. Build trust with your future customers and clients by telling them **why you do what you do.** You don't need to be a superhero to tell great stories, because a great story is the strategic sequencing of facts and emotion."

ESTHER CHOY, *Leadership Story Lab*

2. Your story

Here you'll answer the big questions: *Why are you in this business? How did this company get started? How long have you been doing this? What motivates your team? Why does this service matter?*

You are the only one with your story, so make this a page that sets you apart. Talk about your values, your origin and why this work is important.

3. The video

It's simply an upgraded format for the mission and story. Because it's a video, they'll see your face and hear your voice.

For B2B service company websites, when trust is key, never miss the chance to upgrade the format to video. Video is the most powerful format, so use it for your most powerful message: why you exist as a company.

4. Awards, certifications, memberships and credentials

This is another place to put any kind of visual credential or evidence of legitimacy. Anything that applies to the entire business and not just one service will work. That includes awards, certifications, ratings and association memberships.

To keep the awards from becoming too visually noisy, give them a treatment (such as wrapping them in laurel wreaths) so they look nice.

If you have physical trophies in the office, put them out on display.

5. Faces of key team members, linking to detailed profile pages

Don't be a faceless corporation. Make your brand human. You are the only company with your people, so feature them prominently.

- If you're small, show the faces of your entire team.

- If you're big, show the faces of your key leadership.

Every lead generation website should have pictures of real people. Your visitors want to know who is involved in the service and in the company.

Big companies are always trying to look smaller. And small companies are always trying to look bigger. Really, every business should try to look more human.

6. Community support, volunteer work, philanthropy

Score some goodwill points by showing how you give back. Highlight any donation programs, volunteer efforts and community support.

Example: Orbit has donated $600,000+ in marketing services, together with like-minded partners and friends over the last nine years. We call it, Chicago Cause. We do it for the community, not for our marketing. But we're proud of it and we feature it in our about page.

7. Careers and other calls to action

Unlike a service page, the visitor to the about page may not have any intention of becoming a sales lead. About is an all-purpose page that speaks to everyone. For this reason, non-lead-generation CTAs make sense.

- Careers/See open positions

- Subscribe to newsletter

- Register for an event

8. Embedded social streams

This is a good place to embed an Instagram feed or content from another social network, assuming there's a steady stream of activity there. This is a nice way to give a pulse to an otherwise static page.

Contact page: Where the magic happens

The trick here is to get out of the way. Filling out the form should be as effortless as possible with no distractions. Make it simple. The idea is to start a conversation, not interrogate your visitors (Fig. 4.62).

1. Simple contact form

This is one of the classic lead generation best practices: use a contact form with the minimum number of fields. Don't

"Nobody cares how much you know, until they know **how much you care.**"

TEDDY ROOSEVELT

Elements of a High-Performing Contact Page

Fig. 4.62

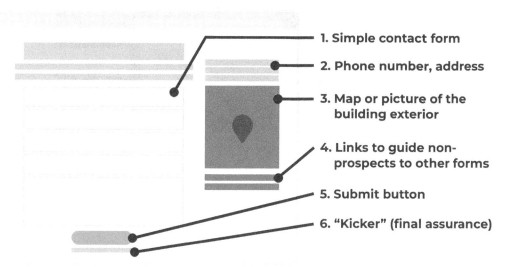

1. Simple contact form
2. Phone number, address
3. Map or picture of the building exterior
4. Links to guide non-prospects to other forms
5. Submit button
6. "Kicker" (final assurance)

make them answer 10 questions now. Don't build a greedy form.

Of course, you'll need a lot of information to qualify them as a legitimate lead *but get it later, during the sales process.*

2. Phone number, address and directions

Not all visitors want to fill out your form. Some want to call. Great. Put all of your contact information on this page: phone, fax and physical address.

Of course, some visitors may just want to send an email. Adding your email address is a courtesy to them. And not showing it may be frustrating. But there is a strong case to be made for NOT putting your email address on your contact page, as we discussed earlier.

3. Map or picture of the building exterior

Here's another chance to show that you're a legitimate business. Make the place of business real and specific. Show a map to your space with a link to get directions. And if you have an attractive location, show a photo of it. It's another indication that you're a legit business.

4. Buttons to guide non-prospects to other forms

Here's your last chance to guide non-prospects toward other conversions. This will help keep your leads flow and CRM database neat and tidy.

It's also good for the accuracy of your Analytics. The fewer non-leads that fill out your lead gen form, the more accurate your lead scoring will be.

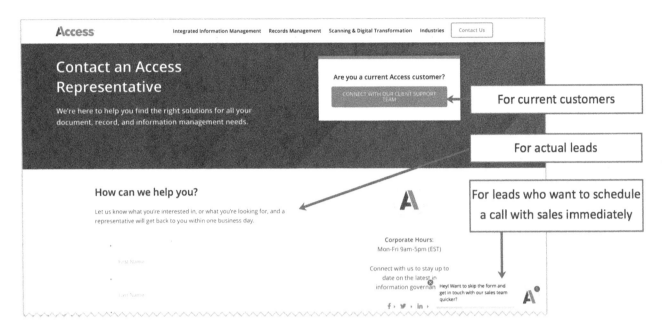

Fig. 4.63

Here's a good example. Access Corp has a B2B lead gen site with several options on the contact form. The big orange button at the top helps keep current clients out of the lead generation funnel (Fig. 4.63).

5. The kicker . . . a final assurance or expectation setting

Notice the text above the form in the example above:

"*. . . a representative will get back to you within one business day*"

In this final moment, the site addresses a final concern.

If you know that the visitor is likely worried about something (Will they sell my data? Will they respect my privacy? Will they ever get back to me?), you can use this final moment to reassure them by adding a little text right next to the submit button.

Measuring the performance of your contact page

The effectiveness of the contact form can be measured using a funnel exploration in GA4. It shows the percentage of visitors who converted from the contact page (Fig. 4.64).

Thank you page: Mission accomplished

On many websites, this page is nothing more than two tiny words: "Thank you."

It might as well say "Good-bye."

This is a big missed opportunity. The thank you page is your first interaction with your newly generated lead. Make it a good one by setting expectations, starting the conversation and building a connection with your new lead.

Fig. 4.64

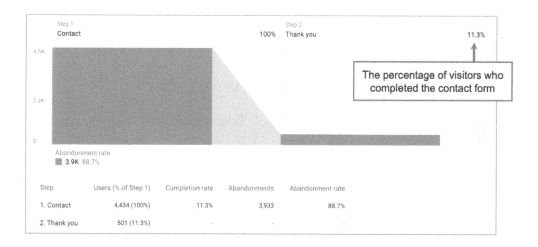

Fig. 4.65

Elements of a High-Performing Thank You Page

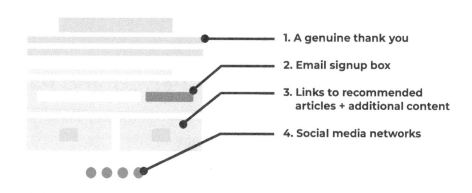

1. A genuine thank you

2. Email signup box

3. Links to recommended articles + additional content

4. Social media networks

If it's a dead end, the visitor is more likely to head back to Google to find more possible partners (Fig. 4.65).

1. A genuine thank you message
Be sincere and use a personal tone. Explain what is going to happen next. *How soon will you be in touch? Who will make contact?*

2. Email sign-up box
If they were ready to reach out, they may already really like you and your brand.

Give them the option to subscribe for more of the content that brought them here in the first place. The results may be excellent (Fig. 4.26).

3. Links to recommended articles
If you don't offer other options on this page, you might as well tell people to leave the site. Why not invite them into your content for a bit more helpful advice?

4. Social media icons
Even if they don't follow you, there's still a chance to show them your latest thinking, to show them a bit of your personality. Include the social networks where you are legitimately active. Don't link to a dead social profile.

Global elements: The header and footer

So far, every one of these best practices was within the design of the page. We've skipped over the global elements (design features that appear on every page) within the header and footer. But of course, these are critical to the experience of the visitor.

Here is a breakdown of header and footer elements on high-performing lead generation websites (Fig. 4.66).

The header

1. Logo, optimized for web
Top-left placement for the logo is a web design standard.[5]

2. Descriptive navigation labels
As with a descriptive <h1> header and meaningful <h2> subheads,

---

5. Web Design Standards vs. Website Best Practices, Orbit Media, /www.orbitmedia.com/blog/web-design-standards/

Fig. 4.66

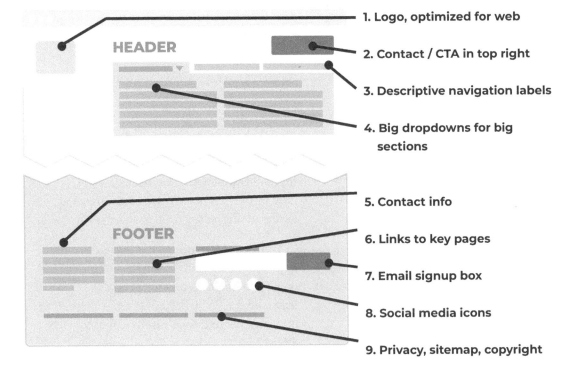

Global Elements of High-Performing Pages

HEADER

1. Logo, optimized for web
2. Contact / CTA in top right
3. Descriptive navigation labels
4. Big dropdowns for big sections

FOOTER

5. Contact info
6. Links to key pages
7. Email signup box
8. Social media icons
9. Privacy, sitemap, copyright

navigation labels should be specific and descriptive, both for your visitors and for search engines. This is a basic website navigation best practice (Fig. 4.67).

If your navigation labels are "services," "about," "blog," and "contact," ask yourself: *why do we have the same navigation as millions of other websites?*

3. Dropdown menus for big sections
Dropdowns have downsides. They are a convenience for visitors, but they also encourage visitors to skip top-level pages. Often, these pages have some of the most compelling content. So the dropdown might be a detour around your best stuff.

This is usually the case for small dropdowns with few items.

But larger dropdowns (often called mega menus) are often excellent for usability when the section has a lot of subsections and pages. They are very useful to visitors, test well in usability studies[6] and support lead generation when used strategically (Fig. 4.68).

4. Contact in the top right
The top right corner is the standard place for contact information. Visitors will look for it here. Use a relevant call to action or a simple button to your contact page. This is also a nice place for a phone number.

6. Mega Menus Work Well for Site Navigation, NN Group, /www.nngroup.com/articles/mega-menus-work-well/

Fig. 4.67

NavCo — Products Services About Blog Contact

❌ Generic navigation common to hundreds of millions of websites

NavCo — About Blog Contact / Compasses Chronometers Charts & Maps

✅ Descriptive navigation that includes relevance to both search engines and visitors

Fig. 4.68

NavCo — Products Services About Blog Contact

- Lighthouses
- Buoys
- Foghorns
- Beacons
- Signals
- Leghorns

❌ Example of a simple dropdown menu

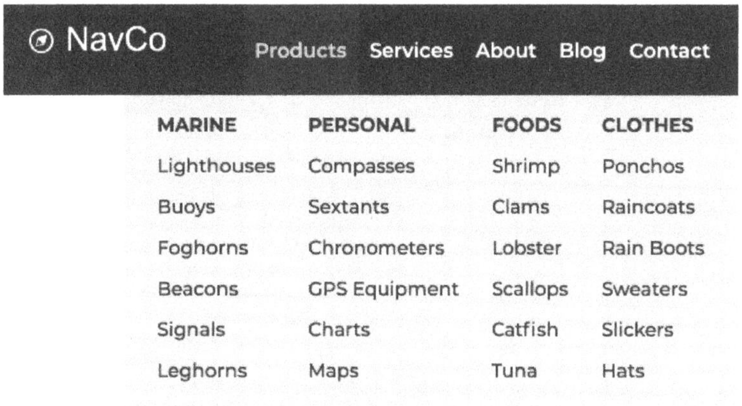

NavCo — Products Services About Blog Contact

MARINE	PERSONAL	FOODS	CLOTHES
Lighthouses	Compasses	Shrimp	Ponchos
Buoys	Sextants	Clams	Raincoats
Foghorns	Chronometers	Lobster	Rain Boots
Beacons	GPS Equipment	Scallops	Sweaters
Signals	Charts	Catfish	Slickers
Leghorns	Maps	Tuna	Hats

✅ Example of a mega dropdown menu

The footer

Here are five of the elements most frequently found in the footers of lead generation websites.

5. Contact information

The footer is a standard place to repeat the contact information. Include the full legal business name along with the address and phone number with the local area code. All together, this global instance of NAP (name, address, phone) is an important part of local SEO and appears in the maps of search engines.

6. Links to key pages

If the visitor came all the way down here, they must not have found what they were looking for, above. Help them by adding links to the pages they are most likely to need—the pages that support conversions and leads.

7. Email sign-up CTA

As above.

8. Social media icons

These are basically exit links that take the visitor to pages filled with distractions. For that reason, we don't really want to encourage the visitor to click these social icons, but we do want them to be easy to find for anyone who's looking.

From the footer, link to any social network where you are legitimately active. That means actively sharing content and actively engaging in conversation. Probably, this is just a few. It's probably not nine (Fig. 4.69).

9. Privacy, sitemap, copyright

Finally, the ubiquitous footer information, common to virtually all websites.

Fig. 4.69

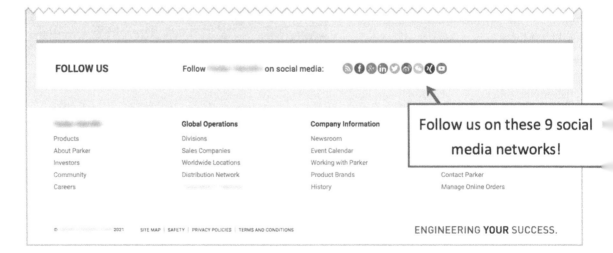

4.8 How to create an AI-powered persona

If the key to conversion is knowing our visitors' information needs, then we have some research to do. Typically, this comes from interviews. The best conversion copywriters know that detailed conversations with clients and prospects are the best way to learn their hopes, the challenges and the buying triggers.

But stakeholder interviews are hard to schedule and time intensive. It's tough to connect with the right people. It takes skill to get them to open up. Often, you have just one chance.

Wouldn't it be nice if you had unlimited time to talk? If they were available at a moment's notice? If you could ask super direct questions, even the questions that make most people squirm?

That's what an AI marketing persona is for.

You can use AI to create a synthetic member of your target audience and ask them anything at all. It's fast and easy. And once created, it's always there for you, day or night, to guide your content and messaging.

A persona is a composite sketch of a target audience or audience segment, describing your ideal customer using all of your customer insights. It guides your marketing strategy by accurately identifying the general traits, concerns and behavior patterns of your potential buyer. It's a guide.

A good persona answers these types of questions:

- What are their primary goals and objectives?

- What problems do they have? How do they manifest? (drivers of the objectives)

- What triggers them to take action and reach out for help?

- What questions do they ask at what stage in the decision process? What do they need to know, and when?

- Where do they get their information? What and whom do they read, listen to and watch?

Even if you have battle-tested documented personas or ideal client profiles (ICPs), AI can still help augment your research by creating a fast alternative or just a second (artificial) opinion. You can create one simply by asking Chat GPT to create a first draft.

It's actually risky to use AI to help with content marketing or conversion copywriting without first training the AI on your target audience. If it doesn't know who you're targeting, responses are all generic and bland. AI might as well stand for "Average Information."

Do not use AI to help with content marketing **until you have trained it on your target audience**.

After it knows who you're targeting, the responses are more focused and aligned with your value proposition and messaging. We'll start with a detailed persona prompt.

Prompt:

Build me a persona of a [job title] with [roles/skills/responsibility] at [industry/company size/geography]. This person is looking for help with [challenge/problem/task] and is considering [product/service].

List their hopes/dreams, fears/concerns, emotional triggers and decision criteria for hiring/contacting a [industry/category/service/product].

Like many of the best prompts, it is detailed. In this case, the prompt asks for some specific elements:

- **Job title**

- **Roles and responsibilities**

- **Industry company size and geography**

- **Challenges and problems**

- **Our product, service or business category**

We'll also add to the prompt the specific output that we're looking for in the response:

- **Hopes and dreams**

- **Fears and concerns**

- **Emotional triggers**

- **Decision criteria for selecting the products or services we offer**

For our example here, we'll pretend we're a social media marketing agency focused on helping nonprofits with fundraising. Our buyer is in a marketing leadership role and has fundraising and event promotion goals.

Here is a prompt that uses the above template as a guide, with the response from ChatGPT.

Prompt:

Build a persona for a Marketing Director of a $10M non-profit in the midwest US with a mission to provide better access to healthcare resources in under-served communities. This person is responsible for promoting events and creating effective fundraising campaigns through digital marketing. List their goals, pain-points and decision criteria for selecting a social media marketing company.

Response from ChatGPT:

Name: Alex Rodriguez

Background: Alex Rodriguez is a compassionate and dedicated Marketing Director of a non-profit organization, Midwest Health Initiative, which holds a mission to enhance access to healthcare resources in under-served communities. Their passion for public health started in college, where they majored in Public Health and minored in Marketing. Taylor later obtained an MBA to gain a stronger business foundation to effectively manage marketing campaigns for non-profits. Taylor has been working in the non-profit sector for 15 years, holding different roles ranging from outreach coordinator to marketing manager. Their lifelong commitment to healthcare access stems from personal experiences growing up in a marginalized community.

GOALS

1. Fundraising: Taylor's main goal is to optimize digital marketing efforts to drive more effective fundraising campaigns. They aim to increase donations by 20% over the next fiscal year and engage more monthly recurring donors.

2. Awareness and Outreach: Another important goal is to spread awareness about the healthcare resource issues faced by under-served communities and the organization's role in addressing them. Taylor also hopes to gain broader publicity for their events, driving a 30% increase in attendance within a year.

3. Volunteer Engagement: As part of their community-focused efforts, Taylor aims to boost volunteer numbers by using effective social media marketing campaigns that target and inspire potential volunteers.

PAIN POINTS

1. Budget Constraints: Working in a non-profit means being careful with how resources are allocated. Taylor is always under pressure to maximize output with limited resources, which often leads to creative, but challenging, problem-solving.

2. Audience Segmentation: Taylor recognizes the power of digital marketing but struggles to effectively segment and target their audience for fundraising, awareness, and volunteer recruitment campaigns.

3. Measuring Success: Non-profits often struggle to measure the impact of their marketing efforts quantitatively. Taylor is often challenged to translate their digital marketing efforts into concrete KPIs.

DECISION CRITERIA FOR SELECTING A SOCIAL MEDIA MARKETING COMPANY

1. Experience in Non-Profit: The chosen company should have demonstrated experience working with non-profit organizations, particularly in the healthcare sector. They should understand the unique challenges and opportunities in this space.

2. Cost-Effective Solutions: Given the budget constraints, the company must be able to offer cost-effective solutions, delivering maximum results for every dollar spent.

3. Audience Understanding: The company should have a deep understanding of the target demographics, their online behavior, and the most effective ways to engage them.

4. Measurement and Reporting: The marketing company must provide robust reporting and analytics tools to track campaign performance and tie it back to Taylor's specific KPIs.

5. Creative Collaboration: The company should be open to collaborating on creative approaches to marketing problems and flexible enough to adapt to the unique brand voice of Midwest Health Initiative.

6. Cultural Fit: Lastly, Taylor is very particular about the company's values. They must align with their organization's mission and values to build a successful, long-term relationship.

It looks like a good start. But is it accurate? We asked our friend Ardath Albee, a persona and audience research

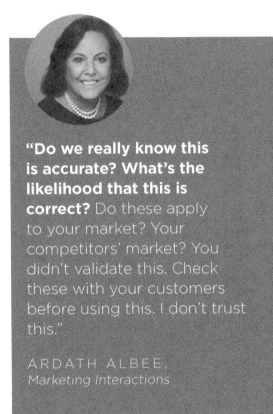

"Do we really know this is accurate? What's the likelihood that this is correct? Do these apply to your market? Your competitors' market? You didn't validate this. Check these with your customers before using this. I don't trust this."

ARDATH ALBEE,
Marketing Interactions

expert with 30+ years of experience in marketing strategy for her perspective.

Ardath is right. We should be skeptical. We don't really know if this is accurate until we check it against our other sources. If anything is incorrect or missing, we need to fix it before moving ahead. We need to tell the AI to add, change or remove things that aren't right.

Only after we know it's accurate can we proceed with confidence. And even then, we'll review every response with a healthy bit of skepticism, just as we would with the output from any tool.

Once we are confident that it's sufficiently accurate, we can start using it to look for insights. Of course, many of the responses will be obvious, off-target or useless for other reasons, but it's likely that a few are extremely helpful.

What was the trigger that sent them looking for help?

There's a true story in the life of every lead. If you know where that story begins, you have a better shot at writing the ending. Knowing the so called "zero moment of truth" is important for conversion copywriters.

Start talking to your AI-powered persona. Ask it what was happening that made it realize that it needed your services.

 Prompt:

What kinds of things might happen that you realize that it needs the help of a marketing agency?

 Response from ChatGPT:

Several signals would alert me to the fact that our non-profit needs assistance from a marketing agency:

1. Overwhelmed Team: If the current team is struggling to

keep up with their tasks, or if their workload is hindering their creativity or performance, it may be time to seek external help.

2. Limited Expertise: If there are areas of marketing that are beyond the expertise of the in-house team, such as SEO, paid social, or advanced analytics, it may be beneficial to bring in an agency that specializes in those areas.

3. Lack of Results: If the current marketing efforts are not yielding the expected results in terms of fundraising, community engagement, or awareness, an agency might be able to bring fresh perspectives and strategies.

4. Limited Reach: If the organization's digital presence and reach are not expanding as desired, a marketing agency with expertise in digital marketing and audience targeting could be beneficial.

5. Major Campaigns or Events: If the organization is planning a significant fundraising campaign or event, they may require additional support or specialized expertise to effectively promote it and engage their audience.

6. Need for Strategic Direction:
If the organization lacks a comprehensive marketing strategy, or if the existing strategy is not aligned with their goals, an agency could help refine their approach.

7. Need for Objective Insights:
Sometimes, having an external, objective perspective can reveal blind spots or provide new ideas that wouldn't have been recognized internally.

These are the initial drivers. Knowing them helps the copywriter and designer craft pages that align with the visitor. All of the marketing materials (plus the pitch and proposal) should all tie back to the original 'why.'

What information do they need to make a decision?

With another prompt or two, we can get ideas for what basic information we need to include in our marketing materials and sales conversations. Anything stories or examples that align with these should improve both our conversion rates and closing rates.

 ## Prompt:

What information about the possible marketing agency would you need before contacting that marketing agency about a potential project?

 ## Response from ChatGPT:

Before contacting a marketing agency about a potential project, I would need to gather specific information to ensure the agency is a good fit for our needs. Here are the key points I would consider:

Agency's Expertise: The area of expertise of the agency should align with the needs of the project.

Experience with Non-Profits: It would be beneficial if the agency has prior experience working in the non-profit sector.

Industry Knowledge: Understanding of the healthcare sector can be a significant advantage as the agency would have a better grasp of the context in which we operate.

Previous Work: Reviewing the agency's portfolio can provide insights into their creative abilities, attention to detail, and whether their style aligns with our brand identity.

Client Testimonials or Case Studies: These help me understand the results the agency has been able to deliver for other clients. It's particularly beneficial if these testimonials come from clients in similar sectors.

Values and Culture: It's important that the agency's values and culture align with ours, for a harmonious and productive working relationship.

Although most of that information may seem general, it's at least a checklist for topics and formats. It suggests that our sales pages should be reinforced with highly-relevant examples throughout the marketing and sales processes. And alignment on values, although not the most important thing, needs to be there.

Marketers everywhere are using AI to generate content.

There are already hundreds of AI startups with tools that write articles, generate web pages and even create videos. And new AI features are rolling out within all kinds of tools you may already be using.

But the process of constructing a high-converting sales page is still a mostly manual process. Don't expect an AI to do an amazing job of gathering the right testimonials, curating the most relevant examples and results or creating the branded visuals.

In later sections, we'll show how to use your AI-powered persona to brainstorm ideas for articles and help with content marketing, but let's start at the bottom of the marketing funnel with our most important marketing asset: our service pages. Let's have an AI check to see if anything is missing from our key pages.

Performing gap analysis on your existing copy using your new AI persona

You can use generative AI to do gap analysis on an existing page, to compare the page copy against the information needs of our persona.

It's very simple. Just copy and paste the text from one of your key pages along with a prompt that asks which of the personas top concerns were not addressed.

For this example, I gave the AI a service page from a social media marketing company's website.

 Prompt:

Which of Taylor's top concerns are not addressed on this webpage?

[copy and paste in the text of a webpage]

 Response from ChatGPT:

While the webpage addresses a number of general concerns related to non-profit marketing,

there are some specific areas related to Taylor's top concerns that are not explicitly addressed:

1. Healthcare Focus: Taylor's non-profit is specifically in the healthcare sector. While this agency states they work with nonprofits, they do not make any specific reference expertise in healthcare.

2. Planned Giving Campaigns: One of Taylor's key initiatives is planned giving campaigns. The webpage does not mention any experience or specialized services related to planned giving campaigns.

3. Values Alignment: The page does not provide information about the agency's values and whether they align with Taylor's organization's mission to provide better access to healthcare resources in underserved communities.

4. Data-Driven Insights: The page mentions tracking and measuring donor engagement but does not elaborate on the kind of data-driven insights they provide to their clients. This lack of clarity might leave Taylor unsure of their approach to analytics and measurement of campaign success.

5. Cost-Effective Solutions: As a non-profit with a tight budget, Taylor is keen on cost-effective solutions. Although the webpage refers to working with organizations large and small, it doesn't speak directly to their approach to budgeting and ensuring their clients get the most out of their investment.

6. Specific Pain Points: Although this agency has a broad range of services, they do not explicitly address Taylor's specific pain points such as increasing donor dollars, building a strong digital presence that aligns with their mission, and creating compelling narratives to inspire donors.

In essence, Taylor would likely appreciate more specificity related to his healthcare focus, his planned giving campaigns, cost-effectiveness, and value alignment from an agency.

Gap analysis is one of AI's superpowers.

You can see that again, it takes the task very literally and basically checks the page against the decision criteria we set in the earlier prompts and responses.

In that example, the page had a lot of misalignment because it wasn't written for our persona. It was a page I picked at random. But you can see how AI is very useful at identifying gaps. Any copywriter could use it as a quick double-check to confirm that nothing big was missed.

Even a single question left unanswered, or a single objection left unaddressed, can hurt conversion rates, as measured in GA4.

Save your new AI persona

Last step. Once you've got your new synthetic prospect in shape, make sure that you hold onto it. Name the chat so you can find it again quickly later. Or copy and paste it out into a document

that can be shared with your team and attached to anyone's future prompts (Fig. 70).

All of your subsequent prompting about this target audience will take place in this chat. You can talk to it on a moment's notice, day or night, for quick ideas or a long conversation about drivers, goals and motivations.

Here are a few more prompts that may reveal conversion optimization insights. Both of these require that you have a ChatGPT Plus account, which allows you to upload images. For both prompts, you'll need to upload a full-page screenshot of the page you'd like to audit, which can be created using a Chrome extension such as **GoFullPage**.

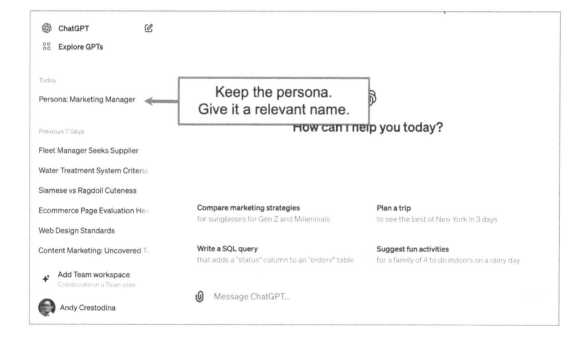

Fig. 4.70

Webpage audit prompt #1

Check for best practices of any service page.

You are a conversion optimization expert skilled in evaluating pages for their ability to both inform and persuade. The most compelling, highest converting web pages share common traits. The following are best practices for B2B service pages.

1. The header clearly indicates the topic of the page, quickly letting the visitor know they're in the right place.

2. The copy clearly answers the visitor's question and addresses their objections

3. The order of the messages generally aligns with the visitor's prioritized information needs.

4. The copy uses supportive evidence to support its marketing claims (testimonials, statistics, case studies, awards, logos, etc.)

5. Subheads for each section are meaningful and specific

6. The page connects with the visitor on a personal level using human elements (faces, quotes, stories)

7. The copy leverages cognitive biases in subtle ways when relevant (loss aversion, urgency, etc.)

8. The page provides compelling calls to action

I'm giving you a web page. Create a list showing the ways in which the page copy does and does not meet the information needs of the persona

Suggest changes that would make the page more helpful and compelling to the visitor.

Highlight the changes in the recommendations.

[attach a full page screenshot of a page in the persona chat, or attach the persona]

Webpage audit prompt #2

Check the extent to which a page uses evidence to support marketing claims.

You are a conversion optimization expert skilled at using evidence to support marketing messages. The following are types of evidence that can be added to webpages: testimonials, reviews, case studies, success stories, data and statistics, years in business, number of happy clients, client logos, awards, association memberships, etc.

The attached image is a screenshot of a webpage. Rate the extent to which the page does and does not use supportive evidence. Which marketing claims are unsupported? Show your thinking.

[attach a full page screenshot of a page in the persona chat, or attach the persona]

Always check for accuracy. Once you find an insight, focus on execution. In later sections, we'll explore other use cases for AI and share prompts along the way.

PART TWO:
LAB

05 Content Creation

I WANTED TO CREATE SOMETHING, TO POINT AT SOMETHING AND SAY "I MADE THAT."

That's why I quit my job in December 1999 and made a new start in the new millennium. It's that exact motivation, the drive to create, that attracts so many people to marketing.

This chapter is about the structure of content, the visuals and the words. It's about aligning the content with your audience and why they'll care enough to pay attention. It's about creating content that's easy to promote later, in search engines, on social media and email.

Step one is to put yourself on a mission.

> Our content is where **[audience X]** gets **[information Y]** that offers **[benefit Z]**.

5.1 Content Marketing Mission Statement

The road to relevance is long. But it starts with this simple first step: you declare your mission. This little bit of text is the foundation of your content strategy. This is where you'll take your stand. It will support or reject every action you take in your content marketing efforts. Not sure about something? Check the mission. If it doesn't fit, leave it out.

The mission statement declares three things: *what you'll be publishing, who it's for and why they'll care.*

Documenting your mission statement is surprisingly simple, yet most content marketers haven't done it. To make it easy, here's a content mission template. All you have to do is fill in the blanks.

By "our content" we are referring to all of your non-sales-focused content. It's not your product or service pages. It's not advertising. It's everything you create, publish and share in your content marketing including:

- Your blog, articles and resources

- Your newsletters and any other emailed content marketing

- Your social media posts

- Your videos, events, podcasts and any other format for content

Unlike a company mission statement, this is specific to your content marketing. It's also different from a more general marketing positioning statement, which states how your company fits into the larger market. A content marketing mission statement is more similar to the kind of editorial mission statements you'd find at a magazine or newspaper.

Now let's take a closer look at X, Y and Z. Then we'll review how to publish your mission and finally, we'll look at some examples.

Audience X

Unlike the target audience for your products and services, the target audience for your content marketing may be very broad. You have two target audiences and two types of visitors:

1. Potential customers you hope to sell to

2. Anyone you can help through your expert advice

That second, much larger audience will drive those huge, indirect benefits. This includes a world of potential visitors, followers, subscribers and influencers. Without this second audience, you are unlikely to attract enough of that first audience to create steady demand.

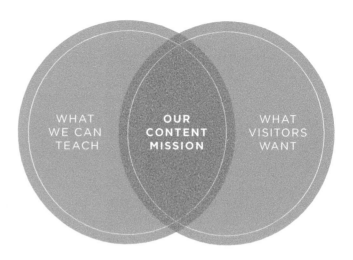

Fig 5.1

Information Y

These are the topics and formats that you will publish. It is the overlap between the topics that you know and can teach, and the topics that your audience wants. When you share this expert knowledge, you pull your audience toward you (Fig. 5.1).

The following words are commonly found in this part of the mission statement. In fact, it's rare to see a content marketing mission statement that doesn't include at least some of these words:

- Tips, advice, insights and strategies (most common)

- Stories (especially common for nonprofits)

- Ideas and inspiration

- Research and reports (often the most effective)

- News and trends

Benefit Z

It has to be helpful. Your mission statement must name the specific benefits that your content offers your audience. If there is no benefit to them, you won't win their attention, you won't attract visitors and you won't generate any demand.

So your mission and every piece of content within it must answer this question: *Why do they care? How does this help them? What task can they complete once they are finished reading this? Why should they click, visit, read, watch, listen, share, subscribe or pay attention to you at all?*

This is the core of your mission.

There are three fundamental benefits of content. These are the standards that you use when you create content. They are also the criteria your audience uses to judge your content when they consume it.

1. **The reader can DO something**
   It's actionable. There are steps they can take or tools they can use. Instructional, how-to content gives the visitor obvious and specific value. The content helps them solve their problems.

2. **The reader LEARNS something**
   It's proven. If you want to teach something, you need supporting evidence. Facts, research and expert input support your assertions. And new, original research makes you the primary source.

3. **The reader FEELS something**
   It takes a stand. You felt something while you wrote it. It's your voice, your perspective and your opinion. Counternarrative, strong opinions are best at triggering emotion.

Unless the post connects on one of these levels, it probably isn't worth the reader's time (and they're certainly not going to share it).

This aligns with Erin Kissane's recommendations in her classic book, Elements of Content Strategy. Erin explains how good content works by relating to the context of the reader

"We always write mission statements from the following two angles: what type of content are we going to create that satisfies audiences and will help our business? We're a B2B healthcare content marketing company, so when we create content we ask two questions:

1. **Does this content help our audience do their jobs better?**
2. **Does this content reinforce the idea that we're a valuable resource?**

If it doesn't do BOTH of those two things, we don't create it."

AHAVA LEIBTAG, *AHA Media Group*

in one of three ways: physical (doing), emotional (feeling) and cognitive (learning) (Fig. 5.2).

To news, or not to news?

Although "news and trends" may be interesting to your audience, it usually isn't something that a company content team can sustain. Can you commit to becoming a real news source? What are the implications for your content strategy?

Follow the thinking through to the end and you'll discover that there are fundamentally **two kinds of content strategies**: "The Publication" which focuses on news and "The Library" which focuses on evergreen content, as in, content that is more timeless than timely. It's a distinction made by Jimmy Daly in an insightful post on the Animalz blog back in 2018.[1]

- **The Publication** seeks to build an audience of repeat visitors by consistently and frequently publishing topics of broad interest to an industry, promoted to subscribers and followers.

- **The Library** seeks to build relevance on more narrowly focused topics with deeper, more interconnected articles, discoverable through search and there when the visitor needs them.

These two types of strategies have very different challenges and opportunities (Fig. 5.3).

1. https://www.animalz.co/blog/library-vs-publication

Fig. 5.2

PHYSICAL
(DOING)

EMOTIONAL
(FEELING)

COGNITIVE
(LEARNING)

"A good content creation purpose explains who you help and how. It's the basis of a content strategy; it energizes both the content creator and their audience. Their audience recognizes a team is writing and sharing to help (rather than just sell), and that's why they'll start following and come back for more.

From a content creation perspective, a mission statement kindles your creativity and enthusiasm, and it helps stay on topic so it's even a good foundation for SEO. Also, it's not fixed. It can evolve over time."

HENNEKE DUISTERMAAT,
Enchanting Marketing

Fig. 5.3

	The Publication (news and trends)	**The Library** (how-to resources)
Content & Cadence	**Timeliness**	
	Fresh content, relevant now	Evergreen and timeless
	Often irrelevant in the future	Often valuable years into the future
	Topics	
	Informative: Bringing new info to readers' attention. Broadly relevant to an industry	Educational: how-to and best practices
		Focused on a more narrow audience
	Headlines	
	Clever, unexpected, emotional	Clear, descriptive, answers to questions
	Success Factors	
	Frequency (more often)	Depth (more detail)
	Consistency (like clockwork)	Formats (videos and guides)
Promotion & Metrics	**Best Channels**	
	Email marketing, social media	Organic search (SEO)
	Traffic Pattern	
	Spikey traffic	Long tail of organic search traffic over time
	Repeat, mobile visitors	New, desktop visitors
	Blog Design	
	Template includes dates, comments and prominent social sharing widgets	Good categorization, search tools, and internal linking
	CTAs in pop-ups	CTAs for gated content
	Example Subscribe CTA	
	Get the top news for zookeepers in a single email, three times per week.	Join the 1000+ zookeepers who get **monthly tips for happy, healthy animals.**
People	**Creator/Writer**	
	Brand journalist	Teacher, technical writer
	Contributors/Collaborators	
	Credible sources, key opinion leaders	Experts with deep advice
	Roundups of social influencers	Interviews with thought leaders

Building a newsroom is a huge commitment. Very few content programs do it well. It's lower energy and lower risk to slowly build a great library of evergreen content for a niche audience. And without evergreen content, you can forget about SEO.

Content marketing mission statement examples

Here are some examples of content marketing mission statements for both B2B and B2C companies. Notice that although they don't all follow the template exactly, each mission statement specifies the audience and the benefits they receive when they consume the content.

Swift Passport
"Where international travelers get travel tips and news to make travel easier."

Enchanting Marketing
"Help small-business owners find their writing voice so they can share their ideas with gusto, connect with their readers, and sell more without selling their soul."

Tellabs
"The best source for info on optical LANs. We show IT buyers how to address tech and business challenges, identify trends, reduce expenses and improve user experiences."

Working Moms Only
"To supply the tools that can give every working mom the ability to lead a healthy, wealthy and more balanced/blended lifestyle."

Digital Photography School
"Simple tips to help digital camera owners get the most out of their cameras."

Home Made Simple
"Enable women to have more quality time with their families."

Indium
"Help engineers answer their most challenging industrial soldering questions."

Inc Magazine
"The place where entrepreneurs and business owners find useful information, advice, insights, resources and inspiration for running and growing their businesses."

Private Equity Firm
"To provide clients, prospects, intermediaries and investors with industry, market and economic insights, original research, and financing strategy stories and outcomes to help them make better decisions about corporate and project financing."

Raptitude
"Raptitude is a blog about getting better at being human—things we can do to improve our lives today. This blog teaches quality-of-life-related skills, such as managing moods, developing habits and enjoying ordinary moments."

Nutanix
What's next in the enterprise cloud? This editorial-driven news site takes an industry insider's perspective, profiling innovative people, sharing thought leadership insights, and reporting on

trends sparked by the enterprise cloud revolution and digital transformation."

Orbit Media

"The Orbit blog is where digital marketers find practical advice on content marketing, AI, GA4 and web design. Our goal is to help you get better results from your website."

3 Places to publish your content marketing mission statement

This is the promise you are making to your audience. Why keep it a secret? There's no reason not to share it publicly. On the contrary, it makes a great call to action to subscribe. Here are three places to post it:

1. The top of the blog

If the top of your blog just says "BLOG" in big bold letters, that isn't really telling your visitors much about your content. You can do better.

Take the [Information Y] section of your mission statement and post it to the top of the blog. This immediately lets your audience know what you've got for them.

This is also an excellent place for an email sign-up box. Put them together and it should look something like Fig. 5.4.

2. Every other email sign-up call to action

In pop-ups, in the footer, next to articles, inside articles and everywhere else your visitors can subscribe. Every email sign-up box will work harder (and grow your list faster) if you adapt your mission statement into a descriptive CTA. This was the second of the three P's of email sign-up forms (prominence, promise and proof) that we reviewed in Section 4.5.

3. Social media bios

A lot of social profiles are really just mini about us statements. Yes, that's relevant, but it's not very compelling. It doesn't really give people a reason to click the follow button.

Fig. 5.4

page 142 | CONTENT CHEMISTRY

Fig. 5.5

Recover Quik ✓
@RecQuik
Backup, Disaster Recovery, and Cloud Mobility Helping Companies Rebound Quickly Since 1994
Boston, MA recquik.com Joined August 2010
1,521 Following **8,752** Followers
Followed by Jo Peterson, Tamara McCleary, and 12 others you follow

❌ Social bio is just "about us" text. Doesn't say what they'll get if they follow.

Recover Quik ✓
@RecQuik
How-to resources, tips from security experts and practical guides on how to project your systems from attacks and bounce back if you get hit.
Boston, MA recquik.com Joined August 2010
1,521 Following **8,752** Followers
Followed by Jo Peterson, Tamara McCleary, and 12 others you follow

✅ Social bio is a mini-call to action. Gives the reader a reason to follow.

Similar to the email sign-up CTA, when you adapt your mission statement into a social media bio, you give people a reason to add you to their social streams. You're telling them what they'll get if they follow you. Just look at the difference in Fig. 5.5.

People are far more likely to do something if you give them a reason to do it. So adapt your mission into a social media bio that works like a mini-CTA. This will grow your following faster.

How does the content mission statement affect success?

The simple act of documenting your mission makes a difference.

According to the 2021 B2B Content Marketing Benchmarks, marketers who document their content strategy are far more likely to report success.[2] In fact, brands that have a documented content strategy are three times as likely to say they're effective at marketing (Fig. 5.6).

2. https://contentmarketinginstitute.com/2020/09/b2b-industry-benchmarks-budgets-trends-research/

Effectiveness of Marketers with Documented Content Strategies

Fig. 5.6

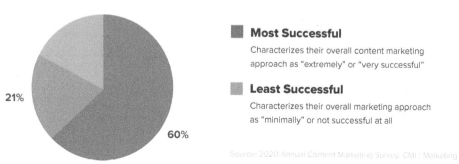

21%

60%

■ **Most Successful**
Characterizes their overall content marketing approach as "extremely" or "very successful"

■ **Least Successful**
Characterizes their overall marketing approach as "minimally" or not successful at all

Source: 2020 Annual Content Marketing Survey: CMI : Marketing Profs

Fig 5.7

Percentage of B2B Marketers With a Content Marketing Strategy

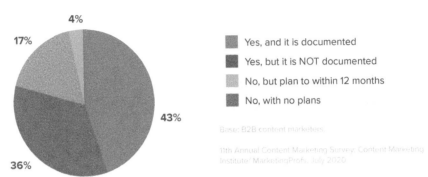

4%

17%

43%

36%

■ Yes, and it is documented

■ Yes, but it is NOT documented

■ No, but plan to within 12 months

■ No, with no plans

Base: B2B content marketers.

11th Annual Content Marketing Survey: Content Marketing Institute/ MarketingProfs, July 2020

So if documenting a content marketing strategy has such a strong correlation with success, you would expect it to be a common practice. It is not. Only 43% of marketers have documented their content strategy (Fig. 5.7).

✦ Use AI to help draft a content marketing mission statement

AI can help. But first, we should teach the AI what goes into a good content mission statement. And as always, we'll do everything within a ChatGPT conversation that began with the persona we created in Section 4.8.

 Prompt:

A content marketing mission statement includes three elements: the target audience, the topics and the benefit to the reader. It should be concise and be adaptable as a call to action to subscribe to a newsletter.

 You are an expert content strategist, skilled in creating content that attracts visitors and builds trust.

Craft a draft content mission statement for the persona based on their information needs. Create three examples of newsletter signup calls to action based on the mission statement.

Whatever it provides will need careful editing. But it is likely to have a few interesting ideas and combinations of words that may be useful. Take what is useful, discard the rest.

5.2 More Marketing Statement Templates

Here are three more statement templates you can use to keep your marketing on track, from the big picture to the small picture.

1. The Marketing Positioning Statement Template

Your content marketing mission statement is specific to your audience and your content.

But what about the bigger picture?

Your marketing positioning statement (also known as a value proposition) describes your place in the market. We highly recommend using Susan Silver's marketing positioning template [3] to sharpen the focus of your marketing in general. Put simply, this describes why you are in business. How you fit into your market.

Positioning Example

Fig. 5.8

TARGET	People who have friends with cancer who are in financial need.
UNMET NEED	Who want to help in a meaningful way.
COMPETITIVE SET	Online medical fundraising tool.
UNIQUE POINT OF DIFFERENCE	Empowers people to help financially.
REASONS TO BELIEVE	Easy-to-use online process. Real fundraising coaches to help you. Has helped people raise $170M since 2008.

Source: Agentum Strategy

To **[target audience]** that has **[unmet need]**, our company is the **[competitive set]** that has **[unique point of difference]** because **[evidence 1, 2 and 3]**.

Fill in these blanks before doing any marketing.

The target audience should be as specific as possible. The unique point of difference explains how you are unique from the other businesses in your competitive set. The brilliance of this template is that it forces you to name the unmet need your business fulfills and how you are uniquely positioned to do it.

Then you have to back it up with evidence. These are the reasons they should believe your claims. Don't go to market without evidence.

Example: GiveForward

To people who have friends with cancer, who are in financial need, who want to help them in a meaningful way, GiveForward, now part of GoFundMe, was the online medical fundraising tool that empowered people to help their ill friends financially.

Fig. 5.8 shows a breakdown of their positioning statement.

3. http://www.argentumstrategy.com/resources/free-marketing-templates/marketing-positioning-template/

The marketing position statement is general to the entire business, not specific to content. And it's typically an internal document; it isn't made public or posted online.

2. The Detailed Content Mission Statement Template

What follows is a mission statement template that goes one level deeper. This expanded template by Meghan Casey pushes you to define your content and outcomes more specifically. The final step in this template is very powerful since it forces you to name the actual tasks that your content will enable your audience to complete.

> The content we produce helps our company accomplish **[goal]** and **[goal]** by providing **[adjective]** and **[adjective]** content that makes **[audience description]** feel **[emotion]** or **[emotion]** so that they can **[task]** so **[task]**.

Fill in these blanks before going deeper into content marketing.

3. The Social Media Mission Template

At this level, it gets easier. Social media falls under content marketing, so this template by Laura Fitton will look familiar. Your social media mission is a subset of your content marketing mission.

Laura encourages marketers to document their mission for each social network, since different content may be shared on different networks.

Filling in these two simple blanks for each social network you use will guide you in what to share and how to engage with each community. Is it inspiration? Share quotes. Is it educational? Share links. Documenting this will help you stay on topic.

> Our social media account is where **[target audience]** can find **[what content]**.

Fill in these blanks before becoming active within a social network.

The most expensive mistake: missing your target

The road to success is lined with burning wrecks of marketing campaigns that targeted the wrong audience, created the wrong content or built relevance in an irrelevant social network.

It takes less than an hour, it correlates with success and it's the best way to avoid a marketing disaster. So before you start producing and promoting content, put yourself on a mission.

Content formats

The mission statement declared the topics, but the **formats for the content** are a separate consideration. These are not usually addressed in the mission statement, but they are key to your content strategy. Great content marketers publish more than an endless stream of blog posts.

The format is the medium and the shape of the content. Content can take many forms:

- Articles, blogs and guest posts
- Guides and whitepapers
- Infographics, templates and checklists
- Interviews and roundups
- Videos and podcasts
- Webinars and live events

Any content on any topic can be published in any format. We're going to look at content formats from two perspectives: how formats align with the stages of consideration (the funnel) and how formats can help you quickly create new content (repurposing).

5.3 Content Formats and Funnel Stages

Content works in many ways. Some writing pulls your audience toward you, building awareness. Other content builds trust, triggering demand. In other words, content can be useful at strengthening different parts of the funnel. Cheese and mousetrap.

The "funnel" is just a metaphor for the path that visitors take on their way to becoming leads and customers, starting with awareness and ending with action.

Every buyer of every product and every service goes through a series of steps: *awareness*, *interest*, *consideration* and then the *actual transaction*. From the impulse purchase of Skittles in the checkout aisle to the government purchase of radar installations, every purchase goes through these stages (Fig. 5.9).

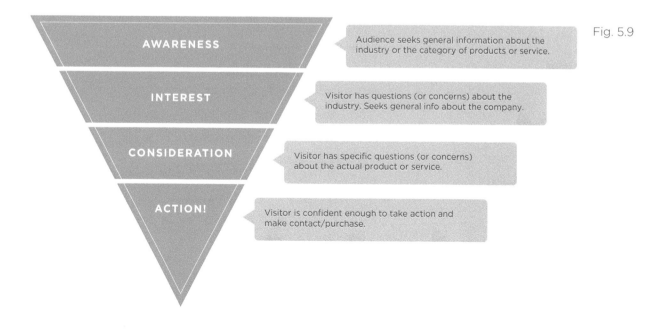

Fig. 5.9

AWARENESS — Audience seeks general information about the industry or the category of products or service.

INTEREST — Visitor has questions (or concerns) about the industry. Seeks general info about the company.

CONSIDERATION — Visitor has specific questions (or concerns) about the actual product or service.

ACTION! — Visitor is confident enough to take action and make contact/purchase.

Fig. 5.10

Formats and the Funnel

17 formats for content. Which are effective at which stage?

Top of the Funnel

Middle of the Funnel

Bottom of the Funnel

1. Search-optimized blog posts
Lots of traffic over many years from (low-intent) visitors.

2. Social media video
Tips, opinion, inspiration drive engagement and interaction.

3. Infographics
They get shared and attract links, but aren't built to sell.

4. Round-ups and interviews
Influencer collaborations can drive both traffic and trust.

5. Guest posts
Pitch and win a shortcut to a lot of visibility, but not traffic.

6. How-to articles
Helps DIY visitors, but is directly related to your services.

7. How-to videos
Same, but more engaging, memorable, and trust-building.

8. Original research
Powerful credibility builder, but often indirect relevance.

9. Gated guides
Long form, subscribe to access, now they're connected...

10. Welcome series emails
... next, send them your best to keep them interested.

11. Webinars and events
Personal format, collaborate with others, engage in the Q&A.

12. Sales enablement articles
One specific traffic source with one specific goal: conversion.

13. Your story
One specific traffic source with one specific goal: conversion.

14. Landing Pages
One specific traffic source with one specific goal: conversion.

15. Case studies / customer stories
Problem solved in the real world. It's evidence and a use case.

Every great content program first gives visitors the information they're looking for and then gently guides them toward the contact page and subsequent thank you page. Content needs to support this process at every step. The format of the content is a big factor. Each format has its own strengths, weaknesses and abilities to affect different marketing outcomes.

Format follows function.

So, the content marketer can make strategic choices about formats and create content specifically to strengthen different stages of the funnel (Fig. 5.10).

Top of the funnel: Content formats for traffic and/ or awareness

Marketing Goals: Brand awareness and visibility. Increase traffic. Establish general relevance. (Fig. 511)

These top of funnel (TOFU) formats make you more visible, but similar to billboards and TV advertising, they don't always reach the target audience. In content marketing, this inefficiency isn't a huge concern because we aren't paying for the reach. There is waste (high bounce rates), but it's inexpensive waste.

Diagnosis: If your conversion rate from visitors into leads is 2% or more, but top-line traffic is low, there is a weakness at the top. Any content marketing that involves these formats will help.

Top of the Funnel: Awareness   Fig. 5.11

Awareness

Diagnosis:
If conversion rates are above 1-2% but overall websites traffic is low, then strengthen the top of the funnel.

Tactics:
Write search-optimized posts, list posts, cross-platform content, more guest blogging.

1. Search-optimized blog articles
You may have a few of these already. They attract lots of traffic over long durations of time. There's no denying that they drive awareness of the brand (these visitors are on your site after all) and "share of search" is actually 83% of a brand's "share of voice."[4] Search visibility is brand visibility.

4. https://www.marketingweek.com/share-of-search-market-share/

"The goal is to be visible to your ideal buyer, so the key is to front-load the beginning of the journey with valuable expert content—and gate as little as possible. If you have expert advice or amazing industry insights, get it out there, and fast."

JENNIFER HARVEY, *VP Marketing at Worksome*

But let's be honest, if the page is ranking for a purely information-intent keyphrase, these are some very low-intent visitors who may subscribe but are unlikely to convert into leads.

2. Social media videos

The social platforms love video. Because video keeps visitors engaged, social media algorithms push video content to the top of everyone's social streams. Videos that are clever in the moment or consistent over time can create a ton of visibility, especially practical tips and counternarrative opinions.

But remember, visibility and website traffic aren't always the same thing. Never expect high click through rates from social media, from any format in any social post.

3. Infographics

They're visual and practical—two factors that correlate with sharing and engagement. They're more scannable than text-based content, so visitors may be more likely to come take a look. When combined with a little research and outreach, infographics can also drive press mentions and links.

4. Roundups and interviews

Click through rates are high when the headline sounds like a list post (as with a roundup) or mentions an influencer (as with an interview). And any content created in collaboration with others may drive more shares if co-promoted with the collaborators. That's called "ego bait" and we'll discuss it later in this chapter.

5. Guest posts

There are publications that have already gathered up the audience you'd like to reach. So rather than build that audience yourself from scratch, borrow it by writing for these publications. Beyond the immediate visibility, guest posts lead to follower growth (social) and links (SEO).

If it's exactly the audience you're targeting, take the time to build relationships with the editors. Turn that one-time post into an ongoing collaboration (a regular column). That means lots of visibility, if not website traffic, over time.

Middle of the funnel: Content formats long game players

Marketing Goals: Keep in touch over time. Demand generation. Connect with tire kickers. Email list growth. (Fig. 5.12)

These middle of the funnel (MOFU) formats are about the long game. They keep your audience engaged. These types of content are especially important when sales cycles are long and multiple decision-makers are involved.

Diagnosis: If visitors aren't returning, your email list isn't growing, and you're not seeing regular referrals for your services, there is weakness in the middle of the funnel. Try these formats:

6. How-to articles

When blog topics are directly related to the services you offer, they move into

Middle of the Funnel: Consideration

Fig. 5.12

Consideration

Diagnosis:
If email and social traffic are low, and there are few shares, comments, and subscribers, then strengthen the middle of the funnel.

Tactics:
Write detailed, how-to posts in a personal tone, link related topics together, and collaborate with influencers.

the middle of the funnel. These often attract DIY visitors who really just want to solve their own problems. But they see your expertise making you a valued resource. They may give up trying to do it themselves and come back. Eventually they may hire you or refer you to others.

7. How-to videos

Similar to articles, but in a more engaging format. Video is inherently more personal, more memorable and better at building trust. Shoot practical tips, upload to YouTube, then embed them on your search-optimized posts. This will give your new YouTube channel a huge boost.

8. Original research

Research makes your website the primary source of new information. It's also a powerful format for winning mentions, press and links. Repeat it annually and promote it aggressively and eventually your website becomes an important industry resource. That repeat traffic and trust is what the mid-funnel is all about.

To learn all about original research as a format, skip ahead to Section 7.2.

9. Gated guides

The workhorse of every marketing automation program, gated content is designed to move the visitor down through the funnel. You give them some value, they give you their email address to get more value. The "lead magnet" that triggers the download is usually a long-form guide.

10. Welcome series email

The next format in the process is email. Once your visitors share their address, you send a series of emails with links to more goodies and maybe, eventually, a straightforward sales message. The emails all happen automatically. They're set up in your marketing automation system or ESP.

Welcome emails are great for deepening engagement with new subscribers. Use the opportunity to share your hardest-working content.

11. Webinars and live events

Live formats are brilliant opportunities to repurpose high-performing articles, roll out research or collaborate with influencers.

- The personal format is both memorable and good for trust-building.

- They have deadlines, which means urgency, which makes for great calls to action.

- They have audience interaction (Q&A) and dialog, which is a listening opportunity.

- They have a networking component and build community, which creates loyalty, relevance and exponential value for everyone.

Each of these is fantastic for the mid-funnel.

Bottom of the funnel: Action

Marketing goals: Build trust. Inspire visitors to act. Start a conversation. Turn "suspects" into prospects. (Fig. 5.13)

These bottom of funnel (BOFU) content formats directly support conversion rates and lead generation. They don't attract new visitors; they simply maximize the percentage of your current visitors who become leads.

Diagnosis: If your site's conversion rate is below 1%, there may be a problem in the bottom of your funnel. Use formats that persuade and build trust.

12. Sales enablement articles

This may overlap with the types of articles already mentioned above, but not always. These articles are written for one specific purpose: sales.

When prospects all tend to ask the same questions, put your best answers into detailed articles with visuals, then show the visuals during sales calls and share them in an email follow-up afterwards. That's the basic idea behind "sales enablement" content. Support the sales process.

This approach creates perfect sales/marketing alignment, which is not always the case with content marketing. And for sales enablement content, traffic and pageviews are irrelevant. Sales enablement articles are created specifically for your current prospects (your most important audience) and delivered to them personally.

These articles are also good fuel for account-based content marketing programs, which we'll explore in Section 6.8.

13. Your story

Your visitor is making a tough decision.

Fig. 5.13   **Bottom of the Funnel: Action**

Diagnosis:
If the conversion rate is below 1% for a simple lead generation site, then strengthen the bottom of the funnel.

Tactics:
Answer the top questions from the sales process, tell your story, use evidence and proof on your service pages.

They're unsure about your company as an option. They don't yet feel a connection to your brand. That's when they visit the About page.

Visitors on your About page are often in serious consideration mode. They know what you do; now they want to know who you are and how big you are. They want to know how it all started. They're looking for your story.

Your About page visitor may be near the final decision stage, but they need a kicker to put them over the top. Share your history, your people and your values. When they feel that connection, they feel validation. They're now more likely to commit.

14. Landing pages
Technically, any entry point into a website is a landing page, but here we're talking about campaign landing pages.

A true landing page has ONE specific traffic source (i.e., PPC, email, display) and ONE specific goal (i.e., lead generation, email sign-ups).

A landing page is an attempt to completely shortcut the funnel and get the visitor to take action on their first visit. Often, the standard header navigation is removed to keep the visitor from getting distracted. The attention ratio is 1:1.

15. Service pages
They say what you do, they explain how you do it, they show proof that you do it well and they offer to help. The product

"The best case studies are focused, customer-centric, and human. While sexy metrics are nice to showcase, it's more important that you're telling a story your audience can relate to in terms of pains overcome and outcomes deeply desired.

- Go beyond the challenge; set the stakes.

- Go beyond the solution; explain WHY that approach was taken or those features played a pivotal role.

- Go beyond the results; showcase the impact on the individual and what was made possible for the business."

JOEL KLETTKE

or service page (aka, the sales page or "money page") is the workhorse of the website. It combines a set of a dozen or more elements, but it really comes down to three things, as we explored in Section 4.2.

- Answers to top sales questions

- Evidence to support those answers

- Clear, specific calls to action

When sales pages are optimized for search (always for the commercial intent keyphrase) the visitor may enter the site here. Even then, they are still fundamentally bottom of funnel content.

16. Case studies/Customer stories

Beyond the testimonial is the case study. This format shows a real-world example. It's a structured, detailed account of an actual problem, solved by the brand.

A case study is a story with characters, conflict and a resolution. Just scanning it makes the value feel obvious, yet surprising. Mix in a few data points and give a case study a killer headline and you have your closer.

5.4 Formats and Repurposing: The Periodic Table of Content

Once you have a growing body of work, you have opportunities to efficiently create fresh content by repurposing and reformatting existing content.

Content is made up of pieces. And pieces can be broken down into smaller pieces

OUTBOUND **MULTIMEDIA** **ON-SITE**

COLLABORATIVE

Fig. 5.14

Elements at the top of the chart are small and tend to have a shorter half-life.

Elements at the bottom are larger, slower to create and last longer.

Elements to the left appear everywhere, on millions of sites and locations.

Elements on the right are more likely to be on your site.

or combined into larger pieces, just like the elements on the Periodic Table. The chemistry-themed periodic table here is what gave the name to this book!

Thinking about content as particles is the key to repurposing your work. It helps you quickly create new work, transforming old posts into high-value content with less effort.

- Atomize your big pieces of content into smaller formats.

- Combine smaller pieces into larger compounds

But before you turn your articles into particles, let's look at what the content universe is made of. Once you know what's on the Periodic Table of Content and all the formats for content, you'll be ready to start smashing particles in the content accelerator (Fig. 5.14).

Here is a description of each particle and examples of how to break it down or combine it with others:

Sp (Social Post)
A tiny particle, which survives in nature for only a short time, typically a few hours. Tweets, Facebook posts, Instagram shots and other social media posts are all variations of this element. They are known for traveling far and in many directions, and they may comprise subatomic links, mentions, hashtags and quotes.

- Any content can be atomized into Social Posts. For best results, use the best quotes, statistics, captions and visuals. Doing so can lead to small

chain reactions of shares and clicks. The simplest way to post (just using the headline) isn't always the most effective.

- Social Posts can be combined into Blog Posts. Ask a question on social media and pull together the answers from the audience into a Blog Post. Or look at your social data to see which posts got the most traction. Use those tiny particles as seeds for bigger ideas.

Bp (Blog Post)
This is the universal building block of web content. Sometimes simply called an "article," the Blog Post is the hydrogen of the website. Unlike other web content, Blog Posts typically have authors, date stamps, social sharing features and comments. Topics may be timely (news) or evergreen (how-to) which determines the longevity of a Blog Post.

- Blog Posts should always be broken down into Social Posts. Share the best sound bites, not just the headlines. Science has found that more visual, collaborative and emotional Blog Posts travel farther and faster in social.

- Combine several Blog Posts on a common topic, or expand on the most successful Blog Posts, turning them into White Papers and eBooks. Once transformed into downloadable content, they can be added to Landing Pages and attract email addresses.

Ne (Newsletter)
An outbound particle that lasts much longer than Social Posts, Newsletters live for days, not hours. Content in the email channel involves more trust and has more properties, including subject lines and open rates. Newsletters require careful handling.

- Newsletters should always link to Blog Posts and articles. Their energy is lower unless this bond is created. If a Newsletter gives the full text of the article and doesn't link to something else, there is no click and no traffic is generated. Never put the full text into a Newsletter. Always combine!

Pc (Podcast)
The Podcast is pure, distilled audio and has very little visual energy. Podcasts are typically less powerful than Video, but more powerful than text, because of their ability to convey tone. Podcasts build trust.

But Podcasts are the dark matter of content marketing, platform-independent, everywhere and nowhere. Listeners may love the content but never visit your website. Results are hard to measure. There is very little data gathered from this particle.

TIP: To turn listeners into visitors and "link" from Podcasts to Web Pages and Blog Posts, mention a diagram, chart or other visual during the recording. Let listeners know where to find it on the website. Also, you can mention a process and suggest that listeners go to the site for more detailed instructions.

- Podcasts are relatively easy to create and publish. The simplest form may be reading and discussing a Blog Post. The most common form is an interview show, which has powerful networking properties.

- Add show notes with links and visuals to turn any Podcast into a Blog Post. Failing to do so would be to limit their power. Give calls to action during the show to guide visitors toward the Blog Post "For more details on this topic . . . to see this diagram . . . visit our website . . ."

Pt (Presentation)
This particle comes in two parts: the live Presentation and the slides. The live Presentation is short-lived, but the slides can always live on. Presentations are most powerful when charged with visual content, such as charts, data and step-by-step instructions.

Here's how to get the longest lasting impact from every Presentation

- Link to Blog Posts on relevant slides. Link to Web Pages in calls to action on the final slide.

- Upload and embed the Presentation in relevant Blog Posts.

- Schedule Social Posts to go out during the live Presentation. Include images, tips and juicy sound bites from the slides. Use the event hashtag sub-particle.

- Record the live Presentation as Video. For conferences, these can be packaged as a virtual pass or gated behind an email sign-up.

- Edit the strongest points into smaller Videos and embed them on relevant Blog Posts.

 Re (Research)
Possibly the most powerful format in all of content marketing, Research reports are difficult to create, but extremely effective. They make the brand the primary source for new data and insights. That data can become useful to the broader industry by supporting common claims, answering a question or providing unexpected insights.

- New Research is news, making it one of the rare events that call for the creation of a Press Release.

- Sound bites from the research become Social Posts and should be kept in heavy rotation on social media.

- Extended versions of the Research can be made into downloads and used as gated content. These can be promoted on Landing Pages, where they attract email addresses from visitors.

 Cs (Case Study)
Also known as a "success story," the problem-solution-result format of Case Studies is easy to spot. Case Studies increase trust by telling a specific, supportive story. They are especially important when sales cycles are long, and there are many decision-makers involved. Here's how Case Studies act as a strong link in a long chain reaction:

- Link from Blog Posts to Case Studies, guiding visitors from advice to stories.

- Link from Case Studies to Web Pages, guiding visitors from stories to sales pages.

- Take the best sound bites (testimonials and statistics) out of the Case Study and use them on the relevant Web Pages to increase conversion rates.

 Pr (Press Release)
These targeted, highly charged particles travel quickly. They are created to attract attention from the media, but in their natural form, they are unlikely to be read by most visitors. Press sections of websites are typically very low traffic areas. But Press Releases are easy to repurpose.

- Rewrite it for a broader audience to turn the Press Release into a Blog Post. Change the formatting by removing more general, less useful sub-elements, such as "For immediate release."

- Share the information from the Press Release with specific bloggers and editors with personal outreach. Offer to discuss the topic or collaborate on a related piece. This can lead to off-site Interviews.

Vi (Video)

Although the content and messaging may overlap with surrounding particles, Video stands alone as the most compelling and powerful format for content. Only in-person meetings (live Presentations) can build more trust. Most content can be atomized into Video in any properly equipped lab.

But it has one major weakness: the messages within Videos can't be crawled by search engines, so compared to text formats, Video has a disadvantage in organic search results. Video's power is in conversion, not attraction.

- Embed Video in Web Pages to increase conversion rates. These Videos should be high quality, tell stories, demonstrate expertise and build trust. Use a pro player like Vimeo or Wistia.

- Embed Video in Blog Posts to increase engagements. These videos can be lower quality, give advice and increase engagement. Use YouTube.

- Embed Video in Newsletters (really just add the image of the Video thumbnail and play button) to increase click through rates.

Wb (Webinar)

The online version of the Presentation isn't limited by the size of the room, and is almost always made available as a Video later. Registrants know that the Video will be shared, so it's common for as few as 20% of registrants to attend the live Webinar. Some Webinars are pre-recorded. Combining a full day of back-to-back Webinars creates a compound called a Virtual Summit.

Webinars are easier to produce and easier to attend than live events, but they do require paid software. Their benefits include attracting email addresses and accelerating list growth.

- Before the Webinar, create a Video of the presenter with a short summary of the topic.

- During the Webinar, trigger the spontaneous formation of Social Posts by specifying a hashtag.

- After the Webinar, summarize the top tips of the Webinar in a Blog Post, an Interview and a Video.

Wp (Web Page)

This is the only element on the periodic table that is created to directly sell products and services. It's the demand generating particle. Remember, there are two kinds of visitors to websites, and visitors to Web Pages have commercial intent.

Guide visitors to them from all other particles. This is the main reason the other elements exist! Be very cautious in linking away from Web Pages. It may be hard to get visitors to return.

- Link to Web Pages from each Blog Post and all other on-site content.

- Link from Web Pages only to credibility building particles such as Case Studies and White Papers.

- Embed Videos into top visited Web Pages to build trust and increase conversion rates.

- Web Pages rarely get shared and can't be repurposed into Social Posts, Newsletters or other formats.

Ro (Roundup)

A popular format for content, the Roundup is a great way to get started with collaborative content. They feature short-form input from a group of experts on a topic. The goal is often to create a chain reaction of Social Posts when each contributor shares the final piece.

- Trigger Social Posts from contributors by mentioning them when sharing the Roundup on social networks or by sending them each a "Click to Tweet" link.

- Transform Roundups into Research by gathering a lot of contributions, then analyzing responses ("4 out of 5 experts report that collaboration is effective").

Int (Interview)

The Roundup asks many experts one question. The Interview asks one expert many questions. It's the deep dive into collaborative content. If the questions are good and the formatting is scannable, the Interview often has higher value for readers.

- Select an expert interviewee whom your audience knows and who is active on social media. This will maximize both credibility and reach.

- Ask questions that relate to past Blog Posts, then link to those posts within the text of the Interview.

- Conduct an email Interview, but add a short Video to make it more compelling.

Inf (Infographic)

A purely visual particle, the Iinfographic is easy to scan, easy to embed and easy to share. This has made it a super popular format for marketers. It usually stands in the place of a Blog Post, but has little more than an intro paragraph.

- A successful Blog Post can be transformed into an Infographic and republished.

- Any Infographic can be pitched as a guest Blog Post.

- If an Infographic is designed carefully, sections of it can be turned directly into social content, adding visual impact to Social Posts.

NOTE! Infographics can drive SEO benefits. Bloggers who publish your Infographic on their blog will typically link back to the original. Some SEOs publish Infographics, then pitch them to bloggers as a way to attract links and build authority. Results depend on the quality of both the content and the outreach.

 Lp (Landing Pages)
The Landing Page is laser-focused on a single goal: convert visitors on their first visit. Landing Pages are designed for a specific source of traffic: a social, paid advertising or email campaign. They promote a specific particle of gated content.

NOTE! Although Landing Pages don't directly promote a product or service, the visitor who converts may get a call from a sales associate.

Great Landing Pages use the same words used in the campaign that attracted the visitor, so visitors know they're in the right place and are less likely to bounce. They offer strong evidence and few distractions. Language is concise. Calls to action are specific.

- Don't link from Landing Pages to anything else!

- Use larger particles from the bottom of the periodic table as the gated content behind a Landing Page: Research, White Papers, Case Studies and eBooks.

- When using a Landing Page to promote a Webinar, be sure to emphasize the deadline and create urgency.

 Wt (White Paper)
White Papers tend to be long, formal and text heavy. They typically go deep into a single topic with a linear flow, establishing the credibility of an expert author. They are a common format for B2B companies with complex products or services. White Papers are prime candidates for atomization.

- Break down a single White Paper into three or more Blog Posts.

- Add visuals and a compelling title to transform a White Paper into an eBook.

- Use the new, more compelling title to pitch it as a Presentation to relevant industry events.

 Bk (Book)
Offline particle with a history of endurance. No particle is older except the ancient Scroll (Sc) and Slab (Sl).

Books increase the authority of the author, but few marketers create them. They are by far the largest element on the periodic table and the most expensive to create. They require editing, design and printing. But through a bit of chemistry, they can be created gradually over time.

- Combine many Blog Posts into a Book through editing fusion. Begin by writing the table of contents.

Guide vs eBook

Fig. 5.15

The "guide" had a 100% higher click through rate

Then gradually write Blog Posts for each section and subsection.

- Break a large Book down into Blog Posts, White Papers and eBooks by adding headlines, visuals and links. Each piece can end with a call to action to buy the complete Book.

Eb (eBook)
Shorter than the Book, less formal than the White Paper, eBooks are an in-between element perfect for repurposing. They are a balance between visuals and text. Marketing eBooks are actually very similar to the slides of a Presentation and can be created using presentation software such as Powerpoint or Keynote.

- Turn Presentations into eBooks by adding text and compelling cover slides.

- Combine the top points of Blog Posts on a similar theme into an eBook. Add a call to action to download the eBook on each of those posts.

- Gate them behind an email sign-up on Landing Pages.

TIP! Call it a Guide, not an eBook. The marketing team at LinkedIn discovered that click through rates were higher with the word "guide," which makes sense. "Guide" sounds practical. "eBook" sounds like homework (Fig. 5.15).

Atom smashing examples

There are millions of examples in the universe of content. But here are a few that come to mind, good and bad.

1. Video into Blog Post
After I gave a Presentation at Content Marketing World, the event organizers asked if I would make a Video. Sure! They used it in their content, social streams and as promotion for future events. For me, the same Video was an

Fig. 5.16

Best Tools for SEO (As voted by 143 SEO and online marketing experts)

#1: SEMrush (63 votes) *[Get one month of SEMrush Pro for free here]*
#2: Ahrefs and Screaming Frog (42 votes)
#3: Moz (21 votes)
#4: Majestic SEO (18 votes)
#5: Buzzsumo (17 votes)
#6: Google Analytics (16 votes)
#7: Search Console (13 votes)
#8: Buzzstream (12 votes)
#9: Google Keyword Planner (9 votes)
#10: LongTail PRO (6 votes) *[Start $1 trial here or read the full review]*

opportunity to publish an article that went deeper into the topics.

So we turned the Video into a Blog Post called *Free SEO Advice for Beginners* (https://www.orbitmedia.com/blog/free-seo-advice/) which has details and diagrams that go far beyond the Video. The Video is embedded at the top.

2. Roundup into Research
Robbie Richards knows a lot about SEO. Of course, there are a lot of bloggers who publish a list of tools. But Robbie saw the opportunity to reach out to other experts and gather their insights into SEO tools. Rather than just make the post live as a roundup, he created a scoreboard of the 10 top tools based on the "votes" of the contributors (Fig. 5.16).

3. Blog Posts into Book
After five years of blogging, I'd written around 75 articles. They were good but, as a body of work, completely disorganized. So I wrote the outline and began shaping them into a Book. Three months later, I had something to send

the editor. Three months after that, it was shipped to a designer. In less than a year, the first edition of this very Book was in print.

"*Duplicate Content Penalty*" are three words that strike fear in the heart of content marketers. Use the same text on two pages and Google will punish you. Use the same paragraph on two pages and both will forever rank lower. Copy and paste an article from your site (or even part of an article) and use it on another website and both sites will be penalized.

This is all nonsense.

Most people shouldn't worry about "duplicate content." If there are two pages of the same content on your website, or if content on your site also appears on another website, Google isn't simply going to drop the rankings for both pages or de-index the websites. If this were true, unethical search marketers could do this intentionally and hurt the rankings of their competitors.

There has been a lot of panic surrounding duplicate content in recent years, but it's something that search engines have dealt with since the early days of the internet.

If two pages have the same text, Google is going to rank the page it likes best. Typically, this is the page that was published first or the page that appears on the website with the higher Domain Authority. And of course, if the pages in question aren't optimized for search or relevant for any particular keyphrase, the question of duplicate or original doesn't matter anyway.

There are rare exceptions. Below is a real-live example of the extremely rare "duplicate content penalty." Hazmat suits and a Reconsideration Request were needed to clean up . . .

> At Orbit, one of our clients launched a site and simultaneously hired a PR firm to promote it. Rather than write an original press release, the PR firm simply copied the text from the website homepage and submitted it to the online newswires. Within minutes, there were more than 1,000 instances of that homepage content on the web.

> Google flagged this as likely spam and blacklisted the domain. Suddenly, the website disappeared from search results, even for searches for the business name. Imagine not ranking for the name of your business. Devastating.

> Although we hadn't caused the problem, we were able to repair it by filing a reconsideration request with Google and explaining what happened. The Google web spam team manually removed the domain from the blacklist.

> This was an extremely rare case. Probably, it happened only because there were hundreds of exact copies (syndicated press releases) of the same page (the homepage) that appeared almost simultaneously (on launch day).

TIP: Syndicate on LinkedIn and Medium. Knowing now that there is no penalty for duplicate content, don't hesitate to take an older article and repost it in other places like LinkedIn or Medium. There is no harm or risk in copying and pasting the article verbatim, assuming that it speaks to those more general audiences. Just make sure to first give it enough time to get social and search traction on your site. A great article may have a successful second life on LinkedIn.

Final thesis

Content marketing is exactly like high-energy physics. Well, not really. But you can accelerate your publishing. Just look at all the content around you. Find ways to combine things and break things down. A webinar becomes a podcast. The podcast becomes a blog post. Combine the blog post with a newsletter. Be a marketing scientist, experiment, atomize and make your marketing go boom.

Create an inventory to see what you have. Group your content into topics and elements. See if anything is missing or if anything can be atomized quickly.

5.5 Keyphrase Research

Right now, someone somewhere is looking for the services you offer, the products you sell or the knowledge in your brain. Literally, *as you read this sentence*, they are typing a keyphrase into Google. Now they're looking at search results. They just clicked on a search listing . . . and they've landed on someone else's website. Bummer.

To get that visitor to land on your site next time, you need to choose keyphrases carefully and then align your content and pages with those phrases. If you know what they're looking for and what you have a chance of ranking for, you'll have a fighting chance of being discovered. So research is the first step in rankings.

Ranking in search results is not as complicated or mysterious as you'd think. In order to rank, a page **must indicate its relevance** and the website itself **must be sufficiently authoritative** in the eyes of search engines.

And it all begins with the keyword. Keyword research is the first step on the road to rankings.

And it's fun. Investigating keywords is like reading the minds of millions of people. It's truly amazing the things you can learn within minutes:

- *What do people really call your product or service?*
  Avoid using jargon and start using top-of-mind phrases.

- *What answers and information is your audience looking for?*
  Align your content marketing with relevant topics and phrases.

With just a few seconds of research, using only free tools, you can find all the most common questions people ask about tree trimming. You can discover which cities in the US have the most people looking for Botox treatments. You can look up which times of year people search for math tutors. You can check whether the demand for vegetarian dog treats is increasing or decreasing. I've seen clients add new products and open stores in new locations based on a bit of keyphrase research.

Commercial intent vs. information intent

In Section 3.1, we looked at the three types of keyphrases: navigational, informational and transactional.

It's extremely useful to target phrases that are broadly relevant to your topics and publish content that is useful to a broader audience beyond potential customers. Although it's unlikely that the visitors who find your blog will become a lead or buy a product, they are still incredibly valuable to your business. The actions they take (subscribing, following and linking) drive traffic (through email, social and search) at levels that would be impossible if you didn't rank for these phrases.

Many industries are so competitive that it's virtually impossible to rank for the commercial intent phrases without having a robust content marketing program. The reason is simple. No informational content means there is nothing useful on your site for other sites to link to. No links, no authority. No authority, no ranking for those competitive, dollar sign phrases. No rank, no traffic. No traffic, no leads.

So even the "low-quality" visitors are valuable. They may share your content, subscribe to your newsletter, follow you on social media, comment on a post or, if they're a blogger themselves, they may link to the article from their site. Every visit is a chance for something good to happen. So go ahead and target those helpful, how-to, question-answering phrases.

Aligning pages with phrases

Keeping in mind that keyphrases align with visitor intent, we can start to align pages with phrases. Let's take a minute to consider the structure of the website and how the pages and overall sitemap fit with a keyword strategy.

A well-planned website has many pages targeting many phrases. The keyword researcher understands that it's all about pages and phrases.

Keyword Research Principle #1
**Every keyphrase is a competition.
Every page is a potential competitor.**

If you don't have a page (as in, a specific URL) that aligns with the keyphrase, you have not yet entered that competition. And if the page is not a detailed, highly

informative page, you don't have a strong competitor.

Fig 5.17 is an example of how pages on a sitemap align with potential keyphrases for SEO.

Notice that **not all of the pages have keyword opportunities.** And that different types of pages target different types of phrases.

- **The homepage** targets the most competitive keyphrase, usually the general business category.

- **Top-level pages** target more general keyphrases.

- **Deeper interior pages** target more specific phrases.

- **About and Contact,** along with many other pages, do not target a keyphrase. They are not relevant in SEO.

- **The blog** gets all the information-intent queries.

Now that we have a sense for the alignment between intent, keyphrases and pages, let's look at the details of keyword research and the criteria for selecting a target keyphrase.

The basic criteria for choosing a keyphrase

The ideal keyphrase checks three boxes: People are searching for it (search volume). Your website has a realistic chance of ranking relative to other sites (competition). And, finally, the phrase

Fig. 5.17

Home

kp: "navigation tools for seafarers"
VIDEO/TESTIMONIALS

PRIMARY NAVIGATION

Compass Repair

kp: "compass repair services"
VIDEO

Chronometers

kp: "primary keyphrase"

Maps and Charts

kp: "primary keyphrase"

Contact

kp: "primary keyphrase"
FORM

Box & Gimble

kp: "primary keyphrase"

Nautical Maps

kp: "primary keyphrase"

Thank You ★

Pocket

kp: "primary keyphrase"

Globes

kp: "primary keyphrase"

SECONDARY NAVIGATION

About

VIDEO

Team

Careers

VIDEO

Blog

Team Bio

Open Jobs

Blog Article

FOOTER NAVIGATION

Contact Us

(link to above)

Sitemap

Social Media

Twitter, Linkedin, YouTube

OFF NAV PAGES

Maps for Pirates

Maps for Explorers

Maps for Migratory Birds

GLOBAL FEATURES

- site search in header
- newsletter sign up in footer

BLOG TOPICS/KEYPHRASES

- "Where to bury your treasure"
- "Compass maintenance tips"
- "How to store old maps"

aligns with the content mission statement you just documented (Fig. 5.18).

Assuming you know what topics and keywords align with the business, let's focus on the first two criteria:

- **Search volume**
  This is the popularity of the keyword. Are people searching for it? A lot or a little? Is it trending up or down? *It's useless to target a phrase if no one is searching for it.*

- **Difficulty**
  How likely is your page to rank for the phrase? Are the other pages that rank for the phrase much more authoritative than yours? *It's useless to target a phrase if you have no chance of ranking for it.*

The goal is to disqualify the phrases with few or no searches (the invisible) or too much competition (the impossible).

Step 1. Check search volume (Popularity)

If no one is searching for it, what's the point?

How many people are searching for the phrase each month? This is known as "search volume" and it's a key criteria in keyphrase research.

The more demand for a keyphrase, the more potential traffic. It is the size of the prize.

You can see an estimate of monthly searches for any phrase, using SEO software. Here's what the report for the

The 3 Criteria for Selecting a Target Keyphrase

Fig. 5.18

phrase "homepage best practices" looks like in **Moz** and **Semrush**, two of the most popular tools (Fig. 5.19).

Fig. 5.19

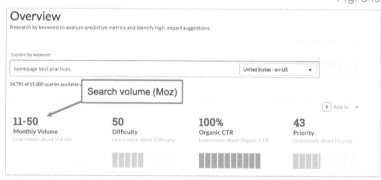

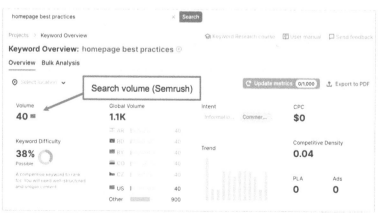

Fig. 5.20

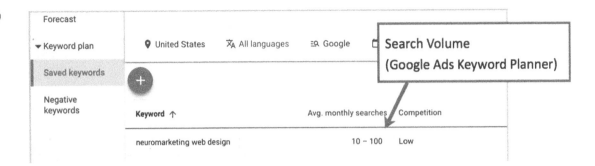

If you don't have a subscription to a paid keyword research tool, you can use **Google Ads Keyword Planner** to check search volume. You will need to set up an account first (Fig. 5.20).

It's time to start capturing the potential phrases.

When writing articles, we capture keyword ideas and their search volume in our content marketing template (you'll find one at the end of this chapter). For website redesigns, they're recorded in a big content strategy workbook.

The estimates in the example above ranged from 10 to 100 searches per month across the three tools we used. Assuming a 30% click through rate for a top ranking, this page could attract

maybe a dozen visitors per month. Sounds low.

Does it make sense to target low-volume keyphrases? How low is too low? Should you target an "unpopular phrase?"

The case for ultra-low search volume keyphrases

Despite the apparent lack of interest in the phrase, we wrote that article about homepages anyway. Eventually, it began to appear consistently as one of the top three positions for "homepage best practices." This is the GA4 report showing the traffic to that page from search. (Fig. 5.21).

Fig. 5.21

Fig. 5.22

Top queries	↓ Clicks	Impressions
homepage	34	34,057
what should a home page include	17	167
homepage best practices	14	460
homepage elements	10	167
what should be on the home page of a website	9	195
homepage checklist	8	58
what to put on the home page of a website	6	94
what to put on a home page		
home page best practices		
what should a homepage include	5	126

That page actually ranks for hundreds of phrases

Rows per page: 10 ▼   1-10 of 1000   < >

You can see that the page actually attracts more than 500 visitors per month on average, which is ten times the amount of demand estimated by the keyword research tools.

How is that possible?

It's because SEO tools drastically underestimate the potential traffic to a page. This is because they show the demand for just that one specific phrase. In reality, any page that ranks high for one phrase also ranks for many closely related phrases.

Here is the Google Search Console data for that page, showing the number of keyphrases for which that page ranks. You can see that, yes, it ranks for the target phrase, but it also ranks for

hundreds of other, closely related phrases (Fig. 5.22).

So how do you estimate the true potential traffic for a given phrase?

Keyword Research Principle #2
Search volume estimates underestimate potential traffic. Multiply the search volume estimates by 10.

This will help reflect the true traffic potential, taking into account the likelihood that it will rank for dozens of adjacent phrases if the page successfully ranks for the target phrase.

Fig. 5.23

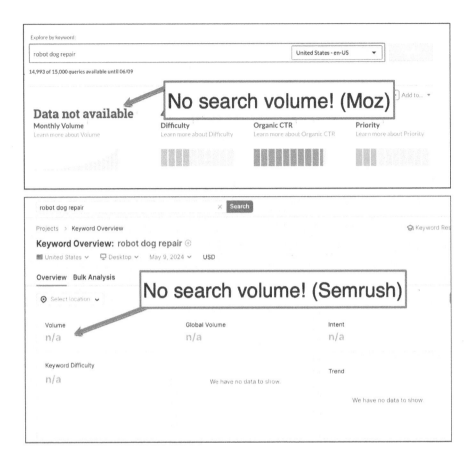

What if the tool shows no search volume at all?

For a lot of niche phrases, the tools won't show any search volume data. Here's what that will look like in Moz and Semrush (Fig. 5.23).

But this does not mean that no one is searching for the phrase. It's likely that even if the tools show no data, that there is still someone somewhere looking for that topic. And there are other places to look for evidence of that demand.

Google Search itself is a great way to check. Just type the phrase you're considering, then hold off hitting the return key. See the keyword suggestions? *If it's suggested by Google, people are searching for it.*

Enter a letter of the alphabet to see more suggested keyphrases (Fig. 5.24).

Getting ideas for phrases to target? Rather than type every letter of the alphabet, you can enter your keyword idea into **Keyword Tool** (keywordtool.io) to see hundreds of suggested phrases, as if you typed the next letter of the alphabet 26 times. You can also see the phrases suggested by YouTube, Bing, Amazon and many other platforms with search suggestions. (Fig. 5.25).

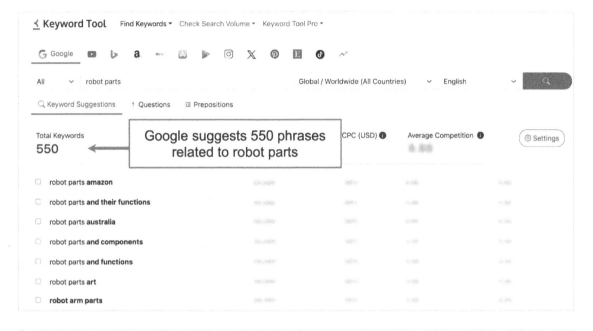
Fig. 5.24

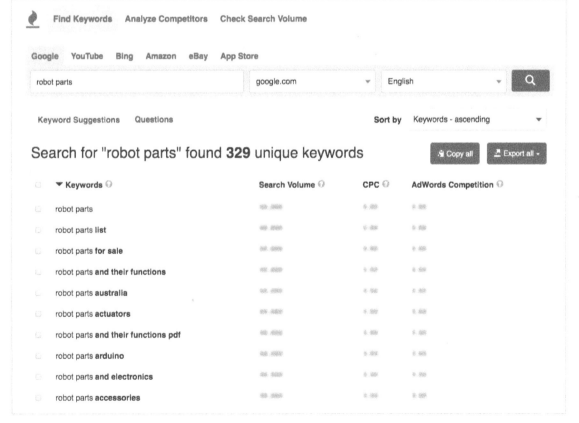
Fig. 5.25

This tool is also great for finding interesting blog post topics. And for the blog posts targeting the informational keyphrases, you aren't necessarily looking for huge demand. Any visibility in search can make a big difference in the performance of a blog post.

Keyword Research Principle #3
If you can find ANY evidence that people are searching for it, it's likely a phrase worth targeting.

A "long-tail keyword" is a target keyphrase of five or more words. These phrases almost always have fewer monthly searches than short keyphrases. **Longer keyphrases have lower search volume.**

But this person is likely deep into their research. They may be getting closer to making a decision. As we know, every keyphrase indicates the searcher's intent. **Longer keyphrases indicate stronger intent.**

The visitor who searches for a very specific phrase is more likely to take action after landing on a website. They may be thrilled to have found you. **Longer keyphrases have higher conversion rates** (Fig. 5.26).

This chart shows the relationship between search volume, competition, intent and conversion rates.

Some very long-tail keyphrases have very little competition. If you target a phrase of six or seven words, such as a complete question, it's possible that you'll have one of the few pages on the internet with that combination of words together in that order. A big advantage.

The short phrase (known as a "head phrase" when it's a single word) is both impossible and useless to rank for. Even if you did somehow rank for one of these super competitive phrases, the visitors who land on your site would have such vague and general needs, they wouldn't stay long.

Fig. 5.26

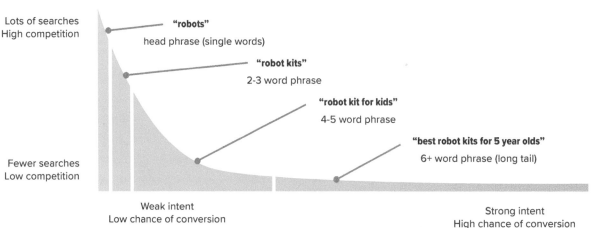

Short vs. Long Keyphrases

Lots of searches
High competition

"robots"
head phrase (single words)

"robot kits"
2-3 word phrase

"robot kit for kids"
4-5 word phrase

"best robot kits for 5 year olds"
6+ word phrase (long tail)

Fewer searches
Low competition

Weak intent
Low chance of conversion

Strong intent
High chance of conversion

The smart SEO looks for opportunities to target longer, easier-to-rank-for, higher-conversion-rate phrases, even when search volume seems to be low.

Keyword Research Principle #4
Low search volume keyphrases are easier to rank for and attract more qualified visitors

A steady trickle of highly interested visitors may lead to a handful of qualified traffic and leads year after year, for many years.

Trends, seasonality and keyphrase comparisons

Tools like Semrush and Moz only show a snapshot of demand based on estimated search volume over the last twelve months. They do not show the ebb and flow of search volume over time. And demands for topics and keywords are constantly changing.

But **Google Trends** shows search demand on a chart. At at glance you can see:

- Trends over time

- Seasonality

- Comparisons of up to five phrases

- Geographic preferences

Let's put three phrases into Google Trends: internet marketing, digital marketing and web marketing. We'll set the date range all the way back to 2004 (that's as far back as it goes) to see the change in relative popularity over time (Fig. 5.27).

Fig. 5.27

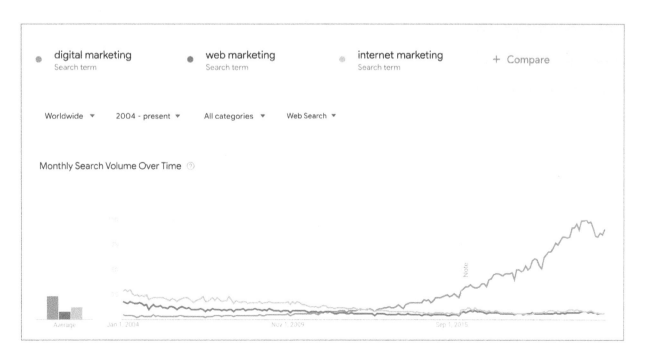

Fig. 5.28

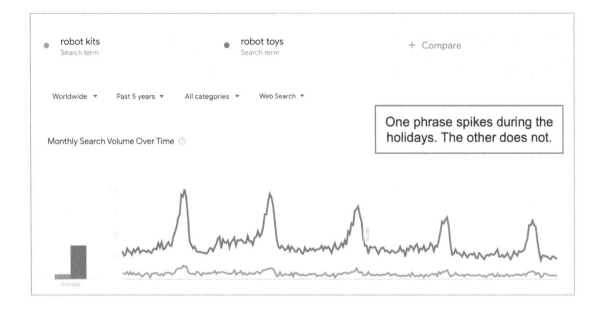

It looks like "digital marketing" wasn't really a thing back in 2004, but over the years has become the dominant term for the industry. Today it has more than 20x the search volume of the other two phrases.

Google Trends also clearly shows seasonal interest in keyphrases. Here you can easily see how one phrase spikes in demand in the holiday season, while the other does not (Fig. 5.28). *Targeting seasonal phrases requires forethought and planning!*

Geographic preferences

Google Trends also shows geographic differences, which can be fun and useful if you're targeting a local audience. By default it shows subregions (that's the state level for the US). If the phrase is popular enough, you can drill down and see demand for metro areas and cities (Fig. 5.29).

It may not be practical or useful to check every phrase in Google Trends. Should you check the trending of every keyphrase for every blog post? Maybe not. But should you check the main keyphrases for your homepage, service pages or product pages? Absolutely.

Fig. 5.29 ● science toys ● space toys

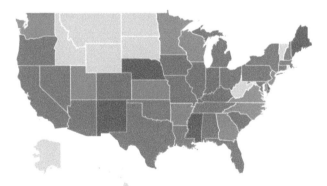

Step 2. Search for the phrases you're considering

To evaluate a potential phrase, you need to search for it.

Keyword Research Principle #5
If you didn't actually search for each phrase (and look closely at the search results), you haven't finished researching the phrase.

Watch a pro do keyword research and you'll see them quickly jump back and forth between SEO tools and the search engine, carefully looking at the SERPs (search engine results pages) as they consider options.

Find a potential phrase . . .

Search for it . . .

Scan through the search results page . . .

Find another potential phrase . . .

Beware of personalized search results

Your search results are always slightly personalized for you. In other words, your target audience may not see exactly the same rankings you do. Here are three tips for seeing more "typical" search results:

1. *Use a browser that isn't logged into any Google products*

2. *Use private browsing or incognito mode*

3. *Use the Google Ad Preview tool, by searching from www.google.com/ adpreview*

There will still be implicit search signals, specific to you and your search history that will affect your search results, so don't spend a ton of time trying to see perfectly neutral results. There is no such thing.

As you scan through the search results for a potential phrase, you're looking for clues, asking yourself questions.

- **Am I in the right neighborhood?**
  If the searcher who is looking for your topic landed on these same search results, what would they do? Would they immediately try again and search for something else? In other words, are the high ranking pages relevant to your brand and your content? If not, you're in the wrong neighborhood. Go back and consider different phrases.

- **Is Google suggesting different or more specific phrases?**
  Google search results are another source of related keywords. Even before you finish typing in the phrase, Google may suggest others (Fig. 5.30). Look at those suggested phrases and the "Related Searches" links at the bottom of the page. Look for question and answer boxes. Getting any ideas?

Fig. 5.30

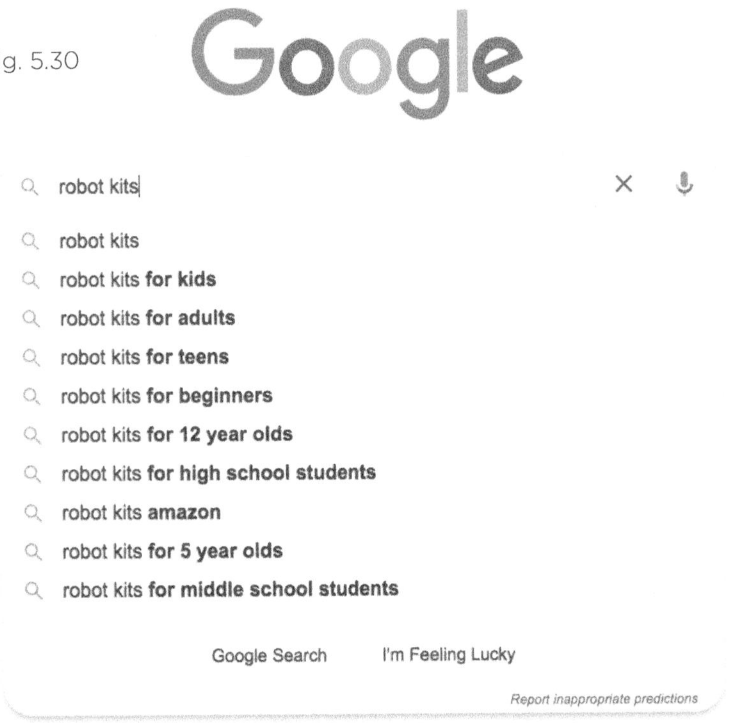

Google

```
Q   robot kits|                                        ×   🎤

Q   robot kits
Q   robot kits for kids
Q   robot kits for adults
Q   robot kits for teens
Q   robot kits for beginners
Q   robot kits for 12 year olds
Q   robot kits for high school students
Q   robot kits amazon
Q   robot kits for 5 year olds
Q   robot kits for middle school students

        Google Search       I'm Feeling Lucky

                              Report inappropriate predictions
```

- **Are there a lot of SERP features pushing down the organic rankings?**
Some search results pages are crowded with ads, images, answer boxes and other features. These push down the high-ranking pages, reducing the likelihood that a searcher will click on your page even if you do rank. This is the big SEO trend we discussed in Section 3.1.

Each SERP feature reduces click through rates for organic search rankings, thereby reducing the traffic potential of a given phrase. If you see a lot of SERP features, you've discovered that Google itself is your competitor and the size of the prize is smaller.

- **What formats for content are ranking?**
Are the search results filled with products? Images? News? Videos?

The SERP features are clues into the content formats that Google has decided are best suited to meet the information needs of the searcher. They can guide decisions about target keyphrases and content formats.

If you see videos in search results, you should create a video, along with a regular web page, to target this keyphrase.

- **Do you see a map?**
If you see a map with a list of businesses below it (known as the "local 3-pack") you are considering a geographically specific keyphrase. You'll need to focus on local SEO to compete in the 3-pack. Local SEO is very different from organic SEO. Those aren't websites that rank under the map; they are local listings.

To improve the ranking of this listing in the local search results, make sure that your business information is up to date in your **Google Business Profile**, within all of the Internet Yellow Pages' websites (IYPs) and anywhere else where your business name, address and phone number (NAP) appear. An instance of your NAP is called a "citation."

When a business has many citations with few inconsistencies, Google has more evidence that there is a relevant business in that location. Therefore,

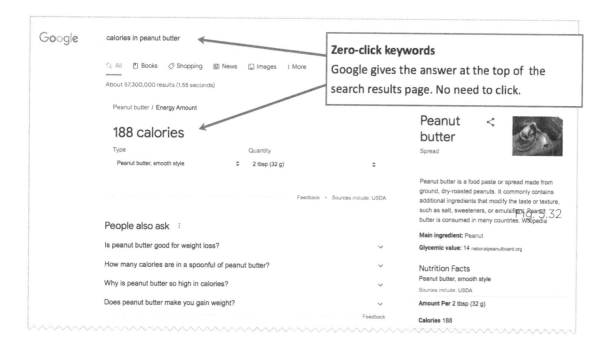

Fig. 5.31

Zero-click keywords

Google gives the answer at the top of the search results page. No need to click.

Google is more likely to show that business listing when visitors in that area search for a related phrase. To quickly improve the number and consistency of your citations and improve your local SEO, consider using a service such as **Moz Local** or **Whitespark**.

- **Does the answer appear right there in the search results?**
  If so, your potential keyphrase has "fact intent" which is short-answer information intent (Fig. 5.31). Google does everything it can to satisfy the searcher's information quickly, even before they click. These "zero-click" keyphrases don't send traffic to anyone. Avoid them.

Step 3. Estimate the competition

You've validated that someone is looking for the phrase. You've looked closely at what is currently winning for the phrase. Next we'll evaluate your likelihood of ranking. It's time to check competition and keyword difficulty.

This is one of the more challenging digital marketing skills. It's a tricky and inexact science. In a moment, we'll show how SEO software can be used to quickly check the difficulty for any phrase.

But we'll start with common sense.

Just search for the phrase and take a look at the search engine results page. The phrase is likely competitive if you see any of these three things (Fig. 5.32):

1. **Lots of ads**
   If there are four pay-per-click (PPC) ads at the top of the page and three at the bottom, this means others have already determined the keyphrase is valuable.

2. **Famous brands ranking high**
   If the top-ranking sites are popular, well-known sites, it's going to be tough. Unless you invent a time machine, you're not going to outrank Wikipedia or Amazon. If the top three or five sites are trusted, reputable websites, they'll have loads of link popularity and therefore powerful domains. You're not likely to compete without focusing serious time and resources.

3. **The phase you searched for is in the links**
   If the top-ranking sites have the target keyphrase at the beginning of the link, then it's likely that those sites have the keyphrases at the beginning

Fig. 5.32

Lots of ads at the top

Famous websites and brands

The target keyphrase often appears at the front of the links (title tag) or immediately after the brand of their page titles, which indicates the owners of these sites understand SEO. Your keyphrase will likely be more difficult, but not necessarily impossible.

Below is the anatomy of a highly competitive keyphrase:

Now let's go beyond the quick visual check and use tools to estimate competition more accurately.

In Section 3.1, we discussed the mechanics of search and the importance of link popularity. We explained that a page is more likely to rank if it is part of an authoritative website, and that a website is authoritative if it has many links to it from many other websites. Now it's time to actually estimate the authority of the websites that rank and therefore estimate the competition for a given phrase.

Keyword Research Principle #6
You will never rank for a keyphrase if you lack sufficient authority.

You need to know your level of authority and compare it to the range of authority of the other high-ranking pages. To do this, you need a metric to compare your specific level of authority (and likelihood of ranking) to other websites.

How authority is measured

Google's authority metric is called PageRank, named after Google founder Larry Page. It's a one-to-ten scale of credibility, link popularity and ranking potential. Until 2013, you could check the PageRank for any website using a Google toolbar that many of us added to our browsers. It's long gone.

Today search optimizers use proxy metrics created by SEO software companies. These companies *estimate* Google PageRank using their own formulas. They all use a scale of 1-100.

Here are some of the more popular metrics and tools:

- Domain Authority, created by Moz

- Domain Score, created by Semrush

- Domain Rating, created by Ahrefs

The cost of each of these paid tools starts at about $100 per month. They all have free trials. Beyond their keyword research tools, they each have many other useful features for search engine optimization: rank tracking, page recommendations, brand mention alerts, etc.

Since Moz offers a free view into its data, we'll use their term, Domain Authority, as we go.

Fig. 5.33

Domain Authority of . . .	. . . is typical for these kinds of sites
0-30	Start-ups, small businesses
30-50	Small biz with strong digital, big biz with weak digital
50-60	Niche publishers, brands with mature content programs
60-70	Daily blogs, enterprise, major brands
70-90	Media companies, global brands
90-100	Digital giants, monopolies

The Domain Authority power curve

Websites with higher Domain Authority (DA) have exponentially greater ranking potential. Authority is plotted on a curve, not a line. Higher DA sites can target far more competitive phrases. Fig. 5.33 shows how it is distributed across types of websites:

This explains why the little blogs rarely rank for the very popular and valuable keyphrases. Search for a general topic or common question and you'll see the heavyweights at the top.

Keyword Research Principle #7
SEO was never a fair fight.

The key to successfully choosing a keyphrase is to compete at or below your own level. Think of SEO as a race. You can't win the Tour de France on foot. But if you're on a bike, you're going to win every marathon you enter (Fig. 5.34).

To properly research a keyphrase (and evaluate your site's potential to rank) you need to know two things: your own level of authority and the range of authority of the other sites that rank for the phrase you're considering.

How to check your own authority

Just enter your domain into any of the tools listed above. Here's what the report looks like in Moz and Semrush (Fig. 5.35).

Fig. 5.34

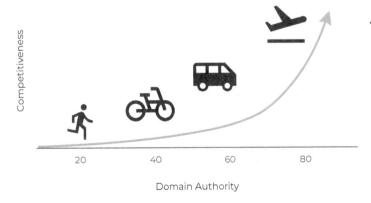

Domain Authority Power Curve

Competitiveness (y-axis)

Domain Authority (x-axis): 20 40 60 80

Fig. 5.35

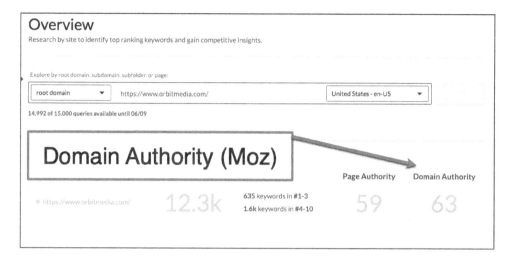

💡 **Improving your Domain Authority** is one of the most valuable outcomes of content marketing. Higher authority leads to a much greater chance of ranking, which leads to huge amounts of traffic and brand awareness. Learn more about Domain Authority and how to increase it here: https://www.orbitmedia.com/blog/increase-domain-authority/

What's a good level of authority? How much authority do you need? It all depends on the competition for the target keyphrase. Remember, every page is its own competitor and every keyphrase is a separate competition.

Check the keyword difficulty

Keyword difficulty is basically the average authority of all of the high-ranking pages for a given phrase.

The SEO tools make it easy to check keyword difficulty, by combining the authority levels of the other high-ranking pages into one easy-to-check metric.

Fig. 5.36

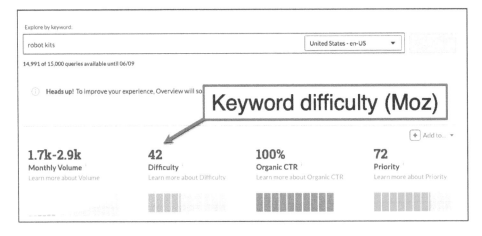

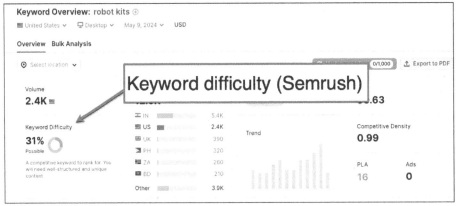

The same report that shows keyphrase search volume also shows keyphrase difficulty. So in one view, you have a lot of the necessary information to consider a phrase. Fig. 5.36 shows what the reports look like.

Now that you know your website's Domain Authority and the keyword's difficulty, you're ready to apply the general rule.

Keyword Research Principle #8
If your Domain Authority is greater than the Keyword Difficulty, you should have a chance of ranking for the phrase.

If your authority is at or below the keyword difficulty, go back and look for a less competitive phrase. In other words, target a longer, more specific, less popular keyphrase.

As you consider possible primary and secondary keyphrases, capture them in a content template, which we'll share at the end of this chapter. For bigger projects, you may track many potential keywords in a spreadsheet as part of a larger keyword plan (Fig. 5.37).

Can I check the competition in the Google Ads Keyword Planner?

No. The Keyword Planner shows competition in pay per click (PPC) to give you an idea for the cost of advertising. It has nothing to do with SEO. Ignore it (Fig. 5.38).

Can I check difficulty without a paid SEO tool?

Yes. For this more manual approach, we'll use Moz because they have a free SEO tool that makes it easy. It's called MozBar. MozBar is an extension for the Chrome browser. Add it to Chrome, turn it on and search for any phrase, and you'll see the authority metrics data for each of the high-ranking pages right below each search listing.

Fig. 5.37

Web Design Requirements

Publish Date: 2/2024

Author: Andy

Editor: Amanda

KEYPHRASE RESEARCH

Record the possible target phrases, including the search volume and difficulty.

Target Keyphrases: as of 2/2024

Keyphrase	Monthly Volume	Difficulty
requirements for website design	0-10	39
website design requirements	11-50	41
Requirements for designing a website	11-50	42
Basic website requirements	0-10	31
Website design requirements checklist	0-10	40

Fig. 5.38

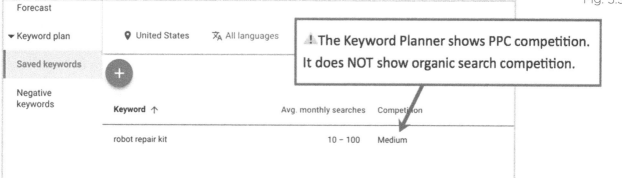

Forecast

▼ Keyword plan

Saved keywords

Negative keywords

📍 United States   🖋 All languages

⚠ The Keyword Planner shows PPC competition. It does NOT show organic search competition.

Keyword ↑	Avg. monthly searches	Competition
robot repair kit	10 – 100	Medium

Fig. 5.39

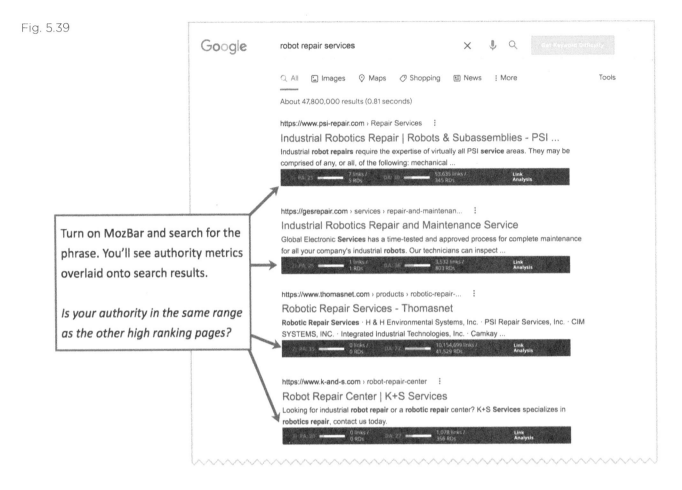

Turn on MozBar and search for the phrase. You'll see authority metrics overlaid onto search results.

Is your authority in the same range as the other high ranking pages?

Here are search results with MozBar turned on. This is another type of "SERP analysis" (analysis of search engine results pages) (Fig. 5.39).

You can see how MozBar shows several metrics under each search listing: the Domain Authority of the overall website and the Page Authority (PA) of the specific page. If you have a paid account, you'll see the number of linking websites/root domains (RD) to both the overall website and the specific page.

You'll soon notice that it's common for pages with lower authority to outrank pages with higher authority. Usually it's because the page (or that entire website) is overcoming it's lower authority challenge with better quality and relevance. These lower-authority/higher-ranking pages are often more focused on the specific topic.

Now that you know both your authority and the range of authority for the competitors, you can look for keyphrases for which your authority is in that same range. And again, if your authority is below the range of the other sites that rank, go back and look for a less competitive phrase. Target a longer, more specific, less popular keyphrase.

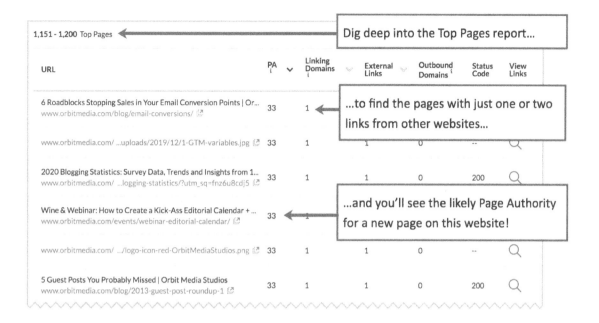

Fig. 5.40

Page authority: The next level of detail in keyword research

Ultimately, the battle for rankings is fought page-against-page, not website-against-website. It's the authority of your specific page versus the authority of their specific page. So **Page Authority**, not Domain Authority is the real test.

Here's a better, more specific rule:

Keyword Research Principle #9
If your *Page Authority* is within the same *range* as the other high-ranking pages, you should have a chance of ranking for the phrase.

This is a more detailed, accurate way to evaluate your ranking potential. But there's a problem. When creating a new page and targeting a new phrase, you don't have a Page Authority to compare to, *because your page doesn't exist yet.*

So there's a time and place for each approach.

- **Use Domain Authority** when creating new content (i.e., writing new articles)

- **Use Page Authority** when optimizing existing content (i.e., during an SEO audit)

Actually, there is one way to estimate the likely Page Authority of a new page that has yet to be published. In Moz, go to the Top Pages report and keep clicking "next" until you see pages that have just one linking domain.

These pages will all have the same low Page Authority. The only authority they have is the authority they inherit from the overall domain. This is the baseline amount of ranking potential of new pages published on this website (Fig. 5.40).

When creating a new page, assume its Page Authority will be the same as the least authoritative pages on that domain. Choose a keyphrase with the same or lower keyword difficulty scores as the lowest Page Authority on the website.

Shortcut!

After researching thousands of phrases for hundreds of clients, we've seen patterns and created benchmarks. Here's one that you can use as a rule of thumb to speed things up.

Estimate your potential to rank using your Domain Authority and the keyword search volume or the number of words in the phrase. (Fig. 5.41) This is oversimplified for sure, but it may help give you an idea of what general range you should be in.

Fig. 5.41

If your Domain Authority is . . .	Target keyphrases with monthly searches of . . .	. . . or keyphrases of this length
less than 30	fewer than 50	5 words
30–50	50–500	4 words
50–70	500+	3 words

What if I really want to target a phrase that is too difficult for me to rank for?

Common question. Often, the outcome of keyword research is a simple conclusion: *there is no SEO opportunity for this page.* When that's the case, you have a few options.

- **Choose a different topic**
  If rankings and organic traffic are that important to you, tweak the topic or abandon it completely.

- **Write for another website**
  If you're writing an article and your site's domain isn't authoritative enough, you can still rank for it . . . just not on your website. Write a beautifully search optimized piece and submit it as a guest post to a blog with a more authoritative domain. You won't win the traffic, but you'll win some brand awareness.

- **Target the keyphrase anyway**
  Organic search is not the only source of traffic. It's just one of many ways to promote a piece of content. Write a great page knowing that you won't likely rank now, but that you may revisit the URL later.

It may rank months or years from now after you've built links to it (better authority) and rewritten it several times (better relevance). In Section 8.2 we'll show an example of how persistence wins for out of reach phrases, along with the process for updating articles for better performance in search.

What should I do with the rejected keyphrases?

During the keyword research process, you may consider a dozen or more phrases. Many you'll dismiss, but the experienced SEO doesn't completely abandon them. They are an opportunity.

Capture them. You can use them to create better content.

Google doesn't simply match words from searches with words on pages. It's doing natural language processing to understand the intent of the visitor and the content of pages. So we need to do "semantic SEO." It's a simple two-step process.

1. **During keyphrase research,** jot down all of the related phrases you find, even if they don't end up being selected as your primary keyphrase. You may have spotted them in keywordtool.io, Answer the Public or in the "People Also Ask" box.

2. **While writing,** work those phrases into your content. But don't be tempted to do keyword stuffing. Think about the visitor. Find ways to cover those subtopics and answer the related questions. The idea is to let the semantically related phrases pull you deeper into the topic, making it a more detailed page.

Keyword Research Principle #10
**Target the topic,
not just the keyphrase**

If you're using our content marketing template, it will look something like Fig. 5.42.

Fig. 5.42

20 Questions to Ask When Interviewing Web Firms

Author: Andy
Editor: Amanda

Target Keyphrases: as of 4/2024

Keyphrase	Searches / month	% Difficulty
How to choose a web designer	0-10	38
How to choose a website developer	11-50	37
How to choose a web design company	0-10	32
Questions to ask a web designer	11-50	25
What to look for in a web designer	0-10	26

Related Words and Phrases:

- How to pick, hire
- how to find
- how to choose, looking for, what to look for
- Web developer, website developer
- web designer, web design company, website builder
- professional

Capture the related phrases, then address those subtopics (and incorporate those phrases) as you write the article

Here again, SEO software can help.

- Semrush has a Google Doc add-on called the **SEO Writing Assistant**. It provides recommendations and tracks keyword inclusion as you write. It's very helpful.

- MarketMuse has a tool called **Optimize** that also makes recommendations and tracks keyword usage as you write. It shows the keyword frequency for your content and compares it to the other pages that rank for the target keyphrase. It looks like Fig. 5.43.

These tools make it easy (even prescriptive) to incorporate related phrases. Hopefully, they also push you to create higher quality content. After all, the best way to incorporate a semantically related phrase is to add paragraphs of detail and deeper explanations, which are good for your readers as well as your rankings.

Fig. 5.43

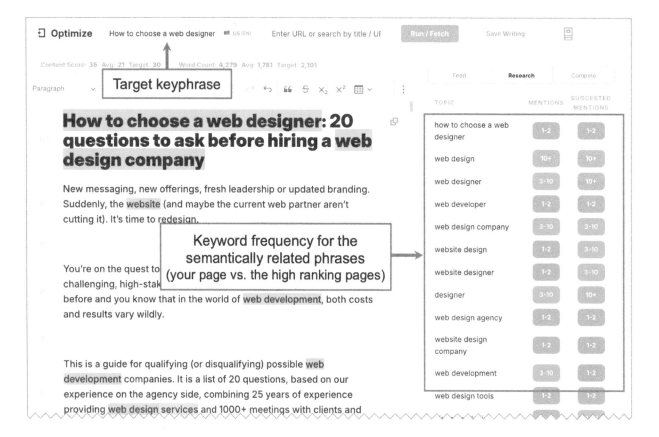

Next step:
Go make something

You did it. You've picked out a target search term. Let's review what you've done and think about what you'll do next:

- You've carefully considered the intent of the phrase.

- You've looked at search volume and found some evidence of demand.

- You've researched the competition and the difficulty of the phrase.

- You've examined the current search results page for the phrase.

- You've collected the closely related phrases.

- You're planning to create a single URL that fits on your sitemap or in your content strategy.

You're ready to write. This brings us to the final principle:

Keyword Research Principle #11
**Make one of the best pages on the internet for your topic . . .
or don't expect to rank**

Yes, you'll need to indicate relevance by using the target keyphrase in the most visible, important places: the title tag, meta description, H1 header and meta description. Yes, you'll need to incorporate the semantically related phrases, answer the closely related questions and cover the related subtopics.

But beyond all of those SEO best practices, you're really just trying to make something excellent. Your goal is to make the best page on the internet for your topic. If you do not create one of the best pages on the web for the topic, *you have no right to rank.*

Should I make two pages to target two variations of a phrase? (closely related keyphrases)

Often, during keyphrase research, you notice several closely related phrases that are relevant to your content. You want to target both. But if you made two pages, one page for each phrase, the writing for the pages might look very similar.

So are they really separate phrases? Or does Google consider these to be the same topic?

There is a quick way to answer this question. Just search for both phrases and look closely at the search results side by side. Is there a lot of overlap? Fig. 5.44 shows an example of two search results pages for two separate phrases.

Fig. 5.44

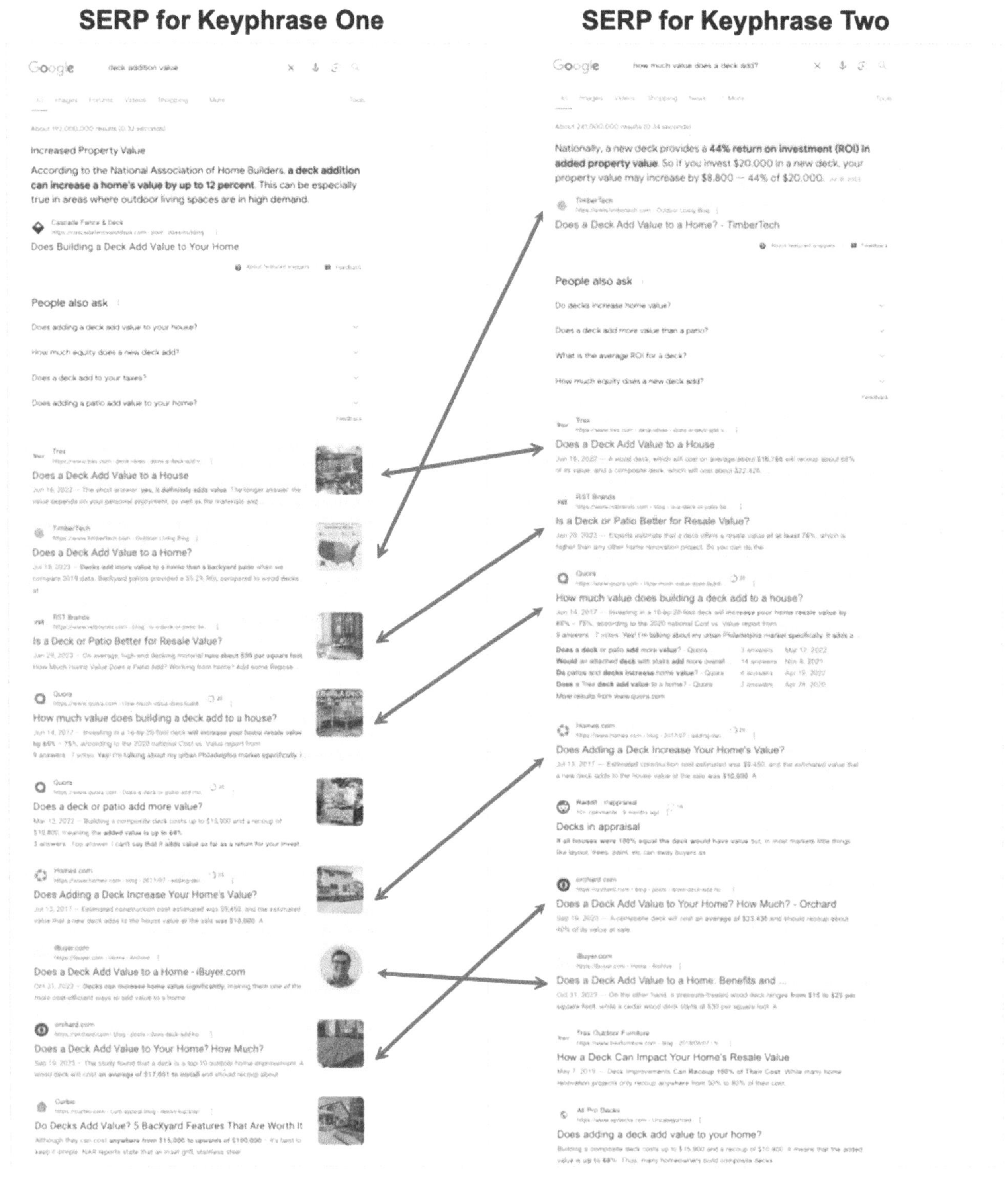
SERP for Keyphrase One
SERP for Keyphrase Two
Increased Property Value
Does Building a Deck Add Value to Your Home
People also ask
Does a Deck Add Value to a House
Does a Deck Add Value to a Home?
Is a Deck or Patio Better for Resale Value?
How much value does building a deck add to a house?
Does a deck or patio add more value?
Does Adding a Deck Increase Your Home's Value?
Does a Deck Add Value to a Home - iBuyer.com
Does a Deck Add Value to Your Home? How Much?
Do Decks Add Value? 5 Backyard Features That Are Worth It
Does a Deck Add Value to a Home? - TimberTech
Decks in appraisal
Does a Deck Add Value to Your Home? How Much? - Orchard
Does a Deck Add Value to a Home: Benefits and ...
How a Deck Can Impact Your Home's Resale Value
Does adding a deck add value to your home?

Fig. 5.45

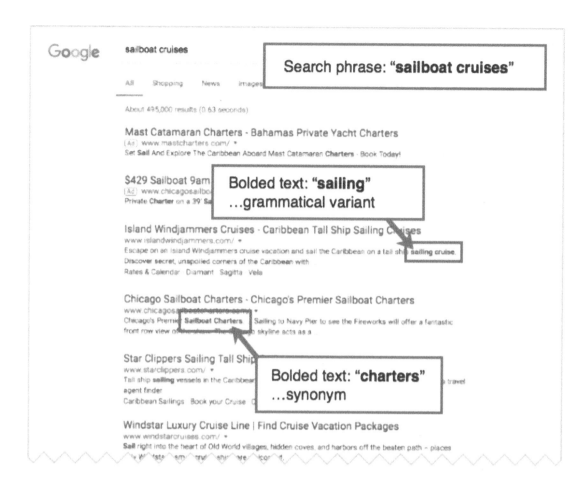

Fig. 5.45

"how much value does a deck add" and "deck addition value."

You can see that the two share many of the same results. This is strong evidence that they are really the same topic within Google's index. One page will target both phrases.

Here's another clue: look for the bolded text within search results when you search. Google bolds the phrase that you search for, making the search results easier to scan. But they also bold closely related grammatical forms and synonyms (Fig. 5.45).

When you see words from your two possible phrases bolded in the search results for either, they are really the same topic. One page can target both phrases.

- If there's a lot of overlap in the search results, the two keyphrases are really one topic. Write one page that targets both phrases.

- If there's very little overlap in search results, the two phrases are two separate topics. Write a page for each topic, targeting the phrases separately.

5.6 Writing Headlines

Scan. Dismiss. Scan. Dismiss. Scan . . . click!

This is what your audience is doing today. This is what we're all doing today. In our inbox, on social media and on blogs, we scan through headlines, dismissing most and clicking a few.

Winning that click depends on the headline, more than anything else. It's impossible to overstate their importance. We are all judged instantly and ruthlessly by this short set of words.

Even if you do everything else right, even if your strategy is solid, your targeting is accurate and you blog your fingers to the bone, *everything will still fail if you get this one thing wrong.*

Before we look at the best practices, let's first look at all the places they appear and how the success factors vary. You can immediately see that a "headline" actually means different things depending on where it appears (Fig. 5.46).

So there really isn't a generic "headline" anymore. There are several and each is written for it's context. A single article has different headlines in different places, each with a specific function and success factors. Do not try to make one size fit all.

With that in mind, we'll look at the psychology of headlines and some general guidelines for writing them, wherever they appear.

Fig. 5.46

What (and where) is a headline?

When the headline is here . . .	. . . it can lead to . . .	. . . especially if you . . .
Article header (H1)	Higher average time on page	Go long with specific benefits
Title tag	Higher rankings	Put the target keyphrase near the front. Use less than 60 characters (SERP snippet truncation)
Email subject line	Higher open rates	Put the most powerful, specific words in the first 5 words (mobile inbox character limits)
Social media post	Higher click through rates, more sharing	Trigger curiosity and emotion, support with hashtags, special characters and even emojis
Video title	more plays/views	Use the target keyphrase and an unexpected word and put the headline into the thumbnail image

1. Make a promise. Be specific.

The key to the click is to understand this: Before any of us click anything, we do a split-second cost-benefit calculation.

Is the benefit of clicking (the value of the content) higher than the cost (two seconds of my time)?

Here's what's happening in your visitor's brain . . . (Fig. 5.47)

The basic job of the headline is to indicate the benefit and to make a promise to the visitor that it's worth it. And to do it in less than a second. The more specific the benefit, the more likely the visitor is to click. Great headlines make specific promises.

Pretend you're the reader and ask yourself, "What's in it for me?" The answer should jump off the page. If it doesn't, get ready to hear crickets. You're about to fail. If you don't explain what's in it for the reader, don't expect them to read your content.

"Content marketing is a war zone. The battle is for attention, and your headline is your weapon. The reader's perpetually asking, 'Why should I read this?' Answer that question. Make it unmistakably clear what the reader gains by investing time in your content. The pulling power of a magnetic headline traces to its promise. Simply stated, it's a benefit."

BARRY FELDMAN, *Content Marketing Consultant and Copywriter, Feldman Creative*

The ability to imagine the readers' perspective is the key to success in writing headlines. *Empathy is the key to getting clicks.*

The Cost/Benefit is Calculated Every Time We See a Headline

Fig. 5.47

```
Open inbox
View social stream  →  See headline  →  benefit > 2 seconds of attention?
See search results

                                         YES → click! → view article
                                         NO → scan / scroll
```

2. Use power trigrams

In 2021, BuzzSumo did a study to discover why some headlines are so much more effective than others in social media.[5] They looked at 100,000,000 articles and found correlations between headlines and engagement. Among the correlations was the use of trigrams, which are groups of three words.

As it turns out, certain trigrams have a big impact.

"The [curiosity gap] technique can easily be overdone—we see brands try to replicate it (badly) all the time. But done right, the so-called curiosity-gap approach can help readers by making it clear what a piece is about.

Keep yourself honest and use such headlines only when they are helpful triggers for your audience. So go ahead and use "14 Surprising Ways You Can Grow Pumpkins," but only if the 14 ways might indeed be surprising to your audience."

ANN HANDLEY, *Chief Content Officer, Marketing Profs, author of "Content Rules" and "Everybody Writes"*

Fig. 5.48 shows the average number of Facebook likes, comments and shares for headlines that include certain trigrams.

They also looked at the placement of the trigrams. When these trigrams appear at the beginning of headlines, the Facebook post is much more likely to get social engagement (Fig. 5.49).

One of the conclusions is that hyperbole works well in social media. But as marketers seeking to build trust with a potential visitor, you should be careful when making promises.

⚠️ WARNING! **No clickbait!** If your first reaction to these trigrams is "this is clickbait," please keep reading. We are not recommending writing clickbait headlines. Do not try to trick your reader. It's good to trigger a bit of curiosity, but don't mislead or overpromise. Your article must deliver on the promise you're making in your headline or you'll hurt your reputation.

But look closely at the trigrams and you can see why they work so well. They all make promises. If you're writing blog headlines that include these trigrams, you're offering specific benefits to the reader.

5. 100M Articles Analyzed, What You Need to Write the Best Headlines, BuzzSumo. https://buzzsumo.com/blog/most-shared-headlines-study/

Top 20 headline phrases on Facebook: 2019/2020

Fig. 5.48

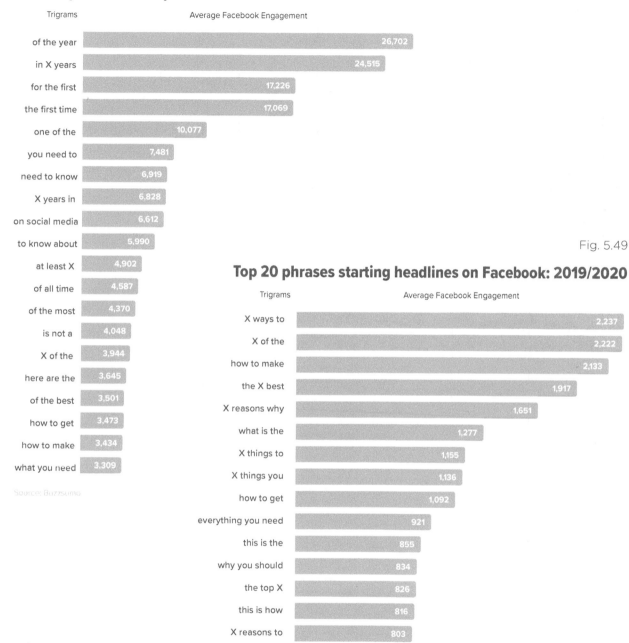

Trigrams — Average Facebook Engagement

Trigram	Engagement
of the year	26,702
in X years	24,515
for the first	17,226
the first time	17,069
one of the	10,077
you need to	7,481
need to know	6,919
X years in	6,828
on social media	6,612
to know about	5,990
at least X	4,902
of all time	4,587
of the most	4,370
is not a	4,048
X of the	3,944
here are the	3,645
of the best	3,501
how to get	3,473
how to make	3,434
what you need	3,309

Source: Buzzsumo

Fig. 5.49

Top 20 phrases starting headlines on Facebook: 2019/2020

Trigrams — Average Facebook Engagement

Trigram	Engagement
X ways to	2,237
X of the	2,222
how to make	2,133
the X best	1,917
X reasons why	1,651
what is the	1,277
X things to	1,155
X things you	1,136
how to get	1,092
everything you need	921
this is the	855
why you should	834
the top X	826
this is how	816
X reasons to	803
what you need	737
the X most	736
the story of	706
what are the	699
what is a	669

Source: Buzzsumo

"At LinkedIn, there's not a campaign that leaves our hands that doesn't have some aspect of A/B testing. Oftentimes, tests reveal that the smallest tweaks can make the greatest performance impact. Using data or stats, especially up front, can imply instant credibility to your post or headline."

MEGAN GOLDEN,
Content Marketing Leader, LinkedIn

3. Use numbers

List posts are popular for a reason: they set expectations about the amount of content, about scannability and variety. If you don't like one thing, you'll be able to scan down and find something else.

Numerals, not just numbers, are part of the magic. *In a line of letters, numerals stand out.* So don't write a headline with "Eight Things," write a headline with "8 things."

Headlines with numbers aren't always list posts. Numbers can also be data and statistics, indicating that the article is supported by research. LinkedIn tested headlines with and without statistics and found that stats had a big impact on click through rates (Fig. 5.50).

Fig. 5.50

Examples:

- 17 Social Media Books That Will Make You a Smarter Marketer

- How to Increase Conversion Rates by 529%

- 101 Ways to Write Top 10 Lists That Increase Traffic by 21%

You get the idea.

4. Ask a question

Question headlines have two benefits. First, they leverage a psychological effect, causing the reader's mind to take the next step: answer the question . . . or wonder. The lack of completeness inherent in questions causes tension and interest in readers.

Search is the second benefit. Google is focused on the *meaning of a search query*, not just combinations of words. It's called "latent semantic indexing" and it's key to search rankings. The natural language of a complete question helps Google understand how the article is useful.

People are using their voices, not just fingers, to search these days. And naturally, they're asking complete, full-sentence questions. Content that includes complete, grammatical questions and answers helps Google connect people to your content.

"Don't buy the argument that 'those headline formulas don't work anymore.' All that old 'cheesy' advice can still be remarkably effective. Numbers in the headline still work. List posts still work.

The secret to staying out of Cheeseland? Make the content *behind* your headline amazing. **Put some love (and work) into it,** to make it compelling and genuinely useful. Bring your own unique writing voice and sincere care for the topic into your written, audio and video content."

SONIA SIMONE, *Chief Marketing Officer, Rainmaker Digital and Copyblogger*

Examples:

- Why Do Dogs Bark at Night? 5 Dog Trainers Offer Tips for Quiet Canines.

- How Does Social Media Affect SEO?

- Which Superhero Are You? Take This Short Quiz and Find Out . . .

5. Put impact words at the front of your headline

In the mobile inbox, subject lines get truncated after just 45 or so characters. In search results, title tags get truncated after around 60 characters. Podcast titles have the same issue.

Consider these examples. These are really the same headline:

- 10 Simple Communication Tips That Can Help You Ace Your Job Interview

- How to Ace Your Job Interview with These 10 Simple Communication Tips

But here's how they look in the mobile inbox (Fig. 5.51):

Fig. 5.51

Put the impact and benefits at the front of the headline

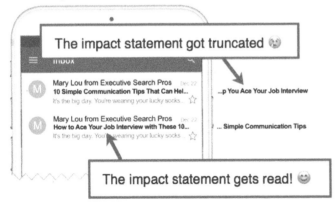

One subscriber sees the impact and benefit of clicking right there in the inbox: "ace your job interview." The other would have to tap to open the email before they see that benefit statement.

Even when truncation isn't an issue, readers will scan your headline from the beginning. So putting those thumb-stopping words toward the front makes them more likely to be seen and more likely to get tapped.

6. Write very long headlines

Just because it's front-loaded with impact words and benefits doesn't mean that the headline is short. According to the research by BuzzSumo, long headlines are winning, at least in social media.

The chart in Fig. 5.52 shows the average number of social engagements based on the number of words in headlines.

That's right. 11-word headlines had the highest average number of interactions. This is actually shorter than it used to be. In 2017, 15-word headlines had the most average interactions. Headlines are getting snappier.

Most marketers don't typically write long headlines. Try it and you'll find yourself writing long, complete sentences. Or maybe two sentences. Check out these examples from some viral content sites:

- A 5-Year-Old Girl Raised Enough Money to Take Her Father Who Has Terminal Cancer to Disney World (17 words)

- Elephant That Spent 11 Hours Digging a Hole Finally Pulled Out Something No One Expected (15 words)

- She Carried a Secret Around for Years. Her Adopted Son Found Out and Loved Her Even More For It. (19 words, two sentences)

Obviously each of these is also exploiting the "curiosity gap" by providing enough information to make readers curious, but not enough to satisfy that curiosity without clicking. Looks like clickbait. But the point here is that longer headlines have more opportunities to entice the reader.

We recommend going long wherever truncation isn't an issue. That's social posts and <h1> tags (page headers). It won't work for title tags or subject lines. Those will always be truncated by Google and inbox providers.

"Place **the most interesting word or phrase** as close as possible to the start of the headline. This becomes even more crucial as people read on their smartphones, where email subject lines can get truncated to 4 or 5 words."

CHARLIE MEYERSON, *News Media Veteran and Principal, Meyerson Strategy*

Fig. 5.52

Optimum headline word count on Facebook & Twitter: 2019/2020

Source: BuzzSumo

Chart shows the most common length of the most shared headlines across Facebook & Twitter, based on average (median) engagement.

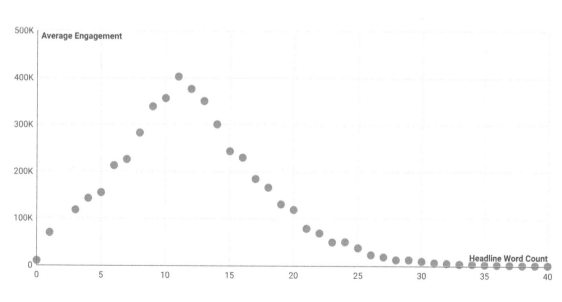

• Powered by **BuzzSumo**

BuzzSumo Research

7. Put the keyword first

Also good at the front of the headlines: target keyphrases.

Using the target keyphrase at the beginning of the title tag <title> and header <h1> gives it "keyphrase prominence," helping to indicate its relevance to search engines. This is not important for subject lines and social posts.

An effective headline works for both search engines and readers. To create headlines that rank and capture attention, **use a colon**. This lets you separate the search-friendly keyword from the social-friendly triggers.

It gives you keyphrase prominence but still leverages human psychology in the rest of the headline.

Check out these examples from past posts on the Orbit Media blog:

- How to Research Keywords: Tips, Competition and Squirrels

- Neuromarketing Web Design: 15 Ways to Connect with Visitors' Brains

- Internal Linking: 9 Best Practices for Internal Links

- What to Blog About: 17 Sources of Fresh Blog Topics

See the pattern? Each post is optimized to rank for the phrase at the beginning of the headline (with perfect keyphrase prominence) followed by a number or words to connect with visitors' hearts and minds.

So, here's Orbit's formula for headlines:

Target Keyphrase + Colon + Number or Trigger Word + Promise

Does it work? *Search for any of those phrases before the colon in the headlines above.* You probably see the post ranking for the phrase . . . and you might just click, thanks to the numbers and the benefit statements.

8. Coin a new phrase

The best headline writers create something memorable. Whenever possible they give their idea a name, as in Mark Schaefer's "Content Shock," Doug Kessler's "Insane Honesty" or Brian Dean's "Skyscraper Technique."

Ryan Law calls these "Coined Concepts." The idea is to create a pithy catchphrase that encapsulates the article's ideas and arguments. Although they have no advantage in SEO (they're new, so no one is searching for them), they may do well in social media.

Write lots of draft headlines before choosing one

The pros aren't writing a headline. They are writing lots of headlines. For any article, you should write a dozen or more headlines. Write several options for each location: title tags, headers and subject lines. Meet with your editor or get input from a friendly marketer.

When I teach classes on content strategy, I give students a sample article and have them write a minimum of 20 alternate headlines.

Once you've got a dozen or more drafts, you can sort them based on their strengths. Keyword-focused headlines are candidates for H1 headers and title tags. Emotional headlines are candidates for subject lines and social posts.

Subject lines, in my view, are the most challenging. After you hit send, you can't go back and change them. There are two techniques that can help:

- If you've built up an engaged social following, use social media to test possible email subject lines. Create social posts from your potential subject lines and see which gets the most engagement.

- If you've built up a large email list, you can use A/B testing tools in your email service provider. 10% get one subject line, 10% get another. The final 80% get whichever subject line performed better in the test.

5.7 Visuals and Content Marketing

Now let's move on to the next most important success factor in content: the visuals.

Blogging is a written, text-based medium, but the text is only part of it. The blog images are critical. They are an all-important ingredient, second only to a great headline. Visuals are a make-or-break factor for successful content marketing. Here's some research that makes the case for strong blog images:

"Coined concepts can be borrowed from adjacent fields, inspired by frameworks and models from science, academia, business, and entertainment. Once-popular concepts can be resurrected and given a new lease of life. If you're feeling creative, you can even create a brand-new concept from scratch."

RYAN LAW, *Ahrefs*

- **Visuals improve social sharing**
  Image posts earn 2.3 times more engagement than text posts on Facebook.[6]

- **Visuals improve clarity**
  People following directions with illustrations do 323% better than people following directions without illustrations.[7]

- **Visuals make content more memorable**
  If you hear a piece of information, three days later you'll remember 10% of it. Add a picture and you'll remember 65%.[8]

Not only do the images make the content more accessible, more memorable and

---

6. http://buzzsumo.com/blog/how-to-massively-boost-your-blog-traffic-with-these-5-awesome-image-stats/
7. http://link.springer.com/article/10.1007%2FBF02765184
8. http://brainrules.net/vision/

Fig. 5.53

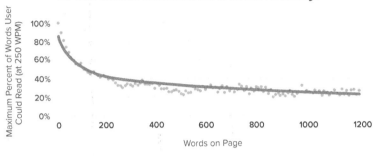

During a typical pageview, visitors have time to read 28% of the words at most. 20% is more likely.

more shareable, but they align with how we humans consume content. According to research by the NN Group , the average visitor reads at most 28% of text on the average website.[9] This calculation is based on the average number of words, the average time spent on a page and the average reading speed of visitors. 28% is actually optimistic. The real number is probably closer to 20% (Fig. 5.53).

9. https://www.nngroup.com/articles/how-little-do-users-read/

Fig. 5.54

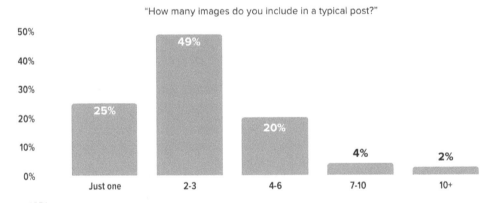

A small minority of bloggers create highly visual content

"How many images do you include in a typical post?"

Fig. 5.55

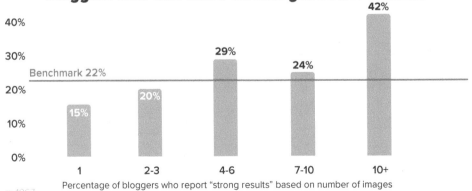

Bloggers who add more visuals get better results.

Percentage of bloggers who report "strong results" based on number of images

n=1067

Your visitor is actually skimming, not reading.

If you have any doubt, just watch your own behavior next time you land on an article.

So how can you slow these scanners down? How can you keep these visitors interested?

First, with formatting. Use short paragraphs, subheaders, bullets, bolding and links. This makes the content easier to scan. But really, visuals are your best chance at pulling the visitor deeper into the content.

Here are a set of guidelines and formats for adding images in blog posts. We'll start with the most important and effective tip:

1. Add many visuals to each article

In our annual blogging survey, we ask how many images bloggers add to a typical post. Most bloggers add just a few, but a very small percentage of bloggers publish highly visual content with 10+ images per post. That's a big investment but it pays off. Bloggers who add 10 or more images are nearly twice as likely to report "strong results." (Fig. 5.54 and 5.55)

Years ago, we recommended using an image on every post. But that's not enough anymore. Now we recommend using an image *at every scroll depth.*

In other words, on the ideal post, no matter how far down the visitor scrolls, there is something of visual interest in their field of vision (Fig. 5.56).

Fig. 5.56

Add visual interest at every scroll depth

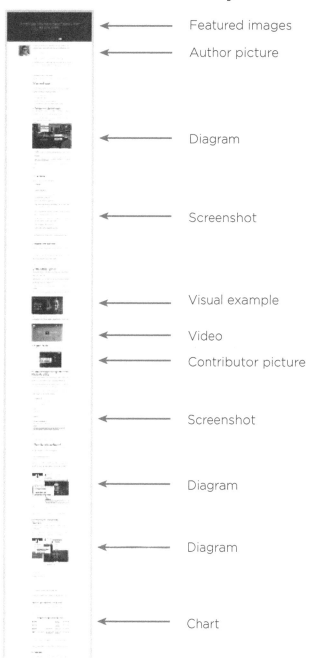

Featured images

Author picture

Diagram

Screenshot

Visual example

Video

Contributor picture

Screenshot

Diagram

Diagram

Chart

We're not suggesting you cram in an irrelevant stock photo after every third paragraph, but there is research on text-to-image ratios. BuzzSumo analyzed one million articles and discovered a correlation: articles with one image every 75-100 words were shared roughly twice as often as articles with fewer images (Fig. 5.57).[10]

10. https://buzzsumo.com/blog/how-to-massively-boost-your-blog-traffic-with-these-5-awesome-image-stats/

The point is, posts with few images generally perform worse than posts with more. So if possible, avoid writing long stretches of written text without visuals. And above all, **never miss the chance to add a visual.**

2. Add charts and graphs

Whenever possible, visualize your data.

Charts, graphs and diagrams are unique among image formats because they contain so much data. An informative chart can be a compelling content asset all its own. One good graph can be enough to make a post engaging.

Bar charts and pie charts are easy to create. Any writer can use a spreadsheet to create a draft image that a designer can then beautify. Other types of charts are less common and more engaging, such as Bubble Charts (Fig. 5.58), Scatterplots (Fig. 5.59) and Flow Charts (Fig. 5.60).

Some charts are so compelling, you can stare at them, transfixed for long minutes. Add a sunburst diagram, a stream graph and some radar charts and your visitor will think you're a genius.

Diagrams are excellent additions to any post, usually by making complex ideas more accessible. They also communicate more quickly than text. Rather than simply telling you that your fingertip is 57 pixels wide, we can show you with a quick diagram (Fig. 5.61).

Although data visualizations are more work to create than other images, they can be used over and over. A single chart

Fig. 5.57

Articles with more images perform better in social media

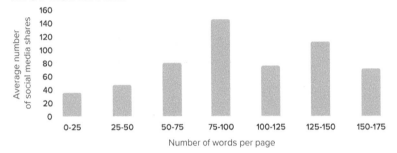

Fig. 5.58

Bubble Chart (Content Quality vs. Longevity)

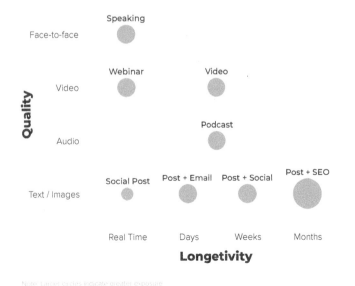

Scatterplot (Types of user research)

Fig. 5.59

Natural use (in context) | Out-of-context use | Scripted use (e.g., in lab)

Behavioral
what people do

Eyetracking | A/B testing | Website analytics (GA) | Sessions recordings (Hotjar)

Usability Lab Studies | Remote Usability Studies | Unmoderated UX Studies

Customer feedback | Focus groups and interviews | Intercept surveys | Card sorting | Email surveys

Attitudinal
what people say

Qualitative
why + how to fix

Quantitative
how many

Flow Chart (Data-driven decision making)

Fig. 5.60

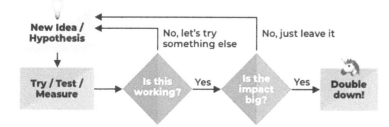

can find a home in multiple articles, presentations and even videos.

Once you've created a set of useful visuals, you can combine them into new articles. We did exactly that in our roundup *55 Diagrams That Explain Content Marketing*. It was one of our most successful posts that year.

Fig. 5.61

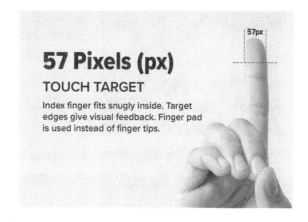

57 Pixels (px)
TOUCH TARGET

Index finger fits snugly inside. Target edges give visual feedback. Finger pad is used instead of finger tips.

When contributing to content on other websites, include a supportive chart. This gives you an additional opportunity to send authority back to your site in the "image source" link. These links are a best practice and great for your site's Domain Authority.

3. Put people pictures on every post

Faces are the other very special type of image. They have a unique magnetic power, unlike any other visuals. From the time we are infants, we have a tendency to gaze at faces.[11] In fact, babies are more likely to look at shapes that resemble faces, even if they're not an actual face (Fig. 5.62).

It is a hardwired visual preference. A cognitive bias built into all of us. Images of faces have a powerful way of grabbing and holding our attention. It's no surprise that the world's most popular social network has the word "face" in the name.

PRO TIP: If you don't have pictures of people in your website's "About" section, add some immediately. Regardless of what industry you're in, it helps to be a person. Humanize your site by adding pictures of your team.

Faces create another subtle marketing opportunity. You can direct the viewer's attention toward specific elements, such as calls to action. Eye tracking studies show that "you look where they look." If the eyes in the image are looking in a certain direction, the eyes of the viewer will be pulled in that same direction (Fig. 5.63).

The team at LinkedIn once shared the results of some A/B tests on images in social posts. In one test, they discovered a 160% increase in click through rates for posts with pictures of faces rather than pictures of objects (Fig. 5.64).

Fig. 5.62

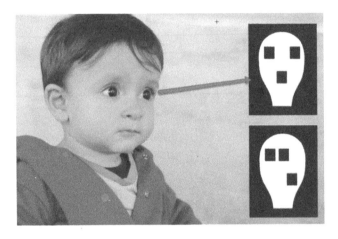

Fig. 5.63

Eyes looking at the camera...
Just 6% of 200 test subjects looked at the product.

Eyes looking at the product...
84% of test subjects looked at the product.

11. http://www.ncbi.nlm.nih.gov/pmc/articles/PMC2572680/

LinkedIn increased click through rates by 89% by using an image of a person looking at, rather than away from, the call to action (Fig. 5.65).

So add faces to your articles, starting with the **headshot of the author**. Use a blog template that puts the face with the name in the byline. Contributor quotes are another opportunity. Add **headshots of contributors** next to their quote, making the article more visually engaging. Usually, contributors like this. It's a boost to their personal brands. We'll review the other benefits of collaborative content in the next section.

Object vs. Face

Fig. 5.64

Control

+160% click through rate
+289% conversion rate

Looking away vs. Looking at the CTA

Fig. 5.65

Control

+89% click through rate

Fig. 5.66

4. Images containing quotes and headlines

Speaking of quotes, here is a type of blog image you can use when there are no charts or diagrams: the quote image. The idea is to simply turn the words into a picture. Take a juicy quote from the article and make it a visual piece of content (Fig. 5.66).

Tools like Canva make it easy to create these from templates. Upload your own background image or pick one from their huge library, pick your font, add your text and save. No need for software or help from a designer.

These visuals are catnip on social media. The team at LinkedIn found images with quotes and faces can have higher engagement than images with statistics (Fig. 5.67).

Images that contain the headline of the article are excellent social media content. The text adds a second opportunity to catch the reader's attention. These images may not appear within the article, but they're often created by social media teams to promote the article.

If the headline is long, the image-text may just be something shorter and simpler. Here's an example of an image that could be used to promote a blog post about blog images on social media. The big red Elmo catches the reader's attention; the text indicates the topic (Fig. 5.68).

Fig. 5.67

Statistic vs. Quote

Control

+30% click through rate

Fig. 5.68

5. Videos with compelling thumbnails

Videos are the ultimate visuals. Adding a video to an article can make it far more compelling, turning your reader into a viewer. On our blog, we've found that adding a video to a post can double the time on page for visitors who view it. They are also far more likely to subscribe (Fig. 5.69).

YouTubers often combine text and faces in the thumbnail images they add to their videos. The face catches the viewer's attention and the text gives them a reason to click. Add a brightly colored background and you have a formula for YouTube custom thumbnail images. Don't overdo it (Fig. 5.70).

Fig. 5.69

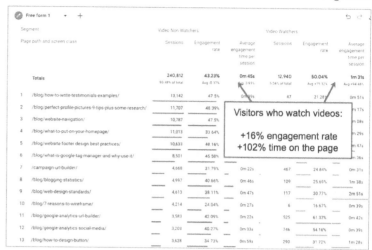

Visitors who watch videos:

+16% engagement rate
+102% time on the page

Fig. 5.70

How do I track social media in Google Analytics? These...
7K views · 10 months ago

How to set your strategy with a content marketing missio...
1.5K views · 1 year ago

How to Generate Website Leads with Conversion...
1K views · 1 year ago

Branded Keyphrase SEO: The 7 Actions for the Fastest Ki...
1.4K views · 1 year ago

The 5 Main Website Traffic Sources - What Are These...
2.5K views · 1 year ago

7 Tips for Writing Killer Headlines (plus, research o...
1.9K views · 1 year ago

Google Analytics website audit: How to use Google...
2.1K views · 1 year ago

Bounce Rates explained: What is a good bounce rate...
2.5K views · 1 year ago

How to Fix Your Website Navigation: 7 Tips on How t...
4.7K views · 1 year ago

How to Research Keywords for SEO: Understanding...
2K views · 1 year ago

How to Track Video Views in Google Analytics Using...
13K views · 2 years ago

How to write a blog post for SEO: The complete process...
9.9K views · 2 years ago

Link Reclamation - Link Building Tip with Andy...
499 views · 2 years ago

How to Set Up Subdomain Tracking in Google Analytics
25K views · 2 years ago

Influencer marketing for SEO
712 views · 2 years ago

Fig. 5.71

Videos embedded on your sales pages should use a professional hosting service and player such as Wistia or Vimeo. But videos embedded in blog posts can use YouTube. The views these videos get on your blog will jump-start the success of your YouTube channel.

Embedded YouTube videos on existing high-ranking articles are basically an automatically successful YouTube content strategy.

6. Infographics

Another highly engaging type of blog image is the infographic.

They are really designed to stand on their own, without any supportive text. So when they appear in blog posts, they often get just a short introduction. But it's far better to surround them with a detailed, informative (and keyword-focused) article.

Infographics shouldn't be overloaded with data or too heavy on design. As with any chart or diagram, the idea is to communicate quickly and clearly.

Infographics are popular in link-building campaigns. SEOs often combine research and infographics when pitching to editors. It usually sounds something like this:

"We conducted some new research and summarized it in this infographic. Would your readers like this? If so, I'd be happy to write a short guest post for you."

The submitted post would include the infographic and, of course, a link back to the SEO's website.

7. Illustrations

Rather than spending hours scouring the web for free images, or struggling with software that isn't part of your skill set, try this crazy idea: **pick up a pencil and draw**.

In minutes, you'll have something original that supports your message. No art degree is required. This is exactly what Henneke Duistermaat does on her blog, *Enchanting Marketing*, and it's wonderful (Fig. 5.71).

All you need are some art supplies and a little bravery.

8. Use consistent images that align with your brand

If you establish your own style, readers will come to recognize it. It also answers a lot of design questions in advance, speeding up the process of making images. You'll have consistent standards for layout, fonts and colors.

Copybloger

Headline overlaid on the right side of the image.

Fig. 5.72

Content Marketing Institute

Orange color, simple illustrations, logo in the bottom left.

Digital Telepathy

Large, colorful header image with center-aligned text on top.

Set standards and follow them. This makes anyone a better designer.

Fig. 5.72 shows examples of how some blogs have created standards for their blog post images:

Here at Orbit, we created a simple style guide that lists the typefaces and colors of our brand.[12] We refer back to this document whenever we reach for a color or a font, and we share it when we collaborate with outside contributors.

9. Size the images to fit in social media

What's the right size for blog images? What are the exact pixel dimensions ideal for Facebook, Instagram or X (formerly Twitter)? There are dozens of articles that detail image sizes for social media networks.

Ignore them.

12. https://www.orbitmedia.com/style-guide

The size doesn't matter. It's the shape of the image that counts. All of the social networks automatically resize photos for their social streams. As long as the image is roughly twice as wide as it is tall, it will look fine on every social network.

If it's taller than it is wide, the social network may cut off the top and bottom. The width-to-height ratio is called the "aspect ratio." Images that are wide are called "landscape," and images that are tall are called "portrait." Give your blog images a landscape aspect ratio, or at least be sure that the focus of the image is centered vertically (Fig. 5.73).

Make your blog images the full width of your blog's content area (usually 800 or 1,000 pixels wide) *and half as tall*. That's really all you need to know about image sizes.

Fig. 5.73

10. Animated GIFs

Be careful using animations. Movement is so effective at capturing attention that it can be overpowering, making the content around the animation hard to consume. There is a fine line between engaging and annoying.

11. Memes

If your content strategy allows for a whimsical tone, then memes may fit well into your blog posts.

These are easy to create using a tool such as Canva. Just upload the picture of your choice or choose one from their catalog, then type in the text. It takes minutes at most to create blog images like Fig. 5.74.

Fig. 5.74

12. Stock photos

No one loves stock images. But they're far better than no image at all. The problem with stock photos (especially stock photos of people) is that they're inauthentic and it's obvious. Avoid stock photos of people if at all possible.

Vince Vaughn and the producers of the movie *Unfinished Business* have very graciously offered some nice stock photos at no charge (Fig. 5.75).

Fig. 5.75

13. AI-generated images

There are many AI tools that generate images from a simple prompt. OpenAI's DALL-E is one example and a very convenient one because you can use it right from the ChatGPT interface.

It takes seconds to have striking and very detailed images generated. Although you can use additional prompts to refine an image, it's difficult to control. That makes it good for blog post images and social media content, but otherwise limited.

Also, it's often obvious when an image was generated by an AI. AI-generated images can be extremely vivid and detailed (Fig 5.76). What human would paint like this?

Fig. 5.76

Keep in mind that images generated by AI cannot be copyrighted in the United States. As with many of the legal issues related to AI, the details of this aspect of copyright law are evolving and often unclear.

Speaking of copyright law…

14. Image rights, licenses and lawsuits

As a content creator, you should have a strong appreciation for creators' rights. And it's always good to avoid legal trouble. It's easy if you know where to look for images. Search tools at all the major photo sites allow you to filter for royalty-free images or images covered by the Creative Commons license.

Google Images' search tool now includes filters for usage rights. Turn them on before searching for pictures of puppies (Fig. 5.77).

You don't want to fall in love with a pooch, then find out you can't take him home!

TIP! If you can find the photographer, reach out, ask permission and offer to credit them as the source. If they agree, you officially have their permission . . . and they'll likely share the post once it's live. Researching photos is an opportunity to build your network and make new friends.

Seriously, don't even think about using an image that isn't Creative Commons. Companies build robots that do nothing but scan the web for images used without permission. PicScout, owned by Getty Images, is one such company.

If their scans find an image used without license on your website, a robot lawyer sends you a "Settlement Demand Letter" . . . and a bill. Depending on

Fig. 5.77

the image, it could be for hundreds of thousands of dollars. Great blog posts start conversations with prospects, not with lawyers.

What you'll need to create great blog images

Selecting and preparing images is a huge part of content marketing. You'll need basic image skills:

- Cropping, resizing and optimizing images

- Applying basic filters and effects (levels, contrast, auto-enhance)

- Adding text and basic typography

- Grabbing screenshots, either with the native feature on your computer (command + shift + 4 on Mac or the "print screen" on the PC) or with Snagit

You'll also need a few tools:

- Photo editing: Pixelmator, Canva, Paint.net, Sketch, Adobe Photoshop

- Screen capture: Snagit

- Screen recording for video: Camtasia, ScreenFlow

- Diagrams and flowcharts: OmniGraffle, Visio, Google Drawings

A great content marketer has basic image editing skills. The ability to crop, resize and optimize images is the necessary minimum. Adding large, uncompressed images to your content can slow load time, hurt the visitor's experience and may even negatively impact search rankings.

Website design and blog writing? Or website writing and blog design?

Visitors to sales pages often have strong intent. They're reading the text closely and getting ready to make a decision. **The writing is the critical element.**

Visitors to blog posts often have weak intent. They're browsing around, looking for advice. They're more easily distracted. **The visuals are the critical element.**

But ironically, we are more likely to say that websites are "designed" and blogs are "written." It should really be the opposite, right?

Investing time, effort and potentially money into blog images is well worth it. On our blog, we put as much time into the visuals as the text. We once tracked the time that went into a typical article and showed the breakdown in a chart (Fig. 5.78).

Fig. 5.78

Time breakdown for the creation of a longform blog post
Total Time: 7 hours, 35 minutes

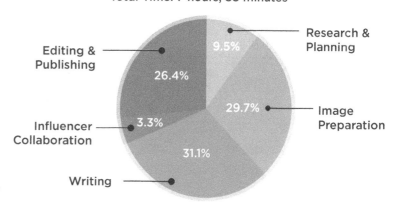

- Research & Planning — 9.5%
- Image Preparation — 29.7%
- Writing — 31.1%
- Influencer Collaboration — 3.3%
- Editing & Publishing — 26.4%

5.8 Collaboration

For a lot of content marketers, the creation process is a solo endeavor. As you read this, there are thousands of bloggers sitting alone in home offices, fingers on the keyboard, tapping out 500-word blog posts in 14-point Arial font. Another day, another post.

For others, it's a team effort of writers and editors—but the team is inside a business, talking mostly to themselves, with little or no input from outside contributors.

In both cases, the marketers are missing an opportunity to collaborate with outside experts on the process of content creation. Adding contributor quotes, curating roundups and interviewing influencers has huge marketing benefits.

- **They make your content better**
  Expert contributions make your content stronger, helping with the research and adding new insights. Their wisdom, expertise and insights are gold. A few nuggets can add serious value to your piece. It's also a fresh voice that breaks up that monotonous thing you were about to publish.

- **They add credibility**
  A reputable source supports your message. And if the contributor is someone readers know and trust, you benefit from the "halo effect," a powerful cognitive bias. Their trust in the contributor transfers into trust in your content.

- **They make your content more visual**
  The pictures of contributors' faces humanize the article and keep visitors engaged, as we discussed in the previous section.

- **They can help drive social traffic**
  Your contributors have an audience too. And since they contributed to your piece, they're invested in it and they are more likely to share it. The technical term for adding contributors with large social followings is "ego bait." But it's better to think of it as having a new ally in the job of content promotion.

- **They can improve your rankings**
  In Chapter 3, we explained how relationships with content creators are a key component in attracting links and growing your website's Domain Authority. Great content marketers build and nurture relationships with influencers (Fig. 5.79).

An ally in **creation** is an ally in **promotion**.

The Traffic Benefits of Collaborative Content Marketing

Fig. 5.79

CONTENT MARKETER

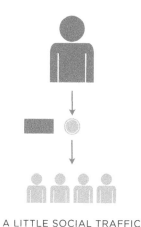

A LITTLE SOCIAL TRAFFIC

COLLABORATIVE CONTENT MARKETER

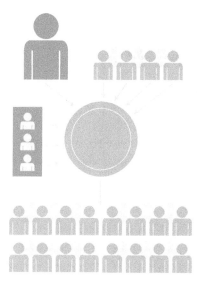

A LOT OF SOCIAL TRAFFIC!

A blog post isn't optimized for social media unless there are people in it.

- **They make marketing more fun**
  And that's important. Maybe the job hazards in this business don't involve forklift accidents. But there is a real risk of burnout. It is a lot of work to create high-quality content consistently, to promote it relentlessly. Anything that adds a social element is a good thing. Working with others keeps it interesting. That's what friends are for.

It doesn't have to be expensive or time-consuming. In fact, "organic influencer marketing" (which is really just collaborative co-creation of content) is actually free and easy. You just need to invite friends, influencers and allies into your content creation process. This may quickly become your favorite part of the job.

Now that we know the secret to better content, more traffic and loving our jobs, let's jump into the practical details. In Section 6.5, we'll share a detailed approach to networking and co-promotion. Here we'll break down five ways to collaborate on content creation, from the simple and quick to the full-on partnership.

> **You're a journalist. Contributors are your sources.** If you can, add a contributor quote to every article. Make it one of your editorial guidelines.

1. The "quote and mention"

This first tactic is less about co-creation and more about ego bait. It's very simple. While writing an article, add a quote that was previously written or said by an expert. The quote should strengthen the writing, adding insight or evidence.

When you publish the piece, send a quick message on social media or possibly an email to let that expert know that you quoted them. Or just tag them when you share the article on social media. This will likely appear for them as a notification. Your hope is that they reshare it with their followers.

The problem with this approach is that since they weren't expecting to be mentioned, they aren't really invested in the content, so they aren't that likely to invest much effort in sharing it.

2. The contributor quote

This is a fast, friendly way to upgrade your content. It's one of my favorite tactics in all of content marketing. As you write, watch for weak spots. Where did you make a claim that needs support? Where is your article boring? These are where the quotes go.

Next, reach out to an expert and ask nicely for a contributor quote. It might be someone who is already in your network. That's easy.

Here is what a contributor quote should look like (Fig. 5.80):

- **Headshot:** It really brightens up the place.

- **Name, title, company:** This is helpful in adding expertise and trust.

- **Link:** Make the company name link back to their website. Or offer to link to something specific, such as a service page or specific article. It gives them more value for their effort.

Fig. 5.80

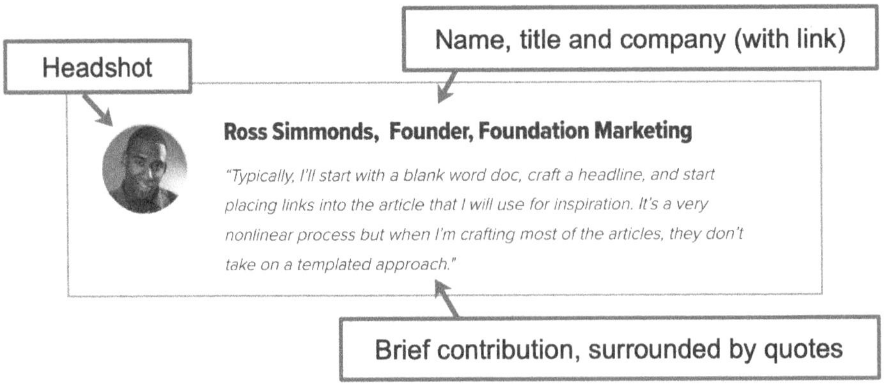

Headshot

Name, title and company (with link)

Ross Simmonds, Founder, Foundation Marketing

"Typically, I'll start with a blank word doc, craft a headline, and start placing links into the article that I will use for inspiration. It's a very nonlinear process but when I'm crafting most of the articles, they don't take on a templated approach."

Brief contribution, surrounded by quotes

- **Short blurb with insights:** Try to keep it down to five lines or less, if possible. Make sure to put everything within quotation marks.

The quotation marks are important. Anything that appears within quote marks instantly sounds different. Rather than the voice of the author or brand, it's a third-party, and another point of view.

3. The expert roundup

Roundups are a popular format for a good reason. They hit all three notes of quality, traffic and networking. They're scannable like a list post, and they're filled with ego bait. But there are two very different approaches:

- **Panel of experts**
  A small group of experts answering a short set of questions on a common topic. The reader can see different but related points of view. The experts might agree; they might not. Since each expert is answering

several questions, the reader goes deeper.

- **The mega roundup**
  Many people answering the same short question. Sometimes dozens or even a hundred contributors, each sharing a short blurb.

As a reader, I'm biased. I prefer the expert panel. Those mega roundups are sometimes so long it's too much. I just scan through looking for familiar faces (Fig. 5.81).

The quality of the roundup depends on the contributions and the curator's ability to organize and add value. Here are ways to do better roundups:

- **Ask great questions.** Ask questions that others are unwilling to ask or that elicit a personal story.

- **Use true experts.** A lot of "experts" give advice so common it's boring.

Fig. 5.81

108 EXPERTS GIVE ADVICE TO NEW BLOGGERS

Fig. 5.82

- **Edit the contributions.** If your contributor sends you a great insight but they start with 50 words of general "throat clearing" language, cut it out and get to the point.

- **Add your own insights.** If you have a lot of contributions, organize them into groups and add a paragraph summary with your input.

4. The deep dive interview

An interview is the opposite of the roundup. Rather than a little bit of info from a lot of contributors, it's a lot of insights from just one.

Most podcasts and webinars are based on this format. So are TV talk shows and many live events. If you get the right expert, you'll want to squeeze every drop of wisdom out of them. Here are tips for better interviews:

- **Do your research up front.** Are they a writer? Read their latest writing. Are they a podcaster? Give a listen. Be ready to jump into their passions. And if appropriate,

congratulate them on something in their personal life.

- **Be quiet.** It's about them, not you. The interviewee should be doing 95% of the talking or writing.

- **Ask follow-up questions.** Q&A isn't always a conversation. Real dialog means you listened to their answers and let things flow from there. Even if it's an email interview, you can send them a question first, get an answer in reply, then send *a follow-up question based on their answer.*

Example: Every month in the Orbit offices, we host a teaching event called Wine & Web. Each year, the last event is me interviewing Gini Dietrich in front of a digital fireplace (Fig. 5.82). It's an hour-long deep dive interview where she shares insights, stories and advice about PR and communications.

5. The guest post

Every guest blog post is a collaboration, almost like a transaction. The guest brings the content and the blog brings the audience (Fig. 5.83).

Together, the contributing writer and the host blog editor agree on the topic, angle, format, length and images. Sometimes the conversation is very brief, but other times it spans weeks, with many emails and phone calls. Once the blog post is live, the collaboration continues as they both likely share and mention each other.

In Chapter 6, we'll go into the specific tactics for influencer marketing, co-promotion and guest blogging.

Zero-waste marketing: content for B2B marketers

Content marketers in business-to-business (B2B) industries have special opportunities in content marketing. It's a surefire way to get value from your content. It's so efficient we call it zero-waste marketing.

These tactics are especially relevant when there are multiple decision-makers, the sales process is long and strategic consultation is necessary. Professional services firms like lawyers, accountants and architects all meet this criteria.

But this isn't just for B2B companies. Whenever the product or service is complex, the sales process is an education process. The company that shares the most expertise has the best chance of winning the client. So content marketing is especially important (Fig. 5.84).

Fig. 5.83

Guest Blogging Collaboration: An Exchange of Value

	Guest blogger brings . . .	Host blog brings . . .
CONTENT	Quality content	Improved quality editing, headlines, images
VISIBILITY	Additional audience social promotion	Audience traffic & visibility

Is the psychology of sales in your industry transactional or consultative?

The goal is to combine sales with marketing in very time-efficient ways, bringing you closer to your prospects and new referral partners. You may quickly discover an opportunity to create laser-focused content and become a thought

Fig 5.84

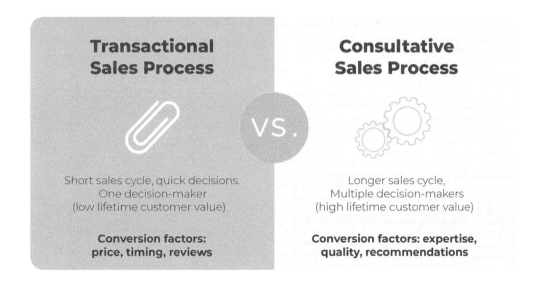

Transactional Sales Process

Short sales cycle, quick decisions.
One decision-maker
(low lifetime customer value)

**Conversion factors:
price, timing, reviews**

VS.

Consultative Sales Process

Longer sales cycle,
Multiple decision-makers
(high lifetime customer value)

**Conversion factors: expertise,
quality, recommendations**

Fig 5.85

YOU

TARGET AUDIENCE

POST AND PRAY

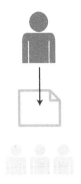

ZERO-WASTE MARKETING

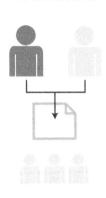

leader in the minds that matter most (Fig. 5.85).

Here are a few ways to get automatic value from your next article, even before it goes live.

Write specifically for your current prospects

Your next customer is your most important audience. Take a close look at the prospects currently in your pipeline. Do they have anything in common? What questions are they asking? What articles would support the sales conversations you're having? Find topics that are relevant to the leads you're already talking to.

- Write articles that answer the questions your prospects are asking (detailed how-to articles)

> This isn't content for marketing. **This is content for sales support.**

- Write stories or examples that address their objections or concerns (case studies)

Spend a few hours writing an article or case study up. Spend another hour editing, adding images and formatting for web content best practices. Within a day or two, you'll be publishing a piece of laser-focused content. Now call the client and tell them you have something you'd like to share. Send it to them directly.

Example:

Your company does logistics management for the dairy industry. There are five companies considering hiring you. Three of them have big questions about how to accurately forecast demand for fresh milk across the supply chain. You're an expert at this. You've explained some of it to them, but it's not translating well to all the decision-makers.

You write a detailed 2,500-word article about how technology has changed forecasting for top dairy producers. The charts, statistics, research and examples are a clear demonstration of your expertise. You call each company personally and ask if they would be interested in taking a look . . .

Beyond improving your closing rate, you've captured two of the benefits of content:

- *You've created something portable.* You can send it to several people at each potential client. People at the client company may even share it with each other. Also, the sales associate on your team can send it to other clients, making your sales messages more consistent.

- *You've created something durable.* This article will live for months or years on your site. You can send it to prospects again and again. This is all in addition to any traction it gets through search, social and email marketing.

TIP! Use interviews to warm up cold leads. They were interested. You had a good first conversation, but then you never heard back. You left a message. Then another. Now months have passed. Instead of making another sales call, reach out with a bit of collaborative content in mind. If they have expertise relevant to your content and your audience, your next article is an opportunity to reconnect. But be authentic. Don't make a sales call in disguise.

Connect with new prospects through a series

Your best prospects check all the boxes: they understand your value proposition, they can afford you, they get huge value from your products or services and they're great to work with. Your business would be more successful if you could connect with more of these companies and people.

Content is actually a great way to connect with those A-list companies. You can interview them for a post or reach out for a contributor quote, but you've got a better chance if you go big. Create a new series of content that puts them

in the spotlight and puts you in front of them.

If you really want to connect with (and impress) your next prospects, upgrade the format beyond text.

- Create a podcast interview series

- Create a video series that features them

- Create an event that puts them on a stage

This works especially well for production companies, because the content itself showcases their talents.

Example:

Echelon Design offers high-end exhibit design and video production. To meet local businesses and show off their skills at the same time, they created a series of videos called 12 for 12. Each episode is a beautiful little short, spotlighting a brand with a tour of a business and an interview with the founder.

These are all brands that Echelon wanted to meet, and the offer to be featured on the show opened the door. Those doors included Goose Island, Vosges Chocolate, Intelligentsia Coffee and Second City. Content started the conversation and created a new relationship that otherwise would have never existed.

Your blog is your **best networking tool**.

Collaborate with your referral partners

About once a month, someone says to me *"Andy, we don't need marketing. We get all of our leads from referrals."* Of course, that's a crazy thing to say because marketing would *add* to their flow of leads, but let's set that aside for now. Even if your plan is to rely completely on referrals from others, content marketing can still increase leads by strengthening those referral relationships.

> Every blogger writes articles. Great bloggers write series of **interconnected articles.**

People refer you to prospects because they met someone who needs your help . . . and they thought of you. So the key is to stay top of mind. Content can help.

Think about your friendly neighborhood referral partner. What do they know a lot about? What content could showcase their expertise on this topic? Got an idea for an article? As you write it, reach out and ask for a quote. Add their face, name, company and link.

Example:

Your company offers sales training. You sometimes get leads from HR directors, so one of your goals is to build deeper relationships with HR directors in your network. They know a lot about culture and retention, so you decide to write an article on this topic in collaboration with a few potential referral partners.

"I'm writing an article about how culture affects retention. I'm including input from several experts in this area. I'm hoping you would be open to being interviewed for this article. Would you be willing to answer a few questions?"

Showcasing their expertise puts you in front of the partner, strengthens the relationship and may even be seen as an act of gratitude. Once the article is live, send them a nice note thanking them for their contribution. Handwritten notes are best.

Use interviews to make connections with new potential referral partners

Beyond your current network of referral partners, content can help create new partnerships. Just find people in noncompeting businesses who work directly with your target audience and include them in your next article.

Example:

You're an architect in Kansas City. You specialize in designing healthcare facilities. If you had more relationships with interior designers, you would likely get more referrals. So you search LinkedIn for "interior design" people in the healthcare industry or near Kansas City. There are dozens (Fig. 5.86).

Note: You don't need to be active on social media to use this approach. If you are, it's a useful place to make the first contact. But it's not necessary to be active on social media to use it as a research tool.

Now we reach out to each of these people and companies. You can use email, their website contact forms or

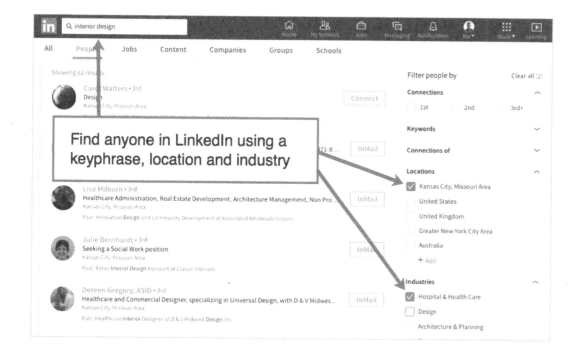

Fig. 5.86

Find anyone in LinkedIn using a keyphrase, location and industry

the phone. Our goal is to build a close relationship, so the phone is always best. Once we connect, ask them if they would like to be interviewed for an article you're writing about interior design trends. You're hoping to feature their expertise and share their insights with your audience.

Once it's live, share the article on LinkedIn and mention them in the post (Fig. 5.87).

Finally, keep the conversation going. Let them know about your services, tell them how you help people and suggest that they keep you in mind.

When networking is the goal and collaboration is the strategy, success is automatic. You get results even before you hit the publish button. In the end, sales is more important than marketing. A few strong relationships can have a far greater impact on your business than all the numbers in your GA4 account.

Fig. 5.87

When you post in LinkedIn, mention the contributors to help build the relationship.

Fig 5.88

Ideal length guidelines
for everything in your marketing

Blog posts (for ranking)	1,500 words
Email subject lines (for open rates)	50 characters or less
Line of text	12 words
Paragraph	4 lines or less
Title tags	60 characters (maximum)
Meta descriptions	155–160 characters
Social media posts (for likes and shares)	65 characters

Fig. 5.89

Content length
(segmented by search volume)

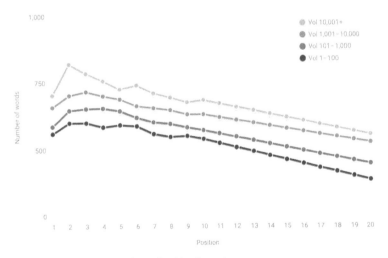

Source: https://www.semrush.com/ranking-factors/

5.9 A Few Words About Content Length

What is the ideal length for your content? "It depends" is not a helpful answer. Of course it depends. But there *are* rules of thumb. There is research and we can analyze what works and draw conclusions. We can create guidelines, especially for things that are measurable such as length.

Fig. 5.88 shows length guidelines for seven types of content. These have been compiled from studies that analyzed the high performers in each category.

Now that you've got the data, let's look at the research . . .

Ideal blog post length

Our focus here is on search rankings, and research shows the average length of high-ranking pages. When Semrush analyzed high-ranking pages, it found more text correlates with high rankings, especially for the popular, high-volume keyphrases (Fig. 5.89).

Think about it this way: Google is a research tool. Longer pages are more likely to include an answer to the question and more likely to be a great page on the topic. More text means more opportunities to indicate relevance.

Another reason is links. When Moz analyzed 3,800 posts on its own blog, it found that the longer posts are more likely to attract links from other websites. If your goal is search engine traffic, longer is better.

The ideal length for a search-optimized blog post is 1,500 words.

⚠ WARNING! Readers appreciate concise writing and tight editing. Don't fluff up an 800-word article to get to 1,000 words. Write a 1,500-word article with lots of details and answers, then edit it down to 1,000 words.

Of course, blog posts vary in length from a few short paragraphs (Seth Godin style) to 10,000+ words (Neil Patel style). But the trend is to write longer articles. The average blog post is more than 1,400 words (Fig. 5.90).

Blogs are still getting longer   Fig. 5.90

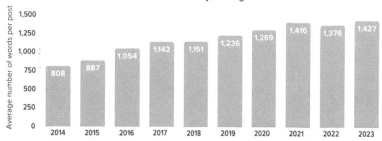

The average blog post is 77% longer than it was 10 years ago

Source: https://www.orbitmedia.com/blog/blogging-statistics/

Ideal length for an email subject line

Surprisingly, the length of an email subject line doesn't have a big impact on open and click through rates. According to a study by MailChimp, shorter subject lines perform only slightly better (Fig. 5.91).

Subject line character count vs. open rate   Fig. 5.91

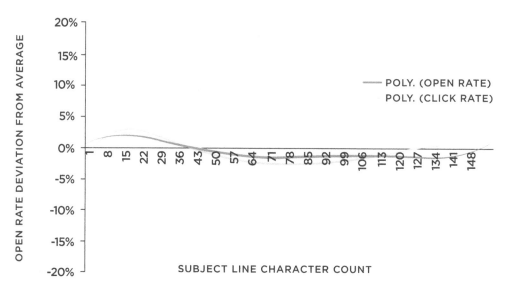

Source: https://blog.mailchimp.com/this-just-in-subject-line-length-means-absolutelynothing/

"**Short paragraphs get read**, long paragraphs get skimmed, really long paragraphs get skipped."

JASON FRIED, *Founder, Basecamp*

Even if the benefits are in the single digits, most experts would say shorter is better. And there is research that suggests shorter subject lines get better open rates. Especially for mobile recipients— longer subject lines get truncated when viewed on a phone. Remember the tip about writing headlines: put the most important words at the front, in the first five words.

The ideal email subject line is 50 characters or less.

Ideal line length

It's all in the biology of the human eye. According to the Web Style Guide (www.webstyleguide.com/), the field of vision for readers is only a few inches. For readers on laptops, if a line of text is too long, they need to use more muscles in the eye and neck. It takes more work

to travel all the way across a long line of text, back and forth, over and over. Readers are more likely to lose their place. This slows reading rates and comprehension.

The length of a line of text is typically determined during the web design process. It's a question of font size and column width. If you want to change it, talk to your web designer.

The ideal length for a line of text is 12 words.

Ideal paragraph length

When you open a book, you expect to hit a wall of text. But books don't have back buttons, so in that format, we aren't as concerned about holding their attention. But in digital, long paragraphs are a problem.

Website visitors are scanning. Short paragraphs give them meaning in short bursts. Visitors often scan down the page, glancing at headers and subheaders, then dive deeper into the paragraphs if something catches their interest.

Designers know that visitors love white space, but somehow, writers didn't get the message. Don't write walls of text. Break up paragraphs to create white space on the page.

The ideal length for a paragraph is 3 to 4 lines maximum.

Ideal length for a title tag

Besides the blog post itself, there are a few other parts of the page that affect SEO. The most important of these is the title tag. Why is it so important? The title tag typically becomes the link when the page ranks in Google (Fig. 5.92).

If the title tag is too long, it gets truncated, and people won't be able to read it all. Guidelines fluctuate slightly over time because of design changes of Google's search results pages. Sometimes the width of search results is a bit wider, sometimes a bit shorter. The cutoff point is always between 55 and 65 characters.

So use the target keyphrase once and keep it short. See Orbit's SEO Best Practices for more info: www.orbitmedia.com/blog/seo-best-practices/

The ideal length for a title tag is 60 characters.

Ideal length for meta description

As with the title tag, the meta description is visible in search results, and it gets truncated if it's too long. The cutoff point here is typically 160 characters. Keep it under 155 to be safe. Your meta description should be a single sentence in plain English, summarizing the content of the page. Use the target keyphrase once and don't make it too long (Fig. 5.93).

The ideal length for a meta description is 155 characters.

Title tags and meta descriptions are managed from within content management systems. For WordPress, there is a very popular and free plugin

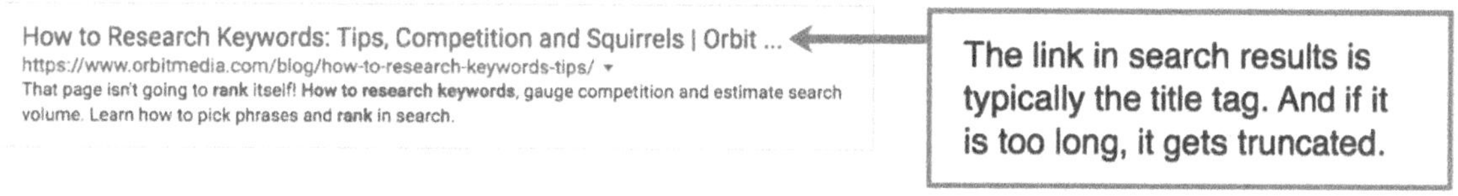

How to Research Keywords: Tips, Competition and Squirrels | Orbit ...
https://www.orbitmedia.com/blog/how-to-research-keywords-tips/ ▾
That page isn't going to **rank** itself! **How to research keywords**, gauge competition and estimate search volume. Learn how to pick phrases and **rank** in search.

The link in search results is typically the title tag. And if it is too long, it gets truncated.

Fig. 5.92

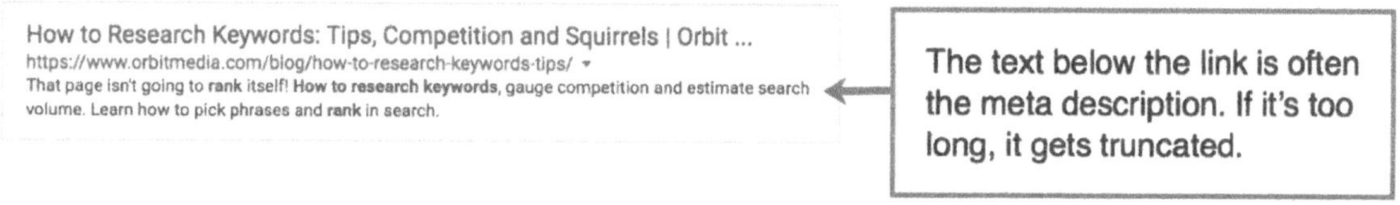

How to Research Keywords: Tips, Competition and Squirrels | Orbit ...
https://www.orbitmedia.com/blog/how-to-research-keywords-tips/ ▾
That page isn't going to **rank** itself! **How to research keywords**, gauge competition and estimate search volume. Learn how to pick phrases and **rank** in search.

The text below the link is often the meta description. If it's too long, it gets truncated.

Fig. 5.93

Fig. 5.94

called Yoast that lets you preview what the search results might look like if the page ranks. As you enter your title tag and meta description, it shows you how long is too long for search (Fig. 5.94).

Ideal length of headlines for social media engagement

For social posts on Facebook or X (formerly Twitter), length has a strong correlation with engagement and shares. According to the research we cited earlier in the headlines section, social media posts with 11 words (65 characters to be exact) generated the most engagement (Fig. 5.95).

The ideal length for a headline on Facebook and X (formerly Twitter) is 65 characters.

Fig. 5.95

Optimum headline character count on Facebook & Twitter: 2019/2020

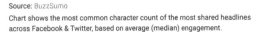

Source: BuzzSumo

Chart shows the most common character count of the most shared headlines across Facebook & Twitter, based on average (median) engagement.

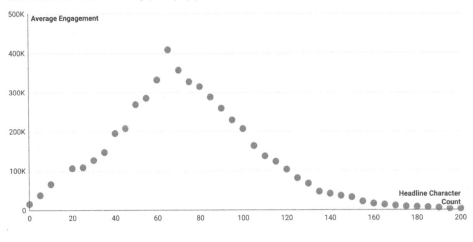

● Powered by **BuzzSumo**   **BuzzSumo Research**

The ultimate rule for content length

These are guidelines, not rules. Making your content longer or shorter doesn't guarantee failure. Making it exactly these lengths doesn't guarantee success.

Inspired? Explaining a complex idea? Giving detailed instructions? Pay no attention to length. Just keep writing in clear, concise language until you're done. Use short paragraphs, short sentences and short words. But don't worry about writing short articles.

There's really only one hard-and-fast rule for content length and it goes like this: *Every piece of content should be as long as it takes to convey the message, and not a word longer.*

5.10 Building Interconnected Hubs of Content

Competition for attention online is fierce. But take a moment to think about the nature of that competition. Competition is specific to topics. In Google, in social media, and in the minds of your audience, the battle for attention is fought topic by topic.

Some categories and topics, like HDTVs and mattress reviews, are insanely competitive. They're crowded with famous blogs and big companies that have invested in content marketing for years. *They're impossible.*

Other topics, such as hedgehog tricks and telescope repair, are much less so. A smaller website can win attention, but it may be such a narrow niche that it's hard to generate enough traffic, leads and sales to thrive. *They're useless.*

So how can you compete and win against the big players for more valuable topics?

No matter the arena, the winner is winning because they have a large body of high-quality, interconnected content, focused on their specific topic, with a body of work that covers all of the related subtopics. They are totally focused on satisfying a narrow range of information needs of their specific audience.

This is how a brand becomes relevant in search engines, in social media and in email inboxes. This is how brands eventually become top of mind with an audience.

To beat the established players, you need to be focused and structured, building up a body of work around a specific topic. You need to build a hub of content.

> **DON'T**: Build a pile of medium-quality blog posts that all say similar things.

> **DO**: Create a well-organized hub of diverse assets, in many formats, in many places, created by various people (Fig. 5.96).

Fig. 5.96

Threshold for being top-of-mind (and visible in search rankings)

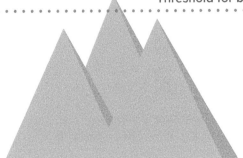

Big central hub supported by a
strong base of related content

Scattered, unconnected articles

When a brand stays focused on a topic, it's as if the content builds up, reaching higher above the competition and gaining greater visibility. Like a mountain, with a central peak surrounded by a wide base of subtopics.

But many marketers just aren't that focused. They publish a bit here and a bit there, deciding what to write based on whim, not publishing a strong central piece, not staying on a topic for long and not connecting content in strategic ways. They create small hills that never rise high enough to be visible.

Why content hubs are so powerful

Visitors might never notice the structure of what you've built, but it doesn't matter. This content strategy helps you in all the most important ways.

Search benefits

Ever seen a little website outrank a big brand? It is possible and happens often. Usually, it's because the big brand was

ranking by accident. They have a page that's relevant and a domain that's authoritative. But the smaller player wins because they have built up a set of highly focused, interconnected pages.

If you've been blogging for a long time, but you're not getting much search traffic, this may be the problem. You're not deliberately creating sets of content organized around central topics.

Social benefits

Your social stream is a curated list of posts. If this stream has a specific focus, you'll gradually win followers and earn attention from people who share that interest. Your followings and influence will grow. You'll also build relationships and friendships with relevant influencers, creating more opportunities to collaborate.

Email marketing benefits

The center of the hub may feature some high-value gated content. Visitors may be willing to share an email address to access this "content upgrade" or "lead magnet." Or you may trigger a pop-up offer to subscribe on the third article that visitors read. There are lots of opportunities to capture addresses once visitors are inside the hub.

Engaged visitors

When a visitor comes to learn about a topic, one page may not be enough to satisfy them. But if they find themselves within a larger hub they'll likely dig deeper. This increases the average pages per visit and average time on site.

Give them more, and you'll keep them longer. You've also got a better chance of being top of mind when people think of the topic. Eventually, when people ask, "What was that site that had all that great information on this topic?" they'll think of you and come back.

Dimensions of a content hub

A content hub (Fig. 5.97) is a set of content organized around a specific topic and a central page. That page is typically a very detailed article or a sales page promoting a product or service. In either case, the central piece is search optimized and targets a relatively competitive phrase. Sometimes it's designed to capture email addresses through gated content.

These pages are sometimes called **"pillar pages"** or **"cornerstone content."** It's all the same idea.

CONTENT HUB STRUCTURE   Fig. 5.97

A. TOPICS

CENTRAL HUB
Main topic, most competitive keyphrase

RELATED SUBTOPIC
Answers to the main questions, "how to"

SUPPORTIVE BASE
Helpful info on broader range of related topics

B. KEYWORDS

CENTRAL HUB
Main topic, most competitive keyphrase

RELATED SUBTOPIC
Answers to the main questions, "how to"

SUPPORTIVE BASE
Helpful info on broader range of related topics

C. FORMAT

TEXT
Search-friendly pages, longform posts, articles

VISUAL CONTENT
Text plus infographics, diagrams and memes

MOTION & AUDIO
Text plus video and podcasts

D. LOCATION

ON YOUR SITE

ON OTHER SITES

E. CREATOR

CREATED BY YOU

CO-CREATED WITH INFLUENCERS

The central piece is surrounded by articles that support that piece in multiple ways. Each of which is a content marketing strategy covered elsewhere in this book. Here you are simply combining the various approaches in a structured, organized way.

A. **Content on interrelated topics:** The posts or pages support each other, inviting the visitor to dig deeper through internal links, like a mini-version of Wikipedia. This triggers longer visits and gently guides visitors toward the center.

B. **Content targeting related phrases:** The center of the hub targets the broadest, most popular, most competitive keyphrase. It is supported by many pages that target more-specific, related phrases, forming a large set of internally linked keyphrase-focused pages.

C. **Content in different formats:** The structure includes many formats from the Periodic Table of Content. It goes beyond blog posts and includes infographics, guides, video, original research or even audio.

D. **Content on other websites:** Not all of the content is on your website. Some of the articles are bylined articles and guest posts, published on other websites. Others may be published on other platforms, such as YouTube and LinkedIn.

E. **Content created together with influencers:** The content isn't created in isolation. It is collaborative, co-created with relevant influencers

and media partners. These may be bloggers, journalists and other people who have already built an audience that you'd like to reach.

TIP! A blog category is often closely related to a content hub. However, it doesn't include the off-site publishing and often lacks other formats and collaboration. Still, if you're building a hub of content, aligning it with a category on your blog is a good idea.

How to build a content hub

Our goal is to be focused, structured and organized around a central hub. This requires forethought, planning and persistence. Some content strategists build a hub each quarter and plan the rollout using a publishing calendar. Depending on the topic, this process may take much longer.

1. Pick a topic that's valuable to you and important to your audience.

Think about the questions your content can answer, the problems your business solves and the phrases your audience is likely to search for. Make a list of these questions, answers and keywords. They should be closely related.

2. Check the competition for the main phrases.

Check your own Domain Authority and use MozBar to see the Domain Authority of the high-ranking sites for your main topics and keywords. Normally, you'd need an authority in the high end of the range of the other high-ranking sites for the phrases you're targeting. But since we're building an entire hub of content, we have a chance of eventually winning for the more difficult phrases.

3. Connect with and collaborate with relevant influencers.

Time to network, then leverage that network. Build a list of potential collaborators and work to slowly win their attention and respect. Join groups, go to events and comment on blogs. Use the Online Networking Guide in Section 6.6, and when the time is right, reach out and ask if they'd like to contribute to your content project.

4. Publish the central hub.

It's time to go big. Create a piece of content that you sincerely believe to be the best page on the internet for the topic. Make it detailed and comprehensive, practical and visual. Original research is a great way to anchor a content hub. All the content around it makes the link-worthy center more visible.

Optimize it for that keyphrase. Include contributor quotes from your collaborators. Give it a clear call to action. In other words, use all of the content best practices found in the article checklist at the end of this chapter.

5. Publish supportive content in various formats.

Next, start publishing on the related subtopics. Write articles that answer the related questions. Start publishing in various formats. Produce an infographic and video. Keep publishing, linking each piece back to the center. Whenever possible, use the target keyphrase of the central hub in the text of these links.

6. Publish on other websites.

Start pitching related posts to relevant blogs, trade publications, association sites and the local media. Write about the topic on Medium and LinkedIn. Answer related questions on Quora. These could be alternate versions of content you've published, repurposed and rewritten (see "Evil Twin" in Section 7.1). And always, link back to the hub.

7. Stay focused, watch your rankings and check Analytics.

As you keep building and promoting, you'll eventually see the growth in traffic and engagement. GA4 will show a slow, steady increase in search traffic, with small spikes of social, email and referral traffic each time something new is published.

If you're not winning, you're not done yet. Keep building. If you are winning, congratulations! You are now relevant. Build it up even higher or go start another content hub.

EXAMPLE: Speedy Bean, an office coffee delivery service

Here is an example of a content strategy for lead generation built around a central hub. We'll use a fictional B2B service company, Speedy Bean. But these concepts will translate to B2C lead generation programs as well. This approach is relevant for anyone in any business focused on search rankings and lead generation.

You'll see how this combines everything we've learned so far, starting with the sales page and content mission statement, then building an interconnected hub of well-promoted content.

1. The optimized sales page

Our main "Office Coffee Delivery Services" page is built to attract and convert qualified visitors. We want to attract and persuade people who need coffee delivered to their business. So this page is optimized in both ways, for search and for conversion.

Optimized to rank (SEO)

It targets a commercial-intent keyphrase for which it has some realistic chance of eventually ranking eventually, based on the Domain Authority of our site.

We'll put our domain into the Moz Link Explorer (Fig. 5.98).

Our Domain Authority is 16. So we should target phrases that are in that general range of difficulty. We are unlikely to rank if all of the other high-ranking sites for a given phrase have more authority than we do.

We'd like to rank for "office coffee delivery" so let's check the competition. We'll put the phrase into the Moz Keyword Explorer (Fig. 5.99).

It looks like it's a bit outside our range. To have a realistic chance of ranking for this phrase, we'll need to build a content strategy designed to attract links to our site and increase our authority. That's our plan!

Optimized to convert

If the conversion rate of this page is zero percent, it doesn't matter how much traffic we generate or how good we are at content. We'll never generate a lead.

Fig. 5.98

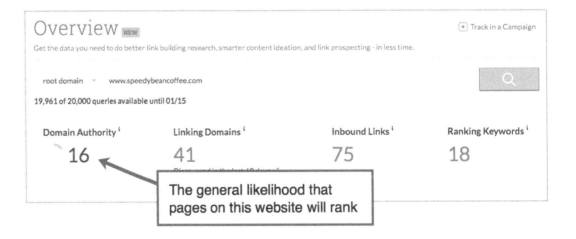

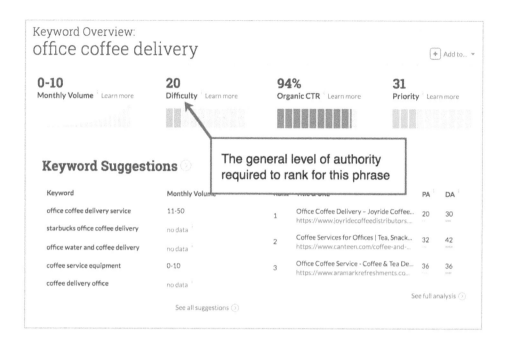

Fig. 5.99

Keyword Overview:
office coffee delivery

[+] Add to... ▾

0-10
Monthly Volume Learn more

20
Difficulty Learn more

94%
Organic CTR Learn more

31
Priority Learn more

The general level of authority required to rank for this phrase

Keyword Suggestions

Keyword	Monthly Volume
office coffee delivery service	11-50
starbucks office coffee delivery	no data
office water and coffee delivery	no data
coffee service equipment	0-10
coffee delivery office	no data

	Title & URL	PA	DA
1	Office Coffee Delivery – Joyride Coffee... https://www.joyridecoffeedistributors...	20	30
2	Coffee Services for Offices	Tea, Snack... https://www.canteen.com/coffee-and-...	32	42
3	Office Coffee Service - Coffee & Tea De... https://www.aramarkrefreshments.co...	36	36

See all suggestions ⊘

See full analysis ⊘

We'll make this a detailed page (which we need to do anyway if we hope to rank) by answering our visitors' top sales questions, addressing their main objections, supporting our marketing claims with evidence and adding clear, specific calls to action.

2. The content marketing mission

Next, we lay the cornerstone of our content marketing: the content mission statement. It declares three simple things:

- The target audience
- The topics to be published
- The benefits of the content to that audience

For our office coffee delivery company, we'll target a narrow audience but cover a wide range of topics and have a light tone. Here is a content mission statement for Speedy Bean's content marketing. Notice how this follows the basic template: audience + topics + benefit.

Where office managers find fun tips for the workplace to build happier, more productive teams.

Now that we've documented our mission, we've basically written our email sign-up calls to action. It's definitely an upgrade from the boring CTAs you'll find on our competitors' sites (Fig. 5.100).

Fig. 5.100

Signup CTA is a repurposed content marketing mission statement...

Get fun weekly workplace tips!
Because no one loves a boring office
email address Sign me up!

Signup CTA is boring, generic and ineffective...

Newsletter Signup
email address Submit

A high-converting email sign-up box will maximize the value of every visitor to the content, by maximizing the likelihood that they'll subscribe and allow us to contact them directly.

3. Original research at the center of the hub

We need to beat every other content program in our industry by being more relevant, useful and differentiated. That sounds hard, but it isn't if we publish original research. New research makes our website the primary source of new data. It's the most link-worthy content we could possibly create, which we'll need if we're going to grow our Domain Authority.

Here's my idea for original research for our office coffee delivery company:

What office perks are offered by the top workplaces in the world?

To conduct this study, we need a list of top workplaces. That's easy to find with a few quick searches. Next, we'll need to reach out to office managers and HR folks at each of these companies and do a quick phone interview. That'll take some time, but that time is worth the effort.

We can start these conversations on social media. The research, outreach and social connections are good anyway because they're our target audience. This social media activity will make future influencer marketing easier. It may even be good for sales if the companies are in our delivery area.

5. Upgrade to visual formats

Every successful content strategy has a foundation of well-written articles (text) and we'll definitely support this strategy with blogging. But the most successful content strategies also use visual formats regularly (images and video) so we'll be sure to upgrade our most successful posts.

Suppose we wrote an article about the amazing benefits of whole bean coffee, a topic that fits squarely within our content strategy. If this topic is successful, it's a candidate for repurposing as a visual. Fig. 5.101 shows what it might look like as an infographic.

6. Collaborate with influencers

To make our link-worthy research visible to other content creators, we're going to include them in the process. A bit of research on social media will help us find people who are relevant (HR pros and office managers) who are also content creators (bloggers and editors).

A paid influencer marketing tool, such as Onalytica or BuzzSumo, makes this simple. You can sort the potential collaborators by the size of their social followings or the Domain Authority of sites they write for (Fig. 5.102).

Fig. 5.101

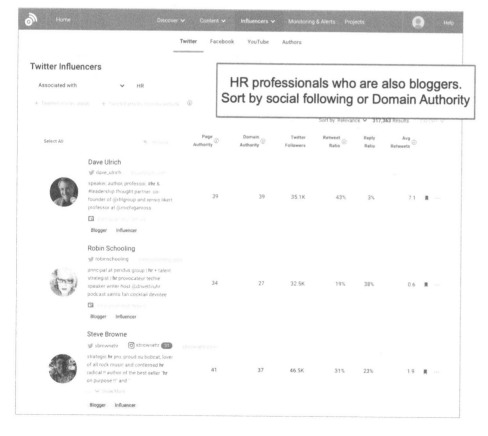

Fig. 5.102

We'll connect with them, start a conversation and invite them to contribute a quote to the final piece.

💡 TIP! Organizations are some of the best collaborators. Consider asking a relevant trade association or media partner to partner with you and co-brand the research. If the research is a survey, getting access to their audience can be a big boost in getting responses.

7. Write for other websites

This tactic directly leads to links and authority. Publishing original research and building relationships with content creators might organically attract links, but when you write for someone's website, you're usually creating a link back to your site, in the author bio if not in the article itself.

Especially for younger content programs, earlier in the process of building an audience, guest blogging and digital PR are so important. We'll talk more about this in Section 6.6.

Fig. 5.103

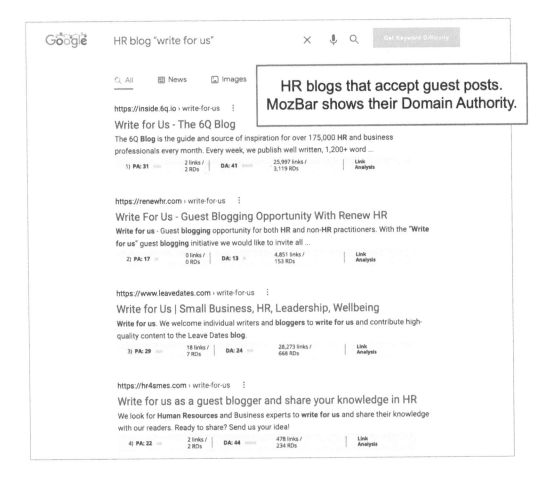

Probably, we already know the top HR blogs, because we live in this niche. But if not, they're easy to find. To find just the HR blogs that accept guest posts, you can add "write for us" to your search. To see the value of a link back to our content hub, turn on MozBar before doing the search (Fig. 5.103).

Connecting the dots

Let's step back and see how all of this content fits together. Fig. 5.104 shows how all of the content connects. Below we'll list a quick description of each piece.

1. **The Service Page:** Optimized for "office coffee delivery service" and filled with answers to sales questions, testimonials and CTAs. Our goal is to

get this conversion-optimized page to rank.

2. **Original Research:** Survey of "Office Perks of the Top 50 Workplaces" includes charts and data, along with contributor quotes from influencers. This is our central hub. It links to the sales page, passing along authority and ranking potential.

3. **The Content Upgrade:** "The Complete Guide to Top Office Perks" is a more detailed, gated version of the research, available to anyone who subscribes.

4. **How-to Article:** "How to retain your top employees" is keyphrase-focused and optimized to rank. It includes charts from the research and quotes from influencers.

Content Strategy for SEO and Lead Generation

Fig. 5.104

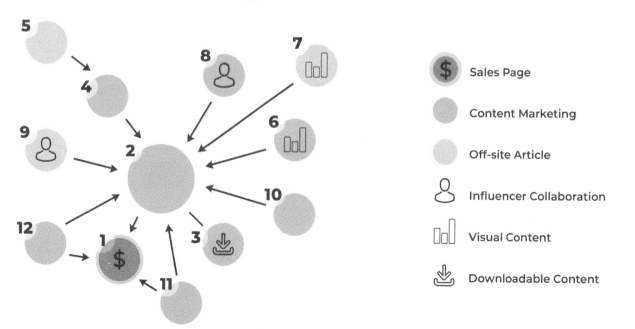

- $ Sales Page
- Content Marketing
- Off-site Article
- Influencer Collaboration
- Visual Content
- Downloadable Content

5. **How-to Guest Post:** "How to lose a top performer in 10 days" is a fun spin on the same article, pitched as a guest post to an HR blog. It's the "evil twin" of the how-to article.

6. **Infographic:** "Top Perks at Top Offices" is a visual version of the research featuring charts, stats and analysis in a short article.

7. **Guest Post/Infographic:** We'll pitch the infographic along with a short, original article to an HR blog. Getting a guest post accepted will support the hub with an immediate link.

8. **Influencer Interview:** "What employees really want" is a text-based or video interview with an HR influencer about employee happiness, retention and the research on office perks.

9. **Contribution/Interview:** In "Office Perks Expert Shares New Research on Top Workplaces" we'll pitch ourselves to an employee benefits or HR podcast with an offer to discuss the research. The show notes will link back to our survey.

And finally we'll do some traditional blogging . . .

10. **Blog Post One:** "5 Workplace Secrets: An inside look into the top offices"

11. **Blog Post Two:** "Coffee, Tea or Beer? What are they drinking at the top companies in the country?"

12. **Blog Post Three:** "The Dirt on Dishes: What's wrong with office kitchens"

This mini-strategy goes far beyond the typical content marketing program. It's more than just blogging. It's a content marketing framework built specifically to build authority and leads. It would work for any brand with a lead generation goal, **but few companies will ever do it**.

Most content strategies do the usual (blogs, newsletters, an occasional e-book) while others use less common tactics (research, influencer collaboration, and video). And a very small percentage of content strategies, about 1%, combine all of these elements to build powerful platforms for high rankings, huge traffic and loads of conversions.

Let's do the math (Fig. 5.105). As we've seen in other sections of this book:

- 39% of content programs have a documented content mission

- 25% are anchored in original research

- 18% have ongoing influencer marketing campaigns

- 60% are PR focused

Multiply those percentages and you get 1%. That is, roughly 1 in every 100 content strategies combine all of these tactics. It's rare, but not expensive. It's not especially difficult, but it does take time.

How long will this take?

"Keep on blogging and eventually you'll create a river of leads." We started by saying that

39 **Mission Driven** **25%** **Anchored In Research** **18%** **Influencer Powered** **60%** **PR Focused**

Fig. 5.105

this isn't true. But this is about content strategy, not just blogging.

We have a mission-driven, research-anchored, influencer-powered, PR-focused content marketing strategy.

And with this strategy, we are 100% confident of success. We have no doubts whatsoever. But how long will it take?

According to the Moz Keyword Explorer, the other sites that rank on page one for our target keyphrase ("office coffee delivery") have 100+ links to them. According to the Moz Link Explorer, we have around 40 links to our website. As we've learned, not all links are of equal value, but for this quick estimate, we'll need 50-100 new links to our site.

Assume that each quarter, we publish a hub of content as shown above. We'll build our marketing around this cadence. Suppose each round leads to just 25 links; in nine months to a year we should have sufficient authority for our sales page to rank for "office coffee delivery." (Fig. 5.106)

Within a year, there will be a steady stream of qualified leads flowing in through our contact form. And in the meantime, we'll have a growing email list, a growing body of repurposable work and growing relationships with influencers.

Fig. 5.106

	Q1	Q2	Q3	Q4
Anchor Piece	Original research (search optimized)	Ultimate guide (search optimized)	Detailed how-to (search optimized)	Original research
Content Upgrade	Full report	Checklist	Resource guide	Full report
Media	Video	Infographic	Infographic	Animation
Collaboration	Influencer interview	Roundup	Panel-style article with 3 influencers	Influencer interview
PR/Guest Post	Article for media site	Guest post on industry blog	Short series for local association	Contribute to media column
Blog Posts	3-5 articles	3-5 articles	3-5 articles	3-5 articles

Fig. 5.107

How long does SEO take?

Result	Timeframe
Crawled	1–2 hours
Indexed	1–2 days
Rank for the brand	~1 week
Rank for low-competition phrases	2–3 months
Rank for high-competition phrases	2–3 years

Too slow? If you don't have time to build a content program, there's always advertising. Remember, content is slow but durable. Ads are fast but temporary.

Search optimization often requires patience and persistence. Although Google may index a page within days, it can take years to rank for highly competitive phrases. That time is spent improving the quality of the content over time (relevance), building links from other websites (authority). An interconnected content hub is key for both (Fig. 5.107).

"I fear not the man who has practiced 10,000 kicks once, but I fear the man who has practiced one kick 10,000 times."

BRUCE LEE, *Black Belt,
Wing Chung School of Kung Fu*

Nothing is hard or easy, but some things take longer than others

When the attention is valuable, it takes longer to win but it's worth the effort. If you're surrounded by mountains, build tall. Be focused and organized. Build a small mountain of helpful information.

Be the Wikipedia for your industry. Be the *People* magazine for the influencers relevant to your audience. Don't make a page, make a section. Don't write a blog post, write a series.

Give the best answers to the questions your audience is asking, and organize those answers into hubs of content. That's how to win online against tough competitors.

5.11 Article Checklist

A simple set of specific things makes the difference between good and great content. Having that list of specific things in front of you will make it easy to include them all. Let's close out this chapter with a checklist (Fig. 5.108).

Fig. 5.108

Search Engine Optimization Elements Checklist

❑	Title Tag	Includes the target keyphrase once, at the beginning of the title tag, if possible. Maximum 55 characters.
❑	URL	Use a URL that is short, simple and descriptive, with no numbers and no formats
❑	Meta Description	A simple sentence summary of the article. Includes the keyphrase once, anywhere. Maximum 155 characters.
❑	Keyphrase Usage	The keyphrase appears in the body of the article two to five times.
❑	Usage of semantically linked words	Words that are semantically linked to the target phrase (such as those that appear in suggestions ot in "related searches") appear in the article once.
❑	Headline	Headline (h1 header) includes the general top and target keyphrase.

Human Psychology Elements Checklist

❑	Secondary Headline	After the first headline (also in the h1 header) but separated by a colon, parenthesis, dash or comma, a secondary headline includes: • Number, if possible. • Clear indication of the benefit of reading the article.
❑	Featured Image	Twice as wide as it is tall for ideal social sharing. Includes the headline of the article within the image (optional).
❑	Subheaders	Each section of the article begins with a clear subheader, formatted as <h2>.
❑	Lists	Bulleted and numbered lists that make content easy to scan.
❑	Formatting	Short paragraphs (four lines maximum). Bolding and italics call out key takeaways.
❑	Links	Link to another article. Link to product ot service page.
❑	Quotes and Mentions	Contributor quote from an expert within the field. Mentions an expert, including a quote from something they've written.
❑	Examples and Evidence	Support for any claims through specific examples and data. Proper citation (link) of any articles or studies.
❑	Call to Action	Invites reader to comment, subscribe or download.
❑	Author Box	Image of author's face. Several sentences about the author's relevance. Link to full bio on-site or preferred social media profile.

Additional Media Elements Checklist

❑	Secondary Images	Additional images appear down the page. Ideally, one image at every scroll depth, so an image is always visible.
❑	Video	Embedded video at the top of the article.
❑	Audio	Embedded audio player at the top of the article.
❑	Click to Tweet	Specific quotes shareable on a single click.
❑	PDF Download	Alternative version available for print or download, available by clicking an email address.

Before you push the publish button on your next article, go through this list and make sure you haven't missed anything. If you do leave something off, do so deliberately, knowing that it wasn't important for that particular article.

This checklist is organized into categories: search optimization, human psychology and media. But of course, there is overlap.

Let's take a closer look at each of these items . . .

Search engine optimization elements

The following elements all indicate the relevance of the article. They are key places to use target phrases and increase the likelihood that the content will rank.

Title tag

It's the text at the top of the browser, in the tab above the address bar, for every page you've ever visited. In the code, it's whatever text is inside the <title> tags.

Title tags are the single most important element for SEO. Not only are they a powerful indication of relevance, but typically the title appears as the link in search results if and when the page ranks (Fig. 5.109).

Use the target keyphrase once in the title. If possible, use it near the beginning of the title. The prominence of the keyphrase (in other words, how close to the beginning it appears) is also important.

It might be tempting to put your business name at the front of the title. Don't. Search engine marketers have a saying: "*brand last.*" Start with your keyphrase, end with your business name. Remember, your first goal is to help people. Promoting yourself comes second.

URL

Keeping in mind that you may update this article later, use a URL that is easy to reuse later. That means keeping your URLs short, simple and descriptive. No numbers. No formats.

Fig. 5.109

Anatomy of a search snippet

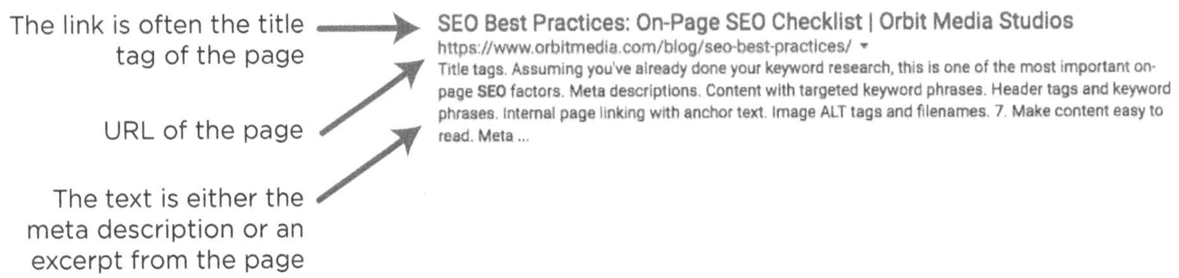

The link is often the title tag of the page →

URL of the page

The text is either the meta description or an excerpt from the page

SEO Best Practices: On-Page SEO Checklist | Orbit Media Studios
https://www.orbitmedia.com/blog/seo-best-practices/ ▾
Title tags. Assuming you've already done your keyword research, this is one of the most important on-page SEO factors. Meta descriptions. Content with targeted keyword phrases. Header tags and keyword phrases. Internal page linking with anchor text. Image ALT tags and filenames. 7. Make content easy to read. Meta ...

- **Never put a number in a URL**
  Example: www.website.com/blog/7-url-best-practices
  That's a problem because if you update it next year, it may have 12 best practices. There will be a mismatch with the title and header.

- **Never put a format in a URL**
  Example: www.website.com/blog/url-best-practices-infographic
  That's a problem because if you update this next year, it may not mostly be an infographic (or webinar or e-book). There will be a mismatch between the URL and the format.

Meta description

The meta description doesn't appear on the page itself, but like the title tag, it's also highly visible in search results. Make your meta description a single-sentence, plain-English summary of the content of the page. Use your target keyphrase at least once, but not more than twice. Limit the number of characters to 155 to be sure that it will fit within the snippet.

In the early days of SEO, search engines paid attention to another tag called "meta keywords." However, spammers abused them, so they are no longer a ranking factor. You can still add meta keywords to a page, but it's not recommended. They're not useful for anything, except telling your competitors what phrases you're trying to rank for.

Keyphrase use in the body text

There is no correct number for ideal keyphrase frequency. But our general recommendation is to use the target keyphrase in the body of the article at least twice, but not more than five times every 1,000 words or so. While writing, you may naturally use various words from the longer phrase in different places. That's good. When possible, use the target keyphrase as one complete phrase.

This should come naturally if the phrase is relevant to the topic. During editing, go back to make sure it's used, but not overused.

WARNING! Don't overdo it. If you compromise your writing so much that it's obvious to the reader, you're guilty of "keyword stuffing." Using the phrase repeatedly in unnatural ways is bad for readers and bad for rankings. This is spam and it's obvious to Google. This won't help your rankings.

Semantically related words

Beyond the specific target phrase, use words that are semantically linked to the phrase. Spread out your meaning by using the words that are closely related to your keyphrase. Indicating relevance for the broader topic is good for search rankings. Any great page on your topic would certainly include those closely related words and phrases, right?

Headline

The headline should be formatted using the <h1> header tag. As we discussed earlier, the headline should use the target keyphrase once, indicating relevance to search engines and stating the general topic to headers. Beyond this, the headline should be written to be compelling to readers.

Human psychology elements

The following elements will align the article with basic, human psychology. Each of these increase the likelihood that the article will be clicked, read and shared.

Secondary headline

A great headline stops the reader in their tracks. Adding a dash, colon or parentheses lets you add a second headline, giving you a better chance at this. For example: "Starship Maintenance: 7 Stellar Tips for a Safe Launch Every Time."

Featured image

Articles with images are more likely to be shared, clicked, read and remembered. Never publish an article without an image. Apply the guidelines in the Blog Image Checklist above for subject, shape, consistency and copyright.

Subheaders

Visitors tend to scan, not read, web content. To make your content scannable, add subheaders into the article, breaking up the article into sections. These serve as mini-headlines for subsequent paragraphs, keeping visitors moving through your content.

These subheads should be formatted using <h2> or <h3> tags, not just bolding (Fig. 5.110).

Lists

Lists give you a natural reason to use numbered headlines, telling readers that the article will be formatted for easy scanning. List articles are successful

Fig. 5.110

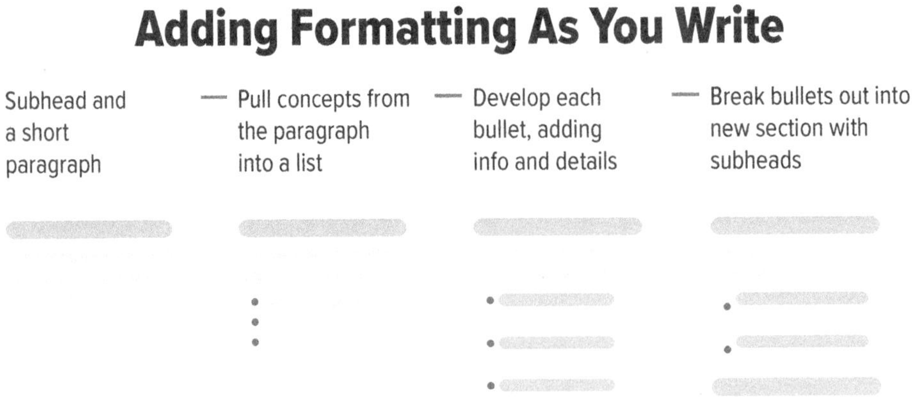

Adding Formatting As You Write

Subhead and a short paragraph	Pull concepts from the paragraph into a list	Develop each bullet, adding info and details	Break bullets out into new section with subheads

because readers are busy. Lists align with their psychology.

- Use bullet lists whenever there are three or more distinct ideas in a section.

- Use numbered lists as a format for the entire article or whenever sequential ideas are presented.

- Avoid list formatting when telling stories with a narrative flow.

Formatting

Format your content so it's accessible and engaging to busy visitors. Never use long, dense blocks of text.

- **Short paragraphs**
  No paragraph should be longer than four lines. Use very short paragraphs of one sentence or even one word to add emphasis (Fig. 5.111).

- **Bolding and Italics**
  These are excellent ways to draw attention to key messages and make content more easily scanned, but don't overdo it.

- **Personal tone**
  Readers are people. Write as if you're writing for one specific person. From you, to them.

While you're at it, add some attitude. Edit that first draft and take out all those qualifying words. They take the edge out of your writing. Make the tone direct. Strengthen those opinions. Do it right, and a group of sentences like this:

"In many cases, blog posts are vague and may not be useful to readers. This is often because they do not provide enough actionable advice."

. . . becomes a sentence like this:

"Vague blog posts aren't useful, since they just aren't actionable for readers."

. . . or even this:

"If a blog post isn't actionable, it's useless."

Fig. 5.111

Lorem ipsum dolor sit amet
Consectetur adipiscing elit. Nunc egestas nunc et nulla rutrum consequat. Etiam eu felis eget lacus posuere ultricies eu a arcu. Nam ornare vulputate blandit. Nam eget tortor eu magna venenatis suscipit. Nam interdum neque quis quam lobortis laoreet. Donec malesuada turpis vitae magna pulvinar commodo. Vivamus blandit libero sit amet eros ornare, at hendrerit nibh dictum. Etiam aliquam nulla eu risus ullamcorper suscipit. Integer eleifend cursus nisl, a sollicitudin mi pretium convallis. Nullam ornare massa id lacus malesuada lacinia. Phasellus rutrum a sapien ac fringilla. Nam ac faucibus justo. Vivamus gravida lacus mauris, sit amet rhoncus est posuere ut. Sed volutpat consequat justo, rhoncus mollis felis.

Duis sagittis vulputate orci vitae volutpat. Ut ac eleifend eros, ut porttitor metus. Nullam ultrices metus et imperdiet scelerisque. Donec tincidunt justo ac sollicitudin ornare. Suspendisse potenti. Phasellus lacus nibh, luctus et leo mattis, volutpat viverra nulla. Nullam sed dignissim velit. Curabitur non arcu id lectus tempus placerat ut non magna. Morbi accumsan malesuada ante, id cursus lectus. Nullam vulputate ultrices tellus ut ultrices. Fusce sit amet mattis neque.

Cras vestibulum, tellus sed mattis finibus, lacus eros molestie sapien, eget finibus ante felis in odio. Lorem ipsum dolor sit amet, consectetur adipiscing elit. Nunc vulputate eget ipsum dignissim pellentesque. Donec blandit aliquet velit, id iaculis metus tempus nec. Etiam interdum eu nisl ut posuere. Nam ut posuere massa. Praesent dictum eget metus at gravida. Aliquam a odio ut diam tincidunt dictum. Morbi posuere nisi ultricies libero condimentum vehicula. Sed sed interdum dolor, sed efficitur diam. Curabitur accumsan in risus ac cursus. Nunc dignissim maximus arcu, vitae dignissim nisi vulputate vel.

Lorem ipsum dolor sit amet
Consectetur adipiscing elit. Nunc egestas nunc et nulla rutrum consequat. Etiam eu felis eget lacus posuere ultricies eu a arcu. Nam ornare vulputate blandit. Nam eget tortor eu magna venenatis suscipit.

Nam interdum neque quis quam lobortis laoreet.

Donec malesuada turpis vitae magna pulvinar commodo. Vivamus blandit libero sit amet eros ornare, at hendrerit nibh dictum. Etiam aliquam nulla eu risus ullamcorper suscipit.

Integer eleifend cursus convallis
Nullam ornare massa id lacus malesuada lacinia. Phasellus rutrum a sapien ac fringilla. Nam ac faucibus justo. Vivamus gravida lacus mauris

- Duis sagittis vulputate orci vitae volutpat
- Ut ac eleifend eros, ut porttitor metus
- Nullam ultrices metus et imperdiet scelerisque.

Donec tincidunt justo ac sollicitudin ornare.

Suspendisse potenti. Phasellus lacus nibh, luctus et leo mattis, volutpat viverra nulla. Nullam sed dignissim velit. Curabitur non arcu id lectus tempus placerat ut non magna.

Links

Your goal is to convert your reader into a lead or a customer eventually. But if you don't help make those connections between the articles and the sales pages, you'll convert fewer visitors. If you don't connect the cheese to the trap, you'll catch fewer mice.

- Link from each new article to an older article

- Link from every article to a product or service page

- Link to each new article from an older article

That last type of link is often overlooked. But the best content marketers know **you haven't finished publishing a new article until you've linked to it from an older article.**

It's easy to find old articles that are candidates for linking to the new one. Use your own site search tool or use Google.

Example: We wrote a research piece about bounce rates and wanted to find older articles to potentially link to it. We can use the site: search operator to search just our own site for "bounce rate" and Google shows us every instance of that phrase on our site (Fig. 5.112).

Quotes and mentions

If optimizing for search means adding keywords, then optimizing for social means adding people. Input from experts adds credibility and will make your article more interesting. It's also more likely to be shared since people tend to share articles that mention them.

Don't expect experts to instantly share articles that they're mentioned in. But most will, giving you a social media boost. If not, it's still great for the quality of your content and great networking.

Examples and evidence

Great writers support their claims with evidence. They add clarity with examples. Here are types of evidence that you can add to your content to make it more compelling.

- Research studies and statistics
- Charts and graphs with supportive data
- Stories and case studies
- Supportive resources
- Relevant (positive or negative) examples

Ideally, there is evidence supporting each point in your article.

Similar to quotes, these are all ways to work other people into your content, and more people means more mentions and possibilities that they will share.

Call to action

Now that you've given your reader a high-quality, well-structured piece of content, it's time to ask for something in return. All great content ends with a call to action, inviting the visitor to become more engaged with your content or your business.

Fig. 5.112

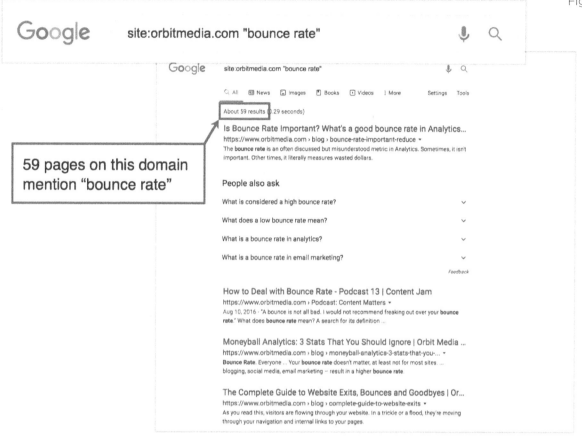

59 pages on this domain mention "bounce rate"

If nothing else, the call to action is simply *an invitation to leave a comment*. Ask a question that they can answer with a comment, ask for other ideas that would complement the article, or even invite the reader to disagree with you.

Another call to action is a one-sentence pitch to subscribe to the newsletter. The moment they finish reading the post is the high point of their appreciation. This is when they are most likely to subscribe.

Author box

Blog software often makes creating the author box very easy. Easy or difficult,

it's worth the effort, since it makes the content more personal and engaging. It has social media and conversion benefits. The ideal author box includes the following:

- Profile picture

- Brief biography (no more than a few sentences)

- Link to the author's bio on the website

- Links to active social media profiles

Additional media elements

Here are ways to improve quality by adding more compelling media. Of course, you won't add all of these to every article. But we recommend upgrading your content with something from this list on a regular basis.

Secondary images

Subheaders and formatting make articles easier to scan, but images are an even better way to keep visitors' attention. Add an image after every three or four paragraphs, so there is no point in your article where the visitor reaches a screen of all text with no images.

Video

The combination of movement and sound make video the most compelling format for content. Adding video to the top of a post is one of the best ways to get visitors to stay. Getting visitors to stay on your page has indirect SEO benefits. Google knows how long they stayed. A long visit (also known as "the long click" or "high dwell time") suggests to Google it's a good page. A short visit, not so much.

Of course, the video thumbnail (default image) should use the same best practices as featured images: faces and headlines.

Audio

Similar to video, audio is a big media upgrade to any post. It's also easier than you think.

1. Turn on the recording software on your computer.

2. Read the post in your own conversational tone.

3. Save as an mp3 file.

4. Upload to SoundCloud or Spreaker.

5. Embed the audio player of the file to the page by copying and pasting in the <iframe> code, just as you would a YouTube video.

Add it to the top of the page. It will look (and maybe sound) like Fig. 5.113.

Fig. 5.113

Click to tweet

The easier content is to share, the more likely it will be shared. This is another simple way to optimize your content for social media.

Take a short, compelling quote from the article (or use a version of the headline) and write it as a tweet, using the link from the article, along with any hashtags and mentions. Put the tweet into clicktotweet.com, then embed it into the article as a link or a little blue bird button.

PDF download

The PDF is really an alternate version of an article, added as a convenience for visitors who may want to download or print it. Large companies doing B2B marketing often add these to white papers or case studies.

More recently, the PDF is a common format for the "content upgrade," available to visitors who enter an email address. This is a cornerstone tactic in marketing automation.

Links to PDFs can include an icon and an indication of the file size, similar to this:

Download a PDF version of this Website Content Checklist (236 kb) >

Eugene's words have never been more true than they are today, in the era of content marketing.

Every great piece of digital content is assembled from many little elements, words, images, tags, media and formatting. Each adds to the results of the whole in its own way.

"Copy is not written. **Copy is assembled.**"

EUGENE SCHWARTZ, *Copywriting Legend*

5.12 Here Is Your New Content Marketing Template

Starting with a blank document? That's hard. *Starting with a content marketing template?* Much easier!

Using this template will force you to plan for promotion. It pushes you to plan for (or at least consider) the various content promotion channels: SEO, social media, email marketing and influencer collaboration.

You can find our content template here: **bit.ly/chemistrytemplate** (Fig. 5.114)

It's a Google Doc, so first click File > Make a Copy. Now it is yours. Bookmark it. Share it. Customize it. It has some helpful instructions at the top. Eventually, you'll want to delete those or add your own editorial guidelines.

Fig. 5.114

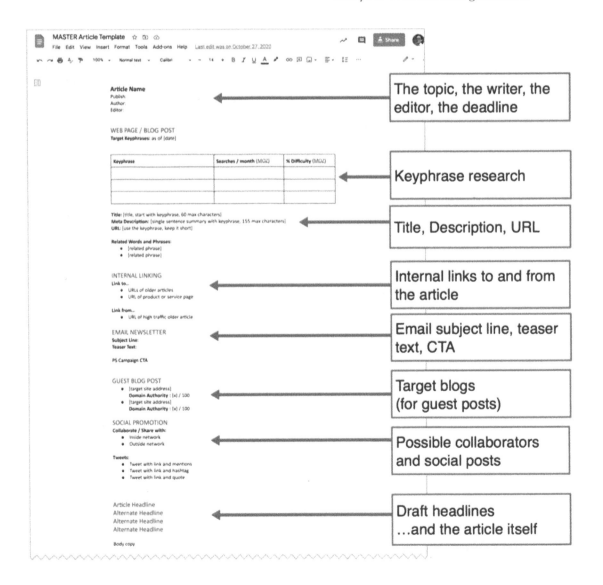

The topic, the writer, the editor, the deadline

Keyphrase research

Title, Description, URL

Internal links to and from the article

Email subject line, teaser text, CTA

Target blogs (for guest posts)

Possible collaborators and social posts

Draft headlines ...and the article itself

At the top you'll find sections for promotion planning. Go through each section, planning the promotion by filling in the text between the [brackets].

Fill in these first and every word you write next will be more likely to be read. Do this every time and you'll never again create content without a plan to drive traffic to it.

1. Copy the template, fill in the basics

For each new article, make a copy of your master template and name it. Then enter the target publish date, the author's name and the editor's name.

2: Do your keyphrase research

If you are writing something that aligns with a keyphrase, use an SEO tool to look up the monthly volume and difficulty and capture those numbers here.

3: Enter the title, description and URL

Watch the character counts for the title (60 characters) and meta description (155 characters) or they'll be truncated. For the URL of the page, follow these best practices if possible:

- Short but descriptive

- Includes the target keyphrase

- No numbers

TIP! Use a URL that is easy to reuse later. If you write a list post that has the number in the URL, you may regret it if you rewrite the post a few years later.

Suppose we write an article called **3 Best Practices for URLs** and publish it at www.orbitmedia.com/blog/3-url-best-practices

Two years later we update the article and it's now **5 Best Practices for URLs** but we want to reuse the same URL because it's been linked to and ranks well . . . we'd regret using the number in the URL because now there's a mismatch with the new title. Oops.

4: Capture the related words and phrases

You want to target the topic, not just the keyphrase. So you'll answer all the related questions and incorporate lots of the related words and phrases.

You can find those words and phrases from within Google itself (refer back to the Keyword Research section earlier in this chapter) or with SEO tools, such as MarketMuse. Capture them here and include them in the content as you write.

5: Plan the internal links

Great content is connected. Plan those connections in advance and you won't miss any opportunities to both guide visitors deeper and pass link equity through your site. Make notes of all three kinds of links listed in the checklist above.

6: Plan the email marketing

Here you'll plan the email newsletter, including the following:

- **Subject line**
  Because it will be truncated in the mobile inbox, make sure it is "front-loaded" with the most impactful words (specific benefits, numbers and unexpected words).

- **Teaser text**
  Write the email copy that will get the subscriber interested in reading more. It may be a short summary or an excerpt of the article.

- **Call to action**
  "Click here" and "read more" aren't really calls to action. A good CTA is specific, restating what readers are about to discover. The link should have campaign tracking code on it so you can track your visitors in GA4, as explained in Section 3.4.

7: If it's a guest post, plan the pitch

If your article isn't a guest post, delete this section. If it will be a guest post, list the host blogs that you plan to pitch to. Look up the Domain Authority of each and make a note here.

Ideally, you've already taken the time to network with the editor. They know you (or at least know of you) already.

8: Influencer collaboration

List your collaborators, but also *anyone or any brand that was mentioned in the article* or whom you contact during the research and writing process.

- Contributors who provided quotes

- Contributors whom you reached out to but who declined to contribute a quote

- Sources of research cited in the article

- Companies that built tools that you mentioned

- Any brand or person you linked to from the article

- People with whom you discussed the topic

This is your list of people to reach out to after the article is live. Once it's live, let them know either with personal emails, direct messages or in social post mentions.

9: Social media promotion

When gathering ideas for social posts, consider at least one of each of these:

- **Questions** that are answered by the content of the article

- **Numbers** whenever possible

- **Visuals** from the post, especially charts and diagrams

- **Hashtags** when relevant.

- **Mentions** of the contributors

10: Write your article!

The planning is done and you're ready to write. Pay close attention to formatting and paragraph length; don't miss opportunities to include images and internal links. Be direct and get to your points quickly. Keep the tone conversational by writing as if you're talking to one person.

11: Share with the editor

Since it's a Google Doc and not a file, you can share it easily. You can collaborate with your team within the document without emailing attachments around. Changes are tracked. Comments added. Together you and the editor hammer out the final details, both for the post and for promotion.

⚠️ WARNING! Avoid emailing attachments whenever possible. Attachments lead to version control issues, viruses, bloated hard drives and confusion.

12: Publish and start promotion

Import the article into your CMS. It should move nicely from the template into your content management system.

💡 TIP! To get images out of Google Docs, go to File > Download as Web Page (.html,zipped). All of the images will be in your zipped file. Rename, resize (if needed) and upload them into your CMS.

Once the article is live, it's time to promote. That process begins by referring back to the notes you added to the content template. These steps aren't possible until you've published.

- Link to the new article from an old article

- Let the contributors know about it with a quick email

- Schedule the social media shares

- Load it into your email service provider

Easy peasy, mac and cheesy.

Content Promotion

PROMOTION ISN'T AN AFTERTHOUGHT. YOU WERE PLANNING THE PROMOTION WHILE CREATING THE CONTENT.

The keyphrases, the headlines, the visuals . . . these were all carefully crafted to increase the reach of the piece you just created. It was designed to get traction. But the biggest part of the job is still in front of you. Getting the content in front of your audience.

The best article will fail if it's not promoted. The best video will never be seen if it isn't marketed. The *New York Times* doesn't keep a list of the best books. They keep a list of *the best-selling books*. The quality of the content isn't the main success criteria; it's the quality of the promotion.

> The best content doesn't win.
> The **best-promoted content** wins.

Yes, poor quality is a deal breaker. No amount of work will help a worthless article get traffic and engage with visitors. But an OK piece of content with brilliant promotion will outperform brilliant content with just OK promotion.

Before the stroke of midnight tonight, the "publish" button will be clicked more than two million times and millions of new blog posts will go live. That is a lot of content. But research shows that most of this content will not achieve any real business results, or at least not get any traction in social media or search rankings.

Steve Rayson, founder of BuzzSumo, analyzed one million articles and found that *most content doesn't get any results in search or social.* 75% of the articles no one links to, and 50% of the articles get two or fewer Facebook interactions (Fig. 6.1). If we assume that one of those is the writer, we can safely round that number down to zero.

This chart shows the stark reality for marketers. *The vast majority of content gets no results.* We also know from the blogger survey that the average article takes more than four hours to write. Do the math and you'll find that hundreds of millions of hours are wasted every day in content marketing. Tragedy!

Content promotion is the difference between a big hit and a wasted effort. It's the marketing part of content marketing.

It's time to focus on the specific, deliberate actions that will raise the visibility of your content. We'll group these actions into our four main promotion channels:

- Email Marketing (Timing . . .)

- Social Media (Integration, Scheduling, Automation)

- Search Optimization (Off-Site SEO, Outreach and Guest Blogging)

- Account-Based Content Marketing

These are the ongoing activities that professional content marketers use in continuous cycles. Although each is a separate skill—and there are specialized marketers and vendors who exclusively focus on one—these techniques are most effective when used in combination.

💡 TIP: As a general rule, you should spend twice as much time and energy promoting content as you spend creating it. If you spend two hours making something, you should spend four hours promoting it.

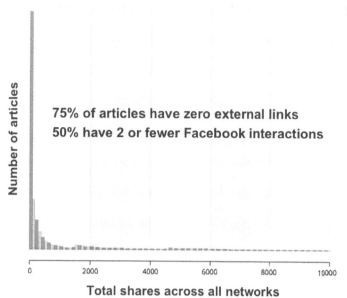

75% of articles have zero external links
50% have 2 or fewer Facebook interactions

Number of articles

Total shares across all networks

Source: https://moz.com/blog/content-shares-and-links-insights-from-analyzing-1-million-articles

6.1 Email Marketing

Email is special. Unlike search and social, there isn't a company, like Facebook or Google, in between you and your audience. Email marketing is disintermediation. You connect directly with your audience in their inbox. There is no need to worry about changing algorithms. No worries about organic reach.

Email is a permission-based relationship between you and your subscriber. They opt-in giving you permission to send them messages. You honor that by sending messages that are relevant and helpful. Like any good relationship, it's built on trust.

A well-run email program builds a loyal and engaged source of traffic, decoupling your destiny from the changing whims of big tech. The factors in success are list growth, the timing, the frequency and the messages themselves.

List growth

Let's start with the list. A big email list is better but a smaller list of targeted, highly engaged subscribers is more valuable than a big list of less-relevant, disinterested subscribers. As always, quality is more important than quantity.

List growth starts with your email signup call to action. In Section 4.5, we showed examples of subscribe boxes that include the "3 P's" which are prominence, promise and proof. When the signup CTA has all three elements, conversion rates from visitor to subscriber will be higher and your list will grow quickly.

Gated content is a common list growth strategy for content marketers. The idea is to simply put high-value content, often in a downloadable form, behind a tiny form, so visitors must provide an email address to access it. This approach is central to marketing automation systems like Hubspot and appears on landing pages all over the web.

Marketers have strong opinions about gated content. Some hate the gate. But how do visitors feel? We asked a few hundred marketers and a few hundred B2B website visitors to see how everyone feels about gated content. We learned that although marketers are divided on the topic, visitors are mostly fine sharing their email address if the content is relevant (Fig. 6.2).

Fig. 6.2

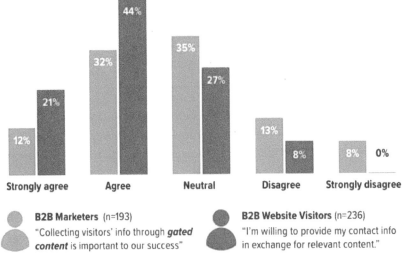

Most B2B visitors are OK with gated content

	Strongly agree	Agree	Neutral	Disagree	Strongly disagree
B2B Marketers	12%	32%	35%	13%	8%
B2B Website Visitors	21%	44%	27%	8%	0%

B2B Marketers (n=193)
"Collecting visitors' info through *gated content* is important to our success"

B2B Website Visitors (n=236)
"I'm willing to provide my contact info in exchange for relevant content."

Source: https://www.orbitmedia.com/blog/website-features-content/

The argument against gated content is that the visitor is really just looking for a single content asset. They aren't actually asking for an endless stream of emails from you. They are a downloader, not a subscriber. So be especially cautious and considerate with your list if you used gating as a growth tactic.

⚠ WARNING! Never send email to people who don't want it. Don't rent or buy lists. That would be advertising, not content marketing. Send email only to people who subscribed either from an email signup call to action or by submitting to receive gated content.

Let subscribers unsubscribe easily. This keeps your list clean and spam complaints low. It is illegal (and inconsiderate) to send unsolicited commercial email if the recipients have no way to opt-out. The unsubscribe link is typically added automatically by the email service provider.

Unsubs are good. Mostly, those subscribers were not engaging with your content anyway. They are dragging down your open and click through rates. We are happy to see them go.

Although "spam" is really any unsolicited mass email, it is only illegal if recipients cannot remove themselves from the list, at least in the US. Check the relevant laws, CAN-SPAM (United States), CCPA (California), CASL (Canada) and GDPR (European Union), to make sure you are compliant.

Is it ever OK to add people without first getting their permission?

Yes, but do so carefully. Seth Godin once suggested automatically adding anyone to your list who would complain if you didn't. For example, our job at Orbit Media is to help our clients with their digital marketing. They would be unhappy if we didn't share our latest web marketing techniques with them, so we add our clients to the list.

The email message

Next we'll look at the message itself. These are the five aspects of email messages that affect performance:

1. Sender name

2. Subject line

3. Preheader text

4. Email body

5. Call to action

The first three are the major factors in open rates. The last two are the major factors in click through rates. Since most email is opened on mobile devices, we'll start there. Here's what the preview looks like in your subscribers' mobile inbox (Fig. 6.3).

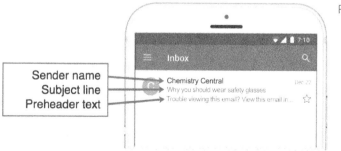

Fig. 6.3

You can instantly see how little information the subscriber has while deciding whether or not to open. Let's try that same email with a mobile-optimized, open-friendly sender name, subject line and preheader text (Fig. 6.4):

Fig. 6.4

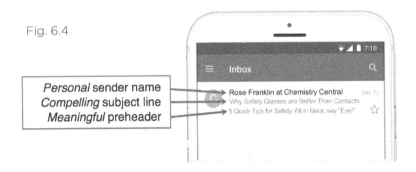

Personal sender name
Compelling subject line
Meaningful preheader

🔆 TIP! Remember to watch your character count for subject lines and preheaders. On most email apps on most phones, you'll have around 60 characters before things get truncated.

1. Sender name

It's the most prominent part of the email preview, so it's a huge factor in open rates. This is your first chance to trigger trust. A lot of marketers forget to check this, but email recipients never forget to look.

If the sender name includes a person's name, the email is more personal and more likely to be opened. For example, an email from "Susan Clark from Zippy Ideas" will have a higher open rate than an email from "Zippy Ideas Company." Somehow it's psychologically more difficult for your subscriber to disregard,

delete or unsubscribe when the sender is a person.

The sender name isn't the same as the "from" address, so never use an email address. Don't make "sclark@zippycpa.com" your sender name. And "Do Not Reply" just isn't a friendly name to call yourself.

The sender name is easy to change from within your email service provider. Your ESP may even make it easy to A/B test different sender names. You'll quickly discover if a more human sender name affect open rates.

2. Subject Line

This is next in the inbox. Your subject line is your hook. If it doesn't indicate a strong benefit or trigger curiosity, it's not doing its job.

All of the headline tips from the last chapter apply. There's no need to include a target keyphrase, since subject lines have nothing to do with SEO. Tailor it for the inbox. It's strictly about empathy and psychology. Be unexpected, helpful, provocative—or all three.

- *Front-loaded*
  The first five words or so is all they're likely to see. So be sure to get the important words and phrases into the beginning of your subject line.

- *Add specifics*
  Use words that are meaningful to your specific audience in the subject line, such as their geography ("Popular in Chicago"), their

interests ("Calling all robot fans") or their job function ("For Lab Technicians only").

- *Use numbers*
  Numerals stand out against letters in lines of text. Those numeric characters can make an email subject line a bit more prominent in the recipient's inbox.

- *Try emojis and ellipses...*
  Emojis help your subject lines stand out in crowded, competitive inboxes, especially if they appear as the first character. Ellipses create interest, suggesting that they'll get more if they click.

- *Use words that indicate visuals*
  If the article you're promoting with email includes a chart, diagram, infographic or video, mention it in the subject line. We've noticed an uptick in open and click through rates when the subject line includes an image word, such as "flowchart," "diagrams" and "video."

- *Use top-performing words*
  Some work better than others. Fig. 6.5 shows a selection of words that appeared in top-performing subject line words, according to the analysis of 48 billion emails by four different marketing research companies.[1]

1. http://www.marketingprofs.com/charts/2015/26984/ five-most-effective-and-ineffective-words-in- email-subject-lines; http://www.clickz.com/clickz/ column/2360657/the-best-and-worst-words-to- use-in-subject-lines-new-research; https://www. smartinsights.com/email-marketing/email-creative- and-copywriting/email-subject-lines-response/; http://content.adestra.com/hubfs/2015_Reports_ and_eGuides/2015_Subject_Line_Report.pdf; http:// www.adestra.com/keywords-for-killer-subject-lines/; http://www.digitalmarketer.com/101-best-email- subject-lines-2014/

Top-performing words

Fig. 6.5

upgrade	snapshot	available	thank you	latest
just	monthly	new	introducing	won't
content	forecast	alert	celebrate	can
go	is coming	update	get your	special
wonderful	get this now	most	what	now

Sources:
http://www.marketingprofs.com/charts/2015/26984/five-most-effective-and-ineffective-words-in-email-subject-lines
http://www.clickz.com/clickz/column/2360657/the-best-and-worst-words-to-use-in-subject-lines-new-research
https://www.smartinsights.com/email-marketing/email-creative-and-copywriting/email-subject-lines-response
http://content.adestra.com/hubfs/2015_Reports_and_eGuides/2015_Subject_Line_Report.pdf
http://www.adestra.com/keywords-for-killer-subject-lines
http://www.digitalmarketer.com/101-best-email-subject-lines-2014

TIP: -Think about whatever question people ask you most often. What's the most common question people ask your sales associates or customer service team? Try using that exact question as your next email subject line. It is very likely to perform well.

✦ Use AI to write draft subject lines for articles

Of course, generative AI can be useful at creating draft email subject lines. An effective prompt gives the AI your own best practices for great subject lines and the draft of the article that you're promoting. Here's an example of a prompt that may work well based on the suggestions above.

 ## Prompt:

You are an email marketing expert, skilled at crafting email subject lines that trigger high open rates. The best email subject lines for emails that promote content marketing articles often meet several criteria:

1. They indicate the specific benefits the article offers the reader without feeling overly promotional.

2. The use numerals, which could be statistics, the year or reference a numbered list in the article

3. They are front loaded with the most interesting, compelling or unexpected words in the first few words of the subject line.

4. They are brief and concise

5. They sometimes use an emoji as the first character and end with an ellipses

6. If the article contains or references visuals, they use a word to indicate that in the subject line, such as "flowchart" "diagram" or "video"

I'm giving you an article. Draft five email subject lines that could be used to promote this article. Briefly explain why each would be effective.

[copy in the text from the article]

---

3. Preheader text

The third and final element in the email preview is the preheader text. This is either the first words from the email message or a tiny bit of text at the top of your email template. Marketers add it specifically to appear in the inbox and increase the chances of getting opened.

Send a test message of your email to yourself and look at it in your inbox. Don't open the email. Just look at the message and ask yourself: *Is the preheader meaningful? Descriptive? Interesting? Is it getting truncated? Would you click on this?*

"Can't read this email? View this in your browser." is common preheader text because it's the first line in many emails, added automatically by ESPs. But it is not helpful for your open rate.

The next two aspects of your email will impact the click through rate and traffic.

4. Email body (design and text)

The design of emails is as varied as the design of web pages. Some emails are visual; others are plain text. Some are focused on promoting a single article; others are a digest-format with multiple links. Whether your emails are long or short, fancy or simple, you can measure their success based on the click through rate to your website.

Everyone loves beautiful design. But it's worth experimenting with sending plain text emails—and comparing the results you get.

When the goal is driving traffic, it's a mistake to put the entire article in the email. The email is really just a teaser for something on your website; it's an invitation to visit. If you put the entire piece in the email, there is no reason to click. Readers may love it but then delete it.

WARNING! Links to other websites, to social media networks or to email addresses may get clicks but not drive traffic. Be cautious and deliberate when linking to anything but your site from your emails.

An email inbox is a crowded, competitive place. Your subscriber is doing a split-second cost-benefit calculation before deciding to click. The design and writing of the email are critical. You are at a disadvantage if the email looks like an ad, if it's a big flashy graphic, or if it's nothing but dense blocks of text.

"Your From line matters more than your Subject line. Why? Your email will be opened (or not) based on your offer (in direct response email) or the promise of value (in an email newsletter). In either case, the relationship and trust between the subscriber and the brand is what triggers an open more than anything else. There are a TON of tools that help you optimize your Subject Line. There's no shortcut to optimizing a From line . . . that's all on you and the value you provide."

ANN HANDLEY, *Marketing Profs*

Here are a few guiding principles of good email design and writing:

- *Mobile friendly*
  Mobile open rates vary across industries. B2B subscribers may be more likely to subscribe using a work address and open emails on a laptop in the office. But everyone has access to email everywhere. Since 2014, most emails are opened on mobile devices.

  Send yourself a test email and open it on your phone. The text should be easy to read, left-aligned and it should wrap nicely. The email should load fast. The design should look good, even when images are turned off.

- *Personal tone*
  Every inbox is a mix of personal and marketing messages. So every recipient is subconsciously filtering emails from people and emails from companies. To keep your emails from going in the company bucket (which is one step away from the trash bucket) write them in a personal tone.

  Use the same voice you would use when writing to a friend. "I thought you might find this one useful…" or "We put a lot of thought and planning into this year's safety guide…"

- *People pictures*
  Just as web pages have a better

chance to connect if they use pictures of people, try using pictures of authors or collaborators in your emails. This is another way to humanize your content.

- *Multiple opportunities to click*
  More opportunities to click can mean a higher click through rate. Even if your email is promoting just one article, give the subscriber a few different places to click. Anything that triggers their interest should be clickable. That might be a headline, an image or a few words within a paragraph of text. And every link or button to your website should get appended with campaign tracking code (See Section 3.4).

💡 TIP! If your email has a company logo in it, it's likely that recipients will click on it. Make your logo and button and consider using it to send visitors to a landing page other than your homepage.

5. Call to action

The headline may link to your article, but you also need a call to action at the end of the email or after the teaser text for the article. And "Click here" and "Read more" are not calls to action. A good call to action uses all the principles of conversion: it draws attention, indicates a benefit and uses a strong verb. Which of these is more likely to win the click?

<u>Click here</u>

or

Show me pictures of the top 5 eye safety mistakes in research labs >

Notice the word "me" in the second example. First person language can also improve click through rates. Think of the button or link text as part of the reader's internal dialog. The text can read like a thought they are having themselves as they consider clicking.

- Start my free trial now

- Save my spot

- Give me the exclusive insights

- Download my guide instantly

💡 TIP! All of us are conditioned to reply to email. So an effective call to action can be to simply ask the recipient to reply. Assuming you can address the implications for the sender's inbox (lots of responses?) and your email service provider (can they track that?) this may be the most effective call to action of all: "Hit reply if you'd like to learn more"

And mobile-friendliness for your CTAs is mandatory. Buttons and links in email must be large and tappable for fingers of all sizes. Research by the MIT Touch Lab shows that the average index finger is 45 x 57 pixels for most screen resolutions. Thumbs are a bit bigger. If you expect people to use their thumbs to tap your button, make it wider: 45 x 72 pixels.

For mobile-friendly emails (and web pages) make sure that calls to action are low and centered. Some areas are right under the visitor's thumb. Others are harder to reach. Keep the "Thumb Zone" in mind (Fig. 6.6).

Fig. 6.6

Source: https://addyosmani.com/blog/touch-friendly-design/

💡 TIP! **The Bulletproof Button.** Some subscribers may have images turned off. This is a problem if your calls to action are image-based buttons, rather than text-based links. But there is a way to design a link to look like a button, using a bit of HTML and CSS code. Email marketers call this the "bulletproof button" because it always displays, even when images are off.

Create your own code-based bulletproof button here: https://buttons.cm/

Email marketing timing

When should you send email? What time of day? What day of the week?

There isn't one best time to send email. If there was, everyone would send at that time, inboxes would be flooded, unsubscribe rates would spike and then a different time would become the best time. Every content program and target audience will have different success rates and should be tested. But there's plenty of research on the topic.

Day of week

Many show that Tuesday and Thursdays are generally good days for open rates. Moosend analyzed 10 billion emails and found that Thursdays have slightly higher open rates and that email is less likely to be opened on weekends (Fig. 6.7).

Fig. 6.7

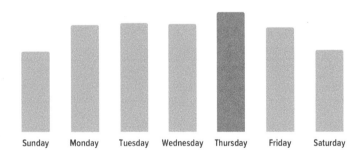

Source: https://moosend.com/blog/best-time-to-send-an-email/

Although weekends may have lower open rates, some studies show that weekend click through rates are slightly higher. Most marketers assume that these are bad days to send email, so a Saturday or Sunday newsletter has counter-competitive timing. Try it as a test for a few months and see how it works for your content and your readers.

Time of day

The research on this is mixed, but suggests that early morning and late afternoon are times when people are active in their inboxes. Emails sent between 6:00am to 11:00 am have slightly higher click-to-open rates, as do emails sent between 4:00 pm to 6:00 pm.

TIP! Avoid sending emails at the top of the hour. 80% of email campaigns are sent out on the hour* so emails sent just after the hour, such as 6:07 instead of 6:00, land in the inbox when it's a bit less crowded.

*Source: Worldata Research Response Rate Campaign Aggregate 2023

Email frequency

How often should you send emails? What is the minimum? How much is too much?

So far, we've looked at the factors that can increase the rate that people open and click, but the *total amount of traffic* you drive also depends on how frequently you send.

Content marketers tend to be empathetic, considerate people, hesitant to bother their audience with a lot of email. Few marketers test their own comfort levels or their subscribers' interest in their articles. Most marketers should try sending email more frequently. There is a clear correlation between frequency and strong results (Fig 6.8).

Remember, they subscribed. They asked you to send them email. They believe in the value of your content and they asked to get it. Send it to them. If and when they're tired of it, they can just unsubscribe, which is good because you really don't want to send email to people who don't want it, anyway.

Yes, if you send more frequently, the percentage of people who click on every email may drop, but your real goal here is traffic, not a high click through rate. Consider this: Even if your click through rates drop by half, sending email weekly rather than monthly will double your

traffic. You'll get half the traffic from each email, but you're sending four times as often.

So how often should you send email newsletters? The answer: *as often as you can consistently produce relevant, useful content.*

- *Minimum frequency*
  Send enough email to stay top of mind with your audience. Consider the length of the sales cycle for your product or service. If it takes one month for a prospect to meet a competitor and buy from them instead, your email frequency should be at least every two weeks.

- *Maximum frequency*
  There is a point at which you may actually annoy people with too much email, but if your content is good, you'll be surprised at how often you can send successful email campaigns. We've heard many people say, "My subscribers don't want to get email

Fig. 6.8

Bloggers who publish more often get better results

Percentage of bloggers who report "strong results" based on blogging frequency

Daily 57%	2-6 posts / week 38%	Weekly 25%	Several per month 28%	Monthly 15%	Less than monthly 15%	Irregular intervals 11%

Benchmark 26%

Source: https://www.orbitmedia.com/blog/blogging-statistics/

that often," but they never tested higher frequencies, or they got a few negative comments or unsubscribes and backed off completely.

💡 TIP! If you want to send frequent emails, consider varying the sender name so they don't all feel like they're coming from the same sender. If you send twice per week, one email can come from "Weekly Lab Safety Tips" and the other from "Dale at Laser Pro"

The real maximum should be based on the upper limit of your company's ability to produce relevant, useful content. If many people within an organization can contribute, and if you have a guest blogger outreach program, the upper limit may be high.

Focus on consistency

Once you find something that works, stick with it for a while. This will help set the expectation that your email is coming. They might not rush to their inbox every Wednesday at 9:30

a.m. ready to click, but they won't be surprised to see your message then, either.

Quality is more important than timing or frequency. If content is relevant and useful, your subscribers read it when they're ready. They may even forward it to a friend or read it more than once. If your email stats show clicks trickling in days or weeks after you send, you're doing something right.

Welcome series emails

The emails with the highest open rates are typically the automatically-sent welcome series emails, that are triggered when you have a new subscriber. They're set up in your email service provider or marketing automation system on whatever schedule you decide.

Ours is a short, 3-email series.

1. Immediately after the new subscriber signs up, they get a welcome email.

2. One week later, a second email goes out, sharing one of our most engaging articles, according to GA4.

3. Two weeks later, they get a third email, with another of our top-performing articles.

Very likely, the open rates for these emails is above your typical campaigns. As you can see from our welcome series emails, open rates are between 30% and 40% (Fig. 6.9).

Fig. 6.9

	Campaign ˄	Last Sent ...	# Sends	Revenue	# Opens	# Clicks	Open Rate	Click Rate
1	Welcom...	2022-08-02 1:	26,487	0.00	10,209	420	38.54%	1.59%
2	Welcom...		0	0.00	0	0	0.00%	0.00%
3	Welcom...	2022-08-02 1:	24,845	0.00	8,412	3,432	33.86%	13.81%
4	Welcom...		0	0.00	0	0	0.00%	0.00%
5	Welcom...	2022-08-02 1:	23,773	0.00	7,382		31.05%	11.83%

Welcome series emails typically have very high open rates

Unlike other emails, the timing of these is triggered by the visitor. They are sent when the subscriber's interest is high. They're new to your list. And you can continue to optimize your welcome series for better open rates, tuning up the subject lines, using words you know to be effective based on results of past campaigns.

6.2 LinkedIn Newsletters

In LinkedIn's ongoing quest to be a content platform and not just a directory of profiles, they added email newsletters for publishers back in 2017. Now, anyone can launch a newsletter and let LinkedIn handle the list growth and email services.

This was a brilliant strategic move for LinkedIn.

No question, their traffic is up. They're sending millions of emails with links to millions of articles on LinkedIn. It's a big opportunity for everyone. Orbit launched a LinkedIn newsletter in January of 2021 with a very simple approach:

Frequency: Weekly
The first week, the article would be from our bi-weekly newsletter on the Orbit website. The next week, the article would be a refreshed version of a previously written article. So the newsletter would alternate weekly, from brand new articles to updated past articles. This strategy worked for us because we had hundreds of old articles that our LinkedIn connections hadn't seen.

Timing: Mornings
In our experience, the best time to send a LinkedIn newsletter is early in the morning. The later in the day, the less engagement our articles get. So we try to get it out by 8am when possible.

Topics: "Practical tips for content strategy, AI, GA4 and web design"
This is the same as the rest of our content program, so the repurposing was easy.

Newsletter Name: "Digital Marketing Tips"
We deliberately gave it a very simple, specific name. We wanted anyone who sees it in their stream to know what it's about. We avoided clever, branded names, opting for simple and specific.

The newsletter grew so fast that people started asking if this was our main channel for marketing (Fig. 6.10).

Fig. 6.10

We know that we don't own that list.

We know that the visitors aren't on our site.

We made the choice deliberately after weighing the good and bad.

LinkedIn is an excellent platform for thought leadership, personal branding and networking. A LinkedIn newsletter makes all of these activities more effective. Because your audience is already there, these outcomes are easier to reach. But there are downsides too.

Let's look at the pros and cons (Fig. 6.11).

First, let's consider the downsides. Here are the disadvantages of publishing a LinkedIn newsletter vs. an email newsletter on your own blog.

1. It's not your website
They're on a site with ads and notifications. You don't control the visitors' experience.

2. It's not your email list
There's no real way to see the list of subscribers and their email addresses. You could hire a VA to crawl through every subscriber's LinkedIn profile and try to harvest the addresses one by one, but that's both tedious and spammy. They didn't subscribe to your email

Fig. 6.11

Should you launch a LinkedIn newsletter?

Advantages	Disadvantages
1. Fast list growth, great reach They can subscribe in one click.	**1. It's not your website** You don't control the experience. It's not your traffic.
2. Engagement is high You'll get more comments here than on your own site.	**2. It's not your email list** There's no way to export subscribers' addresses.
3. Efficient and easily delegated It's easy and fast to publish here. A virtual assistant can do it.	**3. Analytics aren't great** It's very limited compared to Google Analytics.
4. Cost is zero LinkedIn handles everything for you.	**4. No real email marketing tools** It has none of the typical email marketing tools.
5. You can still run your own email newsletter This isn't the exclusive location for your articles.	**5. Not awesome for SEO** Articles are unlikely to rank and links to them don't help.

newsletter. Collecting email addresses isn't the point.

3. Analytics aren't great
You can see the LinkedIn Analytics (impressions, views and engagement), but that's it. You can't see the email open and click through rates. You also don't get website metrics like engagement rate and average engagement time. Data is very limited compared to GA4.

4. No real email marketing tools
You can't split test emails with a/b testing. You can't set up automations. You can't personalize. Really none of the typical features of email marketing services are available.

5. Not helpful for SEO
This isn't a search engine optimization play at all. It is possible, but unlikely, that a LinkedIn article will rank. But if it ranks, it doesn't help you as much. And if someone links to your article, it doesn't help your website's Domain Authority at all.

Now let's look at the upside. This is what makes a LinkedIn newsletter worth it.

1. Fast list growth, great reach
It's an almost frictionless signup process. When you launch a newsletter, LinkedIn will put a call to action in the invitations of your connections and followers. They can subscribe with a single tap. No keyboard or captcha required.

2. Engagement is high
You may have noticed blog comments are down these days. Visitors are looking for answers. They aren't really looking to interact with authors. Ten years ago, it

was different. Blog comments were much more common.

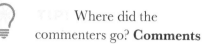 **Where did the commenters go? Comments have moved off of websites and onto social media.** There is still a lot of conversation on content, but it's on social platforms, not on websites. Many blogs have removed the comment section because engagement is so low.

3. Efficient and easily delegated
Once the article is written, it's easy to move into LinkedIn. You simply copy and paste the text, and it preserves all of the formatting. Even a very long article may take just 10 minutes to publish.

If your strategy is to repurpose articles you're already publishing (curating older pieces or distributing new ones on LinkedIn) then this is work that can easily be delegated. A virtual assistant can do it. For the first two years, we delegated the process completely.

If you're publishing from a personal account (rather than a company account), sharing access with a VA is tricky. LinkedIn doesn't like lots of devices in lots of locations logging into one personal account. Too many logins and the account may be temporarily restricted.

4. Cost is zero

LinkedIn handles the hosting and email marketing services at no cost to you. No software needed.

5. You can still run your own email newsletter

This is the main reason to try publishing a LinkedIn newsletter: there is no risk. You can continue to publish your own email newsletter. LinkedIn doesn't need to be the exclusive location for your articles. It is not an either/or question. It is a both/and opportunity.

The idea of having a second newsletter on LinkedIn often raises two concerns:

Could publishing each article twice, once on your website and once on LinkedIn, hurt your SEO? **No.** There is no duplicate content penalty and Google knows that the original is on your website. There is no SEO risk involved.

If a subscriber gets your email newsletter and the LinkedIn newsletter, would this annoy them? **Maybe.** But they can always just unsubscribe from one and keep the other. They have a choice, and they can choose based on their preference.

Publishing your first LinkedIn newsletter

If your LinkedIn newsletter is the beginning of your content marketing program, and you haven't set your content strategy yet, step zero in that process is to create and document your content marketing mission statement.

If you already have an active content marketing program, the foundations of your content strategy are in place. You know your audience, your topics and your frequency. This settles the what to blog about question, because you're simply repurposing your past articles and using LinkedIn to help distribute new articles.

Here are 10 LinkedIn newsletter best practices:

1. Decide: Personal page newsletter or company page newsletter?

Probably, you'll get better results by using a personal page. That human element is great for engagement. But for some brands, this won't work for all kinds of possible reasons: legal, HR, buy-in, etc.

Probably, a personal page newsletter is the best fit for small businesses. The company page newsletter is best for enterprises.

If you want to publish from a company page, you'll need at least 150 followers first. It's also possible to create a newsletter from a LinkedIn showcase page.

2. Give it a very descriptive name . . . even if it sounds boring

We recommend naming your newsletter something that has obvious relevance and value. You only get 30 characters. Don't get fancy. Don't brand it. Just call it what it is. Compare these two examples (Fig. 6.12). Which of these sounds better?

Marketers love to name things, but mostly, readers don't care about names.

Fig. 6.12

Which of these would you subscribe to?

They just want help. So when we named our newsletter "Digital Marketing Tips" we knew that it was a boring name. But it's specific. Clear is better than clever.

3. Write your newsletter description

Again, be very specific. Tell the reader exactly why they should click and subscribe. List the topics and keep it simple. You can write a description of up to 120 characters.

4. Set your frequency

You have four options: daily, weekly, bi-weekly or monthly. Probably, this will align with the cadence of your usual email newsletter. But if you have older content that you can add to the mix, you can go higher.

Setup is done! You're ready to publish.

5. Make the first edition good

That first edition is very important. It's special because when you hit publish on your first newsletter, all of your connections and all of your followers are going to get an invitation. This is the big promotion push. So go big on quality for your first edition. Make it your best.

6. Add some nice preheader text

The top of the newsletter article is going to appear in the subscribers inbox as preheader text. This can affect open and click through rates. So consider putting something special in the first line. We often start the articles with a little hello message with a waving hand emoji. This helps it stand out in crowded inboxes (Fig. 6.13).

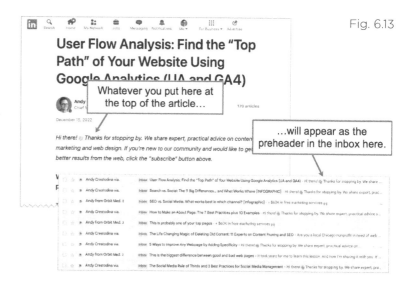

Fig. 6.13

Whatever you put here at the top of the article…

…will appear as the preheader in the inbox here.

"You should also post separately about your newsletter and mention it privately to relevant colleagues via direct messages. If you use other social channels, use them if appropriate to promote your longform content on LinkedIn. There's nothing wrong with a bit of cross-pollination, so long as you're not being spammy."

JOHN ESPIRIAN,
Relentlessly Helpful LinkedIn Expert

7. Always collaborate with (and mention) experts and influencers

If you don't think about social promotion until after the article is live, you're a little too late. The best content marketers *involve influencers and subject matter experts in the process of creating the article.* So include influencers as contributor quotes, then mention them (and thank them) in the post when you create the newsletter.

8. Add a great visual: diagrams, charts or faces

Some will see your article in their inbox. Others who have not yet subscribed will see it in their social streams. The featured image will appear in the social snippet, so it is key to your success. The more compelling the image is, the more likely your LinkedIn content will get traction.

9. Link back to the original on your site

You're committing to LinkedIn, but it's still nice to drive some website traffic. To encourage readers to head over to your site, you can post just two-thirds of an article, then add a call to action, suggesting the visitor goes to your website to get the rest, such as . . .

To read the rest of this article, go to the original on [company blog] >

That link can include the campaign tracking code so the traffic can be tracked in GA4. Unfortunately, links added as embedded media can't use tracking code. But they look nice and likely have a high click through rate (Fig. 6.14).

Fig. 6.14

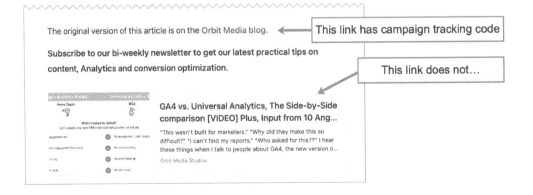

6.3 Social Media Promotion

An email message sits in a recipient's inbox, waiting to be read or deleted. But a social stream just flows past with no obligation for the viewer to act. The viewer is less committed. They're not subscribed and they may not even be a follower. They may be seeing something shared by a friend.

Social media marketing is fast-paced. Share something now and you may get a bit of traffic almost immediately. And since it's built for dialog and messaging, social media is great for starting conversations and networking.

Here are some guidelines for promoting your content on social media. First, we'll make sure your social media profiles are set up and connected to your websites. Then we'll go through best practices for posting, mentions, scheduling and automation. Finally, you'll learn tips for finding relevant influencers and networking online.

Polish your profile

If the email call to action is a mini version of your content mission statement, the social media profile is an even smaller version. Make it more than a tiny "about us." Use it as an opportunity to let possible followers know what to expect. The Social Media Mission Template from Section 5.2 will help.

WARNING Avoid adding hashtags to your social bio. If the visitor clicks one of these, they'll leave your profile and dive into an ocean of algorithm-recommended content. They are unlikely to return.

Use a face in your profile picture. Don't tweet from behind a logo, even for the company's social media account, unless you have no other choice. Faces are more personal and compelling than any other type of image. A company logo doesn't come close.

TIP To grow a company account, share the content first from the brand's social media account, then reshare that post from your personal account (or encourage your team to reshare from their own accounts). This leverages personal connections while guiding our audience toward the brand's page.

Social media/ website integration

There are good and bad ways to connect your website to your social media accounts. You should make it easy for people to find your social media accounts without actually encouraging your visitors to leave.

Remember, website visitors are hard to win and easy to lose.

Sending a visitor to a social media website puts them in the hands of a profit-driven, billion dollar company totally focused on keeping and monetizing that visitor. Those sites are filled with distractions, advertisements and competitors. How is that good for your marketing?

Don't suggest that your visitor leave your site and go to Facebook, X, YouTube and Instagram unless these social networks are a key part of your marketing strategy. Before you add a social media icon to your site, ask yourself two questions. The answer should be "yes" to both:

1. *Do I regularly share content on this social network?*
   There should be as much relevant content on the social network as on your website.

2. *Do I regularly engage with people on this social network?*
   You're not just present on that social network, but you're interacting with people, networking and building relationships (Fig. 6.15).

Now that we know which networks to add, let's consider how best to add them. Be cautious when adding social media icons. They are exit signs. No need to make them too prominent.

TIP! You don't have to be active in a social network to have a profile there. But creating a profile can help people find you. For example, if you choose not to use X (formerly Twitter), you can create a good-looking, descriptive profile and then post once, letting people know that they can find you on LinkedIn or some other network . . . and then link to that network in the social post.

Do not add colorful, candy-like social media icons to the header of every page. Here's what that looks like (Fig. 6.16):

Fig. 6.16

Instead, add social media icons to the footer and remove the color (Fig. 6.17). If a visitor is looking for your social media accounts, they can find them here.

Fig. 6.15

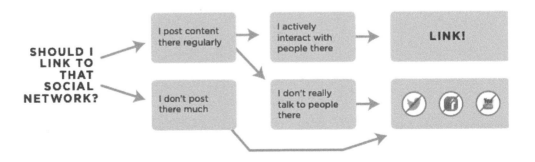

Fig. 6.17

Elements of a great social media post

The more effort and attention you put into your social media posts, the more likely you are to connect with your audience, start conversations and drive traffic. It's not enough to just click the Facebook share button on your article. As with everything else, more effort gets you more reward.

Notice how that the email signup button, which is a more valuable conversion, is more visually prominent than the social media buttons.

Here are guidelines for upgrading your social posts. Adding these elements will increase visibility and engagement on everything you share (Fig. 6.18). It's easy to imagine how this post would get more traction than just a simple share.

> Imagine walking into a store where the **biggest sign says "exit."**

Anatomy of the Perfect Social Media Post

Fig. 6.18

1. Headline best practices (benefit, number, emotion)

2. Secondary headline
3. Power trigram

4. Special characters/ emoji

5. Line Breaks

6. Quotes

7. Hashtags

8. Mentions

9. Visuals

Andy Crestodina @crestodina
Content Promotion Strategies
Here are the 50 ways to drive traffic to your next post
orbitmedia.com/blog/content-p...
How many of these are on your checklist? ✓ ✓ ✓

"Where there's traffic. there's hope."

Features #ContentMarketing insights from @bestofjess and @crazy...
@PmonPurpose, you guys might like this one...

Content Promotion Strategies: 50 Ways to Drive Traffic

Content Promotion Strategies: 50 Ways to Drive Traffic To Your Next ...
Content marketers work hard at content promotion. Here's a checklist of 50 content promotion strategies that will make your life easier.
orbitmedia.com

WARNING! Social media is more than just a dumping ground for your links. It's a place for conversations, connections and new friends. Self-promotional posts should not be the only thing in your stream. Remember the social media Rule of Thirds from Section 3.2.

1. Headline best practices

Numbers, questions, explicit benefits and curiosity will all improve your click through rates.

2. Secondary headline

A second headline or an additional description will give more detail and more reason to click.

> **Andy Crestodina** @crestodina
> 50 Content promotion strategies to drive traffic to your next post. How many of these are you using?
> orbitmedia.com/blog/content-p...

3. Power trigrams

Remember that research from the headline section in Chapter 5? Those lists that show the 3-word phrases that drive social media engagement? Try a few of those and see how it goes. I think you'll be pleased.

4. Special characters/emojis

Special characters add visual prominence. Just notice how these characters stand out on this page:

→ An arrow is an easy way to draw attention to a link in your social post.

☞ A pointing finger may be even better.

★ Using a star can make something stand out.

✓ Adding a check mark shows that something is actionable.

But don't overdo it. Make sure that these more playful, less formal characters fit with the voice and tone of your brand, or you may upset your boss. 😠

> **Andy Crestodina** @crestodina
> Content Promotion Strategies...
> Here are 50 ways to use #ContentMarketing drive more traffic to your next blog post
> orbitmedia.com/blog/content-p...

5. Line breaks

Few marketers do this, so it's a good way to help your posts stand out. Line breaks increase the vertical height of your social post, making it more visually prominent. And the white space keeps text within the post itself from getting too crowded.

> **Andy Crestodina** @crestodina
> Content Promotion Strategies.
> Here are 50 different ways to drive traffic to your next post...
> orbitmedia.com/blog/content-p...
>
> How many of these are you using?

6. Quotes

If there is a compelling sound bite from the article, use it as the text in the social post.

> **Andy Crestodina** @crestodina
> "Where there's traffic... there's hope"
> Content Promotion Strategies to drive traffic to your next post
> orbitmedia.com/blog/content-p...

7. Hashtags

A hashtag is a clickable keyword or topic, such as #contentmarketing, #blogtips or #Chicago. They can increase the visibility of your social posts.

Andy Crestodina @crestodina
Content Promotion Strategies...
Here are 50 different ways to drive traffic to your next blog post
☞ orbitmedia.com/blog/content-p...

When someone clicks a hashtag in any post, they'll see all the posts with that hashtag. If they see yours, that's good! But if someone is looking at your post and they click the hashtag instead of the link to your content, that's bad. The idea is that your content is more click-worthy than the other content on that same hashtag.

TIP! Instagram posts don't include links, so hashtags here won't compete with a link to your content. That may be one reason why Instagram posts often have tons of hashtags. On the other hand, LinkedIn posts tend to have very few hashtags . . .

8. Mentions

Mentioning others in your social media posts is so effective that we're giving it its own section. It's part networking, part promotion and part gratitude. Mentioning or "tagging" someone is so fundamental to social media, that you've likely already done it hundreds of times. But in case you need a refresher, see Fig. 6.19.

If they're active on social media, they'll see the notification and be glad for the mention. They may even reshare your post with a simple click. If you mention someone who isn't active in social media, they'll probably miss it unless they have email notifications turned on. So it's ideal to mention people who are active in that network and likely to engage with the content.

Who to mention

Mention contributors or anyone who helped to create the article. It lets them know it's live, but it's also a small way to say thank you. Here are the types of people you can mention when sharing on social media:

Fig. 6.19

Social Network	Method	Example
X	Enter @, start typing their name, select from the dropdown list	@crestodina
Facebook	Enter @, start typing their name, select from the dropdown list, or tag them within the photo	@Andy Crestodina
Linkedin	Enter @, start typing their name, select from the dropdown list	@Andy Crestodina
Instagram	Enter their account name or let the app tag them within the photo	@crestodina

- *Anyone quoted or cited in the article*
  If you quoted someone, a mention is a way to let them know. Also mention anyone or any account related to the content: *the researchers you cited, the venue you were at, the photographer who took the picture, the designer who made the chart, the makers of the tool you were using, the person who inspired you, etc.*

- *Contributors*
  If you reached out to a person or two to get a contributor quote while writing (the recommended, co-creation approach) now is the time to mention them when you share.

- *Anyone who would sincerely love the article*
  This kind of "targeted sharing" involves finding and mentioning people who are sure to like the article. The idea is to find that tiny slice of overlapping topics or themes, and then use social media to find people who have both in their bio.

Did you write a zombie-themed post about corporate tax accounting? Find and mention people with "zombie" and "corporate tax" in their social bios bio. Did you write an article about changing careers from clinical research to government regulation? Find and mention someone with those titles in their LinkedIn profile.

9. Visuals

As always, images are critical. Research consistently shows that more-visual social posts get more shares, engagement and clicks. The featured image from the article should automatically appear in the social post when the article is shared. If there is a more compelling image from within the article, such as a diagram, add it manually. The ultimate visual is video. More on that in a bit.

TIP! The image suggestions from Section 5.7 can have a huge impact. Images with faces are powerful attention grabbers. And when the headline is included within the image itself, it is much more likely to be read. Create new images for social posts that include the author's picture and a catchy headline.

Use AI to help you make a better social media post

The social post previews the content that you're sharing. The best part of the content to preview is the part that is likely to be the most interesting to the reader. It's often difficult to know what aspects of the content to spotlight in the social post, but AI can help.

If you give the article to AI with the following prompt, it will help you find the most compelling or provocative parts of the article. It also works well for videos if you give it the transcript.

Prompt:

You are a content strategist, an expert at finding which aspects of content and topics are most likely to be engaging to a reader and compelling when used in a social media post. I'm giving you a piece of content. List the top three quotes, soundbites, statistics or sections that are unexpected, memorable and likely to be effective at improving click through rates and engagement when used in a social media post.

[paste in article or transcript]

The response will give you clues into which aspects of the article are likely to make for good social posts. Consider using those quotes or soundbites in the social post. For best results, do this in the conversation that started with the persona prompt, as we showed in Section 4.8.

Of course, you can also have AI write the social post itself, but it will likely need careful editing. AI gets pretty excited when asked to help with social media. Without careful training, it will likely use a spammy tone with lots of emojis and exclamation points.

Prime the social pump before promoting

Some of the most effective content promotion techniques require pre-promotion. The trick is to do a few things *before you publish*. Here's a fun, social way to get more people involved with your content.

1. **Create a social post that asks a question or shares a perspective related to your topic.**
   Use a relevant hashtag. Add an interesting image. Mention people

who have engaged on the topic elsewhere. Don't link to anything. You're just asking a question or raising a topic and asking for input.

2. **Interact with anyone who chimes in.**
   Respond to their answers. Look for opportunities to mention (and tag) more people. Keep the conversation going.

3. **Make a note of the people who engaged.**
   You can write them down. Better yet, grab the link to the actual social media post and save it in the notes in your content template. Fig. 6.20 shows how to find the link to the post in LinkedIn.

4. **Use their input in your article.**
   Let their input inform the article. And if anyone had especially interesting insights, invite them to contribute a quote.

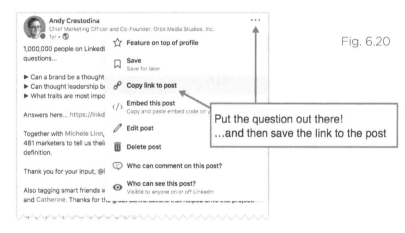

Fig. 6.20

5. **Publish, share . . . and mention.** Now that you know who is interested, you can mention them when you share, just as we described above. Thank them for their input.

Don't just promote an article. Have an open, public conversion. Socialize the topic before you write, while you're writing and after you publish. Listen and learn. (See Fig. 6.21.) Without this conversation and collaboration, the content isn't optimized for social media.

Fig. 6.21

Typical social promotion "Post and pray"	Conversation, Collaboration and Co-Promotion
1. Write article 2. Publish 3. Share on social media	1. Share a question or opinion about the topic on social media. See who engages. 2. Invite people with interesting perspectives to contribute a quote. 3. Write article 4. Publish 5. Share on social media, tag the contributors and people who engaged in the earlier conversation (they may engage or share) 6. Offer to collaborate with anyone who wants to write about this anywhere else.

6.4 Social Media Video

The ultimate upgrade to a social post is video. Videos are effective at catching and holding attention, so Facebook, Instagram and LinkedIn all push video posts to the top of social streams. They keep visitors on the platforms. Video posts win in the algorithms because they win in psychology.

It is *forma maxima*. Marketers who do video do better on social media.

So rather than make a post with a headline, hashtag and link to your article, make a tiny one-minute commercial, where you introduce your article to your followers. You can use your cell phone or webcam, but a little more effort will get you much better results.

What you'll need

In the home office or at global HQ, a little bit of equipment and software do wonders for audio and video quality.

Here is your shopping list to build a tiny studio.

- **DSLR camera with HDMI out**
  Get a cam link so you can connect it through USB. It's an enormous upgrade over a webcam. The difference is amazing.

- **Professional microphone**
  Ideally on a boom so it's easy to move and adjust. Also acoustic tiles are helpful if you're facing a wall.

- **Dimmable LED light or light with softbox diffuser**
  Ring lights are overrated. Who wants to stare directly into a light all day? And the reflection on your glasses is terrible. Get a small, warm, dimmable LED and set it up on an angle.

- **Basic editing software**
  Camtasia is my favorite. It's way better than iMovie and way easier than After Effects. You just need to be able to do basic cuts, captions and transitions.

The total cost of all of the AV equipment in Fig. 6.22 was $1,385. The camera was about half of that. I no longer use that ring light. Those things will give you a headache.

You're making a one-minute social media promotion video. Press record on the camera and on Camtasia. Now sit back, take a deep breath and pretend you're leaving an enthusiastic voice mail. If you mess up, just pause, smile and start over.

Fig. 6.22

1. **Smile** 0:00
   This will be the first frame of the video.

2. **Introduce yourself** 0:02
   Just your name and title are fine.

3. **Tell the viewer what you're doing here** 0:05

   Start with a punchy statement and an extra bit of body language.

   "I'm sharing with you an article about . . ."

   "This is just a quick video to tell you about . . ."

   "Here is a quick summary of our latest advice . . ."

4. **Summarize the article** 0:45
   Quickly go through the key points of the article with a few words about each. Be positive. Use your hands.

5. **The CTA** 0:55
   Invite them to visit.

"If this sounds useful to you, just click the link in the post . . ."

"Click the link and check out the article for the full story . . ."

"The link in this post will take you to the complete process . . ."

6. **Thank them for watching** 1:00
   Stick the landing with a very brief sign-off. It can be one simple word: thanks.

Edit, add captions, export

Press stop. Since you recorded it right into Camtasia, the file is open and ready to go. Make sure your head is big and centered. This is for social media, so on a desktop, your face will appear in just a small part of the browser. On mobile, the entire screen is small. Let your face fill at least 30% of the frame, leaving room for captions below.

Editing is really just cutting out the mistakes and trimming it down to that one-minute mark. Do not try to make it perfect. Imperfections are what make it authentic. Those little breaks are called *jump cuts.*

In the social stream, the video will start playing without sound as viewers scroll toward it. Our goal is to slow them down and catch their attention, so captions are critical. A silent, talking head doesn't have a lot of stopping power. The text of the captions will draw them into the content. Captions are also essential for accessibility.

Once you're done, you export your new video as an MP4 file and upload it to the social network. For the rest of the post, use a headline, mentions, hashtags and all of the other recommendations listed above.

Give the post a nudge

Once the post is live, it's very helpful to jump-start the conversation by sending it directly to a few people right away. This helps trigger the algorithms that push the video to the top of a greater number of social streams. First, grab the link of the social post and get it out to a few close allies (Fig. 6.23).

- Email to a few close friends.

- Share it within a relevant private group.

- Post it in your company Slack board or in Google Chat.

If they're truly close friends, the request will be very short.

Fig. 6.23

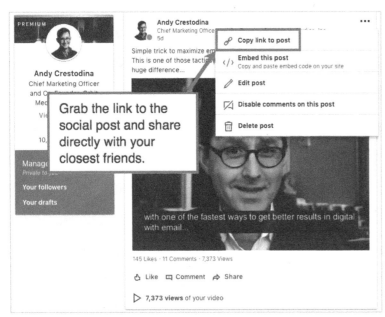

Grab the link to the social post and share directly with your closest friends.

If this all sounds like a strange and indirect way to promote a business, you're right. It is. I'm suggesting sending 1:1 emails to promote a video that promotes an article that promotes your business. It does sound crazy. Things used to be so much simpler, didn't they? (Fig. 6.24)

This approach is a bit derivative, but also very effective. Content is an excellent way to promote a business. Social video is a great way to promote content. And directly sharing the video with close friends is a great way to promote the social media video.

Measure

The social network will show you the number of likes, comments, shares and views. But keep in mind that a "view" in social media is a video playing for just three seconds. Viewers may have just slowed down a little bit as they scrolled past. Social metrics aren't really what we're looking for.

"Super quick favor! Could you please take a look at this post and like it or comment if you think it's deserving. Thanks, buddy!"

If you added campaign tracking codes to the link, you can see the actual website traffic, conversion rate and new email subscribers. Fig. 6.25 is an example from a single social media video.

- 500+ visitors and 10+ subscribers

- The post had an effective life span of four days

Of course, the reach of your video is a function of the size of your network. Larger and more active followings will see greater reach and engagement from any social activity. Results vary.

Throughout the ages, marketing means...

Fig. 6.24

1950-2004			ads that promote...	the business
2005-2009			content that promotes...	the business
2010-2017		promote the...	content that promotes...	the business
Today	promote the...	social video that promotes the	content that promotes...	the business

Fig. 6.25

Fig. 6.26

	Typical social media post	Video social media post
Time to create	3 minutes	30 minutes (10x effort)
Traffic generated	3 visits	300 visits (100x results)

These videos often take 30 minutes to produce, including adding captions. That's roughly 10x the effort of creating a typical social post. But the results were 100x the results of a typical post (Fig. 6.26).

If you can't (or just don't want to) shoot a video for every single article you publish, focus on those major content projects that were 10x the effort to create, such as original research. Or do a content audit (see Section 8.1) to find the articles that convert visitors into subscribers at the highest rates, then use social video to promote those articles again.

In other words, put your best cheese on your best mousetraps.

When to share and how often

Effective social promotion requires frequent and repetitive sharing. You might be surprised at how many times you'll need to share something to make it visible. This is because social streams move fast! The "organic reach" of a typical social media post (the percentage of your followers who see it) is as low as 2% on Facebook and 5% on LinkedIn.[2] Very few members of your audience will actually see anything you post. So you'll need to share the article many times on each network in which you are active.

2. https://www.ignitesocialmedia.com/social-media-strategy/social-media-organic-reach-2021-who-actually-sees-your-content/

Here is an example of what social sharing might look like for a specific article for a company active on several social networks (Fig. 6.27). This might look like a lot, but it's really not. I know social media marketers who post several times per hour on certain networks!

Now let's consider what times of day to share. There are a few ways to think about social media timing, ranging from general advice to actual analysis.

Post when people are active on social media

There is one time of day that makes sense for a lot of North American marketers: 11 a.m. Central Time (Fig. 6.28).

- Noon is lunchtime on the East Coast, a good time for social media

- 11 a.m. is late morning in the Midwest, not a bad time for social

- 9 a.m. is early in the workday on the West Coast, another good time for social

You can apply this thinking for any audience, anywhere in the world. But keep in mind, best practices have hidden risks. Millions of other marketers are using this same thinking. Consider this idea:

Post when others aren't sharing as much

Counter-competitive timing can give you an advantage. Since fewer marketers post on nights and on weekends, these

Fig. 6.27

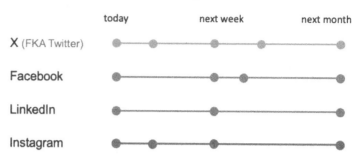

Put Content into Heavy Social Rotation

Fig. 6.28

11 a.m. CT, the "best" time to post on social media

11:00am CT
The East is eating lunch while the West is getting to work

are times when it's easier to rise above the noise. You can get a lot of traction by being active when others aren't, but not if you don't try.

Before you jump in when the pool is crowded, consider sharing just before or just after the hour. If people have a minute just before an appointment (10:58), they're likely to check out their social streams. Or if someone else is late for a call (11:02), they might take out their phone and look at their feed. Credit for this tip goes to Jay Baer, who calls these "micro-opportunity windows."

Post when your specific audience is active

There are tools that tell you when your followers are active and likely to engage with your content. If you use a social media management tool, you may already have access to this report. Here's what it looks like in Agorapulse. (Fig. 6.29).

TIP! Promote your content on social media one day before promoting it through email marketing. Readers from social media may share or comment. Those share numbers may appear next to your sharing buttons and the comment may appear below the article. These can make the post look a bit better when that surge of email visitors arrive.

ADVANCED TIP! If you track the click through rates from social media, you can see which social posts generate the most clicks to the article. You can then use the headline from that social post as the subject line of your email marketing. Your next subject line may be waiting for you in Facebook Page Insights.

Now we know what to share on social media (everything), how to share (with images, links and mentions) and when to share (when our audience is active or when our competitors are not). It's time to get into the mechanics of sharing and scheduling tools.

Fig. 6.29

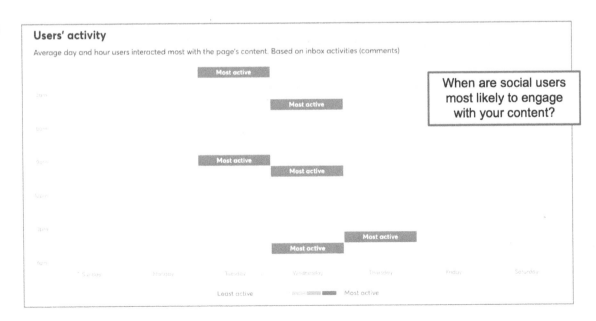

Users' activity

Average day and hour users interacted most with the page's content. Based on inbox activities (comments)

When are social users most likely to engage with your content?

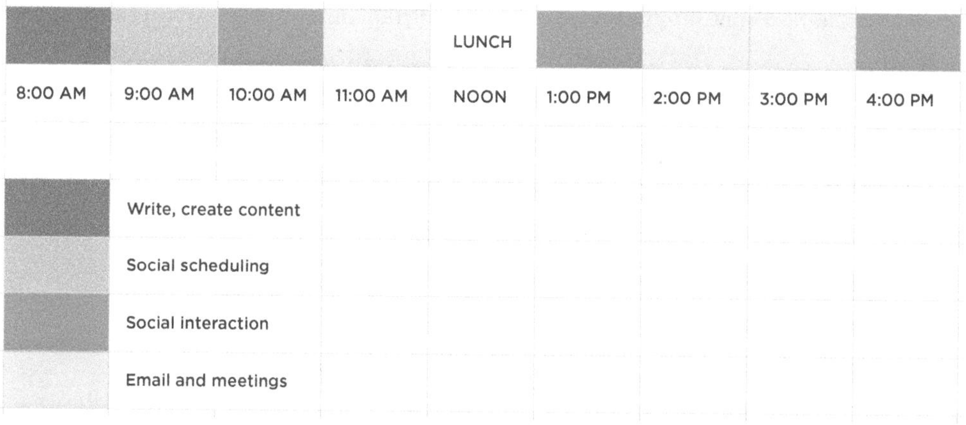

| 8:00 AM | 9:00 AM | 10:00 AM | 11:00 AM | NOON | 1:00 PM | 2:00 PM | 3:00 PM | 4:00 PM |

LUNCH

Write, create content

Social scheduling

Social interaction

Email and meetings

Fig. 6.30

Social media scheduling

There are hundreds of social media management tools out there. They help with things like listening, research, tracking and measuring. Right now you need a tool to get your social media posts scheduled.

It just wouldn't be efficient to go to every social media website several times per day to promote your article. That would be both time-consuming and distracting. The real social media experts are very efficient with their time. They set aside blocks of time a few times per day to share, listen and interact (Fig. 6.30).

A day in the life of a social media marketer

One of the routine tasks for social media marketers is scheduling the social posts for the day (or the week or the month). These posts may be industry news, articles written by friends and collaborators, or anything else that followers might find interesting. In other words, the second third in The Rule of Thirds from Chapter 3.

But your focus now is on content promotion. The most efficient approach here is to schedule many shares over time and to do this all at once using a social media scheduling tool. That way all of the social promotion for your article is taken care of.

The most common tools for this are Hootsuite, Agorapulse and Buffer. These are paid tools, but there are free versions of each with limited durations and feature sets. They allow you to preschedule social shares on different networks months in advance.

💡 **TIP:** You can let the tools decide when to share by using their auto-scheduling features. They will automatically analyze your audience and share when they are the most active.

Once you have all of your posts lined up, with a nice variety of mentions, hashtags, quotes and images, your schedule will look something like Fig. 6.31.

Now that your content is scheduled for promotion, you can focus your social media energy on interacting with people, sharing, answering questions, thanking people who shared and commented on your content, and networking with influencers.

Fig. 6.31

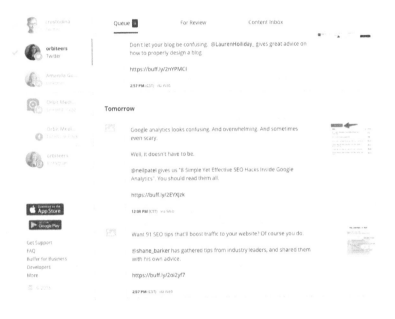

Create an echo chamber

If you've done a good job promoting the content on social media, it's been shared on several social networks. Now you have an opportunity to increase the visibility by creating a mini-echo chamber of conversation. Here's how:

- If the content was on Facebook and LinkedIn, comment on the new shares with a thank you. If there's a conversation happening within the comments, jump in.

- If the content was retweeted, thank the person who shared it. The thank yous and responses can easily triple the number of tweets related to a piece of content.

- If the article generated comments, respond to them. Then find the commenters on the social networks and let them know you've responded.

- If the article generated lots of traffic, shares and comments, tweet about the popularity of the article: "Wow! Everyone seems to like this post . . ."

The idea is to create a small feedback loop and take advantage of any activity by responding. This can extend what is often a very short life of content within social networks. It increases the chance of content appearing at the top of social streams and becoming more visible.

Move quickly. Timing is important since, within Facebook and LinkedIn, posts that have lots of activity (likes and clicks) stay at the top of people's streams longer. Be ready to have conversations, say thank you and respond to comments when social promotion begins.

6.5 Social Media Automation

Ever wonder how some accounts post so much so easily?

The answer is automation. It requires a paid tool such as CoSchedule or Agorapulse, but it's very efficient. When set up properly, the tool promotes your best content over a long period of time. You can schedule social media posts days, weeks and months in advance.

⚠️ WARNING! This is about efficient content promotion. It isn't about spamming the social networks or letting a robot do your job. The days of blasting the same messages across multiple accounts are over. In fact, it's against X's terms of service to do so. Make each post unique. You still have to listen to people and interact if you want to be a good social media marketer.

You're about to fill your social streams with a consistent flow of unique, high-quality well-timed posts.

This is relevant only to the promotion of your own content, the first third in the Rule of Thirds. This won't help you share industry news or build connections with influencers. It will be useful to anyone who meets these criteria:

- You have published a large body of high-quality "evergreen" articles. This method doesn't work well for news or other timely content.

- You frequently interact with your audience on social media.

- You've got the budget for a paid tool.

Automated social posts will be shared multiple times, so only automate your very best content. The articles with the highest value to both your business and your audience. First, you need to find these super engaging posts. Then you'll set up the tool to keep them in rotation. Here is a step-by-step process for automating social media promotion.

1. Find the content that gets reshared most.

Put your own site into BuzzSumo and see which posts have the most shares. Without a paid account, it will show you the top five (Fig. 6.32).

Fig. 6.32

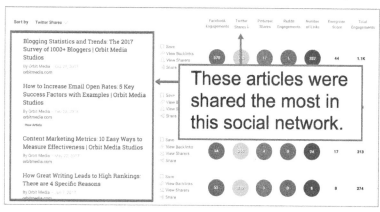

These articles were shared the most in this social network.

These are the posts that are most likely to get reshared. Put them on the list.

2. Find the posts that got clicked the most.

Next, find the posts that are most likely to be clicked. What gets shared doesn't always get clicked, and since our goal is traffic, we are looking for click through rates, not just likes and shares. Likes and shares are vanity metrics. But clicks are traffic.

Each social network has its own analytics that will show you engagement on social posts. Some, like X (formerly Twitter) and Facebook, show you the number of clicks on each post. Paid tools like Hootsuite and Buffer also show this data, so you'll need to look in several places. You'll quickly discover that some posts get much and Facebook, show you the number of clicks on each post. Paid tools like Hootsuite and Buffer also show this data, so you'll need to look in several places. You'll quickly discover that some

posts get much more traction than others (Fig. 6.33).

These are the posts that are most likely to get clicked. Put these on the list.

3. Find the content that converts the most visitors.

Some content does an amazing job of inspiring visitors to subscribe to your list. Other content not so much. So our next job is to find the posts that are most likely to inspire your visitors to subscribe. You'll find a detailed step-by-step process for discovering those high-converting posts in Section 8.1.

Find the posts that are most likely to turn visitors into subscribers. Put these on the list.

4. Find the content that you worked on the hardest.

Some of your content took a lot of time and/or money to produce. Original

Fig. 6.33

research, in-depth guides and video are good examples. Putting these into rotation using automation will increase your return (visibility and traffic) on the investment (the time and cost put into production).

These are the posts that need the boost in ROI. Put these on the list.

Now that you've found all your best candidates for social media promotion, it's time to load them into the automation tool. Here's how to set things up using CoSchedule. It's a paid tool that handles every one of your calendar-related marketing activities, including publishing and social media promotion.

5. Create the posts.

In CoSchedule, click on the plus sign in the top right to create a post. Choose which type of content you would like to share (podcast, article, blog post, video, etc . . .). Now enter your link into the tool and select one or more social networks.

These posts are going to be shared multiple times, so make them good. We recommend using every trick we listed earlier: images, numbers, trigger words, mentions, etc.

So put it all together, and here's what a post looks like when you create the posts in CoSchedule.

6. Create the schedule.

CoSchedule allows you to select which days you would like to share your content: the day it's published, the day after, a week after publish or a month after publish. This will share your

content at those specific times. Since we're automating the sharing of content we've published in the past, just choose several times over the days and weeks ahead.

7. "ReQueue" the content.

CoSchedule Analytics shows you which posts were engaged with the most on social media. This makes it easy to confirm which are the top performers and best candidates for automation.

Toggle the ReQueue switch from the post and select "best time." From here on, that post will be pulled from your content library and shared repeatedly at the best time based on each social media channel (Fig. 6.34).

Fig. 6.34

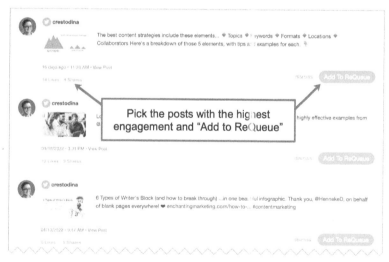

"**Your time is too valuable.** Intelligently automate content and get more mileage out of every message."

GARRETT MOON,
CEO and CoFounder, CoSchedule

That's it! You've loaded your tool with the best posts, scheduled for the best times of day. It will now share automatically until you turn it off and reload with even higher-performing social posts.

This process can easily save you five hours per month picking out content, writing social posts, choosing images and scheduling shares.

The return on investment is very high.

Cost	3+ hours of setup time
	$40 per month for software (CoSchedule or MeetEdgar)
Benefit	Increased traffic from social media (12% increase in our case)
	5+ hours per month of time savings

Now that your self-promotional, traffic-driving posts are all set up, you can focus on finding and sharing other interesting things and online networking.

WARNING! When you set up a tool to automatically and continuously promote content over time, you are also committing to keeping that content up-to-date. Keep a close eye on these articles to make sure they remain current. You'll find tips for updating older content in Chapter 8.

TIP! Remove the dates from your blog. A lot of brands publish advice that doesn't quickly go out of style (so-called "evergreen" content) rather than news or other timely information. If this is your content strategy, removing the date from the template of your blog may increase social sharing and lower bounce rates, because the content won't look old. Those dates really show your age!

If you do remove dates from the blog template, you can still add dates into a headline and body text whenever relevant.

Manual, old-school sharing

Before we wrap up this section on social promotion, let's not forget the least automated, most effective way to share content: the personal email. Send a relevant article along with a personal note to a high-value contact. It could be a prospect, a client, a referral partner, a journalist, a job candidate or an industry thought leader. This should be part of any content promotion checklist.

This is especially powerful when the value of the transaction is very high. If you sell helicopters or provide wealth management services, and you've created an article about the latest in-flight controls or tax law changes, send the article to your current prospects individually via personal email. They are already in your funnel. The prospects in your pipeline are your most important audience.

6.6 Influencer Marketing and Collaboration

They're big names. They're influential. They have an audience that you would like to reach. And it would be great if you could connect and collaborate with them.

But how can you connect with these influencers?

In this section, you'll learn how to use social media to find, connect with and collaborate with influencers in your niche. You'll learn to build the relationships that will power your marketing. It's the relationships with influencers that lead to press mentions, shares, links, rankings and traffic.

According to that annual survey of bloggers we keep talking about, the marketers who collaborate with influencers consistently get the best results. Bloggers who collaborate with influencers every time are twice as likely to report strong results as the average survey respondent (Fig. 6.35).

Influencer marketing. Blogger relations. Digital PR. Whatever you call it, it's one of the most effective approaches to content marketing.

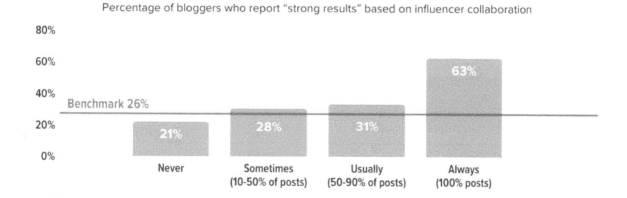

Bloggers who collaborate with influencers more get better results

Fig. 6.35

Percentage of bloggers who report "strong results" based on influencer collaboration

- 80%
- 60%
- 40%
- Benchmark 26%
- 20%
- 0%

Never	Sometimes (10-50% of posts)	Usually (50-90% of posts)	Always (100% posts)
21%	28%	31%	63%

n=1051

Source: https://www.orbitmedia.com/blog/blogging-statistics/

What's influencer marketing?

Influencer marketing is a strategic approach to marketing focused on identifying the people who already have the trust and attention of the audience you want to reach and then collaborating in ways that promote your content and brand to that audience.

Working with influencers is a fast and efficient way to reach a large target audience. It applies to a wide range of marketing tactics. There are *paid and organic* versions of influencer marketing, just as there are paid and organic versions of search engine marketing and social media marketing.

Paid influencer marketing is advertising and is regulated as such. In some cases, the influencer is compensated with free products, but it's always a transaction.

- A car brand pays a famous YouTuber to drive around in their product.

- A travel destination gives a free stay to an Instagram celebrity.

- A baby clothing company sends products to a mommy blogger, hoping for a review.

Organic influencer marketing is about collaboration, but it's still a kind of transaction. Usually, it's an exchange of expertise and exposure.

- Blogger invites an influential expert to contribute a quote to an article.

- Editor accepts a guest post from a blogger who is looking to reach a larger audience.

- Brand interviews thought leaders on a series of podcasts or webinars.

This is a book about content marketing, so our focus here is on earning attention, not buying it. Our goal is to connect and collaborate through content. We're doing organic, not paid, marketing.

TIP! It's not about the size of your following, but the quality of your relationships. Some of the people who can help you are happy to do it. Why? Because they know and trust you. The ultimate outcome of influencer marketing is friendship.

Which influencers have the most value?

When most people think about influencer marketing, they think of Instagram celebrities who post about fashion and travel. That's not really what we're talking about here. We're not necessarily even looking for influencers with big followings.

The influencers who can help the most are the content creators. They may mention us on social media but they may also link to us from their websites. Let's review our list of the types of people who create content:

- Bloggers and blog editors

- Journalists and columnists

- Authors

- Podcasters

- Event and webinar producers

Now let's look closer at their levels of reach and influence. Here I've adapted a page from Mark Schaefer's book *Marketing Rebellion* (Fig. 6.36).

I recommend avoiding that top tier for a few reasons. First, social media celebrities are difficult to reach and collaborate with. Too busy. Second, a social mention isn't likely to drive many visits your way. And third, visitors who come from social media aren't very likely to convert.

TIP! Not all influential people are famous. Consider anyone who is known to and trusted by your audience. They may not be well-known outside your industry or geography, but they're highly relevant in your niche.

In my experience, most content marketers overvalue the benefits of social mentions from internet celebrities. Although an Instagram or YouTube celebrity might have a huge audience, a collaboration with them is unlikely to lead to any search ranking benefits.

- If a **social media influencer shares your content**, the benefits are short-lived. The life span of your mention in their social stream can be measured in minutes. If you do get a traffic boost, it will be over before the day is done.

The Five Types of Influencers

Fig. 6.36

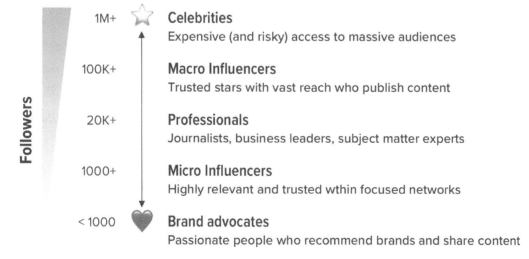

Followers		
1M+	**Celebrities**	Expensive (and risky) access to massive audiences
100K+	**Macro Influencers**	Trusted stars with vast reach who publish content
20K+	**Professionals**	Journalists, business leaders, subject matter experts
1000+	**Micro Influencers**	Highly relevant and trusted wthin focused networks
< 1000	**Brand advocates**	Passionate people who recommend brands and share content

Source: Mark Schaeffer, Marketing Rebellion

Fig. 6.37

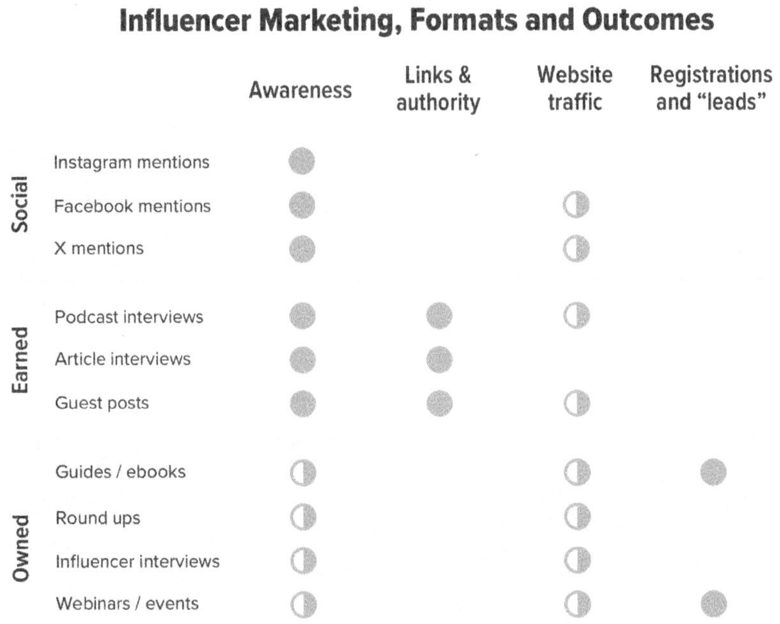

Influencer Marketing, Formats and Outcomes

		Awareness	Links & authority	Website traffic	Registrations and "leads"
Social	Instagram mentions	●			
	Facebook mentions	●		◐	
	X mentions	●		◐	
Earned	Podcast interviews	●	●	◐	
	Article interviews	●	●		
	Guest posts	●	●	◐	
Owned	Guides / ebooks	◐		◐	●
	Round ups	◐		◐	
	Influencer interviews	◐		◐	
	Webinars / events	◐		◐	●

- If a **content creator mentions you on their website**, it has a more durable benefit. The link passes a bit of authority from their website to yours. And that authority can eventually help every page on your website rank for more valuable phrases (Fig. 6.37).

Some collaborative formats, such as webinars, grow your email list. People who want the advice of that influencer may register to watch them give a presentation on your webinar. Now you have their email address and can use it for future content marketing.

Now that we know we're looking for the creators, there are two main criteria for picking influencers to connect with:

Relevant: Will it be an effective collaboration?

- Is this person known and trusted by my audience?

- Are they a writer? Do they create content in my niche?

- Do they have an active social media following?

- Are they likely to share or promote content that we create together?

Collaborative: Is this person likely to work with me?

- Will this person respond if I reach out?

- Are they likely to accept my invitation to collaborate?

- What kind of pitch or outreach would likely be successful?

Salespeople have always known the value of a strong personal network. But marketers have been slower to catch on.

Influencer identification is the first step. If you've been active within the industry, you may already know of some good potential collaborators. You may know them from their content or they might already be in your network.

 **Leverage internal experts.** There are people inside the business with deep subject matter expertise. Some of them may be happy to be quoted in an article. This adds credibility to the business and humanizes the brand. It can also be good for culture, morale and professional development of the team member.

This is a good starting point, but it's not likely that you already know all of the people whom your audience trusts. Go beyond the top-of-mind short list and research new potential collaborators.

How to find influencers using social media

If the names of influential content creators in your niche don't immediately come to mind, don't worry. They're easy to find. Virtually anyone you can imagine can be found in minutes using social media.

Suppose you're a B2B marketer in the aerospace industry. One of your goals is to grow awareness with rocket scientists. Connecting and collaborating with aerospace bloggers could be a great

Social media is the world's greatest phone book.

shortcut. You go to LinkedIn and search for "blogger," then filter for the aviation and aerospace industry. There are hundreds of results. Likely a few of these are potential collaborators.

LinkedIn shows if they have followers and how many. It also shows if you have mutual connections. And the Connect button is right there. You can do your research, identification and outreach all from one platform (Fig 6.38).

Dig deeper into the accounts that look interesting. Are they sharing lots

"You don't have to be connected with the ultra-famous to be successful. The goal should be to **become a micro-influencer** and be known by the 100-200 professionals who are decision-makers in your professional sphere."

DAVID J.P. FISHER,
Sales Expert and Author of Hyper-Connecting Selling

Fig. 6.38

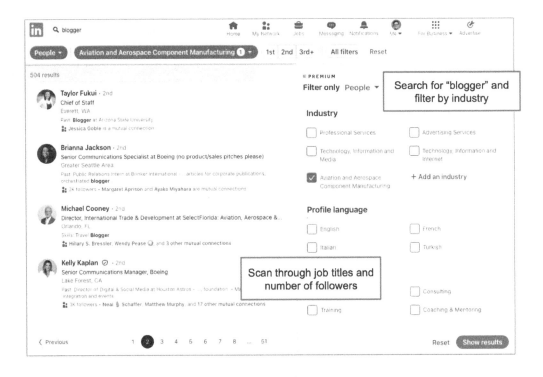

of content? Are they interacting with other people? Are they active on other networks? When you've found a few winners, add them to your list of people to reach out to and collaborate with.

Hesitant to reach out? Don't be. If your outreach message is "Can I feature you?" they are very likely to respond positively. This is not a sales pitch, it's an offer to collaborate on content. Remember, you're a publisher, so to them, your message will feel like an opportunity for publicity. Most people will want to collaborate.

Another way to find collaborators for an article on social media is to first start a conversation on the topic. Post a question or perspective related to the topic and see if anyone engages with your post. If anyone shares an interesting

point of view, consider asking them for a contributor quote for the article. If they have an engaged following, that's a bonus.

Once the article with their contributions goes live, mention them when you share it on that same social network. They may help promote it by sharing it with their audience. You can also reach out to anyone who engaged with your initial post, letting them know that you covered the topic in more detail.

When you "prime the pump" by starting a conversation on social media before you write the article (see Fig. 6.21 again), you are likely to create something of higher value (more perspectives) and with greater reach (more people helping to amplify).

Often the best contributors are those who have views that contrast with those in the article. This makes the content more interesting to the reader and can help trigger discussion on social media. Don't wait for the conversation to start in the social comments. Use conversation elements, such as dissent, in the article itself.

How to find influential bloggers using paid tools

Paid tools, such as Onalytica, can help you discover influencers that you might have missed doing social media searches. These tools have filtering (show people, not companies), sorting (by topical authority) and advanced search features that make it easy to find influential subject matter experts (Fig. 6.39).

Once you've found some good potential collaborators, you can then use the tools to add influencers to lists, create influencer marketing campaigns and track the performance of those campaigns on dashboards. You can watch the share of voice for your brand change over time.

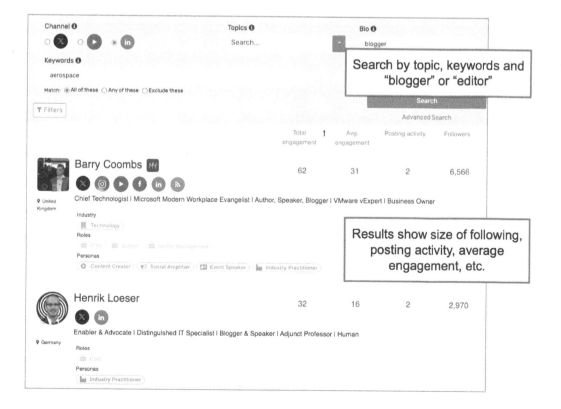

Fig. 6.39

How to find influential bloggers using AI

Here again, AI can help. The services that can crawl the web (ChatGPT Plus) are the most useful for identifying influencers.

For best results, use the conversation that started with the persona. This will help it stay focused on your specific audience. Try this prompt along with the draft article. Either paste in the content or upload it as an attachment.

 Prompt:

You are an influencer marketing expert, skilled at content marketing and B2B influencer identification. The best influencers for collaboration on an article are subject matter experts on the topic and also have an engaged following on a social media platform where our persona is active.

I'm giving you the draft of an article. Suggest five influencers who could provide interesting insights as contributor quotes to this article. Explain why you suggested them.

[Paste in or upload draft article]

The next step is manual. Go to the networks where they are active and look closely at their profiles and posts. Are they collaborating with others? Do they share generously? Do their followers engage with the content?

One or two isn't enough. You should have a list of 10+ potential collaborators. Now let's get on with the process of slowly making friends.

"Make it an everyday habit to build **authentic and meaningful relationships with influencers**. Because I love to meet people, I engage in this sort of activity all the time. I'm not thinking about benefits or results. I'm not thinking about "influencer outreach," I'm thinking instead about "meeting people." My motivation is to get to know someone new, someone I may learn from."

DENNIS SHIAO,
Director of Content Marketing, DNN Software

💡 TIP! A list of influencers and potential collaborators is one of many lists that every good content strategist maintains. Other lists include topic ideas, guest blogging/PR opportunities, keyphrases, common questions asked by your audience, catchy sound bites and quotes, compliments and possible testimonials, etc. Great content marketers are great collectors.

6.7 The 12-Step Online Networking Guide

Building relationships is easier than it used to be. Back in the old days, there were just three ways to connect: in-person (knock, knock), the phone (ring!) and mail. Today, thanks to social media, there are a lot more options. And each little action is visible and can bring you closer together.

Unfortunately, a lot of content and influencer marketers move too fast. Looking for shortcuts, they connect on LinkedIn, then immediately send a pitch in a direct message. Or worse, they scrape email addresses and send batches of cold emails, hoping someone will bite.

The best outreach managers take it slow. Rather than spamming strangers, they take small steps toward visibility, gradually leading to collaboration opportunities that are obvious to everyone. Here are simple steps anyone can take to build relationships with potential collaborators.

1. Follow them on social media

This takes one click if you found them on a social network. If you use X, take a moment to add them to a list. This will make their content easier to keep on your radar.

Create a list called "People who write great stuff" (or something similar) and add the influencers to it. You can make it a public list so they can see that you've added them. Now you can go directly to that list to see what they've shared. This is important because the default home stream is so noisy.

Hootsuite and Buffer are social media management tools that allow you to see several streams in one view. You can add your list of influencers as one of these streams, letting you click, like and reshare their content all from one place (Fig. 6.40).

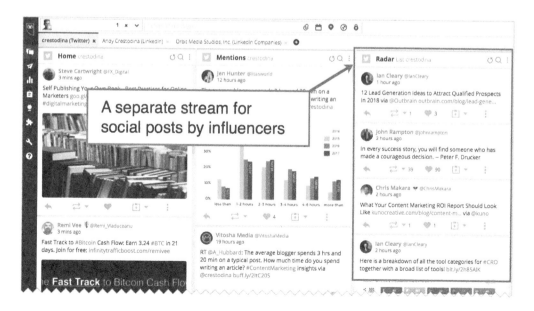

Fig. 6.40

A separate stream for social posts by influencers

Fig. 6.41

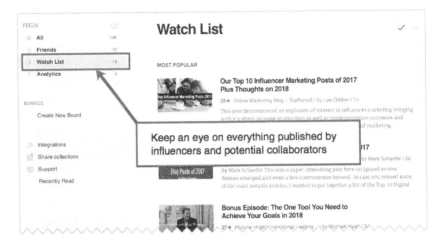

2. Subscribe to their newsletters

Next, subscribe to their newsletters (or YouTube channel, podcast, etc.) so you'll see their content whenever they publish. Use a tool such as Feedly to manage these new email subscriptions in one place. Create a separate category for these influencers to keep things organized. You'll be less likely to miss something and more likely to engage with their content (Fig. 6.41).

Or simply create a new email address for newsletter subscriptions from the influencers you're watching.

💡 **TIP!** Here's another way to manage these newsletters easily without creating a new email address. Just tweak your current email address by adding "+newsletters" to the account name (example: andy@orbitmedia.com becomes andy+newsletters@orbitmedia.com) and then set up a rule in your inbox so that messages to this address are filtered into a separate folder. This will let you easily see influencers' content all in one place.

3. Put their name into a monitoring tool

You can use a free tool to monitor every mention of their name. Talkwalker Alerts (www.talkwalker.com/alerts) will email you weekly with a list of places that the influencer was mentioned in the news. These might be press mentions or guest blog posts that you'd otherwise miss.

4. Start interacting on social media

This is the fastest and easiest way to become visible to someone, to show you're listening and to start building a relationship. Use any network in which they are active.

- Re-share their content.

- Favorite their posts.

- Share their content and mention them.

Repeat these little interactions many times over several weeks and soon they'll begin to notice.

5. Comment on their blog

The best way to engage directly with an influencer is directly through their content. Every writer we know reads every comment they get, assuming the blog has a comments section. So this is an easy way to get a little bit of someone's attention. Great comments are not necessarily positive, but they are always thoughtful. If the author responds, be sure to thank them for the response. Remember, the idea is to start a dialog.

> 💡 **TIP!** Questions often make great blog comments, but big, open questions are sometimes difficult for the author to answer easily. Ask clarifying questions, but don't give them homework.

6. Write reviews

Authors and podcasters all prize one thing above all others: reviews. Reviews are hard to get and very valuable. This is why virtually every podcast ends with a friendly call to action *"If you liked this show, please head over to iTunes and leave us a review!"*

If you're networking with an author or podcaster, you'll score huge points by leaving a book review on Amazon or a podcast review in iTunes.

7. Mention them in your content

You've got a blog, so you're a publisher . . . which means you have an opportunity to give ink to others. Find a quote from your target influencer and

If you're not paying attention to them, why should they **pay attention** to you?

add it to your content. Go beyond a simple quote by adding a few things to it:

- A thoughtful note or additional insights

- A link back to their content

- Their picture

Once it's live, mention them when you share it and thank them for inspiring you and making your content better. You might make their day. And you're one step closer to collaboration.

8. Connect on LinkedIn; Friend on Facebook

By now, everyone knows each other. You've had positive interactions in several places. They won't think it's the least bit strange when you send them an invitation to connect.

> 💡 **TIP!** Don't be too restrictive about accepting connection requests. As we're seeing here, LinkedIn is a content promotion tool, so it's good to have a lot of connections. As a general rule, accept requests from anyone in your geography or in your industry. And if they're in both (see Fig. 6.42), take a minute to send a quick hello!

Fig. 6.42

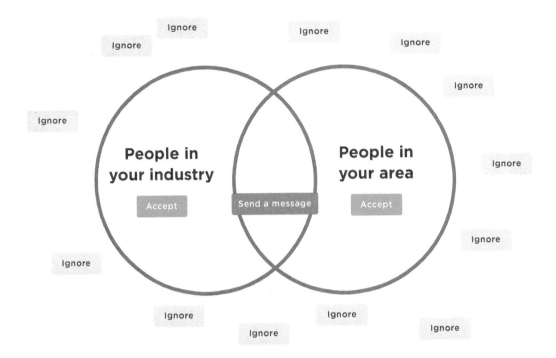

LinkedIn and Facebook, unlike other social networks, require that the other party accept the invitation. So there's more trust involved. That's why this wasn't the first step. Cold connection requests sent to influencers are generally ignored.

- **On Facebook** you need to be especially considerate. Don't click the "Add Friend" button unless you know each other well enough that confirming you as a friend would be an obvious decision for them. So keep it professional and non-creepy.

- **On LinkedIn** people are a bit more likely to accept invitations. Once connected, you can endorse them for their skills or write a recommendation. If it's genuine, don't hesitate to recommend them, even if it's just for their writing.

LinkedIn recommendations are quite valuable, so they're unlikely to forget the favor.

9. Connect on other networks

There are actually hundreds of social networks and places to connect. The influencers you're networking with may be on many of them. Look for them in a few of these places to build a stronger connection:

Quora, Instagram, Medium, Yelp, Pinterest, Tumblr, Meetup, YouTube, Flickr, Reddit, WhatsApp, Snapchat, Runkeeper, Spotify, Peloton, Untappd, Tripadvisor and Friendworld.

We might have made up that last one. But the point is there are a lot of opportunities to connect. Here's a technique that makes it easier to build many connections to a single individual.

10. Cross the streams

Connecting on one social network just isn't enough. Connecting on several networks will help you build a stronger relationship. An easy way to become more visible to someone is to jump across social networks during a single interaction. With apologies to Ghostbusters, we call this "crossing the streams." Here's how it works:

Step 1: Influencer mentions or shares your content within social network A.

Step 2: You share the content again in social network B.

Step 3: Within that social post, mention the influencer, thanking them for sharing it earlier.

When you mention the influencer on social network B, you'll become visible to them there. And since they shared it once already, they might share it a second time on this second network. More importantly, you are now connecting with them in another network, strengthening your bond with them (Fig. 6.43).

Example: Using LinkedIn to thank people who shared on X.

We published an article with detailed instructions for improving your homepage. We actively promoted it as an email newsletter and in social media.

After several days, it had been shared on X by an engaged group of readers, some of whom are quite influential among marketers. Our goal was to be visible to marketers and to build relationships with marketing influencers.

| Post article on your blog | They share on social network A | Say thanks on social network B | They share on social network B |

Fig. 6.43

| 1. Post the article, share it, wait a few days | 2. A few people comment and share on network A | 3. Thank those people when you share on network B | 4. They are likely to share it again on network B |

To cross the streams and get greater visibility and build those relationships, first go to BuzzSumo and enter the URL of the article. Then click "View Sharers" to see a list of people who shared the article on X. You'll see the influencers sorted by the size of their followings (Fig. 6.44).

Fig. 6.44

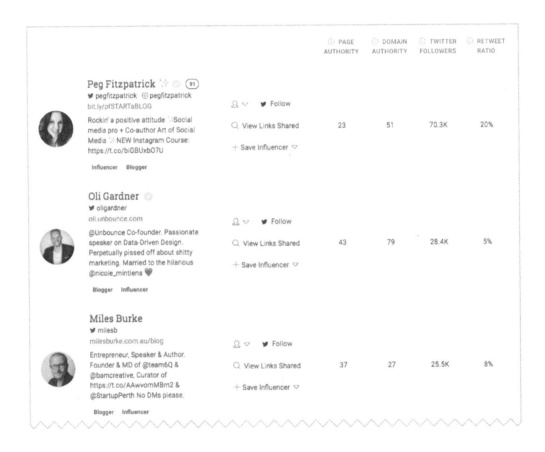

Fig. 6.45

Finally, go to LinkedIn, share the article there and mention some of the influencers who shared it on X. This is also a good time to mention anyone who commented or contributed. The idea is to say thank you, but do it in another place (Fig. 6.45).

11. Attend industry events

Events are a great place to learn, but they're also a fantastic place to meet bloggers, editors and influencers. If they're speaking, go say hello. Be polite and brief. Tell them you have an idea for a quick collaborative project and that you'd like to follow up later.

TIP: Meet the event director and pitch yourself as a speaker. If you'd like to speak at an event, it's a good idea to go once as an attendee and introduce yourself to the organizers while you're there. Every presentation you see is an example of someone they booked, so you'll get a sense for what they look for in speakers, formats and topics.

12. Offline networking

True social media experts don't just interact online. They don't stay behind a screen. They move the conversation offline whenever possible. They look for opportunities to go from social media, to email, to a Zoom call, to a cup of coffee or pint of beer.

The Phone, Zoom and Google Hangout

It's real-time, and it's powerful. Can you really say that you're friends with someone if you've never had an actual conversation with them? End that long string of emails, pick up the phone and dial.

We do calls with bloggers from around the world on a regular basis. The request sounds like this:

"Your stuff is great and we'd love to learn more from you. And there may be a few tricks we've learned that we could show you. Do you have time to jump on a quick Zoom call next week?"

If we've taken the time to build up the relationship properly, the answer will likely be yes. The conversation will be an incredible opportunity to learn and a real chance for collaborative inspiration.

Meet in person

This is why coffee was invented. An in-person, face-to-face meeting is simply the highest-value interaction possible. Nothing is better. Make a habit of doing weekly meetings with other marketers. Here are a few other networking tips:

- Hold open office hours before work.

- Host a regular happy hour after work.

- Form a mastermind group.

- Send handwritten thank you notes . . . and send them via US Post to the "forgotten inbox."

Help everyone you can and your marketing support network will grow. You'll get more done, more efficiently, and have more fun doing it. Try it. It will do wonders for the future of your business, career and personal life.

Fig. 6.46

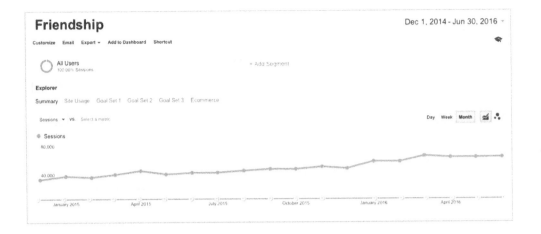

For seven years, we had open office hours every Friday morning at 8:30 a.m. Anyone could sign up and meet in the office in Chicago or on a video call. We'd talk for 45 minutes about any topic they'd like. We met hundreds of people this way.

The benefits from the activities listed here are literally beyond measure. Fig. 6.46 shows one report you won't find in GA4.

Keep it real . . . and take it slow

The key to influencer marketing is patience and humility. The more famous the influencer, the more patience you'll need. If they have a following much larger than yours, go slow. The more similar you are in levels of authority, the faster you can move through the networking process.

Finally, the request . . .

The goal is to work together. So there's a pitch involved. You may want to collaborate on a research project, or get their insights for a post, or contribute to a roundup, or have them accept a guest post from you, or have them join a private group you're starting.

Whatever the idea, a quick email or direct message is a fine way to ask for a quick favor. The tone is light and personal. The request is specific and very easy to say yes to. Fig. 6.47 shows what a simple outreach message for a contributor quote looks like.

You've taken the time to build the relationship, so this is not a cold email. That's the point of all of that networking.

This kind of outreach is often the difference between good and great content programs. So give it a shot. And remember, most people love to be interviewed. You're the press and your email is a press hit.

Helping them share

The co-created content goes live. Now it's time to collaborate on a bit

An ally in creation is **an ally in promotion.**

Fig. 6.47

susan@expertinsights.com

Would you like to contribute a quote?

Hi there, Susan.

You're an expert on laboratory design and I'm a fan of your work! I'm writing an article on that exact subject for my next newsletter. Would you like to be featured in this piece?

If so, just send me a few sentences with your best advice on lab layouts. If you can send something by next Friday, I'll work it into the piece. I'd love to include you.

And if my timing is bad or you're not interested, no worries at all. It's really not a big deal. Either way, thanks for considering this.

Andy Crestodina | Co-Founder / CMO
Orbit Lab Design, Inc.

> Simple, specific subject line

> Message is brief with a personal tone

> Request is specific: length and due date

> No pressure! Easy out if they're not interested.

of promotion. The easier it is for your contributor to share the article, the more likely they are to do it and the more likely you are to get social traffic. Here are a set of progressively more aggressive ways to ask your collaborators to share.

- Send them a link to the article with a polite thank you.

- Send them a sample pre-written social post and encourage them to share.

- Post the article to a community and request that they like or upvote the article there. (Reddit, Inbound.org, Product Hunt, Growth Hackers, LinkedIn Groups, Facebook Groups, etc.)

- Attach an image from the article and encourage them to use it when sharing.

- Ask them to include a link to the article in their next email newsletter. This is the most effective, but it's a big ask (Fig. 6.48).

Fig. 6.48

susan@expertinsights.com

You were featured in my lab design article!

Hi there, Susan.

This is just a quick note that the article is live. Thank you so much for adding your insights. You can see it here: https://www.orbitlabservices.com/blog/lab-design-tips

Would you mind helping us spread the word? You can find it here on LinkedIn.

If you do share it on social media, just let me know and I'll have my team like/share your post to amplify it. And if you'd rather not, no worries!

Andy Crestodina | Co-Founder / CMO
Orbit Lab Design, Inc.

> Start with gratitude

> Politely ask if they would help with promotion.

> Mention the benefit to them

> Again, no pressure if they're not interested.

Here's another interesting tactic we've seen from influencer marketers. Rather than just sending them a link to the article, first post the article on social media and then send them a link to the social post rather than the article itself. We described this approach above in the section about social media video.

Certainly, when the collaborator sees this social post, they're very likely to like, comment and share. This kind of quick engagement may help trigger the social algorithm to show the post to a much larger audience.

There is just no substitute for collaboration with influencers. I sincerely believe it is one of the biggest differences between good and great content marketing. Content marketing is a long road. It's a lonely road if you don't work with others.

Everyone knows that content optimized for search includes keyphrases. But not everyone understands that *content optimized for social media includes people*. In other words, content that does not include collaborators has a disadvantage in social media (Fig. 6.49).

We are moving into a post-single POV era for content marketing. The best content has multiple voices and points of view. Journalists don't write articles without sources. Why do content marketers keep publishing articles without input from experts?

> If you want to go quickly, go alone.
> If you want to go far, **go together.**

Fig. 6.49

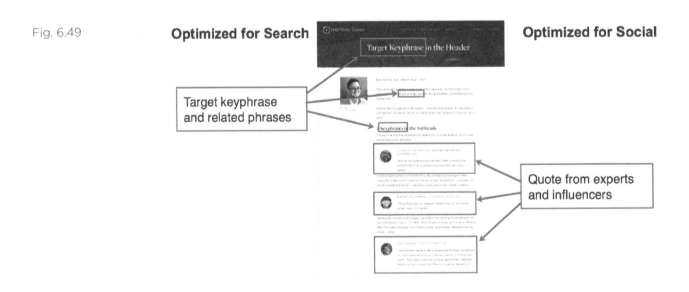

Optimized for Search

Target keyphrase and related phrases

Optimized for Social

Quote from experts and influencers

Influencer marketing examples

The next level of collaboration goes beyond quotes and roundups. A more strategic approach puts industry experts in the center of the content. Here are two examples, one B2B and one B2C, that show how influencers can be more integrated into a content program.

B2B Example: Information Security Company

This service provider has a content strategy with two goals:

- Increase awareness/trust among infosec professionals

- Improve Domain Authority by attracting links and eventually rank for infosec related phrases

But rather than simply making an industry report, they have a more comprehensive plan:

1. Conduct a survey of 200+ cybersecurity experts to discover top threats and trends

2. Conduct brief interviews with five of the most respected experts

3. Partner with an association or trade publication to publish a detailed (and visual) industry report filled with insights from the survey and quotes from the experts

4. Encourage the partner and collaborators to share and link

5. Repurpose the content: produce a short webinar series based on the data and pitch a presentation for industry conferences

6. Repeat annually

Notice how all of the elements of content strategy are covered (Fig. 6.50).

Fig. 6.50

Topic	SEO	Location	Format	Influencers	Promotion
Infosec threats and trends	Keyphrase: "infosec trends" Links: from association partner	Website, association site, conferences (owned, earned)	Research report with visuals (webpage, PDF), webinar, presentations	Top infosec experts, trade association	Email, social, PR, guest blogging, conferences

B2C example: Nonprofit nature conservancy

This donor-driven cultural institution has a content strategy with two goals:

- Increase awareness and attendance for spring programs

- Grow social followings and email list to support future fundraising among small donors

Rather than simply posting photos to social media, they have a more comprehensive plan:

1. Reach out to a well-known nature photographer, inviting them to be the judge in a photo contest

2. Gather submissions from Instagram using a new hashtag

3. Ask a local news anchor to host a live broadcast on Facebook/Instagram to announce the winners

4. Post galleries of winning entries on a web page with a strong email signup CTA

5. Pitch it as a news story to the local media for their newscast and website . . . a natural fit since they're already working with the anchor, right? (Fig. 6.51)

It's easy to imagine how effective these strategies would be. The influencers are fully integrated and the content promotion is built-in. Content at this level isn't possible with collaboration.

6.8 Guest Blogging

Writing content for other websites leverages their audience and influence to improve the visibility of your content and business. That's why we consider guest blogging to be a content promotion tactic. You're promoting your content to an editor so it will be seen by their audience.

Actually, there are two sides to guest blogging: publishing your content on other sites (being a guest blogger) and inviting others to write for your site (blogger relations and guest blogger outreach). They are both powerful content marketing tactics with search marketing and social media benefits.

To understand the benefits of guest blogging, especially when combined, let's imagine the processes and outcomes of two bloggers: one blogger who posts only on his own site, and another who embraces both approaches to guest blogging.

Fig. 6.51

Topic	SEO	Location	Format	Influencers	Promotion
Nature, conservation, photography	Link: from local news media	Website, local news (owned, earned)	Photo galleries, social posts, live TV	Photographer, news anchor	Social (IG, FB), Local media (TV)

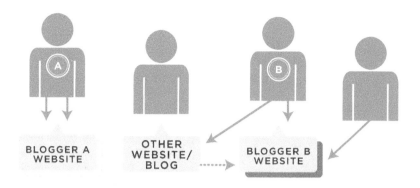

Fig. 6.52

Round 1: Both bloggers create two posts

Blogger A has written two posts and publishes both on his blog (Fig. 6.52).

Blogger B has also written two posts, but rather than post them both on her blog, she connects with the editor of another website who agrees to publish one of her posts. That guest post likely links back to her site in the author bio, or in the content itself. This link is indicated by the dotted line in the diagram above.

Also, she reaches out to another writer in her field. This writer submits a new, original post, and Blogger B publishes it on her site. This guest post is indicated by the red box above.

Let's see how they're doing:

Although Blogger B only wrote two of the posts, she now has three posts associated with her brand. She also has a link and a few new friends:

Scoreboard	Posts	Links	Social Connections
Blogger A	2	0	0
Blogger B	3	1	2

Round 2: Both bloggers have published four posts

Blogger A has now written and published four posts, all on his own blog (Fig. 6.53).

Fig. 6.53

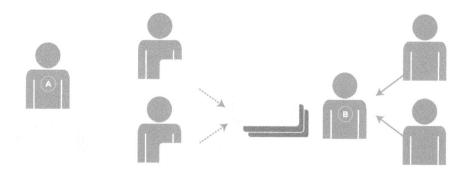

Blogger B has published two posts on external websites, both of which now have links back to her site. She's also connected with expert writers who have contributed two relevant posts that are now on her blog. And she's built connections with the people behind other websites relevant to her business.

Scoreboard	Posts	Links	Social Connections
Blogger A	4	0	0
Blogger B	6	2	4

Round 3: Both bloggers have created eight posts

Blogger A has consistently produced and published content, but . . . (Fig. 6.54)

Blogger B has created a network of content, both on her site and linked to her brand. This has increased exposure to her content. She's also growing a network of connections with experts,

which has increased her influence in her field. **This is what great web marketing looks like.**

Scoreboard	Posts	Links	Social Connections
Blogger A	8	0	0
Blogger B	12	4	8

Remember, search engine optimization is about great content and great links. Social media is about visibility with an audience and strong connections with relevant influencers. Guest blogging provides all of these things.

It's not surprising that most bloggers guest post at least sometimes. If you only write for your own site, you're missing out (Fig. 6.55).

Targeting host blogs

Different blogs have different marketing benefits, so it's important to understand the options and outcomes. There are generally two types of guest blogging

Fig. 6.54

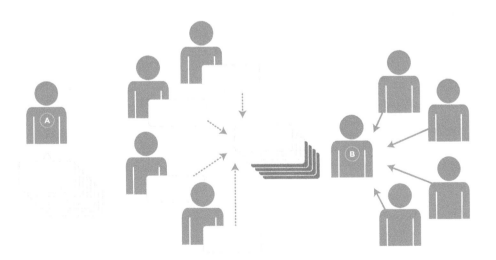

opportunities: local social blogs or national topical blogs.

	Local	National
Primary benefit	Social media	Search engine optimization
Criteria	Large social following and readership	Authoritative domain, linking opportunity

Local and social blogs: Good for networking (social media)

These could be local media websites and blogs. They may cover a broad range of topics, but they are generally focused on your region. They tend to have active social media followers right there in your city or town. The readers are mostly in your area, which is perfect if the target audience for your business is focused on your geography.

Example: Your business installs HVAC systems for companies in your area. Write an article about winterizing your home and pitch it to a local blog. This will make you visible to your local audience through the content and social media.

National and Topical blogs: Good for links and authority (SEO)

Although any guest blogging opportunity has some branding and social benefits, sometimes you are more focused on the benefit of the possible link back to your site. For this reason, the authority of the blog's domain is more important than their social media presence.

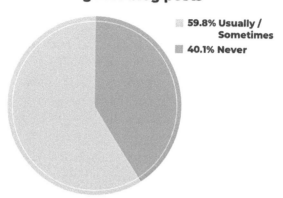

Only 60% of bloggers write guest blog posts

Fig. 6.55

- 59.8% Usually / Sometimes
- 40.1% Never

Source: https://www.orbitmedia.com/blog/blogging-statistics/

These sites may be tightly focused on your industry, such as trade publications or association websites. Or they may be websites of businesses like yours in other parts of the country. Regardless, the topics are highly relevant to your business, and a link from a site that's relevant to your business is better than a link from a random or irrelevant site.

Example: Your business manufactures HVAC systems and sells them to contractors around the country. Write a guide about how to properly install high-tech tankless water heaters and pitch it to a national industry association website. This will make you more visible to your national audience and the link may help your SEO.

If you're able to find a site that meets both criteria—social and search— patiently cultivate a close relationship with editors and position yourself as a regular contributor or columnist.

TIP! There is diminishing SEO value to blogging repeatedly on the same website. The value of a second or third link from the same website may not be as high as a new link from a second or third website. When your focus is SEO and authority, one of your goals is to increase the total number of websites that link to you. So you'd rather have two links from two different sites than two links from the same site.

How to pitch your content

Once you've got a few host blogs in your sights, it's time to reach out and see if they're interested in your content. Keep in mind that the owners of popular sites with powerful domains get a ton of random, cold emails from hopeful guest bloggers. Surveys have shown just how much. A typical Staff Editor gets as many as 53 pitches per day.[3]

You need to separate yourself from the random pitches by being thoughtful and considerate when making contact with sites, just as PR professionals are thoughtful and considerate when contacting journalists.

Read what they've been publishing. Watch what they've been sharing. Listen for the topic and tone that work well with their audience. Do they have guest blogging guidelines? Read them carefully. And *build a relationship first*.

3.   https://www.frac.tl/work/marketing-research/2019-pitching-media-survey/

Here are some DOs and DON'Ts to follow when submitting a possible guest post:

- ### *Don't* waste their time

    A little research goes a long way. Make sure that you're submitting content that would make sense on the site and be interesting to its readers.

    A great way to make this a no-work proposition for the editor is to submit a completed article. That reduces the back and forth that might otherwise be necessary. If they like it, they can run with it.

Aaron Orendorff is a contributor to some of the top media websites and an expert guest blogger. Here is what his pitch sounds like.

"I wrote this for you. **Here it is.**"

AARON ORENDORFF,
Founder, iconiContent

Along with it he sends an in-depth article that was clearly written specifically for that site. It matches the style and formatting. It references other articles on that site. It's well-researched and beautifully crafted.

Even when sent as a cold email to the editors of famous blogs, this approach performs well.

- **_Do_ convey the value of the content**

  Take a moment to explain how the content fits within their blog and how it would be useful to their audience. You'd better sincerely believe in the value of the content! Be confident but brief. A few sentences will do.

  If you added links in your article to other articles on their site, let them know. It will show that you know their blog well and you want to make sure your content fits in with their other content.

  If you optimized the content by aligning it with a keyphrase, mention that here. You can even mention the popularity of the phrase.

- **_Don't_ be pushy**

  Remember, they're the host and you're the aspiring guest. You're inviting yourself over to their home (or at least homepage). You should be very polite. Offer to let them make any edits, change the headline or images, and even remove any links if they feel they're inappropriate.

- **_Do_ offer to help promote it**

  If you have a strong social following, let them know you'll be promoting the article through your social networks and responding to comments. Of course you would do this anyway, but drawing attention to your ability to drive traffic will make your pitch more attractive.

- **_Do_ follow-up**

  Thank the host blog with an email. If the article ranks, let them know and they'll appreciate it. If you feel the post was successful, consider offering to write another. Now is the best time to grow the relationship with your new friends and collaborators (Fig. 6.56).

Fig. 6.56

How many follow-up emails are acceptable?

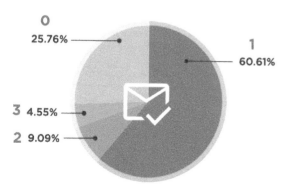

- 0 — 25.76%
- 1 — 60.61%
- 3 — 4.55%
- 2 — 9.09%

When is it acceptable to folow-up after the initial email?

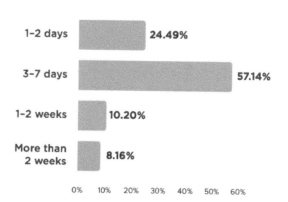

- 1–2 days — 24.49%
- 3–7 days — 57.14%
- 1–2 weeks — 10.20%
- More than 2 weeks — 8.16%

Source: https://www.frac.tl/work/marketing-research/2019-pitching-media-survey/

Don't be discouraged if you have trouble placing a post. If the first blog didn't take it, adapt it for another blog and submit it again. You may submit an article to five or more blogs before it gets accepted.

Link Metrics and Analysis

So what's the SEO value of all this writing, pitching and guest posting? Earlier, we learned how to measure the authority of websites in the context of competition. Here you can use the same tools to measure the potential value of a guest blogging opportunity and potential link.

The MozBar was useful for seeing the authority of all the sites within a search results page, but here, you can just use the Moz Link Explorer because you are evaluating the authority of just one site, the blog we might submit content to. Enter the address of the possible host blog. It will show you the number of incoming links and the Domain Authority. The higher the better (Fig. 6.57).

If the Domain Authority is below 40, a link would have low value. If it's in the 40-70 range, it's worth pursuing. If it's in the 70s or 80s, it's worth pursuing patiently and persistently. Links from sites in the 90-100 range are generally unattainable through guest blogging, but may be possible through "newsjacking" or other clever, well-timed PR techniques. In the end, *any link from a site with a Domain Authority higher than your own site is a good link.*

⚠️ CAUTION! Some media sites add the "nofollow" code to their links, as we explained in Section 3.1. Check this before pitching, if your guest blogging goal is to increase your Domain Authority.

There is more to life than links. And the benefits of guest blogging go far beyond SEO. Here are some other ways to evaluate the potential value of a guest post:

- Is it a high-traffic blog? (good for referral traffic)

Fig. 6.57

Overview

Get the data you need to do better link building research, smarter content ideation, and link prospecting - in less time.   ⊕ Track in a Campaign

| root domain ▼ | https://smartblogger.com/ | Analyze |

Domain Authority [i]
61

Linking Domains [i]
16.9k
Discovered in the last 60 days   808
Lost in last 60 days   850

Inbound Links [i]
233.3k

Ranking Keywords [i]
23.2k

- Does your target audience read this blog? (good for brand awareness)

- Are the social metrics strong? Lots of shares, likes and comments?

- Does the blog have a large email list? Do they promote guest posts through email?

- Is the editor someone you'd like to network with?

If your only reason for guest posting is to get a link, you're missing out on a lot of value.

Be my guest: Finding great guest bloggers for your site

When you let outside experts write for your blog, you add a new voice to your site, you add credibility, you leverage their social networks and *you get an article without spending the time and effort to write it yourself.* But you'll get few or none of these results unless you select your guest bloggers carefully.

First and foremost, you want great writers. They know their subject matter and they write posts with **substance**. They're skilled in crafting compelling content and they write posts with **style**. Read what they submit as if you were a visitor.

Does the headline get your attention? Does the article hold it? Did you learn something from it? Would you be likely to comment or share it?

Beyond the content itself, the ideal guest blogger is active on **social media**. Look them up on X, Facebook or LinkedIn.

Do they have an audience? Are they engaged within social channels? (Fig. 6.58)

Fig. 6.58

Create guidelines for your guest bloggers

If you're serious about guest blogger outreach, you'll save time by providing guest blogger guidelines to set expectations. It will also save time if you post these guidelines on your website, letting possible guest bloggers know what you're looking for. It's really just another version of the Article Checklist from Section 5.11.

Feel free to use this worksheet, or develop your own guidelines based on your standards for content aspects and quality.

- **Types of posts:** Ask for submissions that appeal to your audience and align with other content on your site. Posts should fit nicely within your blog categories.

- **Tone and style:** Conversational, approachable, helpful, useful, interesting.

- **Formatting:** Encourage the use of headers, subheaders and bullet lists.

- **Images:** Suggest (or require) that they submit an image with copyrights and sized to the appropriate width for your site. Ideally, they should include multiple images that support the article with screenshots, diagrams, examples, etc.

- **Search friendliness:** Suggest that they optimize the article for a relevant keyphrase. Provide guidelines for writing search-friendly content if available.

- **Author info:** Ask for two to three sentences about the author along with links to websites and any relevant social media accounts.

- **How to submit:** Require interested bloggers to provide their content to you in a format that makes it easy to review and post. (Word Doc, Google Doc, web form, etc.)

- **Originality and reuse:** Require that the content provided by guest bloggers is unique and has not been, and will not be, used elsewhere. You want to have exclusive use of the article.

TIP: Reserve the right to edit guest posts. If you do make changes, the guest blogger shouldn't mind. In our experience, it's very common for host blogs to make significant changes to our submissions, such as changing the headline. Do we mind? Not at all. Except when they add a lot of bad stock photos.

NOTE: If people often reach out to you to write for your blog, it's likely that they're looking for another benefit. They want the SEO benefit of a link. They are using guest blogging to increase their domain authority. It's not necessarily spammy or unethical, but it's important to understand their motives.

Guest blogging is simply modern-day PR

The outcomes of guest blogging are virtually indistinguishable from the outcomes of PR. Technically, it's just one PR tactic. But as the news media revenue model continues to evolve, crowdsourcing of content becomes more prevalent, and publishing content becomes easier for blogs and brands, guest blogging will be even more important for PR professionals.

Guest blogging falls into a gap between the skill sets of SEO and PR practitioners. Although SEO pros know the value of links, they don't have access to powerful host blogs. PR pros can create compelling content, but they don't typically understand the value of links.

Try it. You'll find that the principles of guest blogging align closely with the philosophy of content marketing in general: create, connect, collaborate and help others. It's fun.

How to use AI to find collaboration opportunities

Here again, there is an opportunity to get help from AI. Here is a prompt that will have the AI find where members of your target audience spend time. Full credit for this goes to AI expert, Liza Adams.

Prompt:

For a [company type] in [industry] we are targeting the following verticals: [list target markets]

You are an expert [B2B industry] marketer who is deeply familiar with these target markets and the buyer persona for [industry] solutions, including where they tend to congregate.

We want to diversify how we reach this market and go beyond search and other digital marketing channels. We want to identify a variety of "watering holes" where these potential customers learn, engage and interact with each other, so we can target and build relationships with them.

Create a table with the categories of watering holes as rows, the verticals as columns and the specific watering holes as the cells. (e.g., the actual names of the communities, industry forums, events, groups, marketplaces, webinars, content platforms, partnerships, financial institutions, associations, etc.) Be as comprehensive as possible with the categories.

Think about this step by step. Do you have any questions for me?

First, look for places and publishers where you already have a relationship. These will be your easiest wins for collaboration pitches.

Next, start researching and networking with editors and community managers using the methods in Section 6.7. Once you have a relationship, offer to help with content in ways that would put you in front of your target audience.

6.9 Account-based Content Marketing

Content marketing is slow. It takes a long time to build up an audience. It attracts a lot of unqualified visitors and leads. A lot of people filling out your forms aren't who you want to sell to.

These are all valid criticisms. But there is a way to use content to target very specific accounts quickly and accurately. It's called account-based marketing (ABM).

Account-based marketing begins with identifying your ideal clients, then targeting this small, specific group directly. So 100% of the audience is relevant. It's automatic sales-marketing alignment. And it engages prospects earlier in their process before they go to Google.

You can catch a lot of fish with a net . . . but most of them you'll throw back.

You'll catch fewer fish with a spear . . . but every one of them is a keeper (Fig. 6.59).

But you still need something to attract these prospects somehow. You need a hook. That's where content comes in. When you combine ABM with content marketing, you're doing *account-based content marketing.*

Account-based content marketing doesn't require a large budget, unlike a lot of software-driven ABM programs. But it does require some content marketing

muscles. Here are the key elements of the strategy we'll be outlining here:

- Ability to produce original research

- Ability to create video, webinars and long-form guides

- Strong presence on LinkedIn

As with any ABM program, we'll still start by defining our ideal client profile (ICP), identifying prospects and building a list of key accounts. Then we'll target that list using outreach and ads, inviting them to an event or sharing a high-value content asset. Then we'll follow up in a high-touch format with personalized offers.

Here's one example of a low-cost content-driven ABM program that is both fast and targeted.

Step 1. Identify top prospects

Our plan is to target marketing decision-makers (managers, directors and VPs) in specific industries. We'll start with

Fig. 6.59

The Net
Traditional content marketing

1. Become relevant to a large audience
2. Maximize the % who will fill out forms
3. (Dis)qualify during the sales process

The Spear
Account-based marketing

1. Identify your top prospects
2. Create content for them specifically
3. Follow up, build relationships / relevance

manufacturing companies and then expand later. We know this audience well and have basic buyer personas in place.

First, we'll define our ideal client profile and build a list of these top prospects. The list came from three sources:

- Research tools/software

- Current database

- Top-of-mind dream clients (Fig. 6.60)

We used LinkedIn Sales Navigator and a tool called Lead411 to do searches and refine a list. Within these tools, "list building" is really just a matter of doing increasingly refined searches. The main criteria for us were industry, company size, contact seniority and job function (Fig. 6.61).

By going through our own CRM, we found more people to add. These were cold leads, past clients, event attendees,

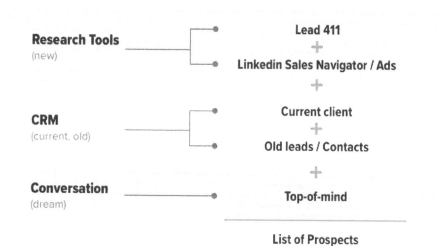

Fig. 6.60

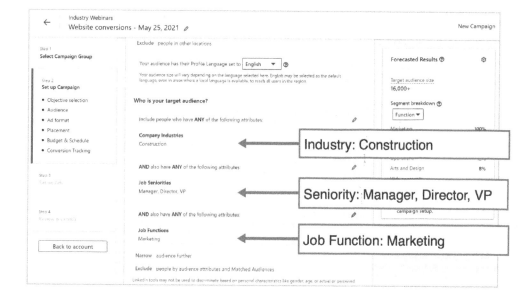

Fig. 6.61

etc. Really anyone we've ever touched that met the criteria. And finally, we mixed in some dream clients. *Who would we love to work with?*

Step 2. Develop the content

We need a hook. We need a topic and a format, just like you'd find in any content strategy. A typical blog post won't do. We need a highly engaging format and a very compelling topic.

Format: Webinar

What format will bring us closest to this audience?

We invited this list of ideal prospects to attend a webinar. We choose this format for a few reasons:

"Since account-based marketing focuses on a finite, clearly defined audience, it's possible to dive deeply into your customer and competitive data and, based on those insights, develop hyper-relevant, resonant content that connects your value proposition to real customer value."

CARMEN HILL, *Principal Strategist at Chill Content*

- *Live video is compelling.* They'll see our faces and hear our voices, building a stronger personal connection and trust.

- *Events drive urgency.* Sign up in time or you'll miss it. That deadline will give us a stronger call to action.

Topic: Research and analysis of top competitors

What kind of content will get their attention?

We decided to produce a little bit of original research. Research is inherently differentiated, giving it big advantages over other topics.

- *Research builds credibility.* It's new. It shows rigor and methodical thinking. It's automatically different from most of the content they'll see on a typical day.

- *It's specific to their industry.* When they see the call to action or hear the invitation, it will feel much more relevant than the other offers they'll see on a typical day.

Our goal at Orbit is to create demand for our web development services. So the research topic is obvious: an analysis of the websites of the top 100 companies in their industry. We found a list of top websites, then reviewed those 100 websites and recorded which sites had which UX features.

The content is tailored and designed specifically for this program. It will make a strong headline and call to action:

What are the top 100 firms doing on their websites?

This data is easy to turn into a presentation for a webinar. To make the deck, you'll turn the data into visuals (simple charts), show examples (good and bad) then discuss best practices (based on other data and your own experience).

Step 3. The promotion video

You need to upgrade the promotion, not just the content itself. The better the invitation, the more likely your ideal prospects will register. Any one of them might be your next client.

The video is produced with the same process and equipment we discussed earlier in this chapter. It's a simple, personal one-minute invitation to attend. To get the maximum value for this effort, you'll use this video everywhere. Here's where (and why).

- Social media outreach messages (improve the click through rate)

- Sponsored content ads (improve the click through rate)

- Landing page (improve the conversion rate for registrations)

Step 4. Ads and outreach

Now you need to connect with this audience and invite them to attend. Here's how we'll get our video invitation in front of these people.

LinkedIn ads

We already built the audience in step one. Now we'll set up the campaign in the LinkedIn Campaign Manager. Our budget is around $1,000. These are sponsored content video ads in LinkedIn, which puts our video invite into the social streams of our target account members. Obviously, this is a component you wouldn't typically find in content marketing.

Direct message outreach

The ads are effective, but outreach is even better. Take the time to send personal direct messages to the first degree connections that appeared on the list. These should be short, simple invitations with a link to the landing page. We send around 50 of these messages. Some lead to conversations. A few turn into registrations (Fig. 6.62).

Fig. 6.62

Short, personal invitation to your first degree connections.

WARNING! Never send a cold pitch to a new LinkedIn connection. It's neither effective nor necessary.

Obviously, this works best if you have some connections with these people already. If you don't, take a few minutes to start engaging with them early using the tips from the Online Networking Guide earlier in this chapter. Then send a connection request. Build up your network, then the next time you do a little outreach, it will be more effective.

Personal emails

If they're in your CRM database, you have their email address. These people should get personal email invitations.

Step 5. The landing page

The next link in the conversion chain is the landing page. If the ads and outreach worked, they clicked and landed here. Fig. 6.63 shows what ours looked like.

It uses a lot of landing page best practices:

- Compelling headline (question format)
- Specific benefits for registrants in both video and text
- Testimonial or some other type of social proof

Fig. 6.63

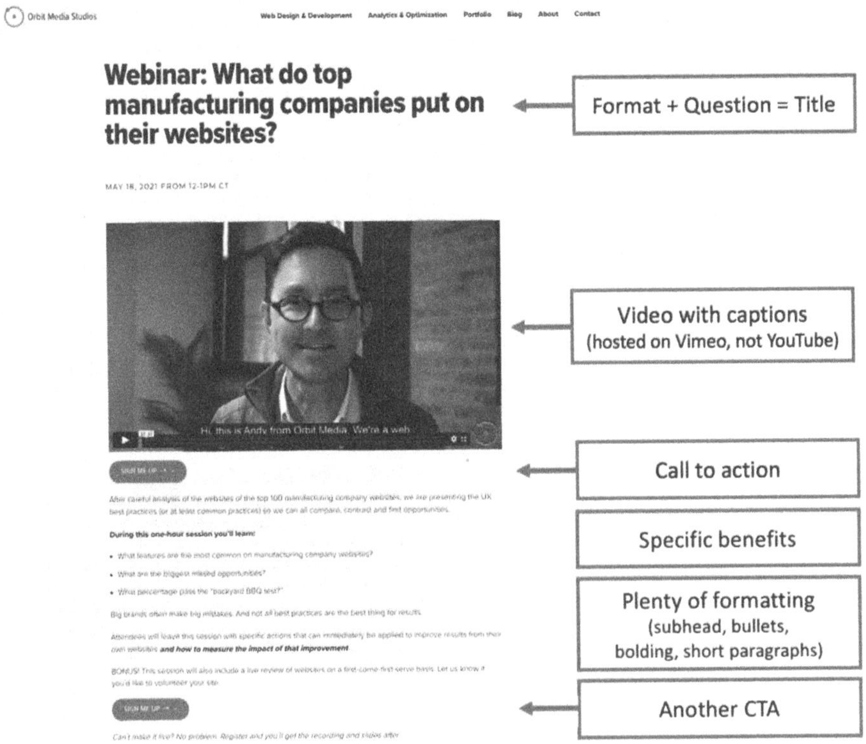
Orbit Media Studios
Webinar: What do top manufacturing companies put on their websites?
Format + Question = Title
Video with captions
(hosted on Vimeo, not YouTube)
Call to action
Specific benefits
Plenty of formatting
(subhead, bullets, bolding, short paragraphs)
Another CTA

- Scannable with lots of formatting (subheads, bullets, bolding, etc.)

- Multiple calls to action, indicating urgency (sign up before your competitors do)

As people register, send personal emails to each. This helps to encourage more 1:1 interaction and relationship building.

Although you can track the success of this page in GA4 users, engagement and conversions from links with that campaign tracking code) it really isn't that important here. Why? Because account-based marketing isn't about quantity (how many), it's about quality (who). Since 100% of the viewers of your CTA fit your ideal customer profile, every signup is a potential client.

ABM is about quality, not quantity

Low numbers are totally fine. This isn't a numbers game. It's about getting the right content in front of the right person at the right time.

Step 6. The webinar

The big day. The live event breaks down into two parts.

The presentation (45 minutes)

Everyone involved in the outreach and follow-up are on the webinar with cameras on. This makes you real to attendees who have only interacted through messages and emails. It also puts a face with the name for all follow-up communication. This is also why starting with friendly, detailed introductions is so important.

The main part of the presentation is a review of the custom research, sharing examples and discussing best practices. It's all custom-created specifically for this audience. They love it.

Fig. 6.64 shows the breakdown of slides and time.

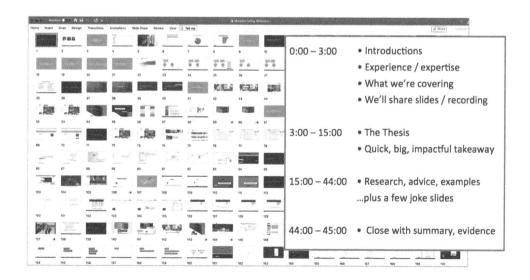

Fig. 6.64

Like any content marketing program, it should be actionable and not salesy. Many of the recommendations will be things the attendees can do themselves, without hiring you. That's good.

Make sure it's not boring. Add a joke slide or short videos in the middle of the webinar, when energy levels usually start to lag. The viewer's attention and retention are high at the beginning and end, but low in the middle. That's called the "serial position effect."

The interactive portion (15 minutes)

This is where the magic happens. It is the most important part of the webinar and your best opportunity to show off your expertise.

Questions and answers

- Take notes on what questions were asked and by whom.

- Optional: Invite a panelist, possibly a relevant client you've worked with.

Live reviews

If you can, go beyond a typical Q&A. Do something that provides real value to volunteers in real time. This kind of live consulting is the ultimate in personalized content. Yes, it's a live event so it has to be based on something non-confidential, publicly viewable or shared with you.

For us, this is real-time website reviews. We do live reviews of websites submitted by attendees.

Promise more value in the follow-up

Time will run out. If you provided a lot of value, they'll naturally want more. Remind them that more value is coming their way.

- "*Send us your questions*. We will answer every question and request made by any of you."

- "*Schedule a time to chat* if you were squeamish about volunteering but would still like us to review something of yours."

- "*We will follow up* with the recording and slides, of course!"

Step 7. The follow-up

Good follow-up will make the entire program much more effective. Weak follow-up and you'll just have to hope that you were memorable. Because the group is small and highly qualified, you can give lots of love and attention to each attendee.

Unlike a typical webinar follow-up (bulk email with a link to the recording and slides), the follow-up from the account-based content marketing webinar is highly personalized (Fig. 6.65). ABM success is all about the follow-up.

Personalized follow-up and nurture

Those who were very engaged during the outreach process or during the webinar will get special follow-up. If they asked a question in the Q&A portion, the

Webinar follow-up actions

Fig. 6.65

Content marketing	Account-based marketing
Upload video / slides	Create post event landing apge
Send bulk email (link to slides, CTA for next webinar)	Send personal email to each attendee (based on level of engagement)
	Reformat presentation into a guide
	Send print piece (printed guide, thank you card or book)
	Offer to consult with subject matter expert (personalized audit, review, advice, etc.)

follow-up email reflects that and speaks to them individually.

These interactions start with email, but don't hesitate to pick up the phone. They know you by now. It won't be unexpected.

The goal of these conversations is to offer more help. For the most engaged and qualified attendees, the offer may be for some free consulting. In our case, this is a review of their website or an audit of their G4 account. We want to give this potential prospect some 1:1 time with a subject matter expert.

The end of the event is the beginning of the nurture process. Save everyone in an event-specific list in Sales Navigator so it's easier to keep in touch. Now you can follow their LinkedIn feeds and comment/contribute when appropriate. Send the following over the next week or two . . .

- *The recording (on the post-webinar landing page)*
  No need to make a new URL. Just flip the webinar signup page into post-event mode. Replace the promotional video with the webinar recording. Change the calls to action from "Register" to "Download the slides" "Get the PDF guide" or "Subscribe for more insights."

> 💡 **TIP** If you have a chatbot, this would be a great page for a new playbook. "Were you able to attend this event? . . . No? Would you like to get a turbo version of it on a quick 1:1 call?"

- *Send a PDF guide from the slides*
  Reformatting the content into a guide gives them a scannable version. This new asset also gives you another reason to reach out. Make it visual and concise. It should also offer to help more with a simple, personal call to action at the end.

- *Send something in the mail*
  USPS is the forgotten inbox.
  Mailing something is automatic
  differentiation because so few B2B
  marketers do it. Send a printed
  version of the guide or just a
  handwritten thank you note. If you
  have something stronger, use it. At
  Orbit, we send a copy of the book
  you're reading now.

Extending the ABM program

One webinar isn't likely to drive results.
A series of webinars presenting industry-
specific original research, with strong
promotion, given to a specific target
audience, with diligent follow-up . . .
that's definitely going to get results.

Fig. 6.66 shows how we've extended
our new ABM content strategy by

doing it for more industries, with more
content, in more formats. The red
indicates completed work, the gray shows
what's next.

For one industry, we found a trade
publication and pitched them an article.
They accepted and ran the piece in a
printed magazine. The article is basically
an 800-word summary of the research.

One of the best ways to get more value
from this content is to keep sharing
this content with anyone new you meet
online. Keep your radar on. If you
connect with someone in a relevant
industry, share the link to the research
and recording with them.

Like any content marketing, it never goes
away. These assets will be on our site for
years. We will never stop getting value
from these programs.

Fig. 6.66

B2B Tech	Financial Services	Architects Construction	Manufacturing	???
Webinar: website research	Webinar: website research	Webinar: website research	Webinar: website research	Webinar: website research
Webinar: digital marketing	Webinar: email marketing		Webinar: digital marketing	
PDF Guide: website research	PDF Guide: website research			
	PR: Trade pub article			

The investment and returns

Unlike a lot of ABM programs, we relied very little on technology or outside services. No fancy marketing automation software required. Account-based content marketing can be low cost, like a typical inbound marketing program, but for a more targeted audience.

Fig. 6.67 shows the breakdown of time, costs and the returns on that investment.

We hope that this example is useful to you. You are welcome to use any or all of it in your own marketing strategy.

The Investment

Fig. 6.67

Task	Role	Time/Cost
Research	Virtual Assistant	4 hours
Prospect identification	Marketing/Sales	4 hours
Presentation planning/prep	Marketing	4 hours
Webinar logistics	Marketing/Sales	6 hours
Paid social (LinkedIn)	Marketing	$1000
Day-of presentation	Marketing/Sales	4 hours
Follow-Up	Sales	8 hours

Total investment: 30 hours, $1000*

*There are a few tools with monthly subscriptions not included here, such as LinkedIn Sales Navigator and Lead411.

The Returns

Task	Time/Cost
1:1 conversations with new prospects	21
Qualified leads	8*
Proposals generated	4
Projects won	2
Revenue impact	$169,000

*We suspect that some leads snuck past us and went straight through the website contact form into our CRM. These leads would be categorized as "web lead" rather than "ABM lead." Oh well!

07 Inspiration, Topics & Process

SCIENCE IS HARD WORK, OFTEN REQUIRING LONG HOURS OF EFFORT WITH UNCERTAIN OUTCOMES. BUT IT'S ALSO PUNCTUATED BY EUREKA MOMENTS. AS A CONTENT MARKETER, YOU'LL HAVE MANY OF BOTH.

The inspiration for new content is part of the joy of content chemistry. Seeing a piece of content planned, created, promoted and measured is satisfying, but for me, nothing beats the big bang of a new idea.

Ideas and topics for content come from all directions. The more you write, the more open you'll be to new concepts. Also, the more you write, the more opportunities you'll have to repurpose content, as described in the Periodic Table of Content in Section 5.4.

But brilliance isn't always forthcoming. So for those moments when it isn't, here are 38 questions to get the content flowing. Your answers to these questions will lead to lists, stories, lessons, strong opinions and a steady stream of articles.

And to make sure that your writing gets read, we've added ideas for driving traffic for each question. Remember, we must always create content with promotion in mind.

Your first step should be writing the answers to these questions. You can think of these as "cornerstone content," "pillar posts" or the center of your next content hub. You'll refer to (and link to) these from many other posts. If these are topics you're more likely to mention in conversation, email and other posts, it's more important to write this content soon.

7.1 Sources of Topics

Teach your reader something

These topics are often great for search engine optimization. People are always looking for practical information. And practical content is also some of the most shared.

1. What are the most important things that your audience should know before buying?
Write a list post with a number in the headline. Use this as a subject line in

an email newsletter. Also share it with prospects during the sales process.

2. What is your best advice? What is the right way to do the job?

If there are several, make a list and use the number in the headline and subject line. Target keyphrases such as "[topic] best practices."

3. What are the common questions in your industry?

Write the long-form piece for the blog, and short answers on your sales pages, and pitch another version as a guest post to an association website.

4. What question should people ask you, but don't?

Make this post your best advice for your buyer, with unexpected help during their decision-making process. Target keyphrases such as "How to find a [product/service]." This post can be shared with prospects in your pipeline.

5. Is it possible for your audience to solve their problems without your help? How?

If there is a DIY approach for your audience, they'll find it. But if you don't publish it, they'll find it somewhere else. Write a practical guide in the same tone you would use if you were talking to a friend.

Sure, you may lose a few people who learn there is a DIY solution, but you'll gain far more in followers, traffic and respect, especially if you target the right keyphrase. Try a phrase such as "how to [solve problem]."

6. What do people who are trying to enter your profession need to know?

What's challenging about your job? What's rewarding?

Although the next generation of professionals may not be prospects, they may be an eager audience for your expertise. These readers may remember you years later. Target keyphrases such as "tips for [industry] job seekers."

7. What is the last professional event you attended? What did you learn?

Every event that you attend is an opportunity to create content. List in a recap post the things you learned at a recent event. Mention the speakers or people with whom you talked. Share the post with these people once it's live. Share the post on social media using the event hashtag.

If the event will happen next year, schedule a social media post to go out around the time registration will open.

If event summaries aren't relevant to your audience, consider making this a guest post on another local blog or industry blog. If there's a website for the event, they may also be interested.

8. What are the tools you use every day? What is the best way to use them?

Whether you use software, services or cement trucks in your business, write a roundup of your top tools and techniques. Mention the brands that make your job easier. Use a number in the title and as the subject line in a newsletter. Mention the brands when you share it on social media. Or if any of the brands have blogs and accept guest posts, submit it! In your author bio link back to a service page on your site.

9. What is the one statistic that best emphasizes the importance of your product/service? Why is this stat important?

Make a graphic of this statistic and use it as the featured image. The post should include some analysis about this number, why it matters and where it's going. Use the statistic in the headline and in your email newsletter subject line. Make sure the image appears when you share it on social networks.

Tell 'em stories

List posts may get lots of clicks, but it's the stories that really connect with readers. Great marketers should be great storytellers. The personal tone gives them an advantage in social media. These are questions you need to answer early and often. Some of these questions should be answered on key web pages, such as "About Us."

10. Why do you love what you do?

This is your passion story. Link to this post from your bio on your website. Also, share this on social networks. Use an image that means something to you.

11. What is the unmet need of your audience? How do you meet this need differently than others? Give an example.

This relates directly to your brand's positioning. Link to this article in your email signature. Share it with prospects during the sales process.

12. What are the greatest successes with the best results that can be achieved by using your product or service?

This story could be about any company that used the type of product or service, and not necessarily one of your customers. If the success is measurable, use a number showing the success in a how-to headline, such as "How FruitCo. Sold 81% More Bananas with Guerilla Marketing." Use this as the subject line in an email newsletter.

If the story is about your service and your customer, make it a case study. Use specific details, quotes from the client and statistics. Make it a web page and also a PDF download.

13. Is there a risky (illegal or unethical) way to solve the problems that you solve without the risk? What could go wrong? What's the worst that could happen?

Use quotes and statistics to add emotion and credibility. Share it on social networks using dramatic excerpts from the article. Link back to your site so visitors can read the full story. These posts can also get traction in search engines. Target keyphrases such as "[topic] mistakes."

If you don't want to go negative on your own site, submit this one as a guest post to an industry blog.

14. How does one of your personal interests relate to your job?

Find people in your industry who share this personal interest by searching social media. Search bios using "[industry] [interest]," then share it with them once it's live.

15. What relevant lessons could your audience learn from a famous person, movie, TV show, book or song?

Write a post that makes the connection. The post will likely be both entertaining and insightful (example: "Web Design Techniques from Jean-Claude Van Damme"). Find people in your industry who also enjoy that character, story or genre. Again, social will help (search for bios that include "martial arts" "web design").

16. When people use your product or service, what are some of the unexpected benefits or side effects? How are these things felt by the customer?

Ask a thought leader in your industry for a quote or example. Add this to the post. Once the post is live, politely ask them to share it with their network.

17. Explain how you have changed your approach (or stopped doing something) since you started out in your industry.

Create a chart showing changing industry trends. Or write a headline that uses the current year, such as "Underwater Archeology in 2024: What's Changed." Use this as an email subject line.

18. What industry blogs or magazines do you read? Which posts there get the most shares and comments? Can you add something to this topic?

Submit your new article as a guest post to a similar blog that hasn't covered this topic. Link from the post to related articles on your site.

Conduct interviews and roundups

These are great formats for writers who are stuck since it's as much curation as creation. Interviews and roundups are efficient to create and have social promotion advantages.

19. Who are the influencers from whom you've learned the most? What have they taught you?

Contact an expert and ask if they would be open to a short email interview. Use the Q&A as the post and add some analysis, opinion and gratitude. Once the article is posted, invite the expert to share it with their network.

Text-based interviews can be an efficient way to produce excellent articles. If you interview an influencer, they may help promote your content through their social networks.

- Email one expert five questions.

- Email five experts one question.

- Invite fans and followers to ask questions on Facebook and X (formerly Twitter). Have experts within your business write answers or answer questions on video.

TIP! Lee Odden recommends asking interview questions that include target keyphrases. If the reply includes the keyphrase, you may end up with compelling, natural-language content that is also search-friendly.

TIP! Video and audio interviews may be more difficult to produce but are often very engaging. If you're considering a podcast or video series, interviews are perfect for those formats.

20. What are the most fundamental questions in your industry?
Send the questions to a handful of relevant experts. Combine the responses in a post that shows off the multiple perspectives. Add your own insights, post it, then let the experts know it's live. To really amplify the reach, partner with an industry magazine and publish it on their site.

"List as many 'truisms' as you're able—the 'best practices' and common assumptions that underpin your industry—and then systematically argue against them. Look for edge cases, flawed logic and real-world experiences that refute each truism, and **use your content to challenge the status quo**."

RYAN LAW, *Ahrefs*

Establish yourself as a thought leader

Here's where you take a stand.

To answer the following questions, you'll need courage and strong opinions. You'll need to remove softening words like "maybe," "probably" and "sometimes." Make bold statements. This voice carries on social media and helps online networking.

You may wake up the next day to long blog comments, new followers and even a few detractors. Connect with respectful, like-minded people on several social networks. They may become long-lasting contacts.

21. What questions are people in your industry afraid to answer?
This gets people talking, so try to spread it to the widest possible audience. If you're allowed, submit it as a guest post to the most popular blog or news site in your industry. They might love the topic. If you post it on your site, check to see if the question is a popular search in Google. (Example: "why do banks charge fees" gets 590 searches/month.) If so, align it with this phrase. Long phrases, such as questions, are often less competitive and easier to rank for.

22. What does nearly everyone disagree with you about?
It's unexpected and it's a strong perspective. So it is automatically differentiated from most content.

Even if you don't change people's minds, you'll influence how they think about a subject, sharpen your own thinking and have a post shared as a discussion point.

The team at Animalz actually has a process for finding these "counternarrative opinions."

23. What do you believe will happen in the future that other people consider impossible or unlikely? Could it happen? You think so. But ask the question on Quora and in LinkedIn groups. Politely email it directly to potentially useful contacts. Publish, start the conversation, then keep in touch with them.

Use AI to identify topics

Generative AI can help you find thought provoking topics that will stand out for your reader. Earlier, we used AI to find gaps in a web page. Here we can use AI to find gaps in content in the blogs and media websites across an entire industry. AI can find rarely-covered topics quickly.

And if we have trained AI on our audience and use an AI-powered persona (Section 4.8), it can help us find the topics that trigger conversation and a bit of emotion. Try any of these prompts to uncover potential thought leadership topics:

 Prompt 1:

What are some relatively mundane, almost trivial [industry] topics that professionals have very strong opinions about?

 Prompt 2:

What questions are people in [industry] afraid to answer?

 Prompt 3:

What false things do people in [industry] believe to be true? And vice versa?

 Prompt 4:

What topics are super interesting to this persona but unlikely to be covered by the industry blogs?

 Prompt 5:

What counter-narrative opinions about [topic] are least likely to be discussed by bloggers and thought leaders?

Of course, it will be up to you as the content strategist to decide which of those topics will fit into our content mission statement. The goal is to be relevant to the target audience, not be controversial for its own sake.

Use tools to find topics

Several sources of data contain powerful clues for content topics. These are questions you can answer using online tools. The answers will lead to new ideas for new articles.

Fig. 7.1

Fig. 7.2

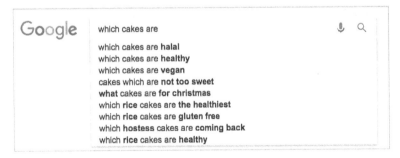

24. What questions are people asking online?

There are free tools that scrape the web for top questions on any topic. Answer The Public (www.answerthepublic.com) is one of the most popular. Just enter a topic and it shows you all kinds of questions people are asking online, each of which is a possible topic for your blog (Fig. 7.1).

BuzzSumo and Semrush have similar features. We'll use BuzzSumo in a minute.

25. What phrases are people searching for?

We've already learned to use the Google Keyword Planner to measure the relative popularity of phrases. It recommends 800 phrases each time you use it. Scroll through looking for topics that you can write about and rank for to establish your brand as an expert.

26. What phrases is Google suggesting?

Whenever you search in Google, you'll see suggested topics as Google auto-completes your query with a longer phrase (Fig. 7.2). This is convenient for searchers, but *it's a gold mine for bloggers.*

Just type in a question word (such as "which") and your topic word (such as "cakes"), and Google will suggest a list of blog topics.

Add a letter and you'll see more suggestions. But it's a long slow process to enter all 26 letters of the alphabet. Fortunately, there are tools that do this for you. One of them is keywordtool.io (Fig. 7.3).

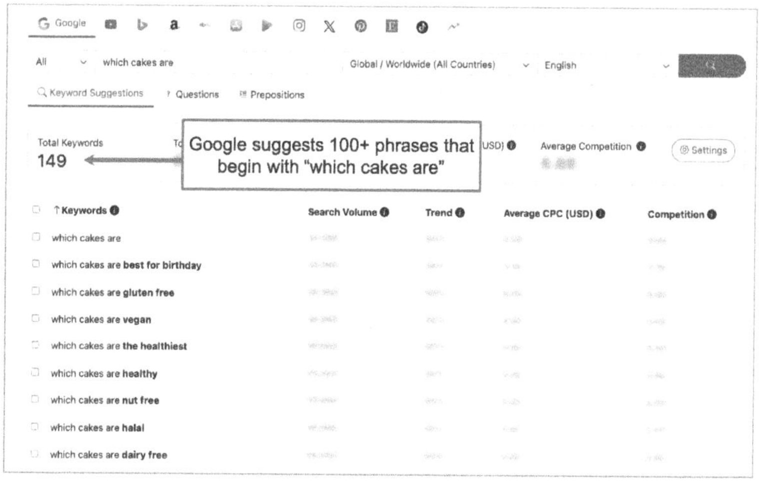

These may be topics you would never have thought of. And each of them is pulled directly from Google, proving there's demand for the topic in search engines. Each of these has an advantage in SERPs.

27. What topics are trending in search engines?

Google Trends shows how phrases trend over time, but it also makes suggestions. It's a great tool for checking seasonality. Here you can see the seasonality of search demand for "baking." It's clearly a holiday thing (Fig. 7.4).

Time your seasonal topics carefully. There are only a few weeks each year that people have any interest in fruitcakes . . . (Fig. 7.5)

Look in the bottom right corner to see a box with a list of 25 recommended phrases. Select "Rising" from the drop-down to see phrases that are suddenly becoming more popular.

Fig. 7.3

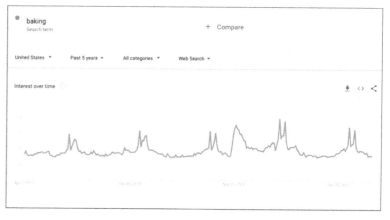

Fig. 7.4

Fig. 7.5

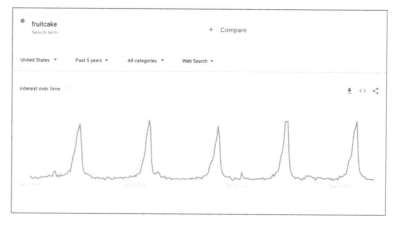

Fig. 7.6

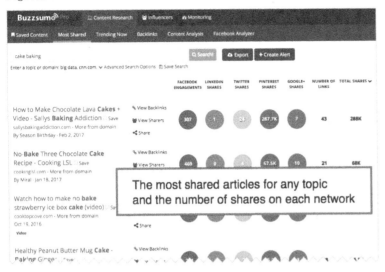

The most shared articles for any topic and the number of shares on each network

Fig. 7.7

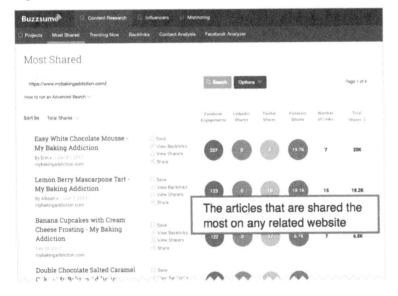

The articles that are shared the most on any related website

Fig. 7.8

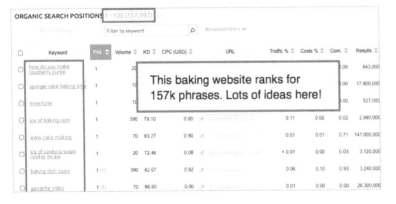

This baking website ranks for 157k phrases. Lots of ideas here!

28. What topics are trending in social media?

You can also quickly find what people are sharing (Fig. 7.6). Enter your main topic into the BuzzSumo **Content Research** tool and you'll find the most shared posts. They are broken down by social network, showing where each piece got the best results (Fig. 7.7).

29. Which posts are getting shared on related websites?

If you want to play follow-the-leader, you can see which posts are getting shared on top industry blogs or competitor websites. Just enter any URL into BuzzSumo, and it will show you which posts are getting shared the most on which social networks. This should quickly trigger ideas for topics, each of which has an edge in social media.

TIP! BuzzSumo also holds powerful clues for effective headline authoring. If you write something similar to a high-performing piece on another site, using the structure or the words from that headline may also work well for you.

30. What phrases are your competitors ranking for?

Since search rankings are public, you can use a tool such as Semrush to view the rankings of your competitors. Just enter their URLs. The free version shows the top ten rankings. The paid version shows all of the rankings (Fig. 7.8).

Getting some topic ideas? Anything you could write about? Why let them win all those visitors?

31. What topics are you already ranking for?

You probably already rank for dozens (or even thousands) of keyphrases. Creating content related to topics you've already written (and pages that already rank) is a fast way both to build up that content hub—which you remember from Section 5.10, right?—and to encourage visitors to dig deeper.

Your rankings can be found in Google Search Console. In the Performance > Search Results report, you can see just the rankings of your blog articles by creating a filter. Assuming your articles are published in a common directory. For example, if your content marketing is in a directory called "blog" create a filter to show pages with URLs containing "blog."(Fig. 7.9)

You are now looking at a list of phrases for which your blog already ranks (Fig. 7.10).

This can be an amazing source of topics. You may already be getting traffic from these phrases.

If you write something new on one of these topics, however, don't forget to link to the new piece from the older post that's already ranking.

32. What relevant topics are getting traction on Quora?

Quora.com is a goldmine of topics. It's filled with *questions*, *answers* and *experts*. If you're a content marketer, that means *topics*, *research* and *collaborators*. Thanks to a system of upvoting, the best of everything rises to the top (Fig. 7.11).

Fig. 7.9

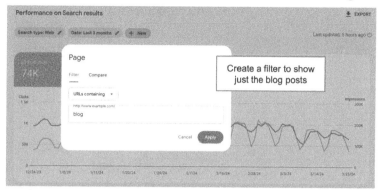

Fig. 7.10

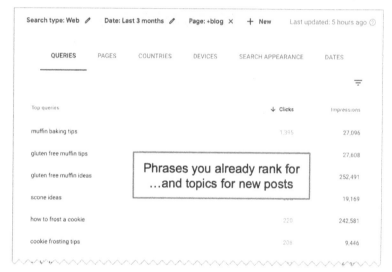

Fig. 7.11

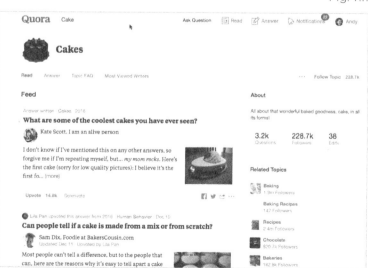

- **Quora questions** are topics that you can use in your content. Top questions are likely the best topics.
- **Quora answers** are a head start on the research for that topic. Top answers are probably the most informative and complete.
- **Quorans** are what members of this network are called. They are possible contributors to the article you're writing.

Quora also makes a great testing ground for new content ideas. *Considering a topic that doesn't appear here?* Post it here and invite relevant Quorans to answer. *Want feedback on your content before you publish it on your blog?* Post it as an answer and see if you get upvotes or comments.

33. Which topics have done well for you in the past?

If it worked well the first time, it's likely to succeed again if you revisit that same topic from another angle.

GA4 can quickly show you which articles readers engaged with the most. These insights are in the Engagement > Pages and Screens report. To see just your blog articles, click the "Add filter +" button and set the filter so Page path contains "blog" (this assumes that your blog articles are in a common directory).

If you don't see columns for "Engagement rate" or "Average engagement time per session," click the pencil icon, then click "Metrics" and add those metrics to the report. Click save.

Now scan through the list and look for articles that have high engagement (Fig. 7.12). Are your visitors telling you something? Are they more interested in some topics than others? Could you write more on these blog topics?

Fig. 7.12

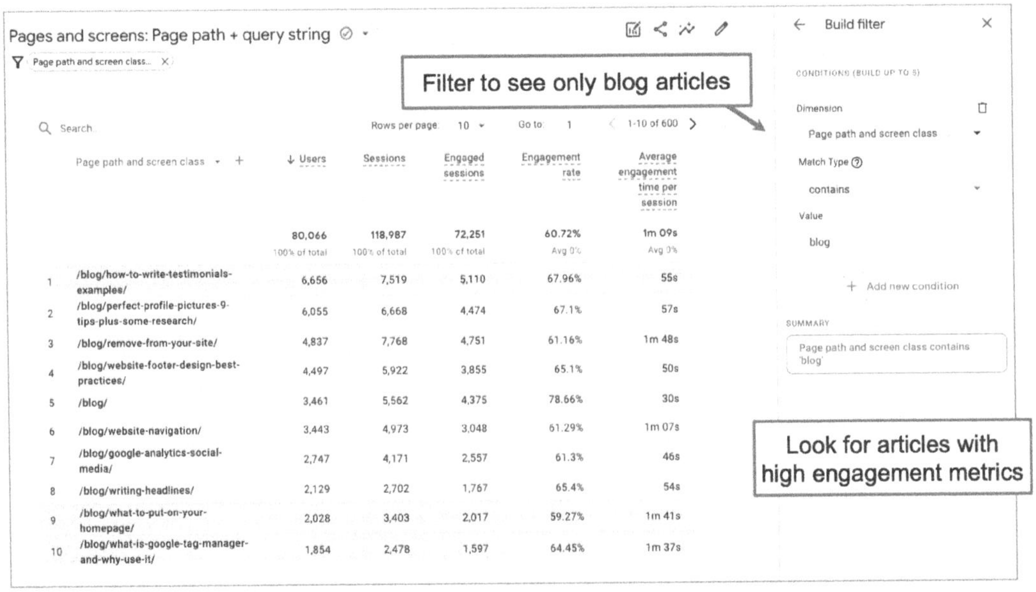

	Page path and screen class	Users	Sessions	Engaged sessions	Engagement rate	Average engagement time per session
		80,066 100% of total	118,987 100% of total	72,251 100% of total	60.72% Avg 0%	1m 09s Avg 0%
1	/blog/how-to-write-testimonials-examples/	6,656	7,519	5,110	67.96%	55s
2	/blog/perfect-profile-pictures-9-tips-plus-some-research/	6,055	6,668	4,474	67.1%	57s
3	/blog/remove-from-your-site/	4,837	7,768	4,751	61.16%	1m 48s
4	/blog/website-footer-design-best-practices/	4,497	5,922	3,855	65.1%	50s
5	/blog/	3,461	5,562	4,375	78.66%	30s
6	/blog/website-navigation/	3,443	4,973	3,048	61.29%	1m 07s
7	/blog/google-analytics-social-media/	2,747	4,171	2,557	61.3%	46s
8	/blog/writing-headlines/	2,129	2,702	1,767	65.4%	54s
9	/blog/what-to-put-on-your-homepage/	2,028	3,403	2,017	59.27%	1m 41s
10	/blog/what-is-google-tag-manager-and-why-use-it/	1,854	2,478	1,597	64.45%	1m 37s

Fig. 7.13

34. The "evil twin" post: what can you rewrite from another angle?

If any of your past, popular posts were a how-to or best practices piece, you can quickly repurpose the topic by taking a new perspective. Write that previous articles' evil twin, such as a "mistakes to avoid" article.

Here are a few examples of how an original topic becomes its evil twin:

- **Original:** How to make muffins
  Evil twin: 3 mistakes that make muffins miserable

- **Original:** The top tips from 5 experts for beginner bakers
  Evil twin: Experts agree that this is the biggest mistake that beginners make in the kitchen

- **Original:** 10 beautiful cakes
  Evil twin: That doesn't look like the cookbook picture!

Fig. 7.13 shows a visual version of that evil twin with viral potential.

Listen to your audience

The best source of topics is your audience itself. When you listen to prospects and customers, you learn their cares, their hopes and their worries. You find out what questions they have. It's the job of your content to answer their questions.

35. What topics are visitors searching for on your website?

If your site has its own search tool, it may be trying to tell you something.

You can set up GA4 to report on what your visitors are searching for. It requires setting up a "custom dimension" and an exploration. Step-by-step instructions can be found here: https://www.orbit media.com/blog/how-to-set-up-site-search-google-analytics/

Once complete, you can see everything your visitors type into that little search box.

This report often shows if there are problems with your website navigation, but it's also an excellent place to find blog post ideas (Fig. 7.14).

Fig. 7.14

Search term	Event count
Totals	30,498
	100.0% of total
1 marketing	547
2 brand	397
3 ethics	187
4 digital marketing	
5 branding	
6 social media	
7 marketing definition	137
8 what is marketing	129
9 green marketing	126
10 advertising	122

All of the things that people search for on your website!

Some of the search phrases may be functional, relating actions the visitor wants to take (such as "jobs" or "donate"), but others will be topical and content related. Your audience is hungry for more content on these topics!

Have you written a post for each of these yet? If not, you've just discovered an unmet content need of your current visitors. Time to publish on that topic.

36. What questions are in your inbox?

They emailed you a question. You wrote a considerate reply. Then you went back to work.

Actually, that moment is a marketing opportunity. Each question emailed to you is a relevant topic (your audience asked for it!) and each reply is potentially

the beginning of an article (it's in a personal tone, which makes for great blog content).

💡 **TIP!** Create an email folder called "content marketing" and use it to store any sent emails that answer questions. I did this for three years and finally moved them into a separate document. It was 92 pages of content. Some of these I immediately repurposed into blog posts. Others I organized into categories, consolidated and finally polished into high-ranking articles.

Your sent mail folder might be filled with topics, ideas and half-written blog posts (Fig. 7.15).

💡 **TIP!** If while reading this book you've said to yourself, "I don't have time to write" or "I don't know how to write," just look at all those messages in your outbox. You're already a writer! You may already be producing 1,000 words of info every day on the same topics and in the same tone that you would use as a content marketer.

37. What are your prospects and customers asking you?

Let's round out the list with the all-time best source of topics: conversations with your audience. Every meeting and phone call with customers and prospects is a chance to uncover topics.

If your company has sales and customer service teams, go talk to them. Find out what people are asking about in sales

Fig. 7.15

EMAIL — Hey, Andy! I just wrote a press release. How can I turn this into an article?

ANSWER — Hi there, Dave! Happy to help. Here is a detailed, 5-step process for turning your press release into a nice little blog post.

KEYPHRASE — press release blog post

HEADLINE — How to turn a press release into a blog post in 5 steps

meetings and on service calls. What are the top questions they're being asked? *What does every prospect need to know before they hire us?*

If a question was answered in a meeting, email or phone call, but never published as a blog topic, the value of your answer is short-lived. But publish that answer, and you can send it to people over and over again. Visitors can find it. It may rank in Google. People may share it.

Three amazing things happen when you write content that answers sales questions.

1. You can send the article to companies that are currently in your pipeline, keeping those conversations going.

2. All sales associates are unified in their messaging; they can send the link to future prospects who have that same question.

3. Put these answers on your services pages to increase your conversion rates. People are more likely to become a lead when their questions are answered.

This is why the best content marketers work closely with sales teams. They ride shotgun to meetings. They jump into sales calls. They listen for questions and answers, then publish accordingly (Fig. 7.16).

Conversations are temporary. Content is forever.

Now that we know the best topics, let's move on to the best format.

Topics flow from sales to marketing

Fig. 7.16

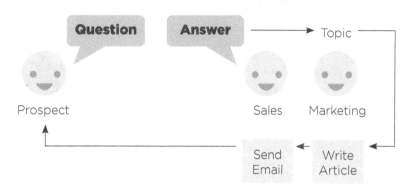

Content flows from marketing to sales

7.2 Original Research: The Most Powerful Marketing Content

The well is deep. There are so many possible topics and formats for content, by now you should have plenty of ideas and a full publishing calendar: helpful how-tos, graphical guides, roundups and rants. But there is one type of content that stands above them all: *original research.*

This format will outperform almost anything else you publish. It's so effective that research is something all serious content marketers should have in their content mix. More than any other type of content, it has a way of making you famous in your field.

Remember Steve Rayson's headline research from Section 5.6? He did another important piece of marketing

"If you want to create content that achieves a high level of both shares and links then you should concentrate on opinion forming, authoritative content or **well researched and evidenced content**."

STEVE RAYSON, *Co-founder, BuzzSumo*

Why research wins

Original research is the most powerful and most effective format for content for a lot of reasons.

1. It's *original and owned by you*, making your website and your brand the primary source

2. Data can support your sales messaging

3. Numbers are convincing and lend credibility

4. Charts and graphs are compelling visuals

5. The outreach involved can help grow your network

6. *Research attracts more links and more shares than any other format for content*

That last point is important since links are the key to search and shares are the key to social. These are two of our main channels for content promotion.

research with an important conclusion: most content gets no links or shares. But Steve's analysis of the top performers revealed one critical insight. There are two types of content that consistently perform well:

- Strong opinion

- Original research

Publishing counternarrative opinion pieces on a regular basis is very difficult. To succeed, you need to be brave, be deliberately provocative and take a stand for (and against) something. True thought leadership is powerful, but it's not a repeatable strategy for most brands. So let's focus on that second group—research.

Most content gets almost no traction in search or social. Original research is the exception.

The 5 types of research

Here are five types of research you can produce, publish and promote. They each have their own challenges and benefits (Fig. 7.17).

Research type 1: Results from experiments

Test, analyze, publish, promote

You tried something. Did it work or not? Anything that you or your company tried is potentially publishable research as long as it produced a datapoint. These are generally not rigorous research studies and your blog is not a peer-reviewed journal. But you tried something and it worked or it didn't. Your audience wants to see your findings.

An experiment is just a case study with a different angle. The key is to publish a conclusion that's relevant to a broader audience. It's not about the results you get for your clients. It's about discovering the truth.

Example: The A/B test results on the Mad Mimi pricing page

Joanna Wiebe from Copy Hackers has a data-driven approach to helping clients. They do conversion optimization experiments and sometimes she publishes the results. Since the results are often dramatic, these articles attract a lot of attention.

Types of Research-Based Content for Marketing

Fig. 7.16

Types of Research	Qualitative	Quantitative*	Process Pros and Cons
Experiments		X	Often easy to perform, results are usually visual
Obervation/ Analysis	X		Fast data collection, doesn't require a survey
Aggregate Existing Research	X		Highly credible, requires careful analysis
Online Survey	X		Big outreach has networking, traffic benefits. Data may support sales.
Phone Survey	X		Big networking benefits, subjects can include sales prospects.

*These are typical, but technically, any of these types of research can be qualitative or quantitative.

Joanna's experiments resulted in a 500% increase in conversions. It also produced a beautiful, visual piece of content (Fig. 7.17).

This experiment and its results have appeared in many marketing presentations. It's also earned 37 links and hundreds of shares.

Fig. 7.17

Control

Variation B

Variation C

Winner on 3/4 Goals

Source: https://copyhackers.com/2014/05/optimized-madmimi-pricing-page/

Research type 2: Observe and analyze

Pick your dataset, gather data, analyze

Just find your data in the wild and run your analysis. Look for patterns, form a hypothesis, gather information and analyze. Steve's research is a great example. He did a statistical analysis on a large set of data: a million posts. He's an expert statistician, but you don't need to be to gather and analyze data.

Example: web design standards

A client once asked me if a site search tool is a standard feature on websites. Not every website has a little search box, right? Do most websites have one? What features are standard on websites? We decided to find out.

First, we built a list of the top 500 marketing websites across a range of five industries. We added these as rows on a spreadsheet.

Next, made a list of design features: site search, calls to action, social icons, mobile responsive design, etc. These became the columns on the same spreadsheet.

For step three, we had a virtual assistant review the sites and record which sites had which features on the spreadsheet. Finally, we analyzed the data and turned it into visual charts, and wrote a detailed article with our analysis (Fig. 7.18).[1]

It was a big success, far more successful than a typical post on our blog. Years later, we updated it and launched it again on the same URL, which is important because it was already ranking for the phrase "web design standards." Over time, that piece has attracted links from 300+ websites. It's also been shared more than 500 times and has 200k pageviews.

1. https://www.orbitmedia.com/blog/web-design-standards/

10 Website Design Standards vs. Best Practices

Review of 500 homepages shows the popularity of various UX features in web design.
But many do not align with web design best practices.

Fig. 7.18

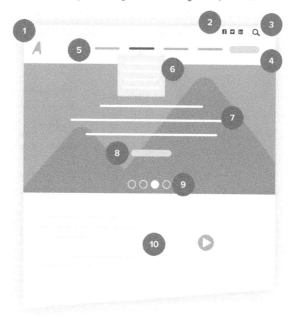

1 **93% of websites have the logo in the top left**
Definitely a standard spot for it. Occasionally, it's center aligned.

2 **13% of websites place social media icons in the header**
Bad idea. Why put colorful exit signs at the top of every single page?

3 **53% of websites have a search tool in the header**
A common place for it, but unnecessary on small or well-organized sites.

4 **55% of websites have a contact button in the top right**
Put it here and it will be easy for everyone to find.

5 **90% of websites have the main navigation in the header**
Why hide it behind a hamburger icon for desktop users? Bad idea.

6 **58% of websites have dropdown menus**
Very common. Handy for websites with a wide range of products / services.

7 **54% of websites have value propositions above the fold**
Don't be clever. Don't use a tagline. Just be specific and descriptive.

8 **33% of websites have a call to action (not just "contact us")**
"Contact us" is not a call to action. Be more specific. Watch your verbs.

9 **42% of websites have a slider / slideshow**
Some sites still do it, despite tons of evidence and research on its ineffectiveness.

10 **18% of websites have video on the homepage**
Uncommon but effective. Why not upgrade the format for key messages?

Research type 3: Aggregate existing research

New insights on a well-covered topic

When the research is already out there, you can combine and repackage it into new metrics and new statistics. This is often faster than gathering data yourself from primary sources. As long as you cite the source, it's a smart and ethical way to build an audience. Malcolm Gladwell, for instance, uses this approach quite well. Here's another example from the Orbit blog.

Example: marketing salaries

Compensation is always an interesting topic. We didn't have any salary data ourselves, but we knew where to get it. To publish a credible article of marketing salaries, we went to two sources: Glassdoor and PayScale. We looked up the top marketing job titles on each site and found averages based on tens of thousands of employees.

By combining these sources, we were able to publish average salaries for the top marketing jobs. By repeating the research every few years, we were able to show a trend (Fig. 7.19).

Fig. 7.19

Marketing Salary Guide

(median salaries from Glassdoor and PayScale)

Marketing Job Title	2016	2018	2020	2022	2024
Marketing Coordinator 0-3+ years experience	$40,718	$46,103	$45,254	$50,171	$55,089
Marketing Associate 1-3+ years experience	$42,102	$47,954	$53,851	$55,701	$57,551
Marketing Manager 5-10+ years experience	$71,352	$76,295	$65,796	$71,713	$77,630
Social Media Manager 5+ years experience	$46,511	$56,687	$50,848	$56,120	$61,391
Content Strategist 5+ years experience	$62,200	$78,780	$65,732	$68,597	$71,461
Director of Marketing 10+ years experience	$93,435	$112,787	$99,913	$104,328	$108,743
VP, Marketing 15+ years experience	$146,860	$166,070	$145,914	$167,002	$188,091

Source: https://www.orbitmedia.com/blog/marketing-job-descriptions-salaries/

The final piece included a compelling headline, a strong visual and search-friendly copy (complete job descriptions for each position). All the ingredients were included.

Every time we update this research, the email gets huge results. The subject line "How much do marketers make?" is like catnip for our audience. Honestly, this piece isn't a perfect fit for our content strategy and mission statement ("Practical advice on content marketing, AI, GA4 and web design") but the results are hard to pass up:

- 4000+ visitors from the newsletter with record high click through rates

- 25k pageviews from search (it's optimized for "marketing job descriptions" and "marketing salaries")

- 127 links from other websites

- 1500+ shares

It also led to press coverage and podcast interviews. No surprise. It's relevant to everyone in our audience and everyone has thoughts about it.

Research type 4: Online surveys

Big outreach, big numbers

A marketing survey is a reliable way to produce something truly original and unique to your website. The data and analysis can make your site a resource for your entire industry. Survey results may even capture the attention of journalists and become news.

The statistics that you discover can also help you sell. Imagine a sales rep for cost tracking software explaining how 40% of companies lose track of their expenses. Or the mouthwash company that shows that 76% of people say bad breath is a "dating deal breaker." (Fig. 7.20)

📋 **NOTE:** Since this was a single multiple choice question, it's really a poll, not a survey.

Fig. 7.20

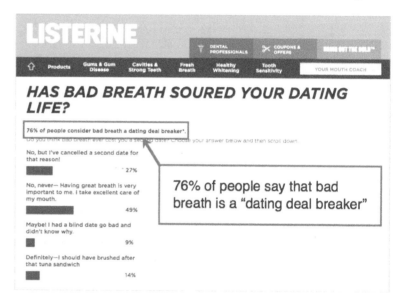

Surveys also offer a special benefit to the content marketer because they involve outreach and interaction with a large group of people.

- **The final results can be shared with the respondents**
  When people take the survey, they can enter their address to get the results. *You are building a list as you are gathering data.* Once you publish the results, email the respondents

a thank you message and let them know the results are live.

- **The massive outreach is good for brand awareness**
  Any project that involves a lot of outreach will cause a spike in attention for your brand.

- **It lends itself to good promotion**
  Survey-driven content includes visuals, numbers and original insights.

And if you repeat surveys year over year, they get even easier to create and promote. You already have your list for outreach. You already know who shared and wrote about it last time. And now that you have trend and longitudinal data, the results are even more interesting.

1. Create a list of survey questions designed to discover a new statistic that supports your marketing message. The fewer the questions, the easier it will be to get completed responses.

TIP! Ask at least one question that allows you to divide the respondents into groups. For example, "What industry are you in?" This will allow you to publish multiple versions of the survey later.

TIP! For the last question, ask respondents to enter an email address if they would like to be notified when the results go live. This will give you an additional list to send the research to.

2. Set up an online survey. Use a tool like SurveyMonkey or QuestionPro that makes it easy to do basic analysis and create draft charts.

3. Build an initial list of potential respondents and places to post and promote the survey.

4. Optional: Create an incentive to take the survey.

5. *Promote the survey aggressively and through any means necessary* until you have a credible dataset.

6. Analyze the findings to discover the missing stat and any other insights you can find.

7. Publish the survey with pretty charts, contributor quotes and an attractive featured image.

8. Make visual, shareable graphics that contain the statistics you created.

9. *Promote the results aggressively and through every channel*, making it visible to influencers, bloggers and the media.

Example: Annual Blogger Survey

Throughout this book, we've referred to our blogging research, so you've already seen how this research has been useful to us and to the industry. Here's a bit more insight into the creation, promotion and results of that research.

- To make sure the research was visible to influencers, we included contributor quotes from the biggest names in content marketing in the research itself.

- To make the research visible in a durable way, we optimized it to rank for "blogging statistics."

TIP: As we discussed in Section 3.1, keyphrases typically have navigational, informational or commercial intent. But there is a tiny set of keyphrases that have actual "linking intent." Ranking for these phrases can attract visitors who are looking for content to link to. These phrases include words such as "statistics," "data" and "quotes."

- To make the original research results more engaging, we made visuals for each chart that included key findings (Fig. 7.21). These work well in social media.

- To increase reach, we pitched related guest posts to top blogs. We republished the findings as an infographic. We made the raw data available to other researchers.

It's a very big job. It takes 150+ hours to create and promote this one piece of content each year. That's more than ten times the typical effort. But the results are far greater than ten times the results of a typical article. Combined, these

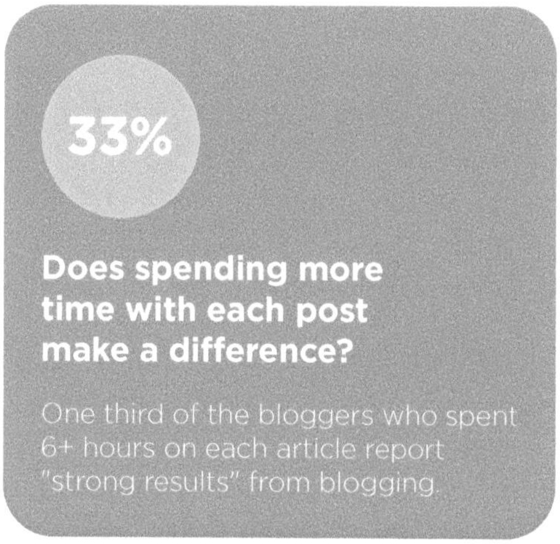

Fig. 7.21

33%

Does spending more time with each post make a difference?

One third of the bloggers who spent 6+ hours on each article report "strong results" from blogging.

surveys have been shared 9,000+ times and linked to from 2,600 websites and counting. They've also led to interviews on many of the top marketing podcasts and blogs.

Translated versions of the results have appeared in Russian, Italian, French, Spanish, Japanese and Hebrew.

Research type 5: Phone surveys

Smaller dataset, higher touchpoint

If online surveys are about quantity and statistical significance, phone surveys are about quality and networking. Rather than getting a little data from a lot of people, get a lot of data from the few people who really matter.

Make a list of 25 people who are experts in your topic *and fit a profile (or job title) of people you'd like to connect with.* They may be from companies you'd like to pitch to someday. They may be potential referral partners you'd like to have in your network. They may be influencers you'd like to collaborate with eventually.

Reach out and ask permission to do a short interview. Call each of them on the phone for a 10-minute interview. The call is a brief interview focused on the main questions, but it can also include follow-up questions. It ends with an offer to share the research once it's complete.

The process itself is an opportunity to create high-value connections. And the research may uncover data that wouldn't have been discovered through multiple-choice questions. Here are some examples of phone surveys, subjects and content outcomes.

- Do you sell social media services? *Call 50 marketing directors and ask about their biggest social media challenges.*
  Possible findings: **68%** *of marketing directors have trouble measuring social media ROI.*

- Do you sell supply chain software? **Call 50 logistics professionals and ask them what tools they use.**
  Possible findings: *Only 16% of logistics companies have a transportation management system in place.*

- Do you do technology staffing? **Call 50 IT directors and ask them about skills gaps on their teams.**
  Possible findings: *4 out of 5 tech hiring managers are looking for QA/testing experience.*

This is a powerful way for B2B marketers to get right in front of decision-makers and connect marketing and sales. The key to success is to be very considerate and follow up.

Example article: "The Seven Skills You Need to Thrive in the C-Suite"

What are the most important skills for succeeding at C-level jobs? It's a subjective question, best answered through interviews, not an online survey. Boris Groyberg produced a high-quality, research-based article on the topic by surveying "several dozen top senior search consultants" and published the findings in the *Harvard Business Review* (Fig. 7.22).[2]

Here is the methodology.

Fig. 7.22

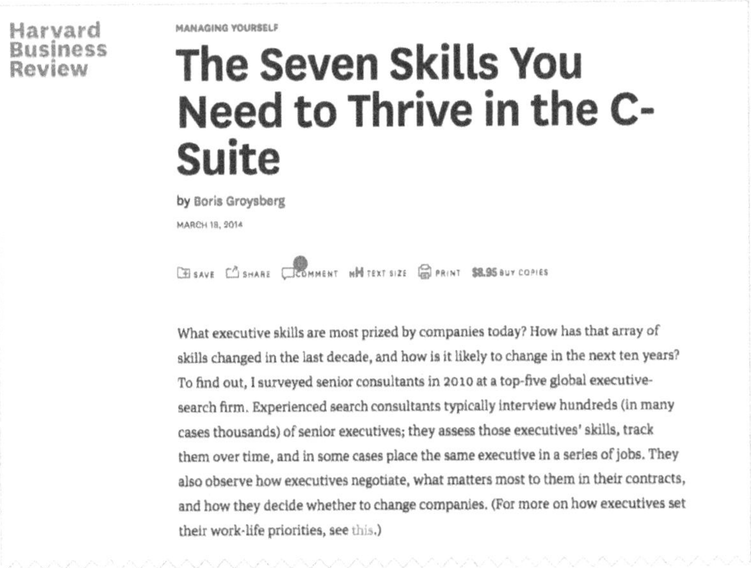

Harvard Business Review

MANAGING YOURSELF

The Seven Skills You Need to Thrive in the C-Suite

by Boris Groysberg

MARCH 18, 2014

SAVE   SHARE   COMMENT   TEXT SIZE   PRINT $8.95 BUY COPIES

What executive skills are most prized by companies today? How has that array of skills changed in the last decade, and how is it likely to change in the next ten years? To find out, I surveyed senior consultants in 2010 at a top-five global executive-search firm. Experienced search consultants typically interview hundreds (in many cases thousands) of senior executives; they assess those executives' skills, track them over time, and in some cases place the same executive in a series of jobs. They also observe how executives negotiate, what matters most to them in their contracts, and how they decide whether to change companies. (For more on how executives set their work-life priorities, see this.)

2. www.hbr.org/2014/03/the-seven-skills-you-need-to-thrive-in-the-c-suite

"To answer these questions, we surveyed several dozen top senior search consultants at a top global executive placement firm. As a group, they were 57% male and 43% female. They represented a wide range of industries . . ."

This page has been linked to from 100+ websites and shared 1,200 times. The networking benefits must have been priceless.

So if original research is such a powerful format for content for building authority, it should be a popular strategy, right? It is not. According to the blogger survey, only 25% of bloggers have published original research in the last 12 months (Fig. 7.23).

What to research: find the "missing stat"

In every industry there are familiar statements and conventional wisdom. It's the common knowledge that everyone agrees on. But it's so commonplace that no one questions it. No one researches it. It isn't supported with data or evidence.

We call these gaps "missing stats" and they are ripe for research. These statements meet two criteria:

1. Frequently asserted

2. Rarely supported

They are the baseless assertions made every day, just waiting for data to back them up. If you can find the gaps, conduct the survey and publish the missing statistic, you'll have supported all of those common assertions. Now, when

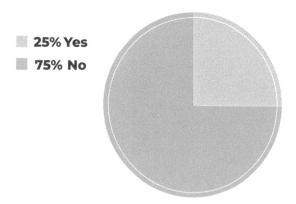

Fig. 7.23

Have you published original research in the last 12 months?

- 25% Yes
- 75% No

people make the claim, your data will be there to support it and your website will be there to link to.

Fig. 7.24 shows some examples of industries, common assertions and hypothetical missing statistics. Each of these could be discovered through research.

Fig. 7.24

Industry	Assertion	Example of the "Missing Stat"
Skin care	People don't wear enough sunscreen	82% of dermatologists agree that people aren't protecting themselves from the sun.
Co-working spaces	Working from home is boring	65% of people who work from home miss the social aspects of working in an office.
Dog training	Dogs and cats don't get along	53% of dogs actually like cats.
Marketing	Blogging takes a lot of time	The average blog post takes about 4 hours to write.

Fig. 7.25

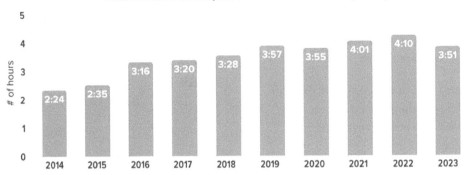

It takes just under 4 hours to write a blog post on average

That's less time than last year, but still 60% more than 10 years ago.

# of hours

Year	Time
2014	2:24
2015	2:35
2016	3:16
2017	3:20
2018	3:28
2019	3:57
2020	3:55
2021	4:01
2022	4:10
2023	3:51

n=1051

That last example is the actual statistic that we originally set out to discover in the blogger survey. Everyone says "blogging takes time" but how much time does it really take? No one had ever answered this question. This was a missing stat in the content marketing industry (Fig. 7.25).

Find this missing stat and support it with original research. You'll have filled an information gap and proved the conventional wisdom. You'll have made your brand a go-to resource for important information. You'll have created something share-worthy, link-worthy and even press-worthy (seriously, you should reach out to the media). You may find your statistic cited in books, presentations and blogs all over the world.

Use AI to find missing statistics

AI can help you find frequently asserted but rarely supported claims. Try these simple prompts.

Prompt 1:

What are the most common assertions in [industry] that are the least likely to be supported with evidence?

Prompt 2:

What new original statistics could be created through research on a [industry] blog that would support the claims made on other blogs?

Publish the missing stat in your industry. The internet will thank you for it.

7.3 The Content Creation Process (in a single flowchart)

So many possible topics. Topics that teach, topics that trigger conversations, topics that align with their decision-making process, topics supported by new research projects.

Inspiration strikes! But before you open up a blank content template and start writing a new article, take a minute to think about the structure and the promotion of the piece.

The diagram in Fig. 7.26 lays out all the considerations for creating content, from first inspiration to the final draft. These are all of the steps in order, with all of the little decisions involved, that a content marketer will consider before the writing begins.

The description of each step reviews lessons from other sections of this book. Here's where the thinking comes together.

1. Inspiration

This comes from all directions, as we explored through the questions earlier in this chapter. Every topic must fit within your content strategy, but beyond that, it's all fair game. Some sources are better than others. The best are focused on the audience, and often come directly from sales conversations.

The Flow of Content Creation   Fig. 7.26

The 17-step process for high-performing articles

DEVELOP THE CONCEPT

1. **Inspiration!**
   Idea for an article!

Is it similar to one of our out-of-date articles? — YES → 2. Plan to rewrite an old article, recycling that URL

Is this a provocative topic? With multiple points of view? — YES → 3. Socialize the topic publicly with your network

Could we conduct a study to support this idea? — YES → 4. Plan the research, analysis, data collection

SEARCH OPTIMIZATION

Is anyone looking for this topic? — NO

5. What keyphrase might they use to look for it?

Do we have sufficient authority to rank for this phrase? — NO

6. Plan to make it the best page on the web for the topic.

7. Forget keywords! Plan to promote through social media, email, etc . . .

8. Create the outline. Plan the sections.

continued on the following page ▶

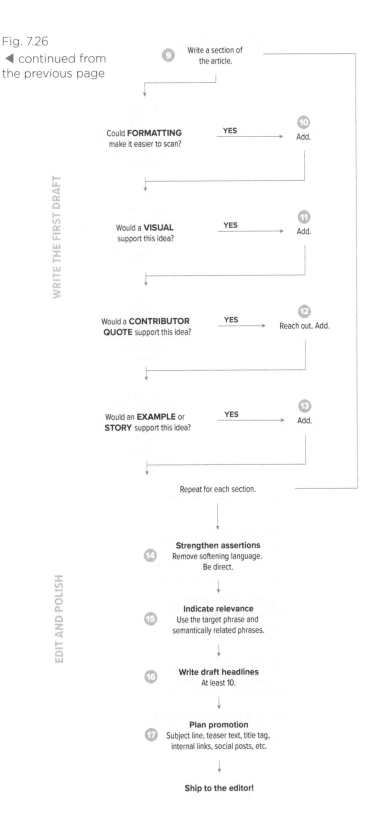

Fig. 7.26
◀ continued from
the previous page

2. Consider rewriting an old article

There's often greater glory in rewriting something old, rather than writing something new. Older content often sits on URLs with strong, unrealized benefits:

- They may already rank, but not yet rank high

- The research and writing process has a huge head start

- You already may have feedback on the topic from your readers

Rewrite an old post that needs some love. Once done, you'll relaunch it just as if it was new. Send it as a newsletter and put it back on top of the blog. In Chapter 8, we'll share a process for finding the posts that need it the most.

3. Socialize the topic with your network

What do people think about this topic? Is this likely to trigger discussion? Drop a relevant question into a social stream and see what happens. Within a few hours, you'll know if it's engaging and who is engaging with it.

This works great if you can find a slightly provocative angle to your topic. This works *automatically* if the topic is a strongly held opinion, especially if that opinion is contrary to readers' expectations.

4. Conduct original research

Produce a new statistic that supports a frequently made assertion, promote it well and it's likely to perform well. As with strong opinion, it's especially effective if the research findings are somehow counternarrative.

Research pieces, especially surveys, are a lot more work than a typical post. But they have built-in promotion advantages, especially if the findings are turned into compelling visuals in step 11.

5. Keyphrase Research

There are two main criteria applied when selecting keyword research: demand (search volume) and difficulty (competition). We learned to answer both of these two qualifying questions in Section 5.5.

- Are people searching for this phrase?

- Do we have a chance of ranking for this phrase?

If yes and yes, you have your primary target keyphrase.

6. You are writing a search optimized article

Your job will be to create one of the ten best pages on the internet for your topic. Then you'll deserve to win a page-one ranking. This means going deep into the subject.

- Touch on the subtopics.

- Answer all of the most important related questions.

- Back up your claims with evidence.

- Include the voices of relevant experts.

It's probably going to be a big one. But don't bother counting words. The writing will be concise, but detailed. Naturally, you'll need to indicate relevance for the topic as you go. So you'll follow SEO best practices but your obsession is quality, not keyword frequency. You'll get fancy with phrases in step 15.

7. You are not writing a search optimized article

Every keyphrase is a competition and every page is a competitor. If your page has no chance of winning the competition (insufficient authority) or if the topic isn't something people are searching for (announcements, opinion), then forget SEO.

You are free! Free to write without any consideration for search. Forget keyphrases entirely. There's no such thing as "a little bit optimized."

You can promote the article through email, social, outreach, or influencers or personally send it directly to people who need it the most. If it's a great article, it will travel through word of mouth.

8. Setting the structure

Start with a template, not a blank document. It will force you to plan for (or at least consider) content promotion. Open up your master content template, copy it and start dropping in your notes. Add links to related articles. Add examples. Some of these notes will evolve into sections. Others will be discarded.

9. Begin writing

You're ready. It's that time and place where you're productive. You've turned off notifications and closed all irrelevant browser tabs. Your deep work mix is playing through your noise canceling headphones. It's time.

- Write a single-sentence summary of the article.

- Expand that into a one-paragraph version of the article.

- Write the outline.

- Write the part that got you excited in the first place.

You might get stuck. You might abandon this idea. That's fine. But save this doc in your big list of partially written articles. You may come back to it one day. And if you ever get ideas or find examples that are related to the topic, just pop open the doc and drop them in.

Eventually, you'll have a list of dozens of articles, slowly growing over time (Fig. 7.27).

10. Add lots of formatting

As writers, we choose words for readers. As content developers, we create an experience for the visitor. That experience is about words, but also visuals, formatting and flow. Remember these items from the Article Checklist in Section 5.11.

- Subheads

- Short paragraphs

- Bulleted and numbered lists

- Bolding and Italics

- Internal links

11. Never miss the chance to add a visual

Remember, your reader came from a place (search engine, social stream or email inbox) that was filled with interesting things to read. And the back button is right there. If you make them slog through long paragraphs of dense

Fig. 7.27

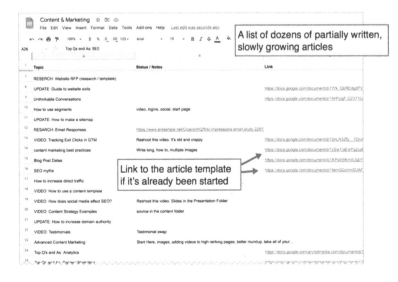

text, they're likely to leave. But give your readers something of visual interest at every scroll depth and they're likely to stay.

12. Reach out to a few experts for contributor quotes

Beyond images, contributor quotes are a way to sneak in another visual. Specifically, a face, which is a magnetic type of image. But a handsome headshot isn't the main reason to add a contributor quote. They add insights and credibility. They can improve social reach and PR.

Don't wait until the last minute to reach out. Give your contributors time to write a thoughtful blurb. When you reach out, let them know the topic, the ideal contribution length and the deadline.

13. Add examples and stories

A lot of content fails because it's just too common. It's boring. Just the usual tips and recommendations. Nothing different. Nothing real. But one good real-world example would rescue this content from mediocrity.

- Add a little narrative with characters and conflict, before and after, cases and evidence.

- Add visual examples, showing the concepts in practice, both good and bad.

- Make it personal, injecting the writer's own experience.

14. Strengthen assertions

Here's another quality check: go back and remove all of that softening language. Cut out the "throat clearing" sentence in the intro. Be direct and concise, even if it feels like you're overstating things a bit.

Compare the before and after:

~~This may have been the most significant finding from the research.~~
This was the biggest insight from the survey.

~~It's generally considered best practices to have each article reviewed by an editor.~~
It's a mistake to not use an editor.

~~It's common for experts to recommend that language be direct and assertive~~
Get to the point.

15. Optimize for search and indicate relevance

If the outcome of the keyword research led you through step 6, you're writing a search optimized article. You've included the primary target keyphrase in the title and header. The text itself covers the topic in detail.

Next, indicate relevance for the broader topic, not just the narrow keyphrase. Find and incorporate the semantically related phrases. They're hiding in the usual places: Google Suggest, "People also ask," related searches, Quora and rivals' rankings. Make a list and then work them into the article, adding depth and detail as you go.

16. Write the draft headlines

Write many draft headlines before picking the winner. And don't use the same headline everywhere. Adapt the headline for the specific location: title tag, header, subject line, social posts, infographic header, video title. Each element has its own opportunities, captured in different ways.

17. Plan the promotion

You made it! You've created an article that's ready for promotion. The process of getting here pushed you to build in

"Content creation is a matter of four disciplines. **First,** you have to have the discipline to be aware of the story ideas bombarding you every day. View your life as possible content that is unfolding. **Second,** you must have the discipline to record those ideas immediately or you'll lose them! **Next,** you need to block out quiet, undisturbed time to create. Actually schedule time, just as you would schedule a meeting or a date. **Last,** it's best to find a way to relax when creating content. Creating content under pressure is never a path to optimal output!"

MARK SCHAEFER,
International Speaker & Bestselling Author

many of the elements that correlate with success.

Social Media

- In step 3 you shared the idea with your network. Once your content is live you can let your network know by tagging them when you share it.

- In step 11 you made visuals.

- In step 12 you added quotes from contributors.

Search Engine Optimization

- In step 2 . . . recycled URL

- In steps 5 and 6 . . . keyphrase research

- In step 15 you indicated relevance

Now you need to get the elements of the newsletter ready. The subject line will be one of the draft headlines (no keywords required) and the teaser text is often an adapted version of the intro. All of your rejected headlines can be used as social media posts.

Structure, forethought and discipline

Let's give the last word to Mark Schaefer, an expert content marketer and prolific writer. Combine his advice about mindset with the tactical recommendations above and you should be all set.

Notes

08 Audit, Update & Optimize

ONCE YOU'VE BEEN PUBLISHING CONTENT FOR A YEAR OR MORE, YOUR OPPORTUNITIES TO IMPROVE BEGIN TO MULTIPLY.

You should have a growing audience—more subscribers, followers and Domain Authority—but you also have more content and more data.

This chapter is about using data to audit the performance of your content marketing program and to find ways to optimize your efforts. You'll discover what worked well and what didn't, giving you insights into what new content to create and what old content to update.

This approach will be useful to content marketers who meet two criteria. If you can check both of these boxes, you're ready to audit, update and optimize your content and content strategy:

1. You've been blogging for several years and have published 50+ articles.

2. Your content is mostly evergreen (educational, how-to articles), not ephemeral (news).

That makes this approach more relevant to more mature content marketing programs, regardless of the experience level of the actual marketer. It's simple, but you need data to do it. And updating older content has become a popular strategy. More bloggers are updating content more often (Fig. 8.1).

Fig. 8.1

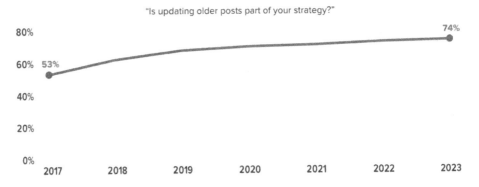

Percentage of bloggers who update old articles

"Is updating older posts part of your strategy?"

Let's face it: A few articles are driving most of the results

The 80/20 rule tells us that 80% of the results come from 20% of the effort. A few things are making the biggest difference. In content marketing, it often seems more like the 95/5 rule. A very small percentage of content is getting a huge percentage of the results. In other words, a small handful of articles pull in the largest percentage of traffic and conversions (Fig. 8.2).

This is true for every website and for every G4 account we've ever reviewed.

Just look at your own data. A report of your top posts by traffic probably looks something like Fig. 8.3. A few posts bring in a lot of traffic, while most articles drive little or no traffic. If you calculate the conversion rate for each piece of content, you'll see a similar curve. A few articles convert visitors at a high rate, while most articles convert few or no visitors.

If a few articles are getting the best results, then why aren't you focused more on these performers? The problem is that you often don't know which articles are the real heroes. To find out, you need to do a content marketing audit.

"For many events, roughly 80% of the effects come from 20% of the causes." —**PARETO**

Fig. 8.2

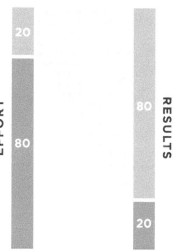

80/20 RULE

Therefore 20% of the effort produces 80% of the results but the last 20% of the results consumes 80% of the effort.

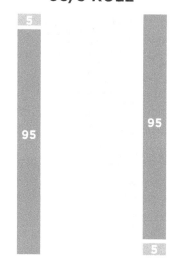

95/5 RULE

Fig. 8.3

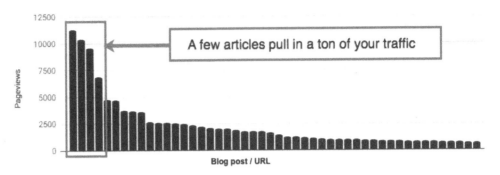

Monthly pageviews for the top 50 blog posts

A few articles pull in a ton of your traffic

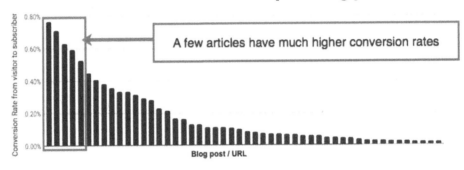

Conversion rate for the top 50 blog posts

A few articles have much higher conversion rates

8.1 The 9-Step Content Marketing Audit

Here's a step-by-step guide for auditing your content marketing efforts. Once you're done, you'll know what's working well for you—and what isn't. You'll also discover some new best practices for adapting your content marketing based on the analysis.

This audit combines GA4 and Google Search Console to find insights, focusing on the top three promotion channels: SEO, email marketing and social media. It includes both the analysis and the actions to take based on the data.

1 Top Performing Traffic Sources

2. SEO: Content that attracts visitors from search

3. SEO: Content with rising or falling search traffic

4. SEO: Keyword performance for any article

5. SEO: Content that has search ranking potential

6. Email: Top performing email campaigns

7. Social: Top performing social networks

8. Social: Content that gets the most traffic and engagement from social media

9. Where did this article perform the best?

At the end of each section, we've added **next steps and action items**, with suggestions for what to do with the data to drive better content marketing outcomes.

1. Which are our top performing traffic sources?

It's a fundamental marketing question. Some content does well on social media. Other content does well in search. You can promote every article everywhere, but content performance varies widely across channels.

We'll start with an easy one. Here's how to check and see, at a high level, where your content is performing best.

1. From the Reports section, go to Acquisition > Traffic acquisition.

2. Click on the pencil icon in the top right to "Customize report" (you'll need to be logged in using an account with more than just "Viewer" level access)

3. Now click "Metrics" to select some useful metrics. We recommend the following:

   a. Users

   b. Sessions

   c. Engagement rate

   d. Average engagement time per session

   e. Bounce rate (less meaningful than engagement rate, but some people still like it)

   f. Session key event rate

Bounce rate and session key event rate won't be on the list. You'll need to add them by clicking the "Add metric" dropdown at the bottom of the list, then searching for them.

Reorder the metrics if you'd like. Fig. 8.4 shows what the customization will look like.

Fig. 8.4

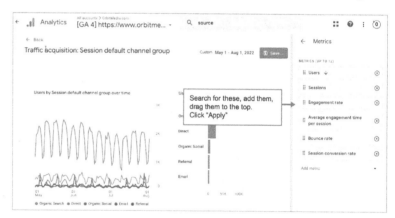

4. Save the customization using "Save changes to current report"

Fig. 8.5

Select a meaningful conversion, such as "subscribe to newsletter"

Session default channel group	↓ Users	↓ Sessions	Engagement rate	Average engagement time per session	Bounce rate	Session conversion rate newsletter_sub...blog_or_footer
	174,906 100% of total	248,741 100% of total	45.54% Avg 0%	0m 47s Avg 0%	54.46% Avg 0%	0.26% Avg 0%
1 Organic Search	135,261	181,298	47.88%	0m 46s	52.12%	0.13%
2 Direct	25,327	37,887	37.31%	0m 37s	62.69%	0.64%
3 Organic Social	7,125	12,589	39.71%	0m 55s	60.29%	0.48%
4 Referral	5,359	8,502	49.54%	0m 59s	50.46%	1.01%
5 Email	4,690	9,799	43.85%	1m 04s	56.15%	0.26%
6 Unassigned	1,418	1,707	18.63%	1m 20s	81.37%	0.23%
7 Organic Video	22	34	47.06%	0m 53s	52.94%	5.88%

Which traffic channels drive... ...the most visibility? ...the most engagement? ...the most conversions?

Fig. 8.6

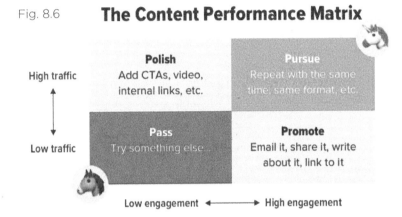

The Content Performance Matrix

High traffic

Polish Add CTAs, video, internal links, etc.

Pursue Repeat with the same time, same format, etc.

Low traffic

Pass Try something else...

Promote Email it, share it, write about it, link to it

Low engagement ← → High engagement

Source: https://www.orbitmedia.com/blog/content-performance-matrix/

5. On the report, select a conversion from the dropdown under "Session key event rate." Because we're doing a content marketing audit, use a content-related goal, such as download or subscribe. This assumes you have conversion events set up in GA4.

Now you're looking at the performance of each "default channel group" which are the high-level sources of traffic. Comparing the metrics for each, you'll see which are most effective in which ways.

You'll immediately notice that some channels are better for attracting visitors. Others are better for engaging and converting visitors. If you're looking for a benchmark engagement rate, our research found that 55% engagement rate is average across channels (Fig. 8.5).

Next Steps / Action Items

This kind of top-line data isn't the best for making decisions. Are email visitors engaged? How are those Google Ads doing? We'll do deeper analysis in a minute.

But the big picture content strategy impact is usually something like this (Fig. 8.6):

- If it's not working, fix it or give up on it.

- If it is working, double down.

Now let's analyze our content and its performance in the three main promotion channels, search, social and email.

2. SEO: Which content is attracting visitors from search engines?

Some pages have durable visibility. People search, the page ranks, people click and the page gets a steady stream of traffic. This traffic is often stable for months and years. Content marketers, like SEOs, should have these on their radar.

The good news is that your top performers are easy to find. Here's how to use GA4 to find your top pages for organic search performance:

1. Go to Engagement > Landing pages. We're looking for content so we'll start here.

2. Add a filter to show just organic traffic. (Fig. 8.7) Click the "Add filter +" button. The "Build filter" options will slide out from the right. In the Dimension dropdown, select "Session medium." In the Dimensions values drop down, check the box for "organic" and click ok.

3. Click "Apply" in the bottom right corner to apply the filter to your report (Fig. 8.8).

4. If your blog content is all within a directory (such as website.com/**blog**) it's easy to filter this report to show only blog posts. Just type "blog" into the search tool above the first column to view just your content marketing URLs (Fig. 8.9).

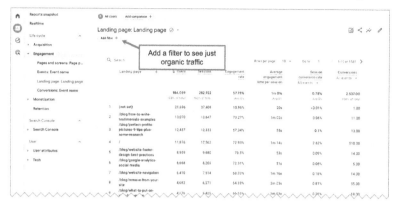

Fig. 8.7

Fig. 8.8

Fig. 8.9

Now you're looking at a list of all of your top performing articles from search. This is an SEO report and these are your winners.

Next Steps / Action Items

Many of these will have 10x the visibility of your other pages. So there's a lot we can learn from them.

- **Make more of them**
  What do these articles have in common? Are they more detailed? Focused on a more specific topic? Are they linked to a lot from other articles? Analyze then emulate.

- **Add CTAs to them**
  These have high-levels of durable visibility (your best cheese). Add internal links and calls to action from these articles to your highest converting articles (your best mousetraps).

- **Exclude them from other reports**
  Some of these outliers produce such huge results, they create noise in other reports. If they're irritating, don't delete them. That would have a cost with no benefit. Just exclude them from GA4 by creating a filter in any report.

3. SEO: Traffic from organic search is rising/falling for which articles?

This is your early warning system. If you're paying attention to changes in organic traffic for specific articles, you can take action before something falls into the abyss. This way you can defend your total topline traffic.

You also won't be surprised when overall organic traffic falls if you've been watching that one random, super high traffic post start to drop in rankings.

To track the changes in search traffic to specific URLs, simply add a comparison to the date range (Fig. 8.10).

Fig. 8.10

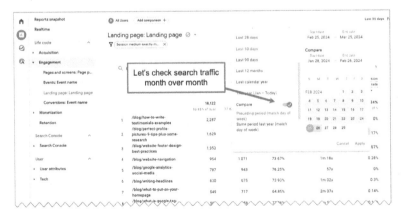

Fig. 8.11

Now the same report shows organic traffic rising or falling. Scanning through, you'll immediately see which ones need a little love (Fig. 8.11).

This is more useful than tracking rankings for specific phrases. Rank tracking is nice, but what if it's a low-performing keyphrase? Or what if that page ranks for other, more popular phrases that you aren't tracking? If so, tracking specific rankings can be misleading. Many SEOs are too focused on rankings and not focused enough on actual organic traffic.

> SEO is not really about rankings. **SEO is about traffic.**

Next Steps / Action Items

Pages that have rising search traffic don't need help. But take a look at them anyway. A lot of other people are. Make sure everything is up-to-date and looking good. It's like tidying up a room that a lot of guests are visiting.

Pages that have declining search traffic do need help.

The best way to reverse the ranking slide is to improve the quality of the page. Use any of the elements we discussed in Chapter 5:

- Add visuals (graphics, video)

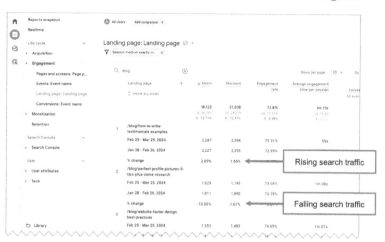

- Add contributor quotes (from subject matter experts)
- Add supportive evidence (charts, examples)
- Add formatting (subheads, bullets, numbered lists)

But there is one specific change that is most likely to improve the declining search rankings. It's all about content quality and relevance.

- Add depth and detail that includes semantically related phrases.

It doesn't help to cram the target phrase in more times. It does help to add content that answers related questions, touches on the subtopics, and goes deeper into the material. Make it a better page.

One great way to improve the relevance of a page is to confirm that it incorporates all of the phrases that it's already ranking for. So let's go find them . . .

4. SEO: What phrases is this page ranking for?

For this part of our content marketing audit, we'll go beyond GA4 and into Google Search Console.

There are lots of SEO tools that will show you the rankings of a specific URL, but the primary source is Google itself. Google Search Console doesn't track changes to rankings for specific phrases, but it shows the "average position" for any phrase for any page over any time period.

Here's how to use Google Search Console to check the rankings of any page on your website (Fig. 8.12).

From the Search results report:

1. Select a recent date range

2. Select the "PAGES" tab

3. Click on the filter icon and then enter the URL (or a word from the URL) to find the page.

4. Click on the URL to see just that page

Now you're looking at the search performance for that specific URL.

5. Check the "Average position" box to add that data to the report

6. Click on the "QUERIES" tab

Now you're looking at the keyphrases for which that URL ranks (Fig. 8.13).

7. Sort by "Position" and scroll down past the top rankings

Fig. 8.12

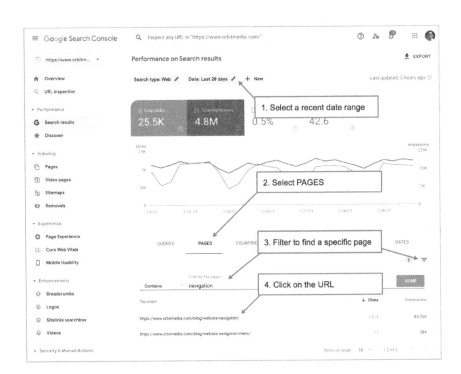

Next Steps / Action Items

Fig. 8.13

Knowing keyphrase performance is part of a content marketing audit, but it's also useful for finding semantically related phrases for making SEO-focused edits to those almost high-ranking articles.

- Improving the relevance of the top queries by updating an article, adding these specific phrases/

- Confirm that the top performing phrase is, in fact, the primary target keyphrase of the article. If not, consider refocusing the article on that top performing phrase and include it in the title tag and <h1> header.

The outcome of these actions isn't just higher rankings for top phrases. It's also about ranking for an even greater number of phrases. This is one of the key outcomes of semantic SEO.

5. SEO: Which pages have ranking potential?

It's possible that you've published articles that have been linked to from other websites but don't rank for much of anything. These are pages with high authority but low relevance.

A URL with authority but low relevance has good ranking potential. It's like a rocket sitting on the launchpad, waiting for the countdown. All it needs is better keyword focus.

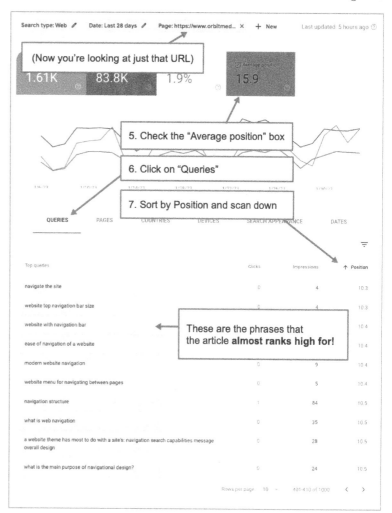

To find which of your URLs has strong ranking potential, we'll use Google Search Console. It will show you the number of websites (quantity) that have linked to any of your articles.

Really, the paid SEO tools are better for this because they show both the number of websites (quantify), but also the authority of each of those websites (quality), which is a key ingredient in the authority of your pages. A link from

MySpace and a link from the *New York Times* aren't of equal value.

But for this audit, we'll stick with the free tool, Google Search Console (Fig. 8.14).

1. Go to the Links report

2. Under External links, click on "More"

3. To see just your content marketing articles, click on the filter icon, then enter "blog" or the name of the directory in which your articles are posted.

4. Sort by linking sites (Fig. 8.15).

Fig. 8.14

Fig. 8.15

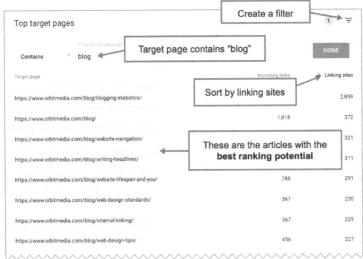

Next Steps / Action Items

The idea is to prioritize these URLs while doing SEO. First, check the current rankings for these URLs

- If it already ranks for something, **sharpen the focus** on those target phrases.

- If it doesn't rank for much, **recycle that URL** by rewriting the article completely, giving it a new keyphrase focus.

Updating existing content, rather than writing new content, is a faster path to greater visibility. We'll show the specific steps for updating content for SEO in section 8.2.

6. Email Marketing: Which of our email campaigns have performed the best?

Now we'll find out which of our email campaigns performed the best.

The beauty of GA4 is that it goes beyond the standard email metrics. Your email

service provider (ESP) will show you pre-click metrics (deliverability, open rates, click through rates). But you'll need to add campaign tracking code to those links and buttons to see post-click metrics (traffic, engagement, conversion rates) (Fig. 8.16).

In section 3.3, we showed how to add UTM tracking codes to the links on your email. If you've done that, you'll now be able to see the behavior of the visitors that come to your website from your email campaigns. Here's the step-by-step process:

1. Use a nice long date range so you can compare the performance of many campaigns.

2. From the Acquisition > Traffic acquisition report, click on the pencil icon in the top right to customize the report.

3. Click on the Metrics dropdown to select your metrics

4. Select Sessions, Engagement Rate, Average engagement time per session and Conversions …or whichever metrics you like best. You can drag these to the top of the list for easy

Fig. 8.16

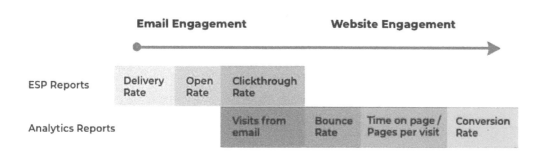

analysis. If you don't see the metric you want, click the "Add metric" and search for it, then select it.

5. Click "Apply" (Fig. 8.17)

6. Save the customization. Again, you can "Save to the current report."

7. Back in the report, we'll add a filter to look at just the email campaigns. Click on the "Add filter +" button

8. Select "Session medium" as the dimension.

9. From the Dimension values dropdown, select "email"

10. Click "Apply" (Fig. 8.18)

11. Last step! In the dropdown above the first column, change the primary dimension from "Default channel group" to "Session campaign"

Now you're looking at the performance of every email campaign within that date range, as long as the clicks were on links that had the campaign tracking code added. This report will show all campaigns, not just email, so you may need to sift through other data.

You'll quickly see that there is a wide variance in the performance of campaigns in terms of both traffic and conversion rates (Fig. 8.19).

Fig. 8.17

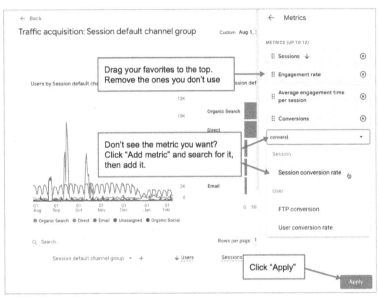

Fig. 8.18

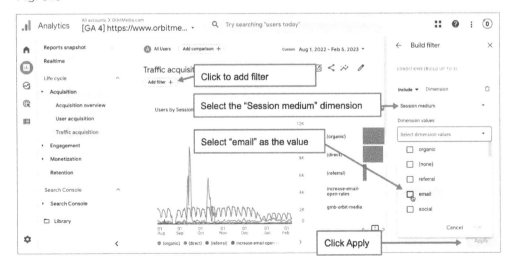

Next Steps / Action Items

Look closely at the top performing campaigns. Review every element, including the topics, timing, subject lines, creative, teaser text and calls to action. What do these outliers have in common?

- Repeat the results by emulating these top performers.

- Simply resend the top performers with new subject lines.

7. Social Media: Which social networks are performing the best for your content?

Moving on to social media marketing, first let's audit the performance of the social networks themselves. Our topics and formats won't perform the same with users across different social platforms. Some social networks will be more effective than others.

To audit the performance of various social networks, follow these steps. We're using the same report customizations we used above, so we'll have those same metrics: users, sessions, engagement rate, conversion rates, etc.

1. Go to the Acquisition > Traffic acquisition report

2. Click "Add filter +" so we can limit the data to just social media traffic

3. Select "First user default channel group" as the dimension

4. Click "Select dimension values" and check the "Organic Social" box

5. Click "Apply" (Fig. 8.20)

Fig. 8.19

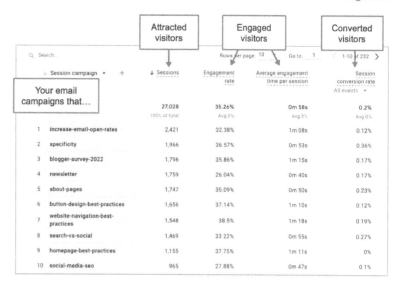

Fig. 8.20

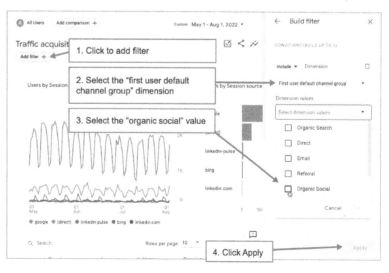

6. Using the dropdown above the first column, change the primary dimension from "Session default channel group" to "Session source"

Now you're looking at the relative performance of every social network that has sent traffic to your website. You may see redundant things (several rows for the same network) and strange things (misattributed campaigns) but sift through the noise (Fig. 8.21).

Next Steps / Action Items

As with the analysis of default channel groups, here we prescribe the same actions based on each social network's performance against your goals.

- If a social network has low traffic, but high conversion rates, get more active there.

Fig. 8.21

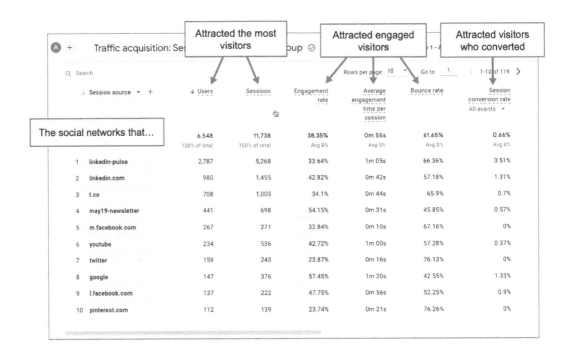

In the report above, you can see that traffic from LinkedIn is roughly twice as likely to convert as traffic from X (formerly Twitter).

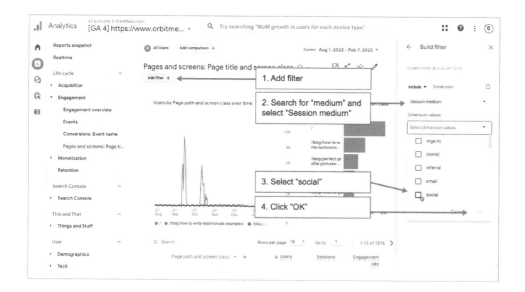

Fig. 8.22

- If a social network has high traffic, but low conversion rates, accept it for its brand awareness support, but don't expect it to help the middle or bottom of your funnel.

- If a social network is high performance all around, double down with greater investment

8. Social Media: Which of my articles performs best on social platforms?

Analysis is always more interesting when you drill down to the next level. Let's look at the performance of each article within social media channels. Because we're looking at specific pages, we'll use the Engagement > Pages and screens report.

1. Click the "Add Filter +" so we can see just the social traffic

2. Set the Dimension to "Session medium"

3. Set the Dimension value to "social"

4. Click "OK" (Fig. 8.22)

5. Type "blog" into the search box to see just the URLs from that directory (Fig. 8.23).

Fig. 8.23

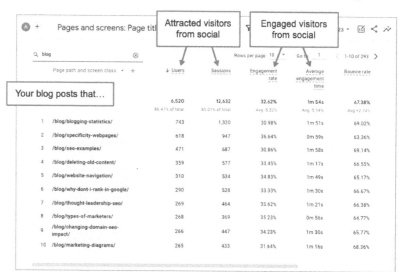

Some of these articles did much better in social media than others. It's immediately clear that articles with lots of visuals did the best here in social media.

Next Steps / Action Items

Analyze the top performers, looking closely at the headlines, formatting and visuals. What do they have in common?

- Produce more content with these same attributes for social media promotion

- For the articles with the highest engagement levels, keep them in heavy social rotation

9. Where did this article perform best?

To see the traction any article got from every traffic source, you don't need to use a filter. We don't want to exclude anything. We want to see ALL of the traffic sources for a given URL.

1. Go to the Engagement > Pages and Screens report

2. Set the primary dimension to "Page path and screen class"

3. Search for the article in the search field above the first column

4. Click the blue plus sign (+) to add a second dimension, select "Session source/medium" (Fig. 8.24)

Fig. 8.24

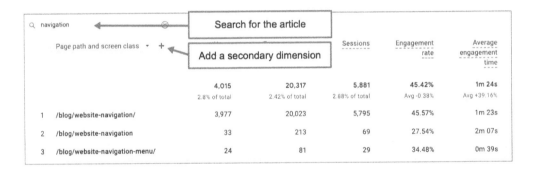

	Page path and screen class		Sessions	Engagement rate	Average engagement time
			5,881	45.42%	1m 24s
	4,015 2.8% of total	20,317 2.42% of total	2.88% of total	Avg -0.38%	Avg +39.16%
1	/blog/website-navigation/	3,977	20,023	5,795	45.57%	1m 23s
2	/blog/website-navigation	33	213	69	27.54%	2m 07s
3	/blog/website-navigation-menu/	24	81	29	34.48%	0m 39s

Search for the article

Add a secondary dimension

Fig. 8.25

	Page path and screen class ▾	Session source / medium ▾ ✕	↓ Users	Event count video_start ▾	Sessions	Engagement rate	Average engagement time
			4,015 4.49% of total	181 0.04% of total	5,881 4.6% of total	45.42% Avg -5.63%	1m 24s Avg +16.34%
1	/blog/website-navigation/	google / organic	2,828	125	3,867	48.69%	1m 07s
2	/blog/website-navigation/	september8-newsletter / email	669	39	1,205	38.01%	2m 23s
3	/blog/website-navigation/	linkedin-pulse / social	206	8	349	38.4%	1m 56s
4	/blog/website-navigation/	rasa_io / email	58	2	98	26.53%	0m 56s
5	/blog/website-navigation/	bing / organic	56	0	64	57.81%	1m 23s
6	/blog/website-navigation/	mangools.com / referral	17	1	29	27.59%	0m 42s
7	/blog/website-navigation-menu/	google / organic	15	0	17	52.94%	0m 29s
8	/blog/website-navigation/	duckduckgo / organic	13	0	19	42.11%	1m 07s
9	/blog/website-navigation	google / organic	11	1	20	20%	2m 45s
10	/blog/website-navigation/	t.co / referral	11	0	12	41.67%	0m 52s

Visitors to this article... | ...from these traffic sources... | ...were this engaged

Now you're looking at all of the traffic from all traffic sources to that article. You can see how the article attracted various amounts of traffic with various levels of engagement (Fig. 8.25).

The example above is for an article with an embedded video, so I've added the "Event count" metric to this report and selected the "video_start" event, which is pre-configured for GA4 (no setup required). That gives me the ability to answer this follow up question:

Q: Which source of traffic attracts visitors who are most likely to watch the embedded video?

A: Email (5.4% of visitors from email watch the video, compared to just 3.9% of visitors from LinkedIn)

Next Steps / Action Items

This report should trigger content promotion ideas.

- If total traffic from an email or social source was unexpectedly low, re-promote it

- Keep promoting the article in any channel where engagement was above average

More examples of content analysis using GA4

We could add another dozen reports to this content audit. But by now, you may be thinking of your own analysis. And hopefully, you feel a bit more confident using Analytics. Test your Analytics proficiency and try answering these questions using GA4:

- Which of your blog readers are more engaged, mobile or desktop?

- Visitors who land on which of your articles are least likely to scroll?

Fig. 8.26

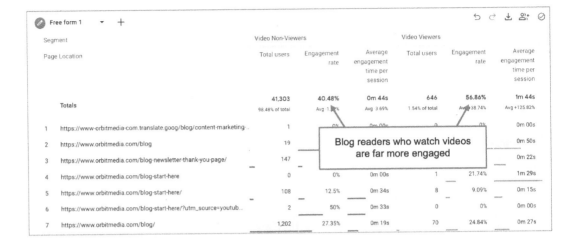

- How are visitors using your site search? What topics are they looking for?

- How much more engaging are articles with embedded videos?

We answered that last question with a free-form exploration. Take a look. at Fig. 8.26.

More juice from every squeeze...

That's the purpose behind this process: to get the greatest potential impact from the smallest possible effort. Since there are so many possible actions we can take in digital marketing, an audit will focus our attention on the actions that matter most.

8.2 Updating Existing Content: How to Teach Your Old Blog New Tricks

You wrote it years ago. It did well at the time. People liked it . . . and clicked, opened and shared it. But then you and your readers moved on. And you never looked back.

Here are a few reasons to revisit and revise old articles:

- **Speed**
  It's faster to update an old post than to write something new since much of the research is already finished.

- **Quality**
  The current article is far better than a rough draft. Also, if there was feedback from your readers on the original (i.e., comments), that can guide revisions and improvements.

- **Traffic**

  The new version will be easier to promote on social media, because you'll know just who to share it with: the people who shared, liked, commented and linked to it the first time. It's also easier to promote in search because the URL may already have some authority.

When you update old content, *you'll get better results with less effort*. Here is an example of how we got twice the traffic in half the time by updating an old blog post.

Example: "Content Promotion" article

In June 2012, we published an article with tips for promoting content. Keyphrase research quickly showed that "content promotion" was a very competitive phrase, so we used a longer, less competitive phrase in the title, header and URL: "content promotion strategies."

It actually ranked well for both phrases, **attracting 150-250 visits per month**. But the rankings gradually declined and it got very little traffic for several years. So we finally sat down and rewrote it in August 2016, adding all of the content promotion tricks we'd learned since 2012.

The headline changed from "33 ways to promote content" to "50 ways to drive traffic" and the rankings and traffic soared. So did the average time on page (see below).

The article enjoyed three years of high rankings and **300-500 visits per month**, always performing a bit better for the longer, less competitive phrase. But eventually, new (and better) articles were written and began to push both rankings down.

But we didn't give up.

We rewrote it in May 2020, this time adding more tactics and more depth. This post headline is now "76 ways to promote content" (did we miss anything?) and the rankings have partly recovered. Here's the timeline of rankings and traffic since 2012 (Fig. 8.27).

Fig. 8.27

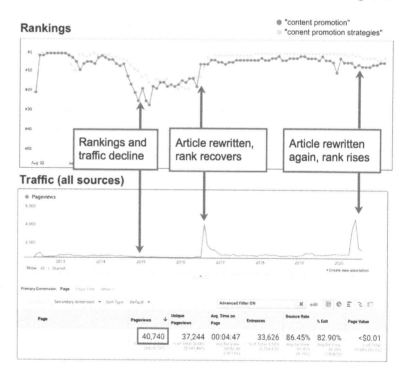

Fig. 8.28

Original June 2012	Updated August 2016	Re-Updated May 2020
33 Ways to Promote Your Content	**Content Promotion Strategies: 50 Ways to Drive Traffic to Your Next Article**	**How to Promote an Article: 76 Content Promotion Strategies for Blog Content**
2,049 words	**4,022** words (+50% previous)	**7,218** words (+55% previous)
2 images	**9** images	**29** images
	12 contributor quotes	**14** contributor quotes
		1 video (not a new one)
3m 59s avg. time on page	**5m 18s** avg. time on page	**5m 26s** avg. time on page
85.24% bounce rate	**86.44%** bounce rate	**83.33%** bounce rate

In Fig. 8.28 you can see the evolution of the article with the headlines, length and assets. Again, we're showing a few behavior metrics so you can see how the content attributes correlate with engagement.

So here was a post with strong potential but declining rankings. Without a little love, it was doomed to irrelevance. It was time to save it, to bring it up to date, to make it new again.

The goal is to make it a better, more current, more useful, more entertaining article. Here's what to change and what to keep when you're teaching an old blog new tricks.

What not to change:

- The topic and focus of the article

- The strongest soundbites, details and examples

- The URL

TIP! To get a sense for what parts of the article to keep, go back and look at the comments, look at the social media shares and listen to your audience. Anything that got people talking is worth keeping.

⚠ Do not change the URL when updating content. If other websites linked to the original, you'll break those links. This is bad for them and terrible for you, because you'll lose whatever authority and ranking potential those websites were passing to you. Hopefully the post has a URL that is easy to reuse. See the recommendations from the Article Checklist in Section 5.11.

What to update:

- Add details, examples and length

- Add media, such as images, audio and video

- Add input from experts, like contributor quotes

- Update older research and citations

- The date

Keep in mind the recommendation in Section 4.8 about blog post dates. If your content strategy is to publish evergreen content (not news) then it is probably best to not use a blog post template that shows the publishing date. But of course, if dates appear in the headline or body text, update them.

Once we learned the power of updating old content, it became central to our content strategy. In Fig. 8.29 you can see the entire history of my own writing and the changes over the years.

⚠ Before you change the keyword focus (title and header) of an almost-high-ranking article, check to make sure you aren't making it less relevant for an even better phrase. Here's a step-by-step process for checking the ranking of any page for free using Google Search Console (GSC): www.orbitmedia.com/blog/what-do-i-rank-for-how-to-check-your-rankings/

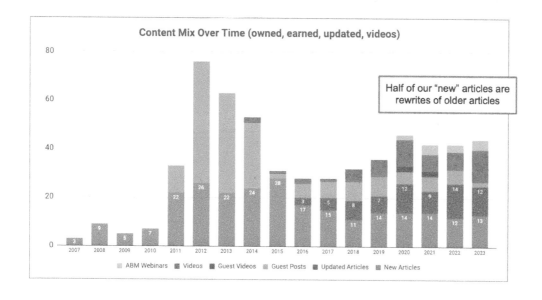

Fig. 8.29

Content Mix Over Time (owned, earned, updated, videos)

Half of our "new" articles are rewrites of older articles

ABM Webinars ■ Videos ■ Guest Videos ■ Guest Posts ■ Updated Articles ■ New Articles

Digital ink is never dry

Publishing an article is just the beginning. Don't stop there. Commit to keeping your content current. Go back and find the top performers, then improve them. Search optimize old posts and you'll drive more traffic in less time than it takes to write a new post. Measurement, and a regular content audit, informs your content strategy, reduces risks of wasting time and focuses your attention on the actions that matter most.

TIP! Repeat this process every three to six months. Make sure you don't miss a content audit, by adding it to your publishing calendar.

You don't need 1,000 articles.
You need 100 great articles.

A few final thoughts:

- **If your blog post doesn't rank, maybe that's because you've only written it once.**
This is what the search engines want you to do: create an amazing piece of content.

- **If your content is search optimized, you've basically committed to this strategy already.**
Your search optimized content has durable visibility. People are still reading it. Don't let them down. Especially if you don't have dates in your blog template (we don't).

- **If you're about to write a new article, first look to see if you can recycle an old URL.**
If it's a URL that has been linked to, it will have a natural advantage in search.

09 Conclusion

SO THERE YOU HAVE IT. YOU SHOULD NOW HAVE A GOOD UNDERSTANDING OF HOW CONTENT MARKETING DRIVES AWARENESS, ENGAGEMENT AND DEMAND.

You should also know how content helps achieve these goals.

Hopefully by now, you're excited to start mixing things up in the lab. You're ready to experiment with keyphrases, discover new connections and concoct a big batch of relevant articles.

Persist

Yes, it's a lot of work. There is no secret formula. Content marketing isn't about just one thing. It's about 100 little things. And it's about doing them well and doing them consistently.

It may take time to find the style that gets a reaction from your audience. You'll need to keep at it if you're expecting big results. Persistence is the biggest factor in success, not just in web marketing, but in every field.

You'll see small results right away—a few shares, more clicks, some new people subscribing to your newsletter—but it will take time before you become an expert.

Some of the greatest content chemists of our time put in tremendous effort to get where they are. It took Chris Brogan eight years to get his first 100 subscribers. Today he reaches hundreds of thousands of readers each month. Lee Odden of TopRank Online Marketing wrote more than a million words over 25 years. Today, he's one of the most sought-after web strategists in the country.

"**Marketing is a habit**, not an event."

JOHN JANTSCH, *Duct Tape Marketing*

"Fortes fortuna adiuvat."
Fortune favors the bold.

You don't need to work for eight years to get 100 subscribers or write a million words to get results. Thankfully, there are plenty of small incremental results to measure along the way. But it will take patience and effort. Keep going—you'll get there.

Fear not

Almost nothing is as high-stakes as it seems. Yes, there are examples of spectacular failures in social media. There are nightmare stories of collapsing search engine rankings. But these stories are rare relative to the millions of businesses doing content marketing.

Don't be afraid to try something new. Don't be afraid to write something provocative. If an article rubs a few people the wrong way, there are probably hundreds of other people who appreciate your candor. If you feel strongly about something, let it show through your words.

Have fun!

To me, web marketing is a game. I play it like a sport, and GA4 is my scoreboard. I've chosen certain metrics that I like best and I try to make them move. It's actually easy to gamify your marketing because there are so many beautiful charts to watch! Thinking of it as a game and making those charts and numbers move helps keep me motivated.

Everything you're about to do is measurable, and the results of your efforts make lovely charts. So pick out a few statistics and watch a few of those metrics. Choose the ones that have an impact on your goals and start obsessing over them a little bit. Call it a "key performance indicator" if you want. Personally, aside from leads, some of my favorite stats are new newsletter subscribers, newsletter click-to-open rates and total visitors. If these numbers are growing, results will come. I'm always trying to break my high score.

So I watch the charts. I measure. I wonder. I tweak. I try something new and I measure again. And somewhere along the way, I forget that I'm working. I'm having fun.

Keep learning

The Orbit blog has dozens of articles on each topic in this book. This is where we add new articles every two weeks that go deeper into each tactic. Feel free to drop by, learn more or share with your team.

- www.orbitmedia.com/blog/

You can also find us on social media:

- www.twitter.com/orbiteers
- www.linkedin.com/company/ orbit-media-studios-inc.
- www.facebook.com/ orbitmediastudios

More resources

Here are some of the writers and resources I've learned from over the years. I still read many of these regularly. One of the wonderful things about content marketing is that the experts are all happy to teach what they know. They do it every day on their websites, in their videos, in their newsletters and at conferences.

I'd like to both thank and recommend the following websites and thought leaders. They've each had a profound effect on me. I'm grateful and, by way of thanks, I encourage everyone to read, watch, follow and subscribe to these wonderful experts, I list here in no particular order:

Mark Schaefer, John Hall, D Fish, Jo Wiebe, Joe Pulizzi, Paul Roetzer, Gini Dietrich, Peep Laja, Wil Reynolds, Jessica Best, Barry Feldman, Heidi Cohen, Robert Rose, Jay Baer, Tom Bowen, Chris Mercer, Michael Aagaard, Rand Fishkin, Jay Acunzo, Andrew Davis, Ardath Albee, Charlie Meyerson, Sonia Simone, Joel Klettke, Justin Rondeau, Will Critchlow, Dan Shure, Henneke Duistermaat, Aaron Orendorff, Nancy Harhut, Dana DiTomaso, Dennis Shiao, Charles Farina, Brooke Sellas, Brian Massey and Rich Brooks.

Also a huge thanks to Amanda Gant for making every bit of Orbit's marketing better, and to Karen Sheets de Gracia, who made this book look beautiful.

Lastly, thanks to my business partners, Barrett Lombardo, Corey Northcutt and Todd Gettelfinger, and the rest of the Orbiteers. The work you do every day for our beloved clients is an inspiration to me.

ANDY CRESTODINA is a co-founder and the CMO of Orbit Media Studios, an award-winning, 55-person digital marketing and web design agency in Chicago. Since 2001, Orbit has completed more than 1,000 successful website projects. The Orbiteers combine talent and experience in developing beautiful, effective sites for businesses in every industry.

Andy is a top-rated speaker at national conferences, a writer for the biggest blogs and gives up to 100 webinars and presentations per year. Over the past 25 years, Andy has provided web strategy and digital marketing advice to more than a thousand businesses. His favorite topics include content strategy, search engine optimization, AI, website visitor psychology and Google Analytics.

Andy graduated from the University of Iowa with a degree in Asian Language and Literature and a certificate to teach Chinese. Today, he lives and works in Chicago in the tree-filled neighborhood of Ravenswood with his lovely wife, Crystal, and their beautiful children, Eli and Ada.